# How to Do Absolutely Everything

# How to Do Absolutely Everything

**Homegrown Projects from Do-It-Yourself Experts**

--------------------------------------------------

Instructables.com, Edited by Sarah James

Skyhorse Publishing

Copyright © 2012 by Instructables.com

All Rights Reserved. No part of this book may be reproduced in any manner without the express written consent of the publisher, except in the case of brief excerpts in critical reviews or articles. All inquiries should be addressed to Skyhorse Publishing, 307 West 36th Street, 11th Floor, New York, NY 10018.

Skyhorse Publishing books may be purchased in bulk at special discounts for sales promotion, corporate gifts, fund-raising, or educational purposes. Special editions can also be created to specifications. For details, contact the Special Sales Department, Skyhorse Publishing, 307 West 36th Street, 11th Floor, New York, NY 10018 or info@skyhorsepublishing.com.

Skyhorse® and Skyhorse Publishing® are registered trademarks of Skyhorse Publishing, Inc.®, a Delaware corporation.

Visit our website at www.skyhorsepublishing.com.

10 9 8 7 6 5 4 3 2 1

Library of Congress Cataloging-in-Publication Data is available on request.

ISBN: 978-1-62087-066-2

Printed in China

# Introduction

Welcome to *How to Do Absolutely Everything*! Inside you'll find hundreds of useful tips and tricks to get you on the path to doing absolutely everything. Whether you're a beginner or a pro, you're sure to find something you never knew before. Learn how to solder, how to bake bread, how to make your workshop more efficient, how to water ski, a dozen new uses for duct tape, and how to turn trash into treasure. Roll up your sleeves and get started!

Instructables.com is the most popular project-sharing community on the Internet. We provide easy publishing tools to enable passionate, creative people like you to share their most innovative projects, recipes, skills, and ideas. Instructables has over 80,000 projects covering all subjects, including crafts, art, electronics, kids, home improvement, pets, outdoors, reuse, bikes, cars, robotics, food, decorating, woodworking, costuming, games, and more.

—Sarah James

# in the
# KITCHEN

# behind the
# BAR

# in the
# CRAFT
## room

# with your
# KIDS

## for your BODY

## with DUCT TAPE

# in the
# HOME

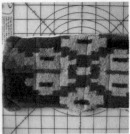

# for your
# PETS

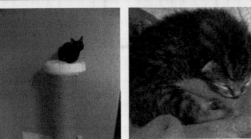

# in the
# GARDEN

# in the
# WATER

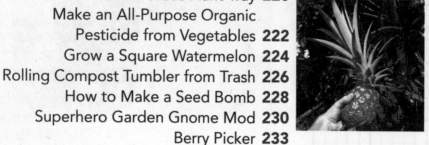

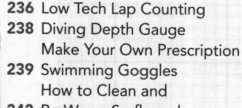

# in the
# GARAGE

# with
# TRASH

# OUTSIDE

# in the
# WORKSHOP

## with SCIENCE

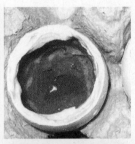
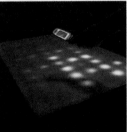

## with ELECTRONICS

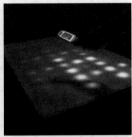
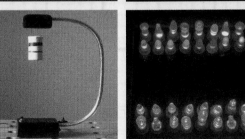

# Editor's note

The wonderful thing about Instructables is that they come in all shapes and sizes. Some users include hundreds of high-quality pictures and detailed instructions with their projects; others take the minimalist approach and aim to inspire similar ideas rather than facilitate carbon copies.

One of the biggest questions we faced when putting this book together was: How do we convey the sheer volume of ideas in the finite space of a book?

As a result, if you're already familiar with some of the projects in this book, you'll notice that only select photos made the jump from the computer screen to the printed page. Similarly, when dealing with extensive electronic coding or complex science, we've suggested that anyone ready to start a project like that visit the Instructables' online page, where you often find lots more images, links, multimedia attachments, and downloadable material to help you along the way. This way, anyone who is fascinated by the idea of converting a car to run on trash can take a look here at the basic steps to get from start to finish. Everything else is just a mouse click away.

Tie on your apron, and let's get cooking! In this chapter you'll learn everything from how to make butter and rice to how to make fresh cheese and milk an almond. Be sure to bookmark the world's best chocolate chip cookie recipe, and everyone will love you once you've mastered the 5-minute cake!

# Five-Minute Chocolate Cake

By **scoochmaroo** Sarah James
(www.instructables.com/id/5-minute-
Chocolate-Cake/)

There are a lot of cake-in-a-mug recipes out there, but I've taken the time to experiment with eight variations on a recipe to come up with the best, tastiest, and most reliable 5-minute chocolate cake on the web. Give it a try—you won't be disappointed!

## Supplies

- microwave!
- coffee mug
- 4 tablespoons flour—make sure you measure it right or the cake is a lie!
- 4 tablespoons sugar
- 2 tablespoons unsweetened cocoa
- 2 tablespoons whisked egg—1 egg is too much, 1 egg white is too eggy, 1 yolk is too dense, but 2 tablespoons is just right! For a fudgier version, omit egg!
- 3 tablespoons milk
- 3 tablespoons oil
- 3 tablespoons chocolate chips
- splash vanilla or other flavoring—try peppermint or cinnamon

## Step 1: Mix Your Ingredients

Add all of the dry ingredients to the mug and mix. Add the egg and combine well. It gets pretty pasty at the point. Stir in milk and oil. Add chocolate chips* and splash of vanilla. Stir well.

## Step 2: Nuke It!

Microwave for 3 minutes in a 1000 w oven, or 4 minutes in a 700 w oven.

It will start to crown over the top of the mug. Don't panic! It will collapse once the heat stops.

## Step 3: Eat it!

*Cuidado! Muy caliente!*

This cake is still good half an hour out of the oven. In fact, I think it gets better the longer it sits, but I can't speak to how it does after that, since there's never any left!

---

* If you don't have chocolate chips, try a broken up candy bar—I can't stress how much this amps the awesomeness of your cake

# How to Make Butter (and Buttermilk)

By theque Jonathan Barton
(www.instructables.com/id/
How-To-Make-Butter-and-
Buttermilk/)

I am about to reveal to you an *ancient* butter making secret: making butter requires shaking, shaking, shaking, *more* shaking, and lots of shaking, but the end result is *fantastic*. Homemade butter can be fun to make (if you are a butter enthusiast) and clean-up is very easy. You only need a few things and the whole process takes about 10 to 20 minutes; the majority of the time is spent shaking.

## Materials
- whipping cream (can be regular or heavy whipping cream)
- 1 jar
- 1 measuring device (not necessarily needed)
- 1 fresh strong arm, able to withstand a lot of shaking

## Step 1: Adding Ingredients
First decide how much butter you really want to make. I used about 1 cup of heavy cream, which yielded about half a cup of butter, (the other half cup didn't go missing, just "turned into" buttermilk). After you've measured out the desired amount of cream, simply pour it into the jar, there are no other required ingredients (and I usually put flavoring for the butter in at the end).

## Step 2: Capping and Shaking
Very, very carefully put the cap on the jar. Phew, glad that's over. Then begin to shake the jar. It will take a while to shake this into butter but it is well worth it in the end.

## Step 3: Nearly Done
About every 3 minutes check the jar by taking off the lid and looking inside. Once the cream reaches the right consistency in the jar you are nearly done.

## Step 4: Butter Sweet Butter
The cream will start to feel thicker as you shake it, making it much harder to shake around. The easiest shaking method is to take the jar by the "neck" or the closest part to the lid, and shake downwards in a stabbing motion back and forth. Eventually the jar seems easier and easier to shake. Open the jar and peek inside. See butter? This is when the butter starts to separate from the buttermilk, once you see the little clumps of butter inside the jar, begin to strain out the extra liquid (I recommend you save this, it is the buttermilk and when homemade it tastes sweet and is often used in baking, i.e., pancakes, biscuits, etc.) After straining the buttermilk you are left with the remaining butter in the jar. Just scoop it into a storage container and pat it down a bit. You'll want to put it in the fridge to harden it a bit more so it's easier to scoop and spread.

# Best Ever Chocolate Chip Cookie Recipe

By **scoochmaroo** Sarah James
(www.instructables.com/id/Best-Ever-Chocolate-Chip-Cookie-Recipe/)

I tested five chocolate chip cookie recipes to bring you what I consider to be far and away the best chocolate chip cookie recipe in existence.

In an exhaustive search to find the perfect chocolate chip cookie—the sole recipe I will use from now on and pass down through the generations—I made sure to test the most popular recipes I could find. Candidates for tastiest chocolate chipper included:

- Nestle Toll House Cookie Recipe
- *New York Times* Chocolate Chip Cookies
- David Lebovitz's Chocolate Chip Cookies
- Perfect Chocolate Chip Cookies from *Cook's Illustrated*
- Allrecipe's Award-Winning Soft Chocolate Chip Cookies

The winning cookies taste like they came from a high-end bakery, I'm not even kidding you. But you can make them yourself—it's easy!

I tell you this, Instructables fans, I hesitated to share the results of this experiment with you. It is now one of the most potent tools in my recipe belt, and I have secretly entertained fantasies of launching my own bakery, based on the inspiration provided by this recipe alone. But, alas, I already have an awesome job here at Instructables HQ, and it would be criminal of me to keep this secret to myself.

If you follow this recipe, you'll soon be known wide and far for your amazing chocolate chip cookie skills and will be called upon to provide them at every function. I recommend making up a huge batch and storing them in the freezer. What could be better than surprising your guests with freshly-baked, bakery-quality chocolate chip cookies in fifteen minutes?

Nothing. That's what.

And here I present to you, David Lebovitz's recipe, the winningest cookie in the world (or at least my kitchen):

## Ingredients

If you have a scale, the whole recipe is made easier by weighing your ingredients. If you don't have a scale, you should get one!

- 2½ cups (350 g) all-purpose flour
- ¾ teaspoon baking soda
- ⅛ teaspoon salt
- 1 cup (8 ounces/225 g) unsalted butter, at room temperature
- 1 cup (215 g) packed light brown sugar
- ¾ cup (150 g) granulated sugar
- 1 teaspoon vanilla extract
- 2 large eggs, at room temperature
- 2 cups (about 225 g) nuts, toasted and chopped

- 14 ounces (400 g) bittersweet chocolate, coarsely chopped
- Sea salt for sprinkling on top (what?)

## Step 1: Secrets Revealed

I did not embark on this experiment lightly. I read everything I could find about what makes a chocolate chip cookie truly outstanding, and gained the most insight from the experiment that inspired this one, performed by David Leite for the *New York Times* in July, 2008. Our results, however, differed, though the few secrets revealed in the article remain invaluable.

The key secret in making amazing chocolate chip cookies seems to be in how long you let the dough sit before baking. Even Mrs. Wakefield employed this technique when she invented the original Nestle Toll House recipe—it just didn't make it onto the package!

Leaving the dough in the fridge for 24 to 36 hours allows the ingredients to fully soak up the liquid and results in a firmer dough which bakes to a better consistency.

A long hydration time is important because eggs, unlike, say, water, are gelatinous and slow-moving. And since butter coats the flour, it makes it difficult for the liquids to get through to the dry ingredients.

Another hint is to rotate the cookie sheet mid-way through baking. This allows your cookies to bake evenly, regardless of where the hottest part of your oven is. This simple trick was a game-changer for me, and I'll never do otherwise again!

The *New York Times* article suggests there's no substitute for a 6" cookie whose dough has been left in the fridge for at least 36 hours. But after this experiment, I care to differ.

## Step 2: The Prep

First you want to toast you some nuts. This makes for the extra yum. If you're allergic, I guess you should skip this part.

In a 350°F (180°C) preheated oven bake 2 cups (about 225 g) nuts (I prefer pecans in this recipe) for 10 minutes on an ungreased cookie sheet. Let cool. If you don't let it cool, your chocolate pieces will get melty in the batter. Which is what happened to me. Which I rather liked and will probably be doing again. So choose your own adventure.

While those are baking, chop up 14 ounces (400 g) bittersweet chocolate.

Insider tip: for the ultimate cookie, use only chocolate with at least 60 percent cacao content and shoot for a ratio of chocolate to dough of no less than 40 to 60.

## Step 3: The Procedure

The primary step in most cookie recipes is to sift together the dry ingredients. So do that. In a bowl, sift or whisk (easier!) together:
- 2½ cups (350 g) all-purpose flour
- ¾ teaspoon baking soda
- ⅛ teaspoon salt

In a separate bowl (preferably with an electric mixer) beat together:
- 1 cup (8 ounces/225 g) unsalted butter, at room temperature
- 1 cup (215 g) packed light brown sugar

- ¾ cup (150 g) granulated sugar
- 1 teaspoon vanilla extract

One at a time, add 2 eggs, beating thoroughly after each addition until each is incorporated.

Slowly stir in flour mixture until fully incorporated.

Finally, stir in chocolate and nuts.

## Step 4: The Hard Part

You know what I'm going to say. It's time to wait. It's time to take all this precious cookie dough you just made . . . and not eat it.

Divide the dough into quarters. Roll each dough into a log about 9" (23 cm) long and wrap in plastic.

Stick em in the fridge for the next 24 hours, and try to forget you knew anything about them.

## Step 5: Let's Be Serious

You are not going to wait the 24 hours. I know this, you know this, who are we

kidding? Nonetheless, it's absolutely worth the wait, so here's my suggestion to get you through the next 24 hours.

Though this is not in the original recipe, I strongly recommend saving a small portion of dough—half of one of the logs maybe—and proceeding to the next step. Not only will this quell your desire to break into the fridge at midnight and eat one whole log straight from the wrapper, it will give you the opportunity to compare and contrast the benefits of allowing your dough to rest.

So do it! Just don't tell David I said so.

## Step 6: The Baking

Preheat the oven to 350°F (175°C).

Line baking sheet with parchment paper or silicone baking mat.

Slice the logs into disks ¾"(2 cm) thick and place the disks 3" (8 cm) apart on the prepared baking sheets. If the nuts or chips crumble out, push them back in.

Scoochmaroo Super Tip: Sprinkle the cookie slices with a small amount of sea salt. This will really make them sing!

Bake the cookies for 10 minutes, rotating the sheet midway through. If you prefer a chewier cookie, scale back the time a bit.

Let cookies cool on the baking sheet until firm enough to transfer to a wire rack.

Baked cookies will store in an airtight container for 4 days. Unbaked dough can be refrigerated for up to a week or frozen for up to a month.

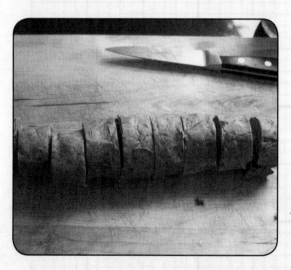

kitchen

# How to Cook Rice

By **noahw** Noah Weinstein
(www.instructables.com/id/How-to-Make-Rice/)

Cooking rice is a valuable skill that you'll use many times over a lifetime of eating. This instructable will show you how to cook both white and brown rice. It's not a strict "recipe" like existing web pages out there. It's the theory behind cooking rice, so that you can become your own expert at cooking rice.

## Gather Materials

Rice is one of the most basic and inexpensive things you can cook, so you won't need many supplies. However, that doesn't mean that it's necessarily easy to make. You'll need a pot with a lid, water, rice (any kind you like, here I'll be using long grain white and short grain brown rice), a measuring cup, and salt and butter (optional).

## Step 1: Rice Theory

Cooking rice is about understanding the proportions of the two ingredients—the rice and the water. People have different preferences as to the ratio of rice to water. The range goes from 1 part rice to 1.5 parts water to as much as 1 part rice to 2 parts water. After you cook it a few times, you'll have your own ideas about how much water to use. For now, we'll walk the middle of the road and use 1 part rice to 1.75 parts water. If you've added in too much water, fear not, simply cook your rice longer and crack the lid, allowing more moisture to escape. If you've added too little water, you're in luck because you can always add more. Ideally you won't need to make the adjustments described above when you're cooking rice, and your batches will come out perfectly fluffy, moist, with just the right amount of chewiness and only enough starchy glueyness to keep the grains clumped together enough to get them into your mouth.

### White Rice vs. Brown Rice

Cooking methods vary slightly for white and brown rice. White rice is, generally speaking, cooked for a shorter period of time (20-30 minutes) with less water. Brown rice is cooked for a longer period of time (30-40 minutes) with more water.

### Rinsing the Rice

Some methods suggest rinsing rice before combining it with water in the pot. This is an attempt to "wash off" the excess starches on the outside of the rice, which purportedly make the rice gluey. I haven't noticed any real difference in the final results between doing this and just going straight to the pot. The real quality comes from the cooking method in my opinion.

### Toasting the Rice

Other methods call for the rice to be cooked in the pot for a few minutes before the water is added in. This technique, known as toasting, is useful when trying to impart additional flavors to the rice. When making a Middle Eastern-style basmati rice or an Italian arborio rice used in risotto, I would fully suggest this process. However, for just making plain, unflavored white or brown rice, as we are in this Instructable, this step is unnecessary. I just find it important to always state that there's no need to follow the recipe exactly when cooking. If you can understand what's going on inside the pot, then there's often many ways to cook something delicious and successfully. Take the recipe with a grain of rice.

## Step 2: Prepare Rice

Measure 1 cup of rice and pour it into your pot. Then, measure 1¾ cups of water and pour that in too. If you're using the same measuring cup for both the rice and the water, make sure you measure the rice first, otherwise the wet sides of the measuring cup will make the rice stick.

Rice expands when you cook it, so 1 cup is usually enough for two people to eat alongside something else. To be honest, if I'm cooking rice for myself, I still make 1 cup because it's so cheap and the stuff sort of has to reach a critical mass in order to be able to cook correctly. In terms of serving sizes, figure on about ½ cup of rice per person. Adjust quantities of water accordingly.

## Step 3: Combine Rice and Water and Bring to a Boil

Once the water and the rice are combined, place the pot on the stove over high heat until the water begins to boil. It should take about 3 to 5 minutes for the water to boil if you're making 1 cup of rice to 1¾ cups water. If you're making more rice, expect longer waiting times.

## Step 4: Cover and Simmer

After the water has boiled, cover the pot and turn the heat down as low as it can go. This is what's known as simmering. The water will still be boiling and bubbling with the cover on, but it shouldn't burn at the low temperature. If it smells or looks like it's burning, turn your burner down even further. White rice will cook like this for 20 to 25 minutes. Brown rice will cook like this for 35 to 40 minutes.

## Step 6: Fluff the Rice With a Fork

Once the rice has sat for 10 minutes, it's time to fluff it with a fork. This basically just means mix it up a bit and let any resident moisture evaporate out. The grains should be plump and hold together ever so slightly.

## Step 5: Let the Rice Sit for 10 Minutes

Once the rice has simmered for the appropriate amount of time, remove the top and check to see if all of the moisture in the pot is gone. To do this, tilt the pot and look for pooling water. If there's no water, the rice is done cooking. If you've cooked the rice with the correct amount of water there shouldn't be any moisture left or burn marks on the bottom of the pot. If you've got too much water left over, you either didn't cook it long enough, or used too much water in your ratio. If you've got burn marks on your pot and on your rice, then you cooked it for too long, cooked it at too high a heat, or used too little water.

Place the lid back on the pot, turn the heat off, and let the rice just sit there for 10 minutes. If you are using an electric stove, switch the pot to a different burner. Electric elements can retain their heat for a long time and can continue the cooking process. This is an important step; letting the rice sit helps it reabsorb some of its starches and results in less gluey rice. So just set a timer, walk away, and build something awesome. Need an idea of something you can make? I know this great website called Instructables.com.

## Step 7: Plate and Enjoy

Plate (or bowl, as the case may be) the rice and enjoy with your favorite foods.

# How to De-Seed a Tomato
## By ale-8-1
(www.instructables.com/id/How-to-De-Seed-a-Tomato/)

If you want to make salsa or perhaps ceviche, you may need to remove the seeds from the tomatoes. There are several techniques, but I like the one I use.

## Materials
- Tomatoes
- Sharp knife

## Step 1: Starting Out
Cut off the top and bottom of the tomato and reserve them. It is somewhat important to make them straight so that the tomato will be able to sit level.

## Step 2: Semi-Circumcision
Depending on the size of the core, you may be able to cut into the spoke area where the seeds are without any obstruction. Do not cut out the seeds directly at this time because you'll make a mess. Instead, cut around the connecting areas. Although it is possible to do it in one go, I recommend you cut the pieces in half first.

We cut from the bottom up to give stability to the cutting process. Starting from the outer spoke, carefully cut around, trying to avoid the seeds as much as possible.

There may be times when you have to cut the tomato into four or more pieces, just repeat the same process of cutting around the seeds.

## Step 3: Surgery
With the exterior gone, you are left with a mass of flesh and some seeds. Take your knife and carefully scoop the seed mass out. Now you can cut up your tomato as you please. I usually do the scooping step over the trash so I do not have to worry about the seeds getting into my food. Don't forget about your tops, they are valuable pieces of tomato.

Now go make some salsa or ceviche!

# Crafting a Bento

By clamoring Kayobi Tierney
(www.instructables.com/id/Crafting-a-Bento/)

Bentos, or boxed lunches, have a long deep history rooted in ancient Japan. They originally began as simple meals that required little or no effort to assemble. Today they are a vibrant art form popular worldwide. This instructable will attempt to provide the basic design principles, resources for obtaining the necessary tools, and some of the traditional rules of making a beautiful and delicious bento.

## Step 1: Know the Rules (then break them!)

Like many other Japanese arts bento making has its own set of guidelines. Traditional bentos follow a couple of basic rules.

The 4-3-2-1 rule: 4 parts rice, 3 parts protein, 2 parts vegetable, and 1 part "treat" (usually either pickled vegetables or something sweet).

Sushi should be prepared with more wasabi than usual. Pack foods with flavors that might run or stick together with a divider. Separate wet foods from dry using a nested or altogether separate container such as a cupcake form. Sauces and dressings go in their own bottles (usually with a lid or cap). Oily foods (like gyoza) should be packaged

on top of an absorbent material. Bentos should not require refrigeration or heating.

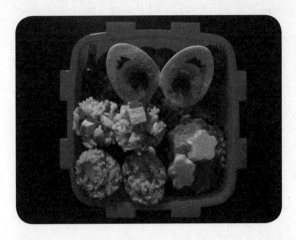

## Step 2: Assemble Hardware

If you're into kitchen gadgets making bento boxes can be a very fulfilling past time. There are tons of super cute accessories with which to decorate your lunches. Many of these items can be found online. If you're lucky enough to have a large Asian market in your town you'll probably be able to find everything you need right there. However, if you don't have one nearby don't fret. We'll talk about options using readily available items you probably already have in your kitchen.

The first thing you need is a bento box. This will influence your portions, your shapes, and even what types of food you use. There are several types. Cute shapes like the bullet train and Pandapple boxes are most popular for kids. Tiered boxes, like the shamrock bento, are more often used for adult lunches. Lock & Lock boxes are fantastic for two reasons. One, they come with individual removable dividers. And two, they lock completely air tight. I've recently started seeing Fit & Fresh brand in stores. The orange one pictured below has a separate ice ring you can freeze as well as a folding spoon. If you want to get started right away and don't have any of these types of boxes there you can also use a standard container. The actual shape of your box will have a lot to do with the final design of your box but we'll talk about that in the design step.

Cupcake forms and dividers are very handy when keeping flavors from mingling. Mini forms fit well in bentos. There are also silicone forms out now that are great if you have something really wet or messy (like spaghetti). The most common divider is the green plastic grass but there are lots of other specialty designs.

Regular shrimp forks are small in size, easy to find in stores, and fit in many boxes. Many colors, shapes, and sizes of specialty forks designed especially for bento boxes are available. Skewers or toothpicks can be cut to size and decorated should you be so inclined. A nice pair of chopsticks will round off your bento set. I like the ones that come with a matching box.

Many of the fancy patterns you see in bentos are made with some form of cutter. A cutter can be a cookie cutter, craft punch, or craft blade. I think I use my craft blade more than any other bento tool! Cutters are especially handy for cutting nori (seaweed/sushi paper), vegetables, or sliced tofu/meat. Who doesn't want little carrot stars on their salad?

Probably one of the more difficult specialty items to substitute for is a sauce bottle. Barring proper bottling, you can also put sauce into a Ziploc bag (towards one corner) and secure the sauce with a rubber band. This would be something like a pastry frosting bag only very small. At lunch you can clip the tip off and squeeze the sauce out. I have also folded tinfoil into a little cup shape. If you go that route just be sure you use it for a thicker substance (like peanut butter) rather than something liquidly (like soy sauce) as it will probably leak.

## Step 3: Gather Specialty Food Items

A trip to your local Asian market is important to a traditional bento. But if you live in an area where you do not have access to such items don't fret. There are lots of creative and healthy ways to make a bento from seasonal local ingredients.

Calrose rice is your first choice for sushi rice. Minute rice isn't going to cut it.

Tonkatsu sauce is simply good on everything. It's mostly used on tonkatsu (fried cutlet, usually pork) but it is also very delicious on steamed veggies. It's similar to Worcestershire sauce.

Furikake is used as a rice seasoning to spice up bland rice. It is usually a mix of dried seaweed bits, sesame seeds, dried shrimp, and various salts (vegetarian options such as the one below are available).

Japanese bread crumbs are primarily used in making tonkatsu and fried shrimp. I think you could use regular bread crumbs in a pinch, but the ones marked Japanese seem to be lighter. (Maybe it's just my imagination!)

Mirin is a sweet light syrup used in making sushi rice and tomago (egg) sushi.

Tempura mix can be used to make tempura batter. You can make your own mix but if you use a premade one you can eliminate the egg.

Wasabi can be purchased in powder or paste form. Don't let the pleasant light green color fool you—this stuff will clear your sinuses!

## Step 4: Stuff to Put in Your Bento: Onigiri

Onigiri, rice balls with filling, are a wonderful comfort food. They are fun to make, fun to look at, and fun to eat. They also serve as a nice parcel to decorate as they have a large surface area. The simplest onigiri, and maybe the most traditional, is simply a rice ball with an umeboshi (pickled plum) in the middle. Umeboshi are extremely popular in bento boxes and especially onigiri.

First you must decide on your filling. Just like sushi, you could put anything you like in an onigiri. Something with a little body is best as anything too fluid will tend to seep. Some commercially packaged onigiris pack the nori separately so that it stays crispy. Some common fillings are tuna, chicken, curry, boiled spinach, umeboshi, or tofu. It is also common to flavor the rice.

After you have decided on your filling take some rice and form a ball. You can make it as large or as small as you like. Using your fingers or a utensil make a pocket. Add your filling and top with some rice. The triangle is probably the most common onigiri shape. Just form with your hands. It's so easy!

## Step 5: Stuff to Put in Your Bento: Tempura

Tempura is a crispy batter coating used on vegetables or shrimp (although you could use it on anything that will hold together in hot oil.) It's fantastically cheap and easy to make.

The batter consists of: 1 egg, 1 cup ice water (it is important that the water is ice cold), and 1 cup all-purpose flour. Mix gently until blended but still lumpy. Use immediately. While you can certainly fry this up at this point it is extra delicious if you also

bread your food. Japanese bread crumbs are light and give a big crunch.

You should have three containers: one with the batter, one with the breading, and a pan with hot vegetable oil. Dip your item in the batter, roll in the breading, shake off excess. Fry the bean in the oil, drain off excess on a paper towel. That's it!

Often served with tonkatsu sauce (see step four for more info).

## Step 6: Stuff to Put in Your Bento: Sushi

Sushi is probably the most versatile food you can put in a bento box. Believe it or not it is quick and easy to make. Aside from cooking the rice making a sushi roll can take as little as 5 minutes.

Sushi could certainly be its own instructable. But instead of trying to cover every type of sushi you could find in a really fantastic bento box I'm only going to cover one just to get you started. Maki sushi is the round, nori-wrapped (seaweed), sushi roll with any number of tasty fillings. Let's use the tempura beans from the last step to fill this one.

Prepare your Sushi rice and let it cool. Calrose rice with a dash of rice vinegar and a dash of mirin is what I like to use. The kind of rice you use is important—use sushi, calrose, or sticky rice.

Now you have your rice, nori, wasabi, and your fried beans. It's time to roll!

Place your nori paper (seaweed) shiny side down on your table or bamboo mat. Prepare a shallow dish of water to dip your fingertips in to keep the sticky rice from

kitchen

13

sticky-ing to your fingers. Cover the entire sheet with rice except for a strip about an inch wide at the top. Place the wasabi and beans about two inches up from the bottom. Roll tightly bottom to top and stop just short of the bare nori strip at the top. Wet the top strip with water with your fingertips and complete the roll. Cut in half and half again.

## Step 7: Stuff to put in Your Bento: Gyoza (part 1 of 3)
### Wrappers

Gyoza is a nice thing to open a bento box and find. They have a pretty fan shape, a nice crispy texture on one side, and a savory filling in the middle. While they fantastic served hot they also keep extremely well.

You can, of course, put anything you like inside your gyoza. Most gyozas have cabbage and pork inside. I happen to be vegetarian so I'm filling these with tofu, parsley, and cabbage. This mix also has a dash of soy sauce, a little grated ginger, and a dash of mirin.

You can find gyoza wrappers in Asian markets or sometimes in a regular grocery store near the tofu. Egg roll wrappers are just slightly thinner than gyoza wrappers but obviously they work just as well. Plus, most grocery stores carry them.

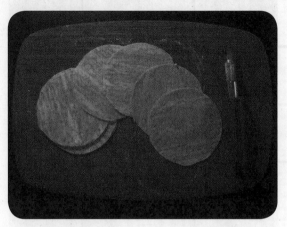

## Step 8: Stuff to put in Your Bento: Gyoza (part 2 of 3)
### Pleating & Filling

After you have your wrappers prepare a small dipping bowl of water. Dip your finger in the bowl to wet your fingertip and run your finger along the edge of the wrapper. Make sure it is wet enough to be shiny, which may require more than one dip. Wetting the edge forms a "glue" to hold your gyoza shut.

Loosely fold the circle in half (not so that the whole thing closes together though) and pinch the corner shut. You want to use enough pressure to just barely feel the gyoza wrapper squish beneath your fingertips.

Holding the corner with one hand, take the half facing you on the same side as the corner you just pinched and make an "s" shape with it. Pinch again. Now you have a pleat. Repeat pleating until you are about halfway closed.

Holding the half-pleated gyoza in one hand like an ice cream cone, put enough filling inside to fill the pocket but not enough to level up to your glue line. Continue pleating until completely closed. It is moderately important that you have no air holes in your gyoza as this will cause your gyoza to leak in your pan while cooking.

## Step 9: Stuff to put in Your Bento: Gyoza (part 3 of 3)

Cooking

Use a light, flavorless oil and medium heat. After the pan is hot place your gyoza inside in a nested line. Be very careful the gyoza doesn't stick to the pan while cooking. This could potentially tear your gyoza and then you have a big mess in your pan! Add more oil if you need to and shake the pan a lot. You may find cooking with chopsticks will add to your dexterity when something small like a corner sticks.

While the bottoms of your gyoza are browning we need to steam the tops. Take a small amount of water (A couple of tablespoons should do the trick) and add it to the hot pan. Place a lid or piece of aluminum foil over the top to trap the steam inside. You may need to do this several times before they're all cooked.

Drain on paper towels. Since we're putting these in a bento box, we want to give them extra draining time. Otherwise, you could serve them right away. In a bento box you would probably want to include a serving bottle of gyoza sauce—soy sauce with a dash of vinegar. You would also place them on a surface that would absorb the oil like a paper doily or paper towel.

Gyoza are often served in groups of five. At dinner in Japan, it would not be uncommon for gyoza to be made in a batch of 30 to 40 for a family.

## Step 10: Design Your Bento!

When I start a bento the first thing I look at is my main item (e.g. sushi or gyoza). I almost always have this in mind before I start cooking. I then choose my bento box and go from there.

As we previously discussed, your bento box will have a great deal to do with your overall design. For example, if you have a traditional lacquerware bento box with rounded corners you are going to need to fill in some odd spaces. Likewise, boxes with dividers built in to them may or may not be the right size for what you want to do.

After space filling, you'll want to consider color. By far, fresh fruits and vegetables are going to have the best colors. Fresh slightly steamed veggies will yield a brilliant spectrum. It is considered unappetizing to have a bento that is uniform in color.

Texture is also very important. Smooth shiny surfaces next to spiky shapes next to billowy veggies treat the eye to a visual array of excitement. Noodles look great furled up into a "bird's nest."

Giving your bento a name or a theme can pull the whole piece together and inspire details. Although you would think it might be the first step in the design process it is often the last. It is surprisingly easy to put together a bento that is full but not finished. Many times just a small pair of eyes cut out of nori, a few carrot hearts, or a tiny little fork can make an ordinary lunch into a bento box.

## Step 11: Inspirational Links

Bento ideas are commonly shared amongst bento makers worldwide. Below are some of the places I regularly go to for supplies and new ideas. JBox, Cooking Cute: Bento, TV Bento, My Bento (a Flickr group), Bento Boxes (a Flickr group)

# Pesto Freezing Method

## By ToolNut Damon Hearne
(www.instructables.com/id/Pesto-Freezing-Method/)

Here is a quick one on how I like to freeze pesto. The short version is that I put the fresh pesto in a decent Ziploc bag, cut a corner of the bag (½" size hole), and squeeze like icing into ice cube trays. I freeze the trays and then transfer them into freezer bags. I freeze mine with the cheese already mixed in. I always see advice not to do that, but I don't know why; I suppose it may taste slightly fresher if the cheese is added when thawed, but I can't tell the difference. When we want pesto in the middle of winter, we just pop out a couple of cubes and toss them into the dish. It's much easier than trying to carve the pesto out of a large frozen block. I have a few tricks to keep it from oxidizing while freezing, etc. I've also included my favorite recipe and a few gratuitous close-ups of the green goop. There is a good instructable on actually making the pesto at www.instructables.com/id/Pesto-2/.

## Materials
- Pesto
- Ziploc bag
- Freezer trays
- Plastic wrap

16

## Step 1: Make Pesto and Put it Into a Ziploc Bag

Make lots of pesto at once. There are many great pesto recipes available online to choose from.

## Step 2: Get Out Ice Cube Trays and Cut Bag

Remove ice from ice trays. Place them in your drink or give to the dog. Line up your ice trays. Cut a corner of the bag (not the corner where the zipper is!) with a pair of scissors—I think a ½ inch size hole is good. Be careful that it doesn't start squirting out as soon as you cut the bag.

## Step 3: Squeeze it. It's Fun

Squeeze the pesto into each ice cube section. Do not overfill. Better to do more batches than overfill it and have a mess on your hands. After the trays are full, level off the pesto, cover with plastic wrap, and press the plastic wrap into the pesto. This reduces oxidation (dark green color).

## Step 4: Freeze and Bag

Freeze in the tray for a few hours, and then transfer to a freezer bag for long term storage. It's best to get as much air out of the bag as possible. Vacuum sealing would be ideal. Now, when you need pesto for one, two, or five you have the chunks ready to go. I buy into the conspiracy theories that microwaving kills the good stuff in veggies so I just let them thaw slowly if I can't just throw them in with the hot food. They thaw pretty quickly anyway because of the olive oil.

# Making Dill Pickles

By **kewpiedoll99** Barclay A. Dunn and Adam Gugliciello
(www.instructables.com/id/ Making-Dill-Pickles/)

In my garden I planted about six times as many plants of each type as was recommended, largely because I was too soft-hearted to throw away the less-hardy of them, and now I have a ridiculous harvest and plants that are taking over the back yard and even trying to get into the house. This created a new problem: What to do with the excess harvest, above and beyond the produce my boyfriend and I could reasonably eat? We decided to pickle some of it, particularly the cucumbers, which lend themselves naturally to such processing. I picked a few green tomatoes as well to try the process on them. I used a recipe by Sharon Howard that I found online. Note: You have to wait 8 weeks after pickling before you are supposed to eat the pickles.

## Ingredients

- 8 pounds cucumbers (cut into spears if too large for the jars); we also used green tomatoes
- 4 cups white vinegar
- 12 cups water
- ⅔ cup pickling salt
- 16 cloves garlic, peeled and halved
- fresh dill weed

## Equipment

It's helpful to have a boiling-water canner (though we didn't).

## Step 1: Chill the Cukes

Wash cucumbers, and place in the sink with cold water and lots of ice cubes. Soak in ice water for at least 2 hours but no more than 8 hours. Refresh ice when it melts. This took all the ice in my freezer and an additional bag that I had to run out to get.

## Step 2: Boil the Brine

In a large pot over medium-high heat, combine the vinegar, water, and pickling salt. Bring the brine to a rapid boil. Note: Although the ingredients called for pickling salt, we used regular table salt and made sure it was completely dissolved in the liquid. This picture was taken when most of the brine was already in jars with cukes. Btw, initially it filled the entire pot, but check out the briny goodness encrusted on the sides of the pot.

## Step 3: Sterilize Canning Jars and Lids

Wash 8 (1-quart) canning jars, bands, and lids in hot soapy water and rinse. Dry bands and set aside. Place the jars and lids in 180° (near-boiling) water for at least 10 minutes. Also sterilize the tongs you use to put them in the boiling water. Don't touch them with your hands after you sterilize them. Keep the jars and lids hot until used. We did steps 3 and 4 in batches of two or three jars at a time.

### Step 4: Load the Jars With Spices, Cukes, and Brine and Seal

Right after you take the jars out of the sterilizing bath, place in each 2 half-cloves of garlic, some dill, and then enough cucumbers to fill the jar (about 1 pound). Then add 2 more garlic halves and some more dill. Fill jars with hot brine. Leave headspace of ¼ inch. Make sure nothing is hanging over the side. Remove air bubbles by sliding a nonmetallic spatula between the jar and food. Clean rim and threads of jar with a damp cloth. Center heated lid on jar. Screw band down to "fingertip tight." Note: If they are too tight, the lids deform when the steam tries to escape during processing (next step).

### Step 5: Process Sealed Jars in the Boiling Water Bath

Process quart jars for 15 minutes as follows.

- It's suggested to use a rack to keep jars from touching canner bottom and to permit heat circulation; we didn't have the right size rack, so we didn't do this.
- It's suggested to put jars into a canner that contains simmering water. We just used the three biggest and heaviest pots we had.
- After adding jars, add boiling water to bring water 1 to 2 inches above jar tops. We couldn't get water above the jar tops, but comments I read online said this wasn't necessary.
- Bring water to a rolling boil. Set timer and process for recommended time.
- Remove jars from canner immediately after timer sounds.
- Cool for 12 to 24 hours on a rack or towel. Or on the counter, as you see in image below.

- Do not retighten screw bands after processing.
- After jars are cooled, remove screw bands, wipe jars, label and date.

### Step 6: Check the Seals

To ensure lids are sealed, remove bands and try to lift lids off with your fingertips. Clean jars and lids with a damp cloth. Label and store jars in a cool, dry, dark place. For best results, wait 8 weeks (*Eight Weeks! That's Two Months!*) before eating. Sorry for you instant gratification junkies, but the flavors won't have melded until then. For best quality, use within one year. When I was checking the seals, I pulled too hard with my fingernails on one and it came off. If a seal comes off, they have to go right into the fridge, and you have to eat them sooner. Oh dang!

# How to Make and Can Applesauce

By **ewilhelm** Eric Wilhelm
(www.instructables.com/id/How-to-make-and-can-applesauce---Canned-applesauce/)

A surprisingly easy way to deal with a surplus of tasty fruit.

## Step 1

Acquire a canning pot. They come with a wire rack for about $18, and for about another $5 you can get the tongs and funnel as well. Jars run about $6 to $9/dozen, depending on size. Fill the pot about ⅔ of the way up with water and start heating—there's enough thermal mass that this will take a while.

## Step 2

Cook down chopped apples with water, lemon juice, honey, and spices to taste. Run the hot chunks through a food processer or food mill, and return to the pot to keep warm.

## Step 3

Meanwhile, prepare jars and lids: Wash jars by hand or in the dishwasher, and then place in a clean sink filled with extremely hot tap water until ready for use. Add clean rings and lids; do not run lids through the dishwasher.

## Step 4

Create a workspace on a clean towel next to the sink. Remove jar from the hot water and shake off excess. Add applesauce to pint jars using the funnel.

## Step 5

Leave about ½ inch headspace for expansion during cooking; this means the big ring on the base of the jar neck. (Useful, eh?)

## Step 6

Wipe threads and top of the jar with a clean paper towel to ensure a proper seal. Place a lid on top of the jar, and gently screw on the ring, leaving it loose enough that air can escape during boiling.

## Step 7

Place jars on the rack in the boiling water as you fill them. Lower the full rack into the water, which should cover the jars by at least an inch or two. Cover, return to a boil, and begin timing for 20 minutes.

## Step 8

Use tongs and/or a spatula to retrieve rack handles from the boiling water, and raise the rack. Remove jars with curved end of tongs, and place on another clean towel to cool and dry. Be sure to leave enough space between jars for air to circulate. Listen for pops as the lids vacuum-seal.

## Step 9

Label with date and contents, then store in a cool, dark place until apple season is over.

# Authentic Pretzels

By **NoFiller** Jaclyn Sharpe
(www.instructables.com/id/
Authentic-Pretzels/)

These pretzels are boiled in a baking soda solution for that unique chewy texture. This recipe makes 16 palm-sized soft pretzels.

## Materials

- 1½ cups water
- 1 tablespoon sugar
- 1 packet yeast
- 1 teaspoon salt
- 1 tablespoon oil or butter
- 4½ cups flour
- ½ cup baking soda
- coarse salt

## Step 1: Prepare Dough

Mix:
- 1½ cups warm water
- 1 tablespoon sugar
- 1 packet yeast and let sit for 10 minutes.

Stir in:
- 1 teaspoon salt
- 1 tablespoon oil or butter
- 2 cups flour

Stir in as much additional flour as you can, then turn onto a floured board and knead for 7 to 8 minutes, adding flour as necessary.

Important: Do not add baking soda to dough!

## Step 2: Rest Dough

Place dough in a lightly oiled bowl and rest in a warm place for 1 hour.

In the meantime bring 8 cups of water and ½ cup* baking soda to boil in a large pot, and heat oven to 450°F.

*Some people have found this to be too much. If you are worried cut it back to ⅓ or a ¼ cup.

## Step 3: Form pretzels

Punch down dough and divide into 16 equal pieces. Roll each piece into a rope 16 to 20 inches long. To form pretzel shape, fold rope in half, twist twice and fold over. Press lightly to stick everything together and place directly into boiling water.

## Step 4: Water Bath

Boil each pretzel for 1 to 2 minutes, turning once. With a slotted spoon transfer to a cookie sheet lined with parchment paper and sprinkle with coarse salt.

Boil or dip? Some recipes call for dipping the pretzels in the baking soda solution but not boiling them. This gives the same chewy texture but allows the pretzels to puff up a lot more in the oven.

## Step 5: Bake

Bake pretzels for 10 minutes at 450°F. Transfer immediately to a cooling rack.

# Easy Doughnuts

### By RealSimple.com
### (www.instructables.com/id/
### Easy-Doughnuts/)

"Our intern Dana Walcott and her college roommates used to make these for late-night study breaks. She topped them with cinnamon. I've tried them with a pinch of cayenne pepper, unsweetened cocoa, and sugar—they were a hit."

—Kate Merker, Associate Food Editor, Real Simple

Warm doughnuts on a Saturday morning are right up there with bubble baths and midday naps on the list of life's greatest pleasures.

## Ingredients
- 1 8-count package large refrigerated biscuits (such as Pillsbury Grands)
- ½ cup vegetable oil
- ½ cup sugar
- ¼ teaspoon ground cinnamon

## Step 1: Cut
Place the biscuits on a cutting board. Using a 1-inch round cookie cutter or shot glass, cut a hole in the center of each biscuit, reserving the extra dough for "holes."

## Step 2: Test
Heat the oil in a medium skillet over medium-low heat. Test the heat of the oil by dipping the edge of a doughnut in the pan. When the oil is hot enough, the edge will bubble.

## Step 3: Cook
Place 4 of the doughnuts and holes in the skillet and cook until golden brown, 1 to 1½ minutes per side.

## Step 4: Drain
Transfer to a wire rack or paper towel-lined plate to drain.

## Step 5: Combine, Toss, Serve
In a large bowl, combine the sugar and cinnamon. Gently toss the warm doughnuts in the mixture a few at a time. Serve warm or at room temperature.

# Cake Pops

By **scoochmaroo** Sarah James
(www.instructables.com/id/
Cake-Pops/)

Made famous by Bakerella and ubiquitous by Starbucks, cake pops are the latest trend in dessert culture. Here I walk you through the steps to make your own cake pops at home! Whether you use homemade or store-bought cakes and icing, you can still customize these adorable treats to your heart's content. Decorate them for any occasion. The process may be time consuming (be patient!) but the rewards are well worth the effort.

## Materials

- A design concept (v. important for knowing what kind of decorating supplies to get!)
- Cake mix (or homemade)
- Frosting (or homemade)
- Lollipop sticks
- Candy melts
- Sprinkles
- Colored icing tubes
- Other neat stuff for decorating
- Styrofoam to stand them up in

## Step 1: Bake a Cake and Mash it Up

Either make your favorite from-scratch recipe or follow the instructions on the box. I chose strawberry. I thought pink would be cute. Next time I'm sticking with chocolate. Once your cake is cooled—really cooled—crumble

it up into a bowl. Stir in your frosting, a little at a time. Once it reaches a nice consistency that will cling together when you roll it in a ball, you're there. Stick it in the fridge.

## Step 2: Ball it Up

Once it's nice and cool, you'll want to start rolling it into balls. This is really baker's choice—how big, what shape and how to make them. I don't have one of those little melon-baller gadgets, but I might get one for the next round—my hands seems incapable of rolling a sphere and they all come out like footballs. It took some work to make the beautiful spheres you see here. Nonetheless! Roll your cake mash into ball-like pieces. Mine were about 1¼" in diameter. Next? Stick em in the fridge.

## Step 3: Melt the Candy Coating

These candy melts from Wilton are super easy to use. Following the instructions on the package, I put them in a bowl in the microwave, on 50 percent power for 1½ minutes. Then I stirred them and zapped them again at 50 percent for 30 seconds.

Repeat until nice and melty, and then repeat once more for superior dipping quality. I melted up some pink, yellow and white.

## Step 4: Dip your Pops

Get those cake balls outta the fridge! Get your lollipop sticks ready, and dip them slightly in the melted candy before inserting them half-to-three-quarters way in to each cake ball. This is where I would usually say "Stick it in the fridge!" but when I did so at this step, I think it worked against me. So don't. Or, try it without sticking them in the fridge at this point, and if it turns out to be a hot mess, then, well . . . stick em in the fridge. Dip your newly-sticked cake pops into the candy coating and rotate to ensure even coverage. Stand the dipped pops into Styrofoam to let drip-dry.

## Step 5: Decorate your Pops

Now it's time to get creative. If you had any pops that didn't turn out so hot, practice on those. I don't have any pictures of my decorating process, but I just used what I had in terms of glitter and confetti and such. The ducks' noses and wings were more melted candy coating, and the feet were little orange stars that came in the confetti mixture. The eyes were dotted on with the tube decorator icing. The eggs were made by using the decorator icing and glitter/confetti. So what should my next ones look like?

## Step 6: Share!

Trust me, these babies are not to be eaten on one's own. They are potent sugar-bombs!

Bring them into work or to the next party you have. Share them with your friends! Bet someone a dollar they can't eat a whole one in one bite!

Then go call your dentist.

## How to Make Great Homemade Mozzarella

By **thomas9666**
(www.instructables.com/id/How-To-
Make-Great-Homemade-Mozzarella/)

I've always been interested in cheese and wanted to make my own. This is my adaptation of the recipe found on www.instructables.com/id/Great-Mozzarella-Cheese/. I used this recipe a few times and it didn't work as well as I hoped. So I took my time thinking through what changes I could make.

I hope this helps everyone who wants to make their own great mozzarella.

### What You Will Need
- whole fat milk—I used approximately 1 quart (one liter) as this was just a quick batch for fun.
- citric acid
- rennet—liquid or tablet. I used a liquid version. Use as the packaging instructs
- bottled unchlorinated water
- cheese cloth/white muslin cloth—for straining curds
- thermometer
- stainless steel pot
- large bowl
- cheese press (optional)
- salt

### Step 1: Gently Heat the Milk
Pour your desired amount of milk into your stainless steel pot (an aluminum pot will affect the reactions later on)

Constantly stir the milk so it does not stick to the bottom of the pan and to prevent a skin forming.

At this stage, DO NOT HEAT PAST 80°F.

### Step 2: Adding the Citric Acid
At this stage, whilst the milk is still under 80°F, you will have to add the citric acid.

The acid will lower the pH of the cheese and give mozzarella its characteristic stretchy texture.

For every quart of milk, you add ¼ teaspoon of citric acid.

I made 1 quart (1 liter) worth of cheese, and used ¼ teaspoon, but if you are making approximately a gallon of cheese (4 liters) you will add a whole teaspoon.

Add the powder and make sure you mix it through thoroughly. You will notice that some of the milk will curdle and stick to your spoon. This is normal.

### Step 3: Adding the Rennet
Now that you have added the citric acid, you have to heat up the milk to 90°F.

Turn off the heat just before the thermometer reads 90°F.

Measure out ¼ cup of bottled (unchlorinated) water. Follow directions of the rennet packaging. My bottle of rennet says "for every liter of milk, add 5 drops."

So for my recipe, 1 liter of milk, I added 5 drops of rennet to a quarter cup of bottled water.

Mix the rennet through the milk for at least 30 seconds. Leave the milk alone, off the heat, for at least 20 minutes to curdle.

## Step 4: Check For A Clean Break

After you have waited for the milk to curdle, you have to test to see if the milk has indeed curdled.

To test this, dip you clean finger into the milk and bring it back out. If you have a clean break, your curds are ready.

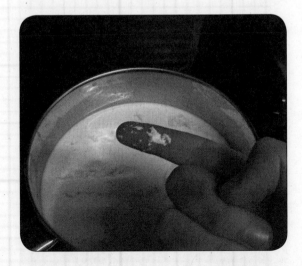

## Step 5: Cut and Cook the Curds

Now cut the curds in a crisscross pattern and turn the heat back on high.

Mix the curds, you don't want them sticking to the pot.

Cook the curds for around 10 minutes.

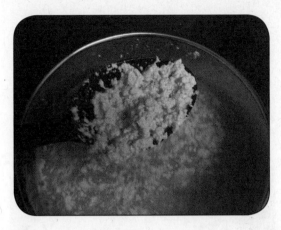

## Step 6: Straining the Curds

To strain the curds, set up your large bowl, with your cheese cloth/muslin over it.

Pour the curds and whey into the bowl. The liquid whey will pass through the cloth and the solid cheese curds will remain in the cloth.

KEEP the whey for later on. Also keep the pot handy.

### Step 7: Cheese Press (optional)

If you own a cheese press, you can use it now.

Place your curds, still in your cheese cloth, inside the mould and insert into your press.

Press for 10 minutes.

Alternatively, I made a quick homemade press with the water bottle used earlier, and a mould that came with a cheese making kit.

### Step 8: Chop and Salt

Now you have your curds, either pressed or not; give them a rough chop (if pressed) and salt the curds.

### Step 9: Prepare to Stretch Curds

Pour your whey from the large bowl, back into your pot on a high heat. Rinse out the bowl and fill with cold water. For ease place the cheese cloth back into the bowl to catch the curds when they are stretched.

Place a medium sized curd onto your spoon and lower it into the hot whey. Leave the curd to heat up to the temperature at which it will stretch. This is around 160° to165°F.

When the curd stretches, you know the whey is at the correct temperature for the rest.

### Step 10: Stretching Your Curds

Add all of the curds into the whey to heat up. Leave them for a few minutes.

You might want to place your cheesecloth back into the whey to catch all the curds again.

When the curds are hot enough, gather them with your spoon then shape them by hand.

The curds will be very hot. Most internet sites recommend wearing rubber gloves to keep your hands cool. I recommend it as well.

I formed my mozzarella balls by kneading the curds in my hand until they started to look smooth. If the curds ever feel more resilient, place them back into the whey to heat them. When you are happy with the smoothness of the mozzarella and it is in an authentic ball form, place them into your bowl of cold water to set the shape.

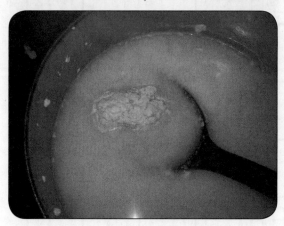

### Step 11: Finished Mozzarella

You have now just made your very own mozzarella.

I don't know how long the cheese will last in the fridge as I always use it straight away.

Mozzarella is best stored in slightly salted water, in an airtight container in the fridge.

Enjoy.

# How to Milk an Almond

By **megmaine** Meg Richards
(www.instructables.com/id/How-to-Milk-an-Almond-fresh-homemade-almond-milk/)

- sweetener of your choice, to taste (optional)

Fresh raw almond milk is delicious, healthy, unprocessed, and economical. There is no waste, no unrecyclable plastic-lined Tetra Pak boxes or cartons to put in landfills and drink BPA out of, and this tastes much, much better than store bought. The resulting almond meal is a free bonus, useful in cookies, crumb crusts, porridge, granolas, or in lieu of bread crumbs in stuffing and dressings, breaded crusts, etc.

## Ingredients

To make a half gallon (or approximately 2 liters) of delicious fresh almond milk, you will need:

- about a pound (or roughly ½ kg) of fresh raw almonds out of the shell
- blender or food processor
- large bowl to strain into
- mesh bag or cheesecloth for first straining
- reusable fine wire mesh coffee cone or fine muslin bag for second straining
- half gallon or 2 liter refrigerator jug to keep it in
- few pinches of salt (optional)

## Step 1: Measure and Soak Almonds

You will be using about 3 cups of water for every 1 cup of raw almonds out of the shell. Soak overnight in enough water to cover with a little more water to provide room for swelling. An easier way to measure if you want to make 2 quarts or 2 liters at a time, is that 1 lb (or roughly a half kilo) of raw almonds out of the shell, makes a half gallon or 2 quarts or roughly 2 liters of creamy, rich almond milk when sufficient water is added after squeezing to equal that volume. You can, of course, halve the water to make an almond cream suitable as coffee creamer, nog base, cream pies, or other uses where milk may be too thin.

## Step 2: Puree in Blender or Food Processor

A quick whir in a powerful blender results in a thick, frothy almond puree ready

27

to be squeezed in a mesh bag, jelly bag, cheesecloth, or something similar. Simply place your cheesecloth or mesh strainer bag over the bowl, pour and scoop your puree into it, draw it closed, and start squeezing until the almond meal is as dry as you can get it. Don't add any more water at this point. The harder you squeeze, the more creamy and nutritious your milk will be, but not to worry, any milk left in the bag will still be eaten in the form of the almond meal, so there is nothing wasted. I use a fine plastic mesh drawstring bag that doubles as a shopping bag for small loose items like garlic or peppers.

## Step 3: Fine-Strain for Perfectly Creamy Results

Pour the undiluted almond milk (just strained through the bag into a bowl) through a reusable gold metal mesh coffee cone filter. When it slows, gentle stirring makes filtering go faster. At the end, I press the bit of almond paste in the bottom of the filter to extract the last and creamiest bit. This finer, white almond meal is good to keep and dry separately and use as almond flour.

## Step 4: Add Water to Equal Your Total Volume

I make this easier by straining it the second time directly into my glass half-gallon refrigerator pitcher and then adding more water to fill the pitcher, but if you are making an amount different from a half gallon, proceed accordingly to get an end result of 3 cups of water for every cup of almond. You may thin it to taste by adding water, but better too rich than too thin, because too rich can be solved by adding water, but too thin is too bad.

## Step 5: Let "Bloom" 24 Hours in the Fridge

Let it sit covered in the refrigerator pitcher for 24 hours. You will notice a creamy layer floats on top, but with a few gentle shaking sessions and a day or so in the refrigerator it will blend nicely and taste superbly creamy. Once that has happened, add sweetener if you choose, and salt, a pinch at a time, shaking in between and tasting, until the flavor goes from a little "flat" with no salt, to "better than any milk I ever tasted" (perfect). If not sure, hold back on another pinch of salt because one pinch too many ruins it. If you accidentally do add that one extra pinch past perfect taste, add more sweetener and it will no longer taste salty. Some like to add vanilla, others add almond extract or other flavors. You can even add dutched cocoa for a creamy sensation.

See how this clings to the glass like the freshest dairy milk? Commercial preparations use thickeners such as guar gum to achieve something similar, but their results are inferior. It's hard not to drink it all up the first day, but it's even better the second. Keeps about a week in the refrigerator, but don't leave it out on the counter unless you want to experiment with raw almond yogurt or kefir.

As for the almond meal, that may be another Instructable, but briefly, you spread it out on a half sheet in a 300°F oven, stirring a few times here and there until toasty and dry. Store in a jar, and use as breadcrumbs, crumb crusts, breading, stuffing, cookies, cakes, and bars, or make into low glycemic granola.

# How to Make a Big Batch of Kombucha

By Tim Anderson
(www.instructables.com/id/How-to-
Make-a-Big-Batch-of-Kombucha/)

Kombucha is a fermented tea beverage popular in Russia, China, and elsewhere. The culture forms a leathery skin called the "mother" that floats on top. Here you'll learn how to wrangle the jellyfish-like "mother" and make kombucha 5 gallons at a time. This method produces a fizzy carbonated kombucha that tastes very much like hard apple cider.

For background on this bizarre beverage, read Arwen's Making Kombucha instructable at www.instructables.com/id/Making-Kombucha/ and the Wikipedia kombucha article at http://en.wikipedia.org/wiki/Kombucha. Some confusion arises from the existence of a Japanese kelp tea also called "kombucha."

I've made hundreds of gallons of kombucha for my friends and myself. I've done a great deal of experimentation and had some serious mishaps. I've killed the culture several times, coaxed it back when it got out of balance, and had a couple of explosions that splattered kombucha far and wide and could have seriously injured someone.

Between the mistakes, mishaps, and disasters, actual Russians and new-age fruitcakes have tasted my kombucha and told me it's the best they've ever had. I work with my culture until I get it tasting like apple cider. So much so that you'll try to figure out what varieties of apples it's from. But there's really nothing in it but tea, sugar, and a festering mass of microbes.

We'll be going step-by step through the process later, but for reference, here is how to make the sweet tea to be fermented.

## Anne's Recipe for Sweet Tea
- 6 teaspoons tea
- 6 cups (1.5 quarts) water
- 1 cup sugar

**Same Recipe for 4 gallons**
- 64 teaspoons (1.3 cups) tea
- 4 gallons (64 cups) water
- 10.66 cups sugar

**Same Recipe for 5 gallons**
- Just under 5 pounds sugar
- 5 gallons water
- 1.5 cups dry tea

## Step 1: Select Your Tea Leaves

Don't ever use Earl Grey tea. The bergamot in it will injure your culture and you'll need to get a new starter. This has happened to me. Anything with citrus in it is bad.

Buy your tea in Chinatown or an Indian grocery store. I pay between a dollar and four dollars for a pound of tea, which will make two or more 5 gallon batches. I've bought many a 6 pound bag of tea, which is very satisfying, walking out with a couple of suitcase-sized bags of tea.

Assam tea, Mamri, or green tea such as "Special Gunpowder" are safe choices.

"Pu Er" tea smells pretty bad at first but makes good kombucha. (The name pu er is actually English, get it? "poo air.")

Don't risk your whole culture with saffron tea, but it can turn out OK.

Early in the fermentation process you'll be able to clearly taste what type of tea it is, but when the fermentation is more advanced, the apple flavors of kombucha will dominate and the flavor of the tea leaf recedes.

Don't use teabags. You'll be shucking them for hours, dealing with lots of teabags and unsure of how strong your tea really is. You'll also not know for sure what's in the teabag; maybe something as bad as Earl Grey.

I made a giant teabag from a piece of a cotton bed sheet.

Types of tea that have worked for me: Assam, Mamri, green (very slow unless you use some brown sugar), jasmine (marginal), coffee (eventually it barely tastes like coffee).

Mother-Killers are Earl Grey, · orange spice, citrus anything, cocoa mix, synthetic fruit punch.

Star likes herbal teas and has successfully tried peppermint (mother was depressed for a long time, but eventually rallied), peppermint-chamomile, and chamomile-Echinacea.

## Step 2: Brew Much Tea

Brew a gallon or two of very strong tea, and then dilute it.

Don't boil all five gallons of water. That wastes energy and time and improves nothing.

Put one or two cups of dry tea in the giant teabag, tie it shut and boil it in your biggest pot. "One *or* two cups?" you ask. "Why not more precision?"

The recipe calls for 1.5 cups, but all tea is not the same.

That's okay because large batches like this are much more forgiving of variations than small batches. If you make a gallon or less you must stick exactly to the recipe in order to get a good result.

If you've got a big thermos, you can let it steep there hot as long as you want. You could also use a hay box or make Arwen-style sun tea.

Warning: The tea *must cool* before you add the culture. The culture has evolved at room temperature. If you put it in warm tea, certain species such as lactobacillus will outbreed the others and you'll get a sour kombucha without well developed fruit flavors. Very much like commercial kombucha, which is usually a weak vinegar.

## Step 3: The Giant Teabag Workout

Wring out the giant teabag into your brewing bucket, soak it with water, repeat until you don't feel bad about throwing out or composting such a large amount of used-up tea leaves. That 1.5 cups of dry tea swells up to become quite an impressive mound.

I cut the top off a plastic spring water carboy to make the brewing bucket seen here. I'm in the process of kneading the last tea-essence out of the teabag. Actually that's impossible, you have to give up some time.

## Step 4: Coffee Screen Method

You can also skip the teabag.

Throw the leaves right in the water and strain them out afterward.

Here, I'm pressure-cooking the tea and then pouring it through a gold screen coffee filter.

This is Mamri tea which stays as little pellets that don't clog the filter. Leaf tea and things with large flakes like "Special Gunpowder" would probably clog the screen and take longer than the big teabag.

I usually soak and pour several times, but it still probably doesn't extract as much tea-stuff as the big teabag method.

## Step 5: Dilute and Add Sugar

This is fun. Open a new 5 pound bag of sugar and dump most of it in. All except 10–15 percent of it.

White sugar is fine, except green tea ferments very slowly unless you add some brown sugar with the white. Otherwise it will take way too long. Other kinds of tea don't need brown sugar, but I usually throw some in anyway. Black tea is just green tea that's been through an oxidation process. That seems to make it easier for the mother to digest.

There's nothing wrong with using just brown sugar except it costs more in the U.S. and the flavor will be a little different. Use whatever sugar gives you the flavor you like.

Add cold water to make it five gallons and mix it all up.

If your batch is bigger than your containers, split it into multiple containers.

Sweeteners that have been reported to work: agave nectar, pineapple juice, honey, brown sugar, white sugar

## Step 6: Add Mother

When the tea has cooled, add the mother. Try to get a solid layer to float on top. That saves time. I save all my mother and add all of it to the new batch.

It grows by a quarter or half inch with each batch and would soon leave no room for tea, but lots of people ask for starters so it's not a problem. I can get starters from them if I make a mistake and mess up my culture, so I don't need to hold any in reserve.

I like lots of mother working. Some people want to only have a single layer of mother and will split the top surface off with each generation. They call the new layer the "daughter" and use it to brew their next batch. If you do that you'll need to add some liquid kombucha or vinegar to your new batch to make it acidic early on and avoid spoiling.

The mother is porous and vinegary. In the quantities seen in these pictures, it will inoculate the new batch thoroughly and leave no ecological niche for opportunistic foreign organisms.

New mother will grow only at the surface.

If part of the mother sinks, a new skin will grow across the area of exposed liquid at the surface. In this picture you can see that the old darker colored mother had puddles of liquid on top of it. The new lighter colored areas grew there.

## Step 7: Cover with Cloth. No Lids!

Warning: *no lids!* You must cover the vat with cloth.

If you have a lid over your vat, even a loose one, there will be moist air over the mother. There will be condensation on the lid and sides of the vat above the mother.

Mold will grow there and spread to the mother. The mother will die and possibly break apart.

If you see fuzz on the mother, throw it away, clean all your vessels, and let them dry out. Bleach them or leave them in the sun if you want to be really careful. Be very alert to this. Some types of mold make poisons. Mold is dangerous, which is to say people have died from it.

If you want to brew in a carboy (big jug with narrow neck, such as spring water vendors use), you need to cut the top off so it's more like a bucket or vat. I've seen it attempted in standard carboys and it ends badly, even if the jug is covered with cloth rather than a cap.

This fermentation is a complex process controlled by the mother. It's an aerobic process at least on the surface layers, and the vessel should not be sealed or you'll end up with problems. There will be another anaerobic stage later for those of you who want more fizz.

## Step 8: Date the Vat

Write the date on the vat. Don't expect to remember how long it's been in there. I expect this batch to be ready for bottling in 9 days or so. Variables in how much time it takes are type of tea (green or black), type of sugar (white or brown), how much mother there is, vitality of mother, and temperature (warm makes it not tasty, but it gets not tasty in a hurry).

## Step 9: Sit Back and Watch the Show

A few days have gone by and good things are happening. A new layer of skin is beginning to form at the surface of the liquid. Where the old mother touches the surface it will be attached to that. This layer of skin controls the environment in the vat.

The tea has gotten a little lighter in color and cloudy. Small bubbles of carbon dioxide are forming in the liquid and under the flaps of mother. Occasionally they burp up from under the mother. That's yeast working, making alcohol and acetic acid vinegar.

Some tentacles are starting to form, hanging down from the mother. I don't know what they are, but they seem to make the apple flavor. A very good sign. The tentacles are structurally very different from the mother. They look almost like algae and are very weak. They're usually darker than the tea and just vaguely greener.

A dusty layer appears on the bottom of the vat. I believe it's largely lactobacillus. It's making lactic acid vinegar. It has the sharp tangy flavor found in yogurt and sauerkraut. It's good for you and should be bottled with the rest. Don't transfer it to the next batch or that flavor will dominate. The same thing will happen if your vats aren't kept cool enough. To correct a culture that's gone sour is simple, wash the vessels and mother with water. Get some starter from someone who's getting more flavors.

The yeast in the vat gets oxygen it makes sugar into alcohol then acetic acid vinegar. That acid has a boingy sort of tanginess to it which is different from the sharp straightforward tang of acetic acid. When it gets less oxygen, the yeast makes sugar into alcohol, which in small amounts gives the other flavors a sense of depth and buoyancy. In larger quantities it's just alcohol.

## Step 10: Apple Tentacles

A batch I recently brewed after letting the mothers sleep in their own juice for a long time had no tentacles and the k'cha had no apple taste. But a bottle of it tasted very apple-icious a few weeks later. I looked and tentacles had grown in the bottle.

Carbonation bubbles float the tentacles to the surface when you disturb the liquid or pull the mother off. The second photo shows what it looks like when it floats to the surface.

## Step 11: Dusty or Cloudy

The dusty sediment building up at the bottom could be acetobacter, lactobacillus, or yeast. It's probably a mix of those. It seems to correspond more with the "straight" sour taste of lactic acid than the "boingy" sour taste of acetic acid.

I try not to transfer this sediment between batches. The flavor seems to be best if these species have to regenerate from the mother. Mostly I look for the tentacles in the previous step and pay attention to what conditions favor those. Don't let your brew get warm because that favors the sour critters in this sediment rather than the tasty tentacles.

I must have been hasty and transferred this sediment. The bulk of the liquid is clear, not cloudy, so it's a few days away from bottling at least and I wouldn't expect this much sediment from liquid this clear.

## Step 12: Cloudy Means Ready

This stuff is ready to taste and bottle. The bubbles mean a somewhat anaerobic environment in the liquid and the yeast is making $CO_2$ and a bit of alcohol. That stirs up the sediment and makes it cloudy. There's a nice growth of tentacles, so it's likely to be tasty!

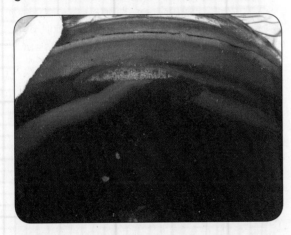

## Step 13: Vegan Leather Anyone?

The mother is surprisingly tough and solid like squid. I tried pretending it was calamari and fried it but it wasn't very good. Then again my fried calamari isn't very good either. Maybe squid isn't supposed to be fried.

Small chunks of mother can be drunk in kombucha and are really good, like the Chinese "pearl" drinks. The mother chunks are slightly more tart than the kombucha they inhabit.

To get a really thick and solid mother, just let a batch of kombucha keep fermenting. It'll get really sour and you'll get comments about the smell. You'll ignore the comments because it smells good to you. The longer you wait, the more sour and vinegary your kombucha becomes and the better the mother grows.

I tried drying the mother; it gets much thinner and very tough like parchment or rawhide. I've read that it's been used to make shoes in wartime but have been unable to find any more details than that.

## Step 14: Ready to Drink, But . . .

You can start drinking your kombucha now if you want to. Some people take out a portion to drink every day and replace it with an equal quantity of sweet tea. That is a traditional method but requires regular habits. Also I like it more fizzy than it gets in the vat, which means bottling it.

## Step 15: Look for Bottles

When it's just the way you want it, or rather *almost*, it's time to put it in bottles. I say "almost" because you should bottle it when it's just a little too sweet. That's so the yeast can make that extra sugar into fizz and just a little alcohol.

Regular PTFE or PET type plastic soda bottles, plastic spring water bottles, or anything like that are fine.

I once had fifteen gallons exactly ready for bottling and couldn't find any bottles to put it in. My friends had found my collection of empty bottles and destroyed them in a frenzy of inventiveness.

So I put it in carboys with rubber glove vapor traps as shown here and let the yeast work while I spammed the institute for empty soda bottles.

You can blend old sour kombucha, young sweet kombucha, and water to adjust the flavor when you bottle it. Set the bottles them aside until they get hard from carbonation. Put them in the fridge drink it.

WARNING:

If you wait too long to drink it the bottles can explode from excessive carbonation. They can puff up until the soda bottle is round on the bottom and rings like a bell when you tap it, and it's scary dangerous. Use bomb squad methods to deal with bottles like that. Three of mine once went off in a daisy-chain. They blew the side out of a Rubbermaid bin and put dripping splatters all over the ceiling.

Bottles like this could cripple, deafen, or blind you. This danger is why commercial kombucha can't be as good as the stuff you make yourself. Commercial bottlers can't be blowing fingers off their customers, putting their eyes out, and deafening them by shipping time-bomb beverages. They'd get sued when a forgotten bottle blew up and hurt someone. They have to terminate yeast fermentation in the bottles. That means high acid, low sugar, or dead culture.

kitchen

So they have to make it sour and not sweet. That way fermentation terminates or gets very slow and they can even put it in glass bottles. If you do it at home, you get to have it all. Sugar, live culture, carbonation, and a potentially dangerous bottle that could blow up if you don't drink it in time. Don't use glass bottles.

## Step 16: Bottling Jug

I cut the top off this water jug and drilled a hole by the bottom for a plastic spigot. I pour the new k'cha in here from the brewing vats. If it's too strong I add water. Be aware that the sweet taste recedes faster than the sour taste as you dilute.

If you lost track of time and your brew got way too sour, you can save it a bit at this step. You can add water and sugar, or younger sweet brew. If you add sugar though you'll need to leave it in the bottles longer before it tastes honest.

New sugar will make your teeth hurt just like candy or soda. After the mother has lived on it for a while, it still tastes sweet, but it won't make your teeth hurt anymore.

I used to screen my brew before bottling, but now I like the chunks and tentacles. Like an Asian "pearl" or "bubble" drink. When this

spigot gets clogged by that stuff, I just work the lever until the chunk comes through.

## Step 17: Decant Over-Fizzed K'cha

The bottles will keep fermenting and carbonating until something stops them. That could be running out of sugar, building up too much alcohol, acetic acid, lactic acid, or exploding.

A more common problem (opportunity) is bottles with so much fizz it's hard to open them without champagning k'cha all over the room instead of into a glass.

Here's one way to deal with that.

First refrigerate it. Gas solubility is higher in cold water. Then rapidly open and pour the kombucha into an angled glass. The angled glass and angled bottle present a much larger area surface for the gas to diffuse out. If you set the same bottle vertical, the upper surface is too small and you can get a volcano effect.

If your stuff has too much fizz even for that, we're in the realm of art, devise your own methods. Freezing is bad. Ice has poor gas solubility and plugs the neck when you open. Some people like to barely open the cap so a slow hiss of air comes out, too slow for bubbles to erupt. I like to open the cap and instantly squish out the remaining air before the eruption. It's amazing how the bottle re-inflates every time you do that. There can be a huge quantity of gas dissolved in the liquid. Enjoy your super-delicious fizzy healthy K'cha!

Make your own infused liqueurs and crystal clear ice cubes to go in them. Show off your mixology skills with recipes for cocktails from simple to sublime! First, master the homemade pomegranate liqueur, then impress your guests with glow-in-the-dark drinks and color-morphing martinis.

# Make Crystal Clear Ice

By isr_Raviv
(www.instructables.com/id/make-crystal-clear-ice!/)

In this instructable I will show you how to make crystal clear ice without any special equipment. It is super easy! You will be surprised.

## Step 1: Use Filtered Water

Dust and extra minerals in the water can cause the ice to cloud. Filtered water is much more pure and clean and therefore is much better for our clear ice.

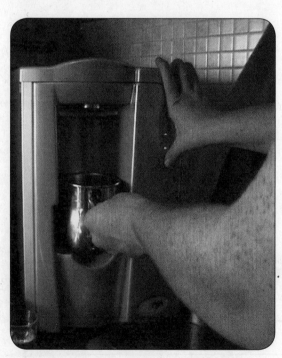

## Step 2: The Main Step—Boiling the Water

This is very simple but very effective. Boil the water, and then let it cool. After it's cool, boil the water again. This is it! You are done! Explanation: Dissolved air + minerals + dust cause the ice to appear cloudy. The double boiling eliminates dissolved air and decomposes minerals in the water.

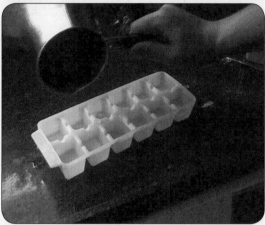

## Step 3: Results!

This is the difference between regular ice (cloudy) and the crystal clear ice after following the process. I hope you find this instructable useful and fun. Enjoy your crystal clear ice!

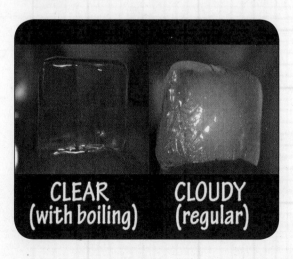

CLEAR (with boiling)     CLOUDY (regular)

# Limoncello Recipe

By **mikeasaurus** Mike Warren
(http://www.instructables.com/id/
limoncello-recipe/)

**limoncello**

Limoncello is a classic Italian liqueur. The process involves using the zest of the lemon peels, which are high in oils, and then steeping in alcohol to impart the lemony-flavor. Traditionally this lovely liquor is made from sorrento lemons, but common eureka lemons are just as good.

You can easily make your own version on limoncello with lemons (or just about any other citrus fruit), splash of sweetener, and a healthy dash of vodka. What are you waiting for? Grab some lemons and follow along to make your own variant of this delicious mouth-puckering drink!

When life gives you lemons, make limoncello!

## Ingredients
- citrus fruit/fruit
- lemons
- limes
- grapefruits
- kiwi
- grain alcohol/vodka (any type) Grain alcohol is ideal as it's high in alcohol content and is flavorless, however it's not available in some places. Vodka works just fine.
- sugar

## Supplies
- cheese grater
- glass bottles/jars

## Step 1: Zest fruit

Using the fine grating side of a cheese grater, take the zest off your fruit. The zest of the fruit is the coloured portion of the fruit skin and the white portion below is called the pith. The zest holds the oil of the fruit while the pith is bitter. You want all zest and no pith.

Fill each jar with fruit zest. For the kiwi, I sliced into small segments and then muddled the pieces in the jar. I then filled each jar with vodka. The remaining fruit can be made into a citrus meringue, squeezed to make fresh juice, or maybe you can find some creative uses.

bar

bottle, but any bottle with a resealable cap will work.

Make sure to squeeze the cheesecloth after straining to ensure all liquid is removed from the zest.

Next a solution of simple syrup (equal parts sugar and water) was added to thestrained liquid, this will make the drink more palatable and less bitter. The amount of syrup to add depends on personal taste. I used about 90 ml (3 fl.oz) of simple syrup for 270 ml (9 fl.oz) of alcohol.

## Step 2: Wait

After filling, each jar was capped and set aside to steep for about 10 days, shake every few days to ensure a good mix.

During this time the zest will infuse the vodka with flavor and color. Ensure your zest (or fruit) is completely submerged in alcohol to prevent the fruit from rotting while it's steeping.

## Step 4: Serve!

Limoncello is served chilled (in chilled glasses) and typically consumed after dinner as a digestif, but is great any time you want a tart refreshment. Try it over vanilla ice cream for a zesty twist on your dessert.

## Step 3: Strain and Sweeten

After the zest has steeped in vodka for a few days, it's time to strain. Using cheesecloth and a funnel, transfer the zesty vodka to a clean bottle. I chose a decorative

# Homemade Pomegranate Liqueur

By **djeucalyptus** David Doctor Rose
(http://www.instructables.com/id/Homemade-Pomegranate-Liqueur/)

Homemade pomegranate liqueur is surprisingly easy to make without any complex or out-of-the-ordinary tools, and the results are both delicious and make perfect gifts for almost any occasion. All you need are a few simple ingredients, a few household kitchen utensils, and some time (it takes about a month and a half to properly age and cure).

## Tools, Utensils, and Ingredients

I went with the simplest utensils, using everyday kitchen implements instead of some specialty items. I always try to make things work with what I have, and this recipe is simple enough that nothing too technical is necessary.

## Ingredients

- roughly six pomegranates, depending on their size (pomegranate juice can be substituted if fresh pomegranates are unavailable, however I've had better results using whole seedpods, as the seeds impart different characteristics to the liqueur and add more depth)
- peel of 1 lemon (I prefer meyers)
- cinnamon stick
- 3 cups vodka
- 1½ cups white sugar (I generally tend away from processed white sugar; however with this recipe—and most liqueurs—white sugar is the best way to go as unrefined, unprocessed sugars fail to yield as successful results.
- ¾ cup water
- other spices can be added as well, like cloves or star anise. My personal preference is to have more fruit flavored and less spiced liqueur (unless I go all out and make one heavily spiced). The spicing is up to you.

## Utensils

- a large glass jar (I used a 3 liter jar)
- large plastic bowl
- paring knife
- vegetable peeler (or knife)
- measuring cups (liquid and dry)
- metal strainer
- cheesecloth
- saucepan
- small funnel

- glass bottles or storage containers for the final product

**Notes on Utensils**

Avoid plastic as much as possible when working with strong alcohol. Glass is always preferable.

A food mill can be used for crushing pomegranate seeds, but certainly isn't necessary. Similarly, a tube siphon can be used to fill the bottles, but I find it just as easy to carefully use a measuring cup or ladle.

## Step 1: Seeding the Pomegranates

There are several different ways to go about getting the seedpods out of pomegranates (some of which are even Instructables!) but I have always preferred the water method.

Cut the pomegranate in half vertically. Fill a large bowl with water. Turn the pomegranate half seed-side down and while holding the edges of the half, push on the center with your thumbs to basically turn the half inside-out. Sometimes it's not entirely successful and you need to pull apart the pods individually.

By keeping the pomegranate underwater, you minimize errant juice spraying when pods are incidentally broken (the stuff stains like crazy!) and the membrane, flesh, pith, etc. all float to the top, while the seeds fall to the bottom.

One final rinse and agitation to free up any extra membrane and you should have a glistening collection of seeds.

## Step 2: Crushing the Pods and Extracting Juice

There's no perfect way to accomplish this one, and I've tried, seen, and heard everything from a potato masher to a blender. A food mill is an option, but the seeds are hard to the point that it makes it difficult.

Keep in mind that the purpose of this step is to crush the pods so the vodka can infuse through the pomegranates and not necessarily to fully extract all of the juice. This is the method I prefer:

Place a fine mesh metal strainer in a plastic or glass bowl. Put seed pods into the strainer. Using a spoon (a slotted spoon works nicely), press the pomegranate seedpods down against the strainer to crush the pods and extract the juice. Continue working the pods around the strainer until all the pods are broken. Remember to reserve the seeds as well as the juice.

## Step 3: Peeling the Lemon

Using a vegetable peeler or a paring knife, carefully peel the lemon. The goal is to avoid getting any of the pith (the white part) with the peel, as you want the oils in the peel. The pith will impart an unpleasant bitterness in the final product. If you peel off too much, you can always scrape off extra pith.

## Step 4: Infusion: Part I

Sterilize the large jar, either in boiling water or by running it through the dishwasher rinse cycle. Add the pomegranate juice and seeds, the lemon peel, and the cinnamon stick. Pour in the vodka, then wipe the rim of the jar to ensure it's clean and seal.

Store the jar in a cool and dark location, agitating the jar every day to ensure everything is properly infusing. A good, solid swirl is sufficient. I let this stage infuse for two to three weeks.

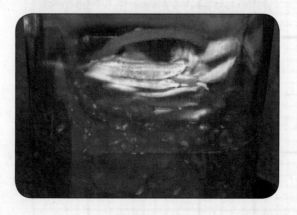

### Step 5: Straining

After several weeks of infusing, it's time to strain the liquid. Carefully strain the liquid through several layers of cheesecloth. It helps to moisten the cheesecloth first so the liquid permeates more smoothly.

Once you get to the point of straining out the pulp and rind, gently wring the cheesecloth to extract all of the liquid and juice. After straining, you can discard all of the rind, pulp and any spices. Return the liquid to the jar.

### Step 6: Making the Simple Syrup

Gently heat the sugar and water to create a simple syrup. Only heat until the sugar is dissolved, taking caution to heat on medium-low so the sugar doesn't begin to burn or caramelize. Give the syrup time to sufficiently cool.

### Step 7: Infusion: Part II

After the syrup has cooled, add it to the jar with the strained liquid. Repeat the process, storing in a cool, dark and dry location, agitating every few days, and allow to age for at least another three weeks, ideally 4 to 5 weeks.

### Step 8: Bottling!

Sterilize the jars or containers either in a boiling water bath or in a sterilizing rinse of a dishwasher. Theoretically, the alcohol should help keep anything unhealthy at bay, but any time you're dealing with fresh fruit juice, it doesn't hurt to be safe. Also sterilize the funnel and whatever cups, spoons, etc. you plan to use to transfer the final product.

Carefully scoop the liquid out of the jar and transfer it into another glass cup. I use a liquid measure so it makes pouring easier. Use caution so you don't agitate any sediment at the bottom of the jar—it's unpleasant at best, and it's best to avoid bottling it. As I mentioned before, some prefer to use a siphon and rack the liquid, as in beer or winemaking, but I find it an unnecessary step and carefully scooping the liquid is just as efficient.

Pour the liqueur into the bottles through the funnel, wipe the lid, and seal quickly. Wipe down the bottles to ensure they're clean, and now you're ready to serve, gift, etc.

### Step 9: Serving Suggestions and Recipe Credits

This liqueur makes an excellent gift! Labeling with serving suggestions as follows is always nice:

*This pomegranate liqueur can be served straight up, chilled. Mix 1 to 1 with vodka (straight or flavored) for a simple pomegranate martini. A splash of fresh pomegranate (or cranberry) juice can add another level. An ounce of pomegranate liqueur in champagne makes for a festive (and stunning) drink.*

While I'd love to take complete credit for this recipe, I cobbled together this recipe after reading through various websites across the internet and a few different books. Most notably, however, is the book *Luscious Liquors* by A.J. Rathbun, and Gunther Anderson's internet musings on Homemade Liquors.

bar

# Skittles Vodka

## By applesticker
(www.instructables.com/id/Shoot-the-Rainbow-Skittles-Vodka/)

## Ingredients

There are just two ingredients in this Instructable: vodka and Skittles.

### Skittles

You need to end up with 180g of each flavor of Skittle. Since Skittles are approximately 1 g each, you can accomplish this with 180 skittles. We used two 450g bags for our experiment—other bag sizes are perfectly acceptable.

Of course, if you want to experiment with making the vodka to be more flavorful, you could definitely try more skittles than this. This was what we found as a good flavor level, without using too many bags of Skittles.

Can you use other candy with this same method? We think it's very likely that this will work well for most fruity candy generally available (like hard candies or chewy fruit candies). We're not sure how gummy candies would work with this—but it's definitely worth experimentation.

### Vodka

The vodka quality is actually pretty important. We found that using middle-quality vodka created an end result that tasted a lot like medicine (particularly the cherry flavor). I would suggest trying a better-or best-quality vodka instead. Several commenters have pointed out that you can try running middle-quality vodka through a water filter pitcher (such as a Brita) to clean up the flavor a bit—we haven't tested this but it's worth a try.

We used one 750 ml bottle for each flavor of skittle—five in all. Larger or smaller bottles will result in more or less flavorful vodka for the amount of Skittles given above.

## Step 1: To Start

Remove the labels from each bottle by soaking them in warm water. This makes it easier to see the dissolving process.

Sort the skittles into different bowls based on color. We weighed ours with a scale to make sure we had approximately the same amount for each bottle (180 grams).

Remove and reserve a small amount of vodka from each bottle—around ⅛ of the bottle.

Drop the skittles by color into each bottle.

Top off the bottles with the reserved vodka (enjoy whatever won't fit in at your leisure.)

Give each bottle a good shake to get the dissolving process started. You should see the liquid begin to color relatively quickly.

## Step 2: Waiting Period

It may take several days for the Skittles to fully dissolve in your vodka. Ours dissolved within one 24-hour period, but your results may vary. Every now and then throughout the dissolving period, give the bottles a shake to move things around.

Over time the vodka will begin to take on the color of the Skittles, while the Skittle bodies will turn white and start to break apart.

If you look at a package of Skittles, you'll notice that besides sugar and flavoring there's also a number of ingredients that give the candy its texture and chewiness. As your Skittles dissolve more and more, you'll get a thicker and thicker layer of white "scum" on the top of the liquid. This scum layer is pretty horrible and generally not tasty, so it needs to be filtered out before the drinking can commence.

## Step 3: Filtration

Once all the skittles have mostly dissolved in each bottle, it's time to filter out all the extra leftover ingredients that we don't want in our finished product.

The original method that we used for this was to run the liquid through a filter made of several layers of paper towels pushed down into a strainer. As several commenters pointed out, it is likely that coffee filter might be a better solution than the paper towels. We haven't tried this ourselves, but it sounds quite reasonable and we see no reason why you shouldn't try it.

It will take some time to get all the liquid through the filter—be patient. The stuff left in the filter will be pretty gross. We couldn't think of a good use for it, so we chucked it in the garbage.

## Step 4: End Result
### Color

You should end up with five bottles of relatively clear liquid. The purple will probably stay pretty opaque. The red, orange, and yellow will be pretty see-through. Green will most likely be in-between the two extremes.

There were some commenters who noticed problems with long-term storage of the purple variety—they reported that over a period of days the purple color broke into a red with some blue mixed in. We didn't store our finished product for more than a day, so we can't speak to their experience. However, we don't think it's all that strange a result. The purple bottle was much cloudier than the others and we're sure they had to mix red and blue dyes to get that color in the first place. You may want to drink this bottle quickly, rather than storing it long-term. (We liked the purple flavor a lot, so we didn't have any left after our tasting.)

### Taste

So, how does it taste? We found that we liked the green flavor best of the lot—it was probably the closest to the original Skittle flavor and it mixed well with the vodka. Purple was a definite runner-up in the flavor contest. We didn't have any of these two bottles left after our tasting party.

Red tasted like cough syrup, which is pretty reasonable since it's a cherry + alcohol mix. Not our favorite, but if you like the taste of cough syrup, this is your winner.

Orange and yellow were definitely pleasant, without the cough syrup taste of the red.

# How to Make Delicious Chocolate Liqueur

By **brawns214**

Stephen Brawner

{www.instructables.com/id/How-to-make-delicious-chocolate-liqueur/)

bar

This comes from a typical Italian recipe for chocolate liqueur. Funny how those Italians love to add pure alcohol to normal everyday beverages and call it a liqueur. Well, it works because this stuff is extremely delicious and perfect for ice cream, coffee, or just sipping straight. At over 25 percent alcohol, most people will probably prefer to mix it with something. Perhaps, some cream and a little cinnamon? Warning! For those of you looking for a quick way to get drunk, just skip the chocolate and buy Everclear. It will save you a few steps. Good, now that I got that warning out of the way, we can proceed.

## Ingredients and Materials to Make 750 ml

- 4 oz baking chocolate (Make sure it says baking chocolate, I've had bad luck with stuff like Lindt chocolate bars.)
- 1 cup sugar (I prefer raw or turbinado, but if you wish you could use white.)
- 1 pint whole milk (the wholer the better.)
- 1 cup grain alcohol (190 or 151 proof— 75 to 90 percent. It's hard to find 190

proof in the States, it generally can only be found as 151 proof. The typical American brand is Everclear. It probably shouldn't be too hard to find elsewhere.)
- You'll need a large pot for melting the chocolate into milk.
- A fine meshed strainer (I have yet to find one I like, but I found a non-disposable coffee strainer at Vons Supermarket that worked pretty well.
- Spoon
- Funnel Bottles (0.75-1 liter is good size). I'm not sure what to call these kinds of bottles, but I found the ones used in this instructable at Sur la Table (it's close to work, don't judge me)

## Step 1: Caramelize Sugar (mostly optional)

Since you are a fan of instructables, I suggest you make the most out of this and caramelize your sugar. It's not absolutely necessary, but if all you want to do is get drunk, you're best off skipping this instructable entirely. Also, if you're capable of multitasking, you can do this while you mix the chocolate and milk, and just turn off the heat to the one that finishes first.

To caramelize the sugar, mix the 1 cup of sugar and about 1 cup of water in a separate pot then what you are using to melt the chocolate. The sugar will dissolve easier as you heat the mixture, so don't try to mix it before setting it on the stove. Basically just keep stirring the mix as it heats up even once it's mixed. It will start boiling and bubbling and will require much more frequent stirring. I guess there is a fine line between making caramel and making candy, but it will all dissolve into the end mix anyway. It's tough to tell when enough is enough (OK, I'm not a professional caramelizer), but you'll notice eventually that the stuff is thickening. That's probably a good point to add it to the chocolate mixture.

Like I said, it's difficult to determine the point of caramelization because you are stirring while hot when the stuff tends to flow the best.

*Uhh*, I guess I looked it up, and this is not the way to make caramel. It's the way I made it for the liqueur, so I'm going to leave it until I try differently. There isn't an instructable that gets at it, but Wikihow suggests just melting sugar www.wikihow.com/Make-Caramel.

## Step 2: Mix Everything but Alcohol, Then Add Alcohol

Heat up the milk on a stove, careful not to burn it. Mix in the baking chocolate. It will start melting into the milk as the temperature increases. Also mix the caramel and ensure that everything is well mixed before taking off the heat.

Reduce the temperature down to about ambient. Placing the pot in the sink and running cool water around it can help to bring down the temperature.

The last step is to add in the alcohol and again ensure everything is well mixed. Like I said, wait until the temperature is low, because the alcohol will tend to vaporize off if it's too warm.

## Step 3: Filtering

I haven't quite discovered what this stuff is, but without fail a crust of sediment forms on the top. It takes about 4 to 5 days for the stuff to fully form, but you'll notice it after a day or so. Take all your chocolate liqueur and run it through the filter/strainer. It will go pretty slowly and will probably be a messy painful process, but it's pretty important. Wash the bottle to remove any sediment that didn't escape. You'll probably lose a small amount of this stuff during the process as it tends to stay behind in your pots and funnels. Re-bottle your concoction and notice its glamorous appeal.

## Step 4: Let Sit and Wait

It's that easy, just let this amazing bottle full of sin and alcohol sit on your shelf well-sealed for a couple weeks to a few months. This is a confectionery Italian product, and can be extremely delicious depending on how well you make it. I gave you the basic recipe, but there is much more to it that I haven't quite yet discovered. If anyone else has done this before and has further suggestions (especially any Italians with secret family recipes!), please feel free to post comments.

For consumption, drizzle a small amount over your ice cream (or gelato!). Pour on top of fresh fruit. Mix it with coffee, or sip it straight. There are plenty of uses to get this stuff from the bottle to your belly.

The most important step is creating your own labels. I bought printable packing labels from Office Depot and designed what you see here. It's pretty simple, but it sure adds your own authenticity.

# How to Brew Beer

By moaner70 Mark Summers
(www.instructables.com/id/How-to-
Brew-Beer/)

This is a step by step guide to brew beer from scratch using the raw ingredients. The method explained here is a "full mash" meaning that the extract is made from crushed malted grain and not pre-prepared extract which can be bought in a tin. Total preparation time until ready to drink is approx 3 weeks (worth the wait!).

## Equipment

The main kit you'll need is a container in which to heat the liquid, another large bucket/bin-type container to transfer the liquid into, and a final beer barrel to store (rack) the beer. You can also store the finished product in beer bottles (bottle conditioned).

**Full List of Kit**

- boiler/mash tun to hold 5 imperial gallons*/25 liters. One used in picture is metal with a heating element in the bottom. I think you can buy plastic ones also. Also a large pan would work
- fermentor/bucket to hold 5 imperial gallons/25 liters
- sterilizer (e.g. sodium metabisulphite, chlorine-based iodophor, San Star)
- water treatment, calcium chloride, Epson salts, Gypsum (see step 4)
- stirring implement
- large jug
- thermometer
- hydrometer
- scale to weigh ingredients
- straining bag (mashing and sparging bag)
- barrel and/or bottles
- siphon tube
- metal bottle tops (if using bottles)
- gadget to get metal tops onto bottles (if using bottles)

## Ingredients

These are all available online or at your local brew shop. This is a "London Pride" recipe from Dave Line's book *Brewing Beers Like Those You Buy* by Dave Line. This will make 5 gallons (25 liters).

- 7 pounds (3.5 kg) crushed pale malt (I used Maris Otter)
- 8 ounces (350 g) crushed crystal malt
- 3 gallons (15 liters) water
- 1 teaspoon (5 ml) Irish Moss
- 10 ounces (310 g) demerara sugar
- 1 ounce (30 g) Fuggles
- 2¾ ounces (85 g) Goldings hops

---

\* Note on gallons: 1 imperial gallon = 4.456 liters; 1 U.S. gallon = 3.785 liters

- 2 ounces (60 g) brewer's yeast (I used a dried packet mix of 11.5 g)
- ½ ounce (15 g) gelatin

## Step 1: Sterilize

Make sure all equipment is sterilized. This will stop bacteria and wild yeasts messing up the beer. I used sodium metabisulphate, but I read that a chlorine-based sterilizer will be better at killing wild yeast rather than just inhibiting the growth (also I'm told that Iodophor and San Star work well). Rinse well. Keep all equipment sterilized at all times, don't sterilize too early and if something is used or put down on a surface then sterilize again.

## Step 2: Add Water

Add 3 imperial gallons (not U.S.!) or 15 liters of water to the mash tun/boiler. The water is then treated depending on whether you live in a hard- or soft- water area.

**For Hard–Water Areas**

- Add 1 teaspoon of flaked calcium chloride or lactic acid solution (or boil water for 15 minutes then use when cooled).
- Add 1 teaspoon Gypsum (calcium sulphate)
- Add ½ teaspoon Epsom salts (magnesium sulphate)

**For Soft-Water Areas**

- Add 1 teaspoon Gypsum (calcium sulphate)
- ½ teaspoon of Epsom salts (magnesium sulphate)
- Stir the mixture

## Step 3: Prepare to Add Malt/Start Heating

Put your "Sparging bag" over the top of the mash tun. This will stop the malt touching the element in the boiler. Turn on the boiler and start to raise the temperature to 60°C (140°F).

## Step 4: Stir in the Malt

Stir in the correct amount of both the crushed pale malt and the crushed crystal malt (gives color). Keep stirring as the malt is added. Keeping the temperature at around 66°C (151°F), leave for the next 1½ hours. Putting the lid on the boiler should keep the temperature constant. Keep checking every 20 minutes or so to ensure temperature is correct. This is the stage where the fermentable sugars are obtained from the malted grain it's "mashing."

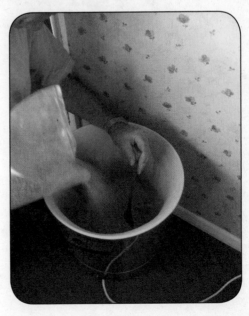

## Step 5: Drain Wort into Fermenting Bucket

Open up the tap and drain the wort into the fermenting bucket.

## Step 6: Sparging

With the boiler tap still open keep topping up the boiler with mains water which has been heated to slightly hotter than the mash, rinsing through the malt until the fermenting bucket is topped up to 4 imperial gallons or 20 liters. This is called "sparging."

## Step 7: Measure out the Hops

As per ingredients in Step 2.

## Step 9: Add Second Lot of Hops

Switch off the heat and add ½ ounce (15 g) of Goldings hops. Leave for 15 minutes for the hops to soak in.

## Step 10: Transfer Wort to Fermenting Bucket

Peg the cleaned and sterile cloth used earlier for sparging over the top of the fermenting bucket. This will prevent the grain and hop debris from entering. Another tip is to slightly obstruct the tap from the inside to prevent hops clogging the tap. Turn on the tap and let the wort drain from the boiler to the bucket.

## Step 11: Top Up Fermenting Bin With Cold Water

Top up the fermenting bin with cold water up to 5 imperial gallons (25 liters). At this point you can take a hydrometer reading. This will be the original gravity (o.g.), the reading on this batch here was taken at 1040 o.g.; the recipe said it should be 1042 o.g., so not far off.

## Step 8: Add Wort Back to Boiler and Add Hops

Pour the wort from the fermenting bin back into the boiler and add all the Fuggles hops and just 2 ounces (60 g) of the Goldings hops. Boil the mixture and then add in just 8 ounces (250 g) of the demerara sugar (the rest is used later on). Also add in 1 teaspoon of Irish Moss. Then leave to boil for 1½ hours.

### Step 12: Adding Yeast

Once the wort has cooled to about room temperature you can add the yeast. It can get a better start if you cool a pint of the wort in a separate glass and then add the yeast to the pint of wort. Once it's given a start in there, you can add it to the room temperature wort. In this case we waited overnight before the pint of yeast mix was added to the fermenting bin. This is also known as pitching the yeast.

### Step 13: Fermentation Begins

The beer started to visibly ferment about 1½ hours after the yeast was added. This picture was taken after about 6 hours. The fermentation will continue now for around 3 to 5 days. Take some hydrometer readings throughout this time and you will see how it's coming along. We are looking for a hydrometer reading of about 1012. Read the next step though, as there is something to do before the fermentation is finished.

### Step 14: Skim Off the Top of the Yeast

You have to take the dark head of yeast off or it sinks back into the beer and makes it taste too bitter. Once skimmed, the beer carries on fermenting with a lighter coloured head. This was done after about 12 hours of fermenting.

### Step 15: Fermentation Slows

This was taken after around 24 hours. Hydrometer reading taken at 1020.

### Step 16: Siphon Beer in Barrel

After about 4 or 5 days the beer should be fully fermented. The gravity should read 1012. Use the siphon tube to siphon the beer from the beer to the barrel. Make sure the fermenting bucket is higher than your barrel (as per next picture/step).

### Step 17: Siphon Beer in Barrel—Another View

### Step 18: Prepare the Last of the Hops and the Finings

Prepare the finings (gelatin) and the last of the hops to add to the barrel. That's ½ ounce (15 mg) of gelatin mixed with water in a cup. The finings are used to clear the beer. The final flavoring of ¼ ounce (60 g) of Goldings hops is also added directly to the beer in the barrel.

### Step 19: Add Hops and Finings and Leave for 7 Days

Add hops and finings (gelatin) and leave for 7 days.

### Step 20: Drain Beer Back into Fermenting Bin

Drain the beer back into the fermenting bin. This will ensure the hops added are filtered out of the beer.

49

## Step 21: If Using Bottles, Sterilize Them

Sterilize the bottles and leave upside down to drain.

## Step 22: Get Ready to Put the Bottle Tops On

You will need a gadget like this to put the bottle tops on:

## Step 23: Add Sugar and Siphon Beer into the Bottles.

Add ½ teaspoon of demerara sugar into each bottle. Using a funnel will make it easier. I used (15x) 500 ml beer bottles. Make sure they are proper beer bottles, other bottles/containers may be libel to explode under the carbon dioxide that will be produced within the bottle. Siphon the beer from the bin into each bottle.

## Step 24: Siphon Remainder/All the Beer Back into Barrel

Siphon the beer back into the barrel. You need to prime the barrel with 2 ounces (60 g) of demerara sugar (less if you used some of your beer for bottles like I did). I took some of the beer to one side in a glass and mixed the sugar in and then reintroduced the beer/sugar mix with the main batch of beer. Leave for a week in the barrel before sampling your beer.

bar

# Make Your Own Damn Sports Drink

By **fungus amungus** Ed Lewis
(www.instructables.com/id/Make-Your-Own-Damn-Sports-Drink/)

Sports drinks are awesome. They have electrolytes and sugar and quench that thirst. Gatorade pioneered the field and now they're everywhere, but why pay them a ton for what is just salty sugary water with artificial flavoring?

So stop dropping all that money on the glorified bottled water and make some on your own! You could end up paying up to 90 percent less.

While this isn't a perfect recipe that will taste exactly like Gatorade since matching their artificial flavors is impossible, it will be just as effective.

Did I mention that this stuff has electrolytes? Oh, man, does it ever have electrolytes.

It's got electrolytes!

Hydrate!

Save money!

## Why to Do It?

Buying a premade sports drink is practically the same thing as buying bottled water since a sports drink is mostly water with some sugar and a tiny bit of other stuff added.

Let's do a quick breakdown of why you shouldn't do this:

You can get perfectly good water from the tap.

The stuff you get in the store is just coming from someone else's tap anyway.

If your tap water tastes bad, get a filter. It'll pay for itself, trust me. It takes a lot of gas to move all that heavy fluid around the country. More waste and more emissions.

Even if you don't care about the wasting of fuel and the extra emissions, do you really want to pay for it?

By the way, you aren't drinking bottled water either, right? There's just no good reason for doing that unless you're too lazy to chill water by either putting it in the fridge or adding ice, and that would just be sad.

## What's in a Sports Drink?

The basic breakdown of a sports drink is easy. In fact, Gatorade puts all the information you need on its nutrition label so let's look at that:

- 14 g sugar
- 110 mg sodium
- 30 mg potassium

The 14 grams of sugar make sure that the total make-up of the liquid is 6 percent carbohydrates. Gatorade claims that this is the optimal level to enhance the water being absorbed into your body.

To get the sodium and potassium is easy. Sodium comes from any salt (sodium chloride) you drop in water. As for the potassium, just look for a "lite" salt like Morton's Lite and you'll find it there.

For the flavoring, we're going to go the easy route here and simply use a Kool-Aid packet. It's cheap, comes in many flavors, and is the fastest route to getting a similar experience to commercial sports drinks. We're never going to be able to match the flavors of a commercial product, but it is close enough.

## Doing the Math

Since we're using a Kool-Aid packet for the flavoring and one packet is meant for 2 quarts (64 oz.) of liquid, we'll be making

2 quarts of sports drink. You could cut the dry ingredients in half for 1 quart batches, but if you're going as far as making your own sports drink you'll likely be able to put away 2 quarts pretty quickly. You will probably want to make a double batch or more in the future.

So let's go back to the original numbers from Gatorade and convert them to a 2 quart batch.

Thus:
- 4 g sugar
- 110 mg sodium
- 30 mg potassium
  becomes:
- 112 g sugar
- 880 mg sodium
- 240 mg potassium

Since white sugar weighs about 190 grams per cup, we'll just use one heaping ½ cup of sugar and call it a day. If you're super picky, use a scale or add a heaping tablespoon to ½ cup of sugar.

Next is the sodium and potassium. If we add ¼ teaspoon of the Morton Lite salt to ¼ teaspoon of the sea salt we get:
- 880 mg sodium
- 350 mg potassium

This is 50 percent more potassium than Gatorade, but, hey, more electrolytes! Also, this is for a 2 quart mixture so when we go back to the original serving size we get:
- 14 g sugar
- 110 mg sodium
- 44 mg potassium

Since the recommended daily amount for an adult is 2,000 mg of potassium a day, this will work just fine. Now, let's make some sports drink!

## Ingredients
- Kool-Aid packet
- ¼ teaspoon Morton Lite salt
- ¼ teaspoon sea salt
- heaping ½ cup sugar
- 2 quarts water

Throw it all together and stir. Chill it and prepare to guzzle it down when you're sweating a ton from sports or working outside on a hot day.

## Cost Savings
Now that you've seen the recipe, here's the cost break down:
- Kool-Aid packet—25 cents
- Morton Lite salt—1 cent
- sea salt—1 cent
- sugar—15 cents (based on 5 lb package)
- Total for 2 quarts: 42 cents!

But remember 2 quarts is 8 servings, so that's about 5 cents per 8 oz serving.

Gatorade has a few different bottle sizes, but the 32 oz. size often retails for $1.99. We just made it ourselves for 21 cents. Even compared to the Gatorade powder we still come out ahead. In my local grocery store I can get a plastic container with enough powder to make 32 servings for $4.99. If we want to make the powder on our own, it would cost $1.68.

And for all of you who aren't losing those precious electrolytes through exercise, there's an even cheaper option: water. You don't need a sports drink to drive, walk around, or work on a computer all day. You also don't need all the sugar in these drinks either. So unless you really need that optimal 6 percent of carbohydrates that Gatorade insists improves your hydration, just fill up a glass of water and drink it up.

bar

## Sweet & Sassy: Candied Bacon and Spiked Cantaloupe Granita & Bubble Tea Brunch Cocktails

By Susie_Q
(www.instructables.com/id/Sweet-Sassy-Fun-Brunch-Cocktails-Treat/)

The way we celebrate brunch is by having sweet treats, but spiked.

There's nothing better than sharing a fun morning cocktail or light dessert with friends.

This is what I came up with to keep things sweet, yet make it fun and different.

## Candied Bacon and Spiked Cantaloupe Granita

A fun dessert-like take on the typical Prosciutto-wrapped Melon.

### Ingredients
**Spiked Cantaloupe Granita**
- 1 cantaloupe
- ½ cup sugar
- vodka (your preference)

**Candied Bacon**
- 4 strips bacon
- ½ cup brown sugar
- 1 tablespoon maple syrup

### Step 1: Make the Granita

Cut the cantaloupe into 1 inch cubes. Puree the cantaloupe in your blender, a bit at a time until it is smooth and with no visible pieces. Add the sugar and pulse a couple times to mix.

Add your vodka (if desired). Pour the mix into a freezable vessel (ours was 12" × 6"). Cover with plastic wrap and place in the freezer overnight.

The next day scrape at the granita with a fork to scratch the mix into small crystals. Place back into freezer until ready to serve.

### Step 2: Making Candied Bacon

Preheat oven to 350° F. Mix brown sugar with maple syrup and add slices of bacon. Toss bacon a couple times to coat and then lay the each of the slices flat onto a parchment paper-lined cookie sheet. Sprinkle the remaining brown sugar/maple syrup onto the strips of bacon. Place another sheet of parchment paper on top and cover that with another cookie sheet (this will keep the candy flat).

Place into preheated oven and bake for 15 to 20 minutes. Once the sugar has caramelized and the bacon is cooked, remove for the parchment paper and place onto a rack to cool. As it cools the caramel will harden into a sweet, salty, smoky candy bacon delight.

# Bubble Tea Brunch Cocktails

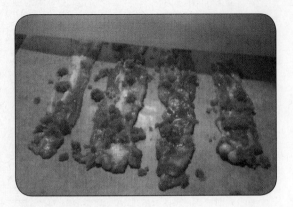

### Step 3: Put it Together

Scoop out the Spiked Cantaloupe Granita and serve it with a slice of Candied Bacon.

Granita: Cool, Light, and Fruity
Bacon Candy: Sweet, Salty, and Smoky.
Together: Amazing

For the uninitiated, bubble tea is a sweet, oftentimes fruity (tea) beverage that contains small chewy balls of tapioca or fruity jelly (the bubbles). Invented in Taiwan, it has now become hugely popular worldwide.

We made three different cocktails for our lunch (each without tea, though feel free to add tea to yours).

Each cocktail theme was a cocktail within a cocktail.

## Ingredients

**White Sangria with Red Sangria Bubbles**
- white sangria
- white wine
- lemon-lime soda
- cut up oranges, lemons, berries

**Red Sangria Bubble**
- 1½ cups red wine
- ½ cup lemon-lime soda
- lemon and orange zest
- 2 envelopes of gelatin

**Mojito with Pomegranate Vodka Bubbles**
- mojito
- lemon-lime soda

bar

- white rum
- mint sprigs

**Pomegranate Vodka Bubbles**
- 2 cups pomegranate juice
- few shots of vodka
- 2 envelopes of gelatin

**Mimosa with Cranberry Champagne Bubbles**
- mimosa
- champagne
- orange Juice

**Cranberry Champagne Bubbles**
- 1½ cup champagne
- ½ cup cranberry juice
- 2 envelopes of gelatin

## Step 1: Make the Bubbles

We followed a standard recipe for each cocktail.

Warm the juice component over medium heat until a light simmer.

Add into a bowl along with the alcohol and packages of gelatin.

Gently whisk to dissolve the gelatin completely and pour the mixture into a nonstick pan.

Place into the refrigerator to set overnight.

Once completely solid, turn out of the mold (pour some boiling water over the bottom of the pan to facilitate this).

Cut the jelly into small ½ inch cubes.

Voila! Bubble tea cocktail jellies.

## Step 2: Assemble Bubble Tea Cocktails

For the next step, just assemble the main cocktail in your favorite way. You can add some green or black tea as you like to make a more authentic bubble tea.

TIP: Add the cocktail jelly bubbles to the bottom of the glass and slowly pour the main cocktail into the glass along the side.

Disrupting the jellies too much may cause them to break, though they are very firm. Better safe than sorry.

To get the fat bubble tea straws, just go to your favorite bubble tea place and ask for them. Or you could probably find them in an Asian grocery store.

## Step 3: Sit back, Relax with friends, and enjoy

bar

# How to Make Glögg

By natalina Natalie Walsh
(www.instructables.com/id/How-to-Make-Glogg/)

Glögg is a Scandinavian Christmas drink. The recipes vary widely, but all of them use either red wine or port as a base with the addition of mulling spices, sugar and usually other liquors such as brandy or vodka. It's great to get you through the cold winter season!

## What you Need

For this version of Glögg, you will need the following:

- 2 bottles of tawny port (the cheap stuff is fine)
- half liter of brandy
- mulling spices: cinnamon, cardamom, and cloves
- 1 orange peel
- 10 sugar cubes
- raisins
- slivered almonds

## Step 1: Mulling the Port

In a large pot, add port, mulling spices, and shavings from an orange peel. For the mulling spices, I had a pre-mixed version, but it would be the equivalent of roughly 10 cloves, 10 cardamom pods, and two cinnamon sticks. You can also add some raisins for added flavor.

Warm the mixture to right before boiling, and let it sit at low heat for an hour or so. It is important to not allow it to boil or bubble in any way, as that will burn off the alcohol.

## Step 2: Set the Sugar on Fire!

Now for the fun part. Once your Glögg has steeped sufficiently, it's time to add the final ingredients: sugar and brandy. I use around 10 sugar cubes, which I find plenty sweet. Add more or less depending on your taste preferences.

Place a few sugar cubes on a metal grate or pan, and pour a heavy splash of brandy over them. Quickly light the sugar on fire, and ladle the port over the sugar until it is fully dissolved. If desired, add more brandy to taste.

## Step 3: Ready to Serve

Strain the mixture into mugs, and serve hot with toasted almonds and raisins. Traditionally served with ginger snap cookies. Enjoy!

# Ogden's Old Firewhiskey

By **starshipminivan**
(www.instructables.com/id/Ogdens-Old-Firewhiskey/)

Favored by the mighty and the meek the wizarding world over, Ogden's Old Firewhiskey will put hairs on your chest or at least a smoldering sensation in your belly.

I was inspired to create this libation after reading about it in Harry Potter. I remember dissolving red hots in vodka and apple cider in my college days. So I pulled out the red hots, dusted them off (OK, I bought fresh at Wal-Mart), and tossed them into some whiskey. Then I added cinnamon sticks to create the whole cinnamon round-up of flavor. It's spicy and warm—perfect for cool autumn nights and Halloween in particular.

## The Stuff
- whiskey—your favorite brand
- Red Hot cinnamon candy—about 6 to 7 candies per ounce whiskey
- coffee filter and holder
- 3 to 4 large cinnamon sticks

## Step 1: The Process

Find a clean glass container with a lid such as a bottle or mason jar. You can also use the bottle your spirits originally came in—you just have to take a few swigs to make room for the candy. Measure how much you are adding and be sure to leave at least $\frac{1}{10}$ of the container empty.

For every ounce of whiskey, add 6 to 7 red hot candies to your container. I used a 750 ml (about 25 ounces when full) bottle of bourbon, poured out about ½ cup, and added 135 red hot candies. Shake your container occasionally. It only takes a few hours for the candy to dissolve.

The candies are coated with carnauba wax so once the candy is dissolved you'll want to filter it through a coffee filter to keep the whiskey smooth.

Bottle the filtered whiskey and drop the cinnamon sticks in the bottle. Leave them in there one week or more. You can also keep them in the bottle indefinitely.

Optional: Label your bottle. (I decided to label it "Ogden's Olde . . . " with an "e" in the "Olde" because it seemed more appropriate, though the name of it from Harry Potter fame does not include the "e")

## Step 2: How to Take Your Firewhiskey

You can, of course, drink your Ogden's straight-up.

Other options include:
- Fire and Ice—Ogden's layered in a shot glass with Irish Cream
- Spattergroit—Odgden's added to cranberry juice
- The Hungarian Horntail—Ogden's added to hot cider
- The Mediwizard—Ogden's added to Dr. Pepper
- The Time Turner—Ogden's added to cold sweet tea
- The Collapsed Cauldron—Ogden's added to hot tea
- The Red Eye—Ogden's added to hot coffee.

# The Color-Changing Martini
### By makendo
(www.instructables.com/id/The-Morphing-Martini/)

This drink smokes elegantly, changes from a calm blue to fuchsia as it cools from room temperature to drinkably cold, and tastes like a dirty martini.

Dry ice is the sedate, well behaved little brother of liquid nitrogen. Put some in a drink and it burbles away quietly, producing fog-filled bubbles that pop attractively. It won't even freeze your drink. So how do you make a dry ice cocktail compete visually with the fierce crackling and raw cooling power of liquid nitrogen? Read on . . .

## Ingredients
You'll need:
- gin (or vodka, for a vodka martini)
- vermouth
- dry ice
- baking soda
- red cabbage

## Step 1: Red #$@%! Cabbage?

Yes. Red cabbage contains a water-soluble anthocyanin that is a pH indicator. At low pH (acid), it's red. It's purple at neutral pH, and goes blue then green as the solution becomes alkaline. You're not going to see the full range here, because we want the drink to be, well, drinkable.

To get the indicator, chop up a cabbage leaf, put it in a bowl with some water, and microwave until it's boiling (or just add boiling water and allow to steep). A purple pigment will stain the water.

## Step 2: Build

Add a teaspoon of cabbage juice—I mean indicator solution—to the martini glass. Then add very small quantities of baking soda, just enough to turn the solution blue. Add gin (or vodka) and vermouth (~6:1) to the glass. You should have a pale blue clear liquid.

## Step 3: Present

Give the recipient the drink. Tell them to watch closely, then add a chunk of dry ice. It will sink to the bottom of the drink and bubble away happily, slowly cooling the drink. It will also neutralize the baking soda and change the colour of the martini.

This drink was mostly made as a way of keeping three small children entertained while their mother was out Christmas shopping. They liked the look of the cocktail, but thought the mocktail version was "really disgusting." (I did warn them that it was just salty, cabbage-flavored water.)

## Step 4: Taste

In the interests of science, I tried some of the baking soda/indicator mix straight. Baking soda tastes salty on its own and rather overpowers the cabbage juice. The latter by itself doesn't taste of much; a slightly sweet, vegetable taste, nothing like what its violent colour suggests. Overall, it flavors the martini in a way reminiscent of a dirty martini (martini with olive brine added). So you'll only like it if you like dirty martinis, probably a pretty small constituency.

# Creamy Pear "Pudding" Cocktail

By **Angryredhead**
(www.instructables.com/id/Creamy-
Pear-Pudding-Cocktail/)

This instructable shows how to make a cocktail with a floating cream top. While drinking, sip the juice cocktail through the cream top. The taste of this cocktail is like a nutty pear pudding, and because this is a mixed drink with such a heavy fruit juice, you definitely do not need expensive liquors/liqueurs.

## Ingredients

- 1 pony (1 ounce or 2 tablespoons) white brandy
- 1 jigger (1.5 ounces or 3 tablespoons) amaretto
- 3 to 4 ounces (⅓ to ¼ cup) pear juice
- ⅛ teaspoon (or a few drops) vanilla
- ¼ cup heavy cream
- white chocolate
- ice (not shown)

## Tools

- Collins or a highball glass
- large glass (for chilling)
- soup spoon
- vegetable peeler
- strainer
- liquid measuring cup
- jigger/pony combo (or tablespoon/teaspoon set)
- long stirring spoon/swizzle (or a butter knife)

## Step 1: Base Ingredients

Add ⅛ teaspoon vanilla to ¼ cup heavy cream and gently stir.

Note: I don't have a ⅛ teaspoon, so I approximated it. It's a few drops of vanilla.

Pour 1 pony of white brandy and 1 jigger of amaretto.

Top with pear juice until glass is ⅔ full.

## Step 2: Ice and Strain

Pour mixture into a large glass filled with ice and stir.

Strain mixture back into the Collins/Highball glass once chilled.

## Step 3: Top with Vanilla Cream

With a soup spoon against the far side of the glass, carefully pour the vanilla cream mixture onto the back of the spoon so it rides down the side of the glass.

Note: Cream wants to float, but it's good to be careful.

## Step 4: Garnish

Using a vegetable peeler, garnish the top of the drink with curls of white chocolate.

Alternative Garnish: You can also top with a swirl of caramel or crushed toffee.

## Alternative Directions

- Combine 1 cup heavy cream with ½ teaspoon vanilla, stir, and return to the fridge.
- Mix ¼ cup brandy, ¾ cup amaretto, and 2 cups pear juice. Chill in the fridge.
- Pour pear mixture equally between 4 Collins/highball glasses.
- Follow steps 5-6 for each glass.

bar

# Glow in the Dark Drinks

By ModMischief
(www.instructables.com/id/TRON-inspired-glow-in-the-dark-drinks/)

Most people are probably familiar with the fact that gin and tonic glows under black lights (there's even a great instructable about it) but what if you're not a big fan of g&t?

Thanks to the fantastic Kryptonite Candy instructable, I learned that vitamin B2 (also known as riboflavin) glows yellow.

I decided to experiment to see what adding tonic water and B2 could do to some of my favourite drinks.

## What You'll Need

The magic glowing ingredients are riboflavin and quinine. You can find them in vitamin B2 pills and tonic water.

You can make pretty much any clear or light coloured drink glow by adding either B2 or tonic water, so choose ingredients that suit your tastes.

I made 4 different drinks:
- Classic gin and tonic
- Red Bull and vodka
- Vodka and sprite
- Sobe pina colada with white rum

To get them to glow you will need a black light.

To create drink umbrellas, I used bendy straws and the bottoms of plastic martini glasses (I've used these disposable glasses for parties and have noticed that the tops are more likely to break than the bottoms, so even though I try to wash and reuse them, I usually end up with a surplus of bottoms)

## Step 1: Make Some Futuristic Drink Umbrellas

To create a stir stick, I used a drinking straw and the bottom of a disposable martini glass. The bottom part of a plastic wine glass would work just as well but would be a little smaller.

First pierce a hole the middle of the disk. Using a lighter, I heated up a nail and pushed it through with pliers. You could also use a drill.

Next, thread the straw through the hole up to the bendy part. The bendy elbow lets you tilt the umbrella to a jaunty angle.

Trim the straw to the desired length and you're done!

## Step 2: Mix the drinks

Now the fun begins!

**Yellow & Green Drinks**
- Crush up a B100 complex vitamin. One pill is good for many drinks as you will only need a tiny pinch of powder to make the liquid glow. Add some powder to the bottom of your glass and pour in the desired drink. Red Bull or similar energy drinks are a great choice as they already contain a small amount of riboflavin. The vitamin powder has a bit of a medicine taste to it, so strong flavored drinks are better at masking the bitter taste.
- To make the drink green, add a drop of food coloring and stir.

**Blue Drinks**

In addition to the classic gin and tonic, try adding tonic water to other mixed drinks. Tonic water has a bitter taste, so I found that sweet mixes worked better.

Learn how to make candles, organize your sewing tools, hand wind a ball of yarn, and more. Make your own candles, bind your own books, screen-print and tie-dye t-shirts, make amazing things out of paper, and put Martha Stewart to shame. Store-bought gifts will be a thing of the past once you've mastered this chapter.

# Hand Wind a Ball of Yarn

By **scoochmaroo** Sarah James
(www.instructables.com/id/Hand-Wind-a-Ball-of-Yarn/)

This simple tutorial will show you how to wind a center-pull ball of yarn without any special equipment.

I have several hanks of really beautiful yarn in my stash that I don't even think about using because I imagine having to take them to a yarn shop so they can be wound into balls on their nifty little swifts and winders. And really, when am I going to do that?

So one day when I was home sick, I decided to crack out a few hanks I'd just purchased for a summer project (missed the boat on that one. . . ) and wind them up by hand.

It's easy! And it's a nice project to do while you're home doing not much else and watching silly television online.

The advantage of wrapping a center-pull yarn ball is that the yarn stays neat and won't get tangled. Also, if you pull the working yarn from the center instead of the outside, the ball will stay put and not roll around as you unwind it!

## Step 1: Prep Your Yarn

Some yarn comes already wound into center-pull balls. Some comes twisted in hanks, like in the picture here. If you purchase this kind, take the paper off and open the yarn up into a big loop. Drape the loop of yarn over two chairs or the edge of a desk, or between the hands of a helpful friend. This keeps the yarn from getting all tangled up while you're winding it.

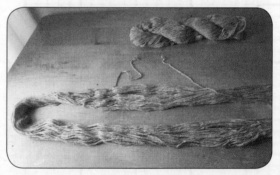

## Step 2: Begin the Ball

62

You start winding from the center of the ball (obviously). Hold one free end in your hand and drape the long end around your thumb . Make your hand into a gun, and wrap the yarn in a figure 8 around thumb and finger. Continue in this method until you run out of room on your fingers!

into the center of the yarn where I started wrapping so I don't lose the free end. Then I just wrap and turn, wrap and turn all around the ball until I'm out of yarn.

Finally, tuck in the end of the yarn you've been wrapping so it doesn't unravel. Now you have a center-pull yarn ball. Take the center end that you kept free, and start your knitting from there!

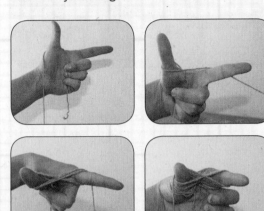

## Step 3: Wrap

Slide the stack of figure 8s off your finger and thumb and pinch together in the middle. Pinch the yarn stack between finger and thumb, keeping the starting end draped over your thumb. You want to make sure as you wind the ball that this end remains free and accessible! Start to wrap the yarn around this bunch in a circular motion to form a ball. Keep your thumb pinched into the middle as you wrap.

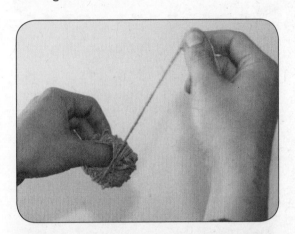

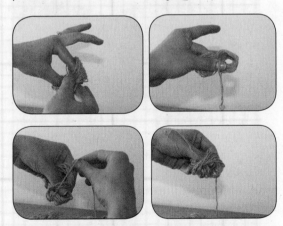

## Step 4: Keep Wrapping!

Continue wrapping the ball of yarn. You will quickly see it begin to resemble a proper ball and it will be easier to understand what you're doing. I like to keep my thumb stuck

craft

# How to Make Candles!

By **Weissensteinburg**

Micah Weiss
(www.instructables.com/id/How-to-make-Candles!/)

My mom loves candles. This year for Hanukkah, instead of spending eighteen bucks for a candle or two from Yankee, I've decided to make her some candles! I ended up spending $12 for enough wax/wicks for 16 candles. However, I only made two so that she can decide on her own scent/color combination when I make more. I had a lot of fun making these, and I know she's going to love them.

## What You'll Need
- wax—a 4-pound block for something like $14
- wicks
- crayons (if you want your candle colored)
- scent (I used vanilla extract)
- olive oil (optional)
- Double boiler (or two nesting pots)
- Knife
- Molds (I used a soda can, and a Dixie cup)
- Mixing Spoon

## Step 1: Caution
This project does require a few safety/mess preventions. Wax is very hard to clean up from counters. In order to help with cleanup, use as few tools as possible, and cover your work space in newspaper. I wish I had done that. Wax is flammable, for this reason, it's very important that you don't use any setting higher than medium on your stove, and use a thermometer if possible. Wax's flash point is 300°F, don't let its temperature exceed 250°F.

## Step 2: Preparation

Turn on your double boiler, and if you have a large block of wax like me, rest the wax over the boiler. This way, it will soften, and be easier to cut. Lay out newspaper over your work space. Take the wax off, and cut a chunk off, use the double boiler to melt that chunk of wax. I used about half a pound, and there was some wax left over after making my two candles.

As the wax melts, prepare your molds. Both of my molds were disposable and tearable. If you are using something like glass as a mold, rub the inside with oil on a paper towel, this will make it easier to remove the candle.

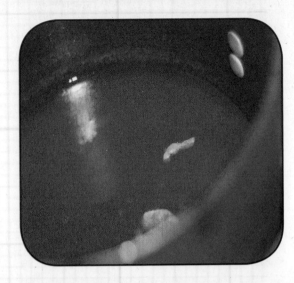

## Step 3: Additives

I made my candles yellow and vanilla scented. For my half pound of wax, I put in half a yellow crayon, and a splash or two of vanilla. For help matching colors with scents look at www.candletech.com/general-information/color-suggestions/. For help making the scents you want go to www.candletech.com/general-information/scent-mixing-ideas/.

## Step 4: Wicks

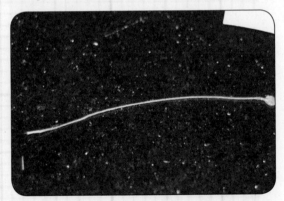

Cut off a piece of wick (cotton string) that's about an inch longer than your candle will be. Dip this into the wax, and then take it out. Use two paper towels, tongs, or anything else to pull the string taught while it dries for the most part . . . now your wick will be straight. You can put the wicks in the fridge to harden while you finish the candles, if you'd like.

## Step 5: Pour the Wax

Use the double boiler to pour wax into each mold, and then stick the candles into your fridge. This will speed up the cooling process. Once they are starting to firm up and the top of the candle looks firm, use a tooth pick to poke into the center of the candle.

You'll notice that the inside of the candle is still melted. Position the wick straight up and so that it touches the bottom. Melt a small piece of wax over the wick's hole to seal it.

Leave the candle in the fridge until fully hardened. When they are hardened again, either peel off the mold or slip out the candle (depending on your mold).

## Step 6: Clean Up

Wax spills are inevitable. One of the best ways to clean them up is to lay a brown bag over the spill, and use an iron set on high to melt the wax onto the paper bag—voila! Your tools are going to be a huge pain to clean up. My only suggestions are use few, use hot water, and use a rough brush to scrub it off. Good luck!

# How to Tie-Dye an Old White Shirt

By **stinkymum**

(www.instructables.com/id/How-to-tie-dye-an-old-white-shirt-or-a-new-shirt-/)

Take an old white shirt suffering from the "dingies" and turn it into a rainbow masterpiece! I'll show you how.

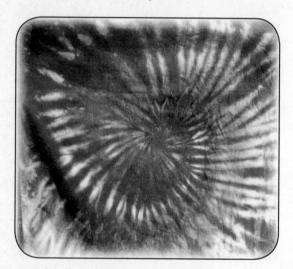

## You'll Need

**The Shirt, Fit to be Dyed!**

The shirts that work best are 100 percent cotton, although you can use 50 percent cotton/50 percent polyester (although the. results will not be so vibrant.) I once tried to dye a 100 percent polyester garment and when it was unwrapped, all the dye washed off! The dyes only bond well with natural fabrics like cotton, silk and rayon—but we're talking cotton here.

**Presenting Your Choice of Dyes**

You can buy dye kits which come with everything you need very easily in the craft stores. They include rubber gloves, rubber bands, soda ash, urea, and complete easy to follow instructions. The dyes are already in the squeeze bottles; all you have to add is warm water (not hot).

Other alternatives include buying single packages of dyes. These also come with the necessary urea and soda ash and instructions for mixing. However you would need to purchase some squeeze bottles separately if you don't have any.

**The Tools You Will Need for Success**

If you are like me and not using a prepackaged kit, you will need the following;. Procion dye, rubber bands, rubber gloves, squeeze bottles for the dye, urea and soda ash. Oh yes, don't forget to have paper towels and old rags to mop up the spills. Tie-dying does not have to be messy!

## Step 1: Soaking the Shirt

To enable the dyes to bond with the shirt, you need to soak it in a solution of *warm* water and soda ash for about 10 minutes. Follow the instructions given with the soda ash so that you have the right mix. Do not use water that is too hot or too cold, and add a couple of tablespoons of common salt to the mix too

Make sure the mixture is thoroughly dissolved before adding the shirt. The temperature of the water should be about the same as a baby's bath. As the soda ash is slightly caustic you may want to wear rubber gloves at this point, especially if you have a cut on your finger—it will sting!

After soaking, wring the shirt out thoroughly. The more liquid you can squeeze out, the more dye will be able to get in. I usually spin my shirts on the spin cycle of the washing machine. (Note: if you use a brand new shirt, wash it first to remove the newness, which I think they call "size." This "sizing" will prevent dye from bonding properly and you may get a streaky effect.)

## Step 2: Tying a Rainbow Swirl Pattern

After you have soaked and wrung out the shirt (by the way, if you don't do it in the washing machine, try wringing it out with a friend!) place the shirt on a flat surface. Place it right side down, as you will then get a sharper pattern on the front of the shirt. Of course if you want the sharper pattern on the back—well, you know!

Place the dowel rod (or your finger, or a wooden clothes pin) in the centre of the shirt and start turning clockwise until you have a nice flat pie shape. You can also turn counter-clockwise if you prefer, it makes no difference really.

### Step 3: Achieving Pie

This what your shirt should look like at this stage. Do not allow the shirt to creep up the dowel rod, make it behave with the hand not turning the dowel rod.

You are now ready to remove the dowel and put on the rubber bands. The trick is to place the bands, without disturbing the shirt. It can be done! However, be careful removing the dowel. You do not want to pull the shirt up in the middle—thus un-achieving pie! This part of the process is the most important step of all. Believe me, if you do a sloppy "tie" you will achieve a sloppy and messy "dye" and live to regret it.

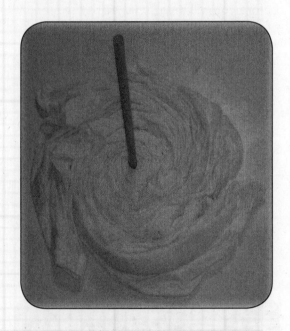

### Step 4: Join the Band

With your lovely pie shape achieved, you can now put on the rubber bands. Slip several bands on (see the picture), and then turn the shirt over and put on some more. This keeps its shape. Keep the whole thing as flat as you can. You are now ready to dye!

### Step 5: To Dye For

When doing the actually dying bit, you will need to cover your working surface with plastic. Something like a plastic tablecloth will work fine. You also need to wear old clothes, old shoes, etc. The dyes will stain your clothes, the floor, the walls, the ceiling, etc. So if you are not working outside, please be careful. The dyes are harmless to your skin, but if you don't wear rubber gloves you will achieve red, yellow, or blue dyed hands, which won't wash off. (Wears off in a couple of days but can be a amazingly embarrassing!)

### Step 6: Actually Using the Dyes

Place your shirt "pie" on a couple of thicknesses of paper towels on top of a paper plate on your plastic protected working surface. It's less messy and easy to flip the whole thing over when dying the other side. Wear rubber gloves.

Just a note: When I tie-dye I usually only use three colours: fuchsia red, turquoise, and lemon yellow. With these three colors you can make any colour you like.

To make the rainbow swirl shirt, imagine that your "pie" is an actual pie chart. Working from the centre of the shirt and holding the bottle low over the shirt, dye one third of the shirt lemon yellow. Do not wave the bottle around as you will make a mess.

Dye the second third of the shirt fuchsia red and the final third, turquoise. Do not leave any white spaces showing—the "white" is hiding within the folds! If you overlap the colors at the edges of each section you will get the other rainbow colours, i.e. green, purple, and orange. It's magic!

Hint: Always put yellow (or other light coloured dyes) on first. Once you "lose" or cover it up by mistake, it is changed to something else (either orange or green) and you can't get it back.

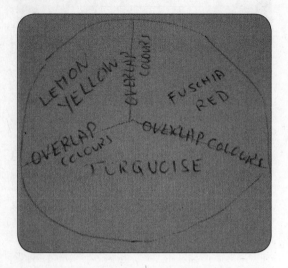

## Step 7: Turn the Pie Over

When you have finished putting the dye on the first side, turn the whole thing over. This will be easy to do, if you just flip the plate over onto another paper plate with clean paper towel all ready for you.

Throw the first paper plate and towel away (clean up as you go along whenever possible).

Apply the dye on this second side in a similar manner. If you are making the rainbow swirl, you need to be sure to put the three colors behind the same colors you used on the other side (i.e. red behind red, blue behind blue, etc.). If you don't do this, you will not get a rainbow spiral, but a sort of rainbow spider pattern (which is quite nice actually).

## Step 8: Now Comes the Hard Part—Waiting!

After you have completed putting the dye on the shirt, pop it into a zip lock bag and seal it up tight. Put the bag in a warm place and leave it for AT LEAST 24 HOURS! The dye needs this length of time to "prove" and allow the beautiful colors to really bond with the fabric

For you desperate "have-it-nows," you can unwrap after 8 hours—but . . . you can also leave the shirt for as long as 36 hours if you are very patient. If you leave it much longer, I have found the colors go sort of fuzzy (don't know why).

When you unwrap your shirt, wear rubber gloves and old clothes again. Don't make a mess!

Note: You have-it-nows should try the bleach tie method at www.instructables. com/id/Transforming-a-boring-old-black-t-shirt-using-blea/.

## Step 9: Unwrapping Your Masterpiece—Wear Rubber/Latex Gloves!

I love this part! This is the moment you have been waiting for. It's time to unwrap and discover your beautiful (we hope) creation for all to see.

Take the shirt out of the bag!

You can either take the bands off first, unwrap and start running the shirt under a cold water tap, or just run it under the tap for a while and then take the bands off!

BEWARE, if you have never tie-dyed before you will be astonished at the amount of dye that pours out as you are rinsing. The water will turn black. Fear not, this is normal. Not all the dye you so lovingly applied will bond with the fabric. Enough dye will remain, well and truly bonded.

Keep rinsing until the water runs clear (it may take a while). Hopefully, if you have done it right, your pattern will be revealed in all its glory. It's like a butterfly emerging from a chrysalis.

You may now wash your shirt in the normal way in a washing machine (on its own the first time). I usually wash my shirts two or three times on their own before I trust them with other "coloureds."

# How to Bind Your Own Hardback Book

By **KaptinScarlet**

Chris Barnardo

(www.instructables.com/id/How-to-bind-your-own-Hardback-Book/)

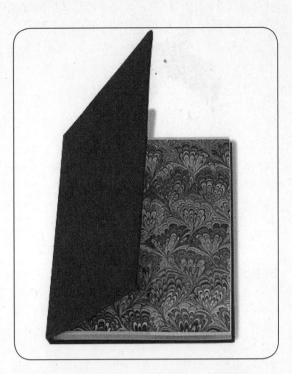

The art of book binding is an ancient craft, but actually it is not very difficult to do and with almost no practice you can get really awesome results. There are other instructables on the art of book binding, but this project is meant to be a simple quick project that will give a very acceptable finish and a book that looks like it has been professional made, yet without the need for any special equipment.

## All You Will Need Is

- Some paper; minimum really is about 32 A4 or U.S. letter-sized sheets to make a half A4 (half U.S. letter–sized) book, although smaller books can be made as can ones with more pages. You can use tracing paper, thick, or thin paper, and, of course, colored or even preprinted or written-on paper.
- PVA (Elmer's White glue) or a rubber fabric adhesive (in the UK that is called Copydex, perhaps someone could tell me what it's called in the U.S.) A glue gun, if you have it, would help with one of the stages, but it's not mandatory.
- Some stiff cardboard or corrugated (fluted) cardboard.
- Some fabric or leather. Any old stuff will do for the cover. I have used the fabric from some old pairs of trousers that were being thrown out (actually nothing gets thrown out in my house, just put to one side for later use). You could use a bit of leather, some old curtains, cushion covers, etc., I'm sure you get the idea.

## Step 1: Stack Your Paper Neatly in (at least) 4 Piles of 8 Sheets

You are going to be binding your paper in 8-sheet folios. Of course you could do more or less. I have found 8 sheets to be a good number because you are folding each sheet in half and each sheet will make 4 pages of your book, so this 8-sheet stack is going to make 32 pages. Your book should have at least 4 of these 8-sheet folios which will therefore make 128 pages (apologies to all the math wizards out there). You can use just plain paper or paper upon which you have already printed a header and footer (remember to get this the right way round and remember that there will be 4 headers and four footers per sheet of paper). If you want to mix in different papers then remember that they will appear further into the book as well. (Don't worry, this all becomes obvious as we go through the project.)

## Step 2: Fold Each Stack in Half

As neatly as possible and keeping the paper as lined up as possible, fold each pile of 8 sheets in half cross wise.

## Step 3: Unfold the Paper and Turn Over

Making sure you keep the paper nice and straight, unfold each stack of 8 sheets and turn over.

## Step 4: Staple the Pages Together

I have a long arm stapler ("bully for you," I hear you say), but if you don't have one of those, then no worries—just do the following:

Open out your stapler.

Place the upturned paper stack on top of an eraser (positioned where you want to staple, which will be about 2 inches from the edge of the page, exactly on the crease).

Slowly but firmly push down on the stapler until you have stapled the pages.

Turn over the pages and pull off the eraser and then fold over the staple ends with the blunt end of a dinner knife or your thumb nail, being careful not to break it/stab yourself.

Repeat at the other end of the crease so that each page has just 2 staples in it.

If you have a long arm stapler, simply staple the 8 sheet stack in two places. I knew there was a good reason for borrowing that thing from work.

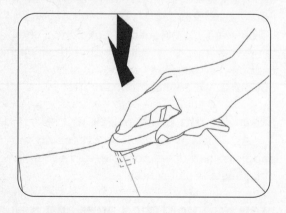

## Step 5: Glue the Binding onto the Folios

You are now going to make the heart of the book. You have made at least 4 of the 8-sheet/32-page folios and they need to be stuck together.

Firstly, cut a piece of thin fabric to the same length as the page height and about 5 times the thickness of all the folios held together. Hold the folios tightly together and all lined up. Either get a friend to help or clip the folios together using giant paper clips or bull dog clips (or even a rubber band, I guess).

When they are all nicely aligned, apply glue to just the spines of the folios. You can use white glue for this (this was what white glue was originally made for) but you must be careful not to let it drip down into the gaps between the folios (maybe painting the fabric would be better). Alternatively, you can use hot melt for this part. Again, hot melt is used in industry for book binding so it is perfect for the job.

Before it has a chance to set, quickly turn over the wad of folios and glue them to the piece of fabric so that some fabric sticks out each side (i.e. that is not glued to the pages)

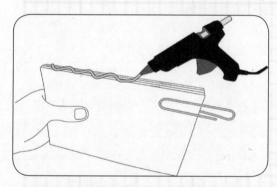

## Step 6: Trim the Bound Folios

As "Fugazzi" has pointed out in another instructable, you may be able to get your bound pages trimmed by a proper guillotine at your local one-stop print or copy shop. Failing that, read on. . .

If you want (and you don't have to) you can trim the folios a tiny bit. Beware that the first time you do this you might end up making more of a mess of the edge of the paper than if you just left it. It takes a bit of practice and a sharp craft knife or scalpel (definitely NOT something for children to do on their own). If you want to trim, then the most important edge to trim is the edge opposite the binding. This is because when the paper is folded over, all the pages get to be slightly different lengths depending on where they are in the folio stack. The trick is to hold the rule very steady and take many repeated cuts being careful to cut in the same groove and try to make sure that at each cut the paper on at least one layer is cut from edge to edge.

Trimming is by no means necessary. Trimming or not, you have now finished the paper part of the book and it's time to move on to the cover.

## Step 7: Mark and Cut Out the Cover Boards

Place the bound folios on a piece of stiff card so that the bound edge lines up with one straight edge and then draw around the paper allowing about a ¼ inch/5mm border on the three other edges. Cut the card out and then cut a duplicate. Corrugated card is fine as the cover, as is thin foam core (foamboard), but the best kind of card is the stiff card that is used as the backing for drawing and sketching pads.

## Step 8: Make the Book Spine

Loosely assemble the bound paper and the covers. Pressing them together, measure their combined thickness and mark off on a piece of scrap card. Cut the spine so that it is the thickness of the covers and the paper together and the same length as the height of the book covers.

## Step 9: Mark and Cut the Material

Position the book covers and the spine on the reverse of your chosen fabric or leather and mark out so that there is a border of about 1 inch/25mm all round. Cut out the material. As already mentioned, you can use any material you want really, but a very

thick material will be difficult to fold and glue (although, who knows how patient you are?).

## Step 10: Glue the Cover Board and Spine in Place

Using white glue or rubber solution glue, smear an even coating over the boards and place face down on the wrong side of the material (i.e. the side of the material that you don't normally see, which has the pattern the wrong way round, etc.). Make sure you stick them neatly in a row so that they are aligned with each other and straight and that there is a gap of about 1 or two thicknesses of the card you are using between the spine and each of the cover boards.

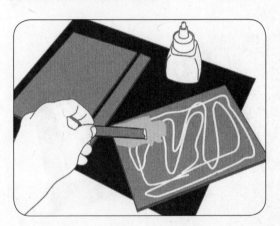

## Step 11: Finish the Edges of the Cover

Smear an even layer of white or rubber glue round the edge of the boards and fold over the material to cover the edge. Work on one edge at a time. Do opposite ends first and then fold the other ends over on top so that all the folds go the same way. Make a neat job of the corners. If you are using thick material, you may well have to cut away some of the material that is going to be hidden under the fold over to stop the corners getting too bulky.

## Step 12: Glue the Paper into the Covers

Things are starting to shape up now. Smear some white glue (or rubber solution glue) in two stripes down the middle edges of the cover boards being careful not to get any glue on the spine board. Then place the bound paper wad so that it is centrally resting

craft

on the spine board and ONLY the thin cotton "wings" are glued to the cover boards.

The spine should NOT be glued to the bound paper wad, although you should make sure that it IS glued to the cover boards right up to their edges because this is the join that makes the book strong and stops the page block falling out of the cover.

It is best if you wait for this part to dry before moving on to the next step. It is probably a good idea to leave the book lying on its back with the paper was supported by two food cans while it dries because if you leave it to dry closed, bits of it might stick together that you don't want sticking together.

## Step 13: Cut Out Your Lining Paper

Your book is nearly finished. Functionally it is already a hardback book, however the next step will make it look like a real book and cover up all the bits of folded over material.

For the lining paper you can use almost any type of paper. Traditionally marbled paper was used. Now you can make this yourself (hey, I feel another instructable coming on already), buy it in sheet form from most good craft shops, or download a sheet of marbled paper from my site (where you'll see loads of other projects just like this). Alternatively, you can use a bit of old gift-wrapping paper or even just plain old brown packing paper.

Be as creative as you can here, the lining paper is like the lining of an expensive suit; hidden until it is revealed by someone opening it. Ideally you want the lining paper to be a fraction smaller than the paper wad's height (so that you can line it up neatly) and

twice as long as the paper wad's width (so that it covers the inside of the hard cover).

## Step 14: Glue the Lining in Place

Fold the lining paper sheet in half crosswise.

Smear the inside of the cover and the first page with white glue or rubber solution glue.

Carefully place one half of the folded lining paper on the glued first page so that it lines up neatly with the edge of the paper.

Then, making sure that it goes in to the corner of the join between the paper and the cover, fold the liner out and glue it to the inside of the cover so that it covers up all the folded over material and the inside of the cardboard covers.

Repeat for the back of the book.

That's it . . . you're done. If the first paper goes a bit wrinkly as it dries out, wait for at least a day for it to dry really thoroughly and then iron over the page using a medium iron. It won't get all the wrinkles out, but it will make the page a whole lot flatter. Just try to use a bit less glue for the next book.

## Step 15: Experiment and Make Loads of Different Books

Make books as presents, make them for school, make them for friends. Keep a pictorial journal—you never know, one day you might be famous. Think, how cool would it be when they unearth your journal, which is not only full of angst and perceptive youthful insights into the unfairness of it all, but is also embodied in a book that you yourself made and not some cheap (or expensive) notebook/diary that you bought from the store like millions of other people.

# Down and Dirty Screen Printing for Under Ten Dollars

By **woodenshoepress**
(www.instructables.com/id/
down-and-dirty-screenprinting-for-
under-10/)

As a seasoned printer, friends and acquaintances consistently ask me if I can print shirts, cards, etc., for them. Usually, however, they only need a few things printed at a time, and it doesn't really justify the time/cost of doing it the "right way." I conceived this method of printing so it could be shared with anyone who wants to print short, inexpensive runs on any substrate, without having to deal with the space and economic constraints of setting up a whole studio. Most of the supplies for this project would usually end up in a landfill and can be found completely for free. Usually one can get 20 or more successful prints with this method, which seems to be sufficient for most small projects.

## Supplies

For this project, we will need some tools and supplies that are easily available and a few that might require the tiniest bit of searching. Recycling is key here. Most of the supplies can be found as trash, including the ink. What isn't direct waste can be recycled from thrift stores or garage sales.

**Tools**

- staple gun (almost any size will do)
- X-acto or utility knife (you could use a plain razor blade in a pinch)
- heat gun or a hair dryer
- scissors
- plastic putty
- knife
- small container for mixing

**Materials**

- spray adhesive
- staples
- any old picture frame as long as it is bigger than your image (ideally you can find this in the trash).
- water-based paint or ink of any type (recycle! use old house paint that would end up in the landfill/water table without you!).
- Some sort of ink retarder—I used "Floetrol," which is sold in most hardware stores as a latex paint wetting agent. It is around $6 for the bottle. You can also use straight glycerin, which is available at most drug stores for a dollar or two for a small bottle.
- Adhesive Backed Sign Vinyl (any color)— This is available from many arts and crafts stores, but sign shops generate so much scrap every day that if you ask them nicely, they will almost certainly just give you some. If you don't want to ask, check the dumpster, because that's where it will end up. This material is the garbage left behind by the modern printing industry. it is a shame that it doesn't get reused more.
- Screen Printing Fabric (a piece bigger than your old picture frame). This is available in various mesh counts from www.dickblick.com. Again, screen printing shops can help you out if you ask nicely, and their dumpsters can be messy, but fruitful. If you are adventurous, you can experiment with different fabrics from the scrap bin at the fabric store and use that instead of genuine screen fabric. Substrate (stuff to print on)—Paper, Shirts, other textiles, bags, napkins, underpants, and just about anything else that is reasonably flat will work fine.

## Step 1: Making the Screen

Starting in the center of one of the long sides of our picture frame, use the staple-gun to attach the edge of the screen fabric. Then, stretch the fabric tight across the frame, and staple it directly opposite the first staple. Move to the shorter side of the frame, and do the same thing on each side.

Once there is some tension in the screen, slowly work around the frame, stretching and stapling until the whole screen is evenly tensioned, with no weird ripples, bumps, or saggy spots. Once there is a staple about once an inch all the way around the frame, and the screen is nice and tight, you have an almost completed screen frame!

## Step 2: Taping the screen

It is important to cover the edges of the screen to keep the ink from seeping in and making a huge mess all over the substrates. Cut some of the scrap vinyl into strips, and stick it to the screen and the frame so there is no empty space for ink to get through. Cover the fabric all the way around about 1. 5" from the edges of the frame. Start with the top of the screen, and then do the bottom. The vinyl might not want to stick to the fabric very well, which is where the heat gun comes in. Once the vinyl is all in place, quickly hit it with some heat and burnish it flat to the frame and the screen with your fingers. The heat will set the adhesive of the vinyl and make it stick firmly to the frame and the fabric.

## Step 3: Preparing the Image

This is a one color process, so think stencil, think contrast, and think monochrome. Some images work better than others and some skill is required to cut out detailed or highly shaded images. Start simple. If you are a stencil master, then make it as detailed and complex as possible. Measure the space on the screen still available for your image. Choose an image, drawing, photograph or whatever, and use either a computer or copy machine to print it out at that size. This will be going on the bottom of the screen, so remember to print out the image backwards, especially if you are using text. Once the image is printed, trim it to rough size. Now the fun begins!

## Step 4: Cutting the Stencil

So, we went to the sign shop to get scrap vinyl right? They use a lovely machine called a plotter to cut their vinyl. Making friends with them, or at least dropping them a few dollars, or a six pack of beer, or something, can allow you to skip this step. Take them your prepped image, have them cut it out, and skip ahead. . .

Otherwise, it's time to cut the stencil. Cut out another piece of vinyl a little bit larger than the printed and trimmed image. Use the spray adhesive (not too much) to stick the image onto the vinyl. Start cutting. But not too deep!!!!!!

Cut out the parts to be printed. Leave the parts that remain the substrate color. Be sure only to cut through the paper and the vinyl, do not cut through the paper backing, or everything will fall apart! If a photograph is being used, as in the example, it can be confusing. If the stencil is held up against a light, or viewed on a light table, you can get a better idea of how things are going. Once the stencil seems satisfactory, it is time to adhere it to the screen.

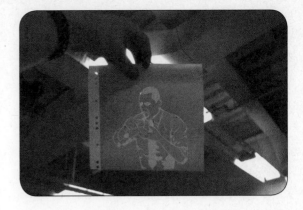

## Step 5: Adhering the Stencil to the Screen

Peel the vinyl stencil and stick it directly to the bottom of the screen in the space you have provided. Remember how that pesky vinyl didn't want to stick to the screen? Time to get out the heat gun again.

Lightly hit the stencil with heat and carefully burnish it. It will stick. Once the stencil is nice and stuck to the bottom of the screen, begin filling in the empty space with more vinyl.

Cover everything that won't be printed, using the vinyl to cover the edges of the stencil. Once the top is done, flip the frame over, and do the same thing on the bottom. Again, use the heat gun to help the vinyl set up nicely and stick to the screen and itself. You now have a completed screen, almost ready to print.

craft

## Step 6: Mixing Ink

Depending on humidity, temperature, paint quality, age, etc., ink will have to be mixed differently. Too dry, and the ink will dry up in the screen in between passes. Too wet, and the ink will run through the screen and ruin our substrates. It will probably take some time to get the perfect consistency, be patient.

Here in the very dry desert, I mix about 1 part retarder for 10 parts paint. Dark colors printed on light colors work best for this method because there is only one opportunity to pull the prints before moving the screen, and no way to layer lighter colored inks. Everything is ready. . .

Pour a thin line of ink directly above the stencil on the screen. Using the plastic putty knife at a 45 degree angle to the screen, firmly pull the ink across the image. This forces the ink through the stencil and onto the substrate. It may be necessary to pull the ink through multiple times, but be sure the frame does not move on the substrate, otherwise the image will get blurred and smeared.

Carefully lift the screen off of the substrate and move it to the next item to be printed. Continue until you are finished, or until the screen blows out.

## Step 8: Print!

Lay out all of the items to be printed upon so they are easily positionable and moveable. Start with a clean, clear work area, and be ready to move quickly. There is no need to rush, but no lollygagging either. Set the screen in place on top of whatever is to be printed and hold it down firmly. A friend can help immensely here.

## Step 8: Clean Up

Clean the screen and putty knife with dish soap and water. Peel off all the vinyl if you want to use the screen again. Be sure the ink is out of the mesh, because once it dries hard there, it will never come out. Let the finished prints dry overnight. Make more. Feel satisfied that you are creating something beautiful out of what was already considered refuse.

# Duct Tape No-Sew Tote

By **scoochmaroo** Sarah James
(www.instructables.com/id/Duct-Tape-No-Sew-Tote/)

Make this unique duct tape and fabric tote with absolutely no sewing—no kidding! This project, inspired by the awesome book *Simply Sublime Bags* by Jodi Kahn, takes less than an hour to whip up and will garner *oohs* and *ahhs* from all who see it!.

With a few simple supplies (get your stapler loaded!), a little time, and absolutely no prior experience needed, you can make your own gorgeous custom tote bag today!

## Materials

- fabric—something a bit sturdy works better. I used a donation scrap of what I think was upholstery fabric. I made the bag as big as the scrap would allow, which turned out to be 10" × 18".
- duct tape—get a color you like to coordinate with your fabric. This was my first go, so I just used what was around. The next one will get something fancy!
- scissors to cut your fabric
- stapler + staples (oh yes)
- optional (but awesome)—two tiny strong magnets

## Step 1: Cut Fabric

Whatever size you decide to go with, fold the fabric in half vertically. Cut two squares out of the bottom corners, about 1" high and 1½" wide. If you make a bigger bag, or want it to be wider at the base, increase these measurements.

## Step 2: Tape

Open the fabric, party side down. Start layering strips of duct tape over the wrong side (inside) of the fabric, slightly overlapping each strip. Continue until piece is covered. Trim away excess tape.

## Step 3: Cut Handle Opening

Now you're going to mark where the opening for your handle will be. In this instance, I made a 4" × 1" opening, centered near the top. This is how: Fold the fabric in half, party sides together, to mark the center on the tape, 1½" down from the top. Draw a line 2" to each side of this mark, and 1" down on each side. Finish the box by drawing the bottom line. Mark a line horizontally across the center of the box. Make a mark ¾" from each side on this line. Draw diagonal lines from the corners to these marks. Repeat on other end. These are your new cutting lines. If you ever have sewn, you may recognize how much these look like welt pockets or bound buttonholes.

## Step 4: Make Handle

Now we make the handle. Cut carefully along the new lines you've made. Fold back the flaps and secure with pieces of tape. Repeat on other handle

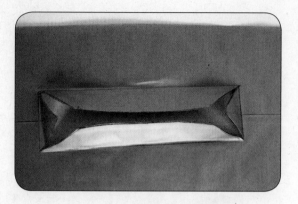

## Step 5: Finish Top Edge

You want to turn the top. ½" of fabric to the inside and tape down. I did it this way: Lay a piece of tape to cover ½" of the top edge on the party side of the fabric. If you're using magnets as a latch, insert them under the tape in the center of the top edge. Fold this edge over to the inside and tape down. Trim away the tape covering the handle opening. Repeat on other side, making sure magnets are in correct alignment.

## Step 6: Staple Together

Now we make the "seams." Fold fabric in half, right sides together. Staple the sides of the bag. ½" from the edge. Clip the corners at the top. Repeat on other side.

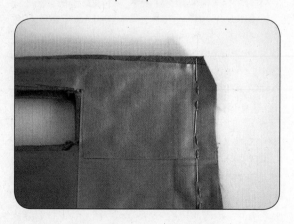

## Step 7: Tape Over Edges

Now we'll seal the raw edges. Using a block or book inside, press the seam allowance

open with your fingers. Cover the edges with tape and trim. Repeat on other side.

## Step 8: Close Bottom Corners

Close the bottom of the bag at the corners by matching up the raw edges. Staple together ½" from edge. Fold seam allowance toward the bottom of the bag and cover with tape. Trim and fold edges for a clean finish. Repeat on other side.

## Step 9: Turn Tote Right Side Out

Well, that's pretty self-explanatory. Turn bag right side out. Test out your awesome magnets. Fill it with goodies. Send some to me.

# Sewing Organizer

By **saleyla**

(www.instructables.com/id/
Sewing-Organizer/)

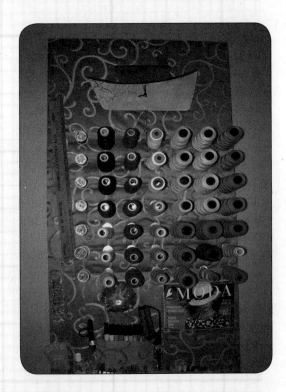

## Materials

- 2 Masonite pegboards 48" L × 24" W
- upholstery material—51" L × 27" W, plus another pockets and pin cushion
- batting—48"L × 24"W
- sewing machine
- scissors, thread, iron, pins, pliers
- staple gun
- 12" long wire
- 1 yard ribbon
- 3 bolts—1" length
- zinc fender washers

## Step 1: First Step

The first thing you do is put both pegboards together, matching the holes. Then measure about 4" from the top. Take two 1" bolts, two nuts, and wire 12" long. Screw the bolts in about 9" apart from the middle center and tight around the both ends of the wire.

Next thing you do is use that ½ yard of material and cut the pockets. Here I made 3 different size pockets—1st pocket— 3"W × 15" L; 2nd pocket—7"W × 4"L; 3rd pocket—9 ½" W × 6"L (you can use different sizes or variations of pockets).

Hem the top edge of each pocket, use pins, and place it in about 5" from the bottom of the material (for the board 51" by 27") you leave the extra 3" that we are going to fold on the back of the board; sew the pockets and iron for better look, then place the ribbon at the back edge of the pockets and sew the top of the ribbon at each side of all pockets.

Now you have a little organized area where you can hang pens, markers, notes, cards, safety pins or anything you like.

## Step 2: Second Step

Next, place the materials with sewn pockets at the bottom side of the pegboards and the batting in between.

Measure 5" down from the top middle: make a little hole with scissors and place a 1" nut and secure it with a bolt in the back side: here you can hang a clock (in this case, also possibly a calendar, monthly planner, or painting).

The next step is to start putting bolts and nuts together through the material to create the spools holder. Measure from the top 14½" down; you start from right to left placing a 3" bolt with nut, fender washer in between and tighten up with a nut on the back; screw the nuts as tight as possible; the holes are already in the pegboard but you have to make a little hole in the material.

Starting from right to left, you build the first row going down; leave 3" space between the bolts and make 6 rows with the 3" bolts, and one last row with 2" bolts to fit the smaller spools (the 3" bolts also fit the smaller spools but it is more comfortable with 2" bolts).

## Step 3: Final Step

You are almost done! Now you have all the bolts on, check the back of the board and make sure the bolts are tight. Fold the extra material on the back, grab the staple gun, and start stapling the material on the back; make sure you fold the corners tightly; look at the front and check the material if its tight enough. And there you are!

# Packing Tape Dressform

By **stijky**
(www.instructables.com/id/Custom-Dressform-from-Paper-Packing-Tape/)

Make a custom dressform, display mannequin, body double, cast, or a big piñata with some help and a little paper gum tape. You could also use this technique to make paper casts of other body parts, objects, or people! I got the basic directions and idea from here: www.taunton.com/threads/pages/t00002.Asp. But since they didn't really go into that much detail, I've made an instructable (my first! yippee!) since I was originally looking for one here anyway. Making the dressform is pretty easy, and only took us about 2 hours to complete.

## What You Need
- roll of kraft paper
- gum tape (it's the kind with dry glue on one side) I got mine relatively cheaply at Staples. To make my form (I am a size 4), we used less than half the roll; if you are larger, you will need a bit more tape. If you can't find the paper tape, I think you can also use duct tape, but you will need a few rolls to make the layers stiffer since it is flexible. The beauty of using the paper tape is that it shapes itself after drying like instant papier-mâché strips. And later on you can put pins through it without lots of sticky residue getting on your sewing pins.
- scissors (make sure they can cut through fabric)
- a rag or sponge to wet the tape, maybe a bowl to hold a little water (or just do it by the sink, and keep the rag damp)
- an old turtleneck or fitted T-shirt that you are willing to sacrifice to this project. The shirt should be as close fitting as possible and not too thick or textured. Crew neck or turtleneck is ideal, and the length should not be too short. If you don't have a turtleneck or longer shirt, don't fret, it is easy to extend the length of the form to cover your hips and neck.
- hairdryer
- marker
- someone to help you.
- optional, a hanger (to make a hanging dress form); an old pillow or Poly-fil to stuff it when finished, or a bag of packing peanuts, packing foam, or a few cans of spray foam (if you want to stuff/coat the inside for reinforcement—not necessary since it holds itself in shape but maybe it keeps the thing more durable); old lamp base, tripod or music stand (to make a standing dress form)

## Step 1: Cut the Dry Paper Tape
Before you begin taping, it helps to prepare a bunch of cut pieces in different sizes. The trick is to use smaller strips for curvier areas like breasts, collar bones, neck, and larger strips for flatter areas like the small of your back and your shoulders. We mostly used a lot of 1. 5" by 6" strips, but cut some long (3" × 18") and super short (5" × 3").

## Step 2: Tape the Torso
Now it's time to start taping. The "tapee" should be wearing the fitted turtleneck and his/ her usual undergarments. He or she should probably be standing up. Wet each strip as you need it because they dry fast and

are extremely sticky when wet. To wet the glue, lightly run a damp (not sopping, just damp) rag or sponge over the shiny (glue) side of the tape. Do not put the tape under running water, as this usually causes too much glue to be washed off and it won't stick later.

Begin with a horizontal strip running around the midsection below the chest. Make sure that it is not too loose; we want the shape to be as close to the body as possible.

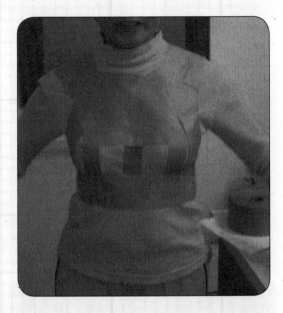

Next, tape the chest and shoulders, like making a harness. Use small pieces in all different directions over curvy parts, and try to keep them laying flat against the body. If you encounter a fold or wrinkle happening in the tape, you can notch it to keep it laying flat. Lastly, tape around the stomach and lower back and neck area. It helps if you tape symmetrically so in the end all areas are evenly covered.

Ultimately you need about 2 to 3 layers of tape to create a sturdy shell. The tapee can help by cutting more tape or taping the front sections within reach. Try to avoid twisting and bending so the torso shape isn't crushed or distorted too much; eventually they won't be able to move anyway.

## Step 3: Tips for Taping Shapes

I already mentioned about using short thin strips to cover rounded areas like the chest, some other areas you should watch out for are the dips by the collarbone,

area between the shoulder blades in the back, around the waist (love handles?), and underarms to shoulders.

To keep the integrity of a depression area, push the tape into the valley part first, then smooth outward letting the edges of the strips fall where they may. I used a V-shape pattern to tape the back between the shoulder blades. If you notice an area tenting too much, don't be afraid to cut it off (just the tape, not the shirt) and re-tape that area with smaller pieces. Having the tape overlap in all different directions will create a stronger contoured shell. You might also want to create "spines" (such as a cross shape over the front and back) to support the entire structure more.

To create extensions (say, if you are using a crew neck shirt instead of a turtleneck) use a vertical strip, tape to the inside of the shirt with the sticky side out. Then fold it over onto itself so that the ends are sandwiching the shirt but the tape sticks out to the length you need the form to cover. Space these extension prongs a few inches apart, and then tape them together using the same method (folding the tape over onto itself, but sandwiching the tape next to it). Use a hair dryer to dry any pieces that are still wet.

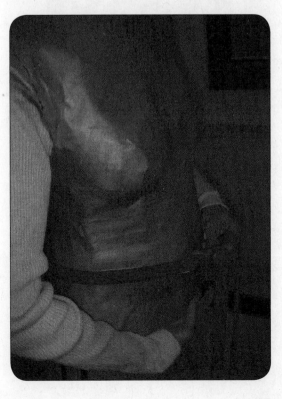

## Step 4: Draw Guidelines

If you are making a dress form for sewing, now is when you want to use a marker to draw your own waistline, hip line, shoulder line, center line, etc., on the form. You can use a ribbon or string to measure the line. Now is also a funny time to add tattoos.

## Step 5: Remove the Shell

Using the scissors that can cut through fabric, carefully cut through the center of the back, vertically. You are cutting through the paper tape AND the shirt underneath (which is now a part of your dress form). Be careful not to cut the person or their undergarments by accident. They should be able to wiggle out of the shell without bending it too much.

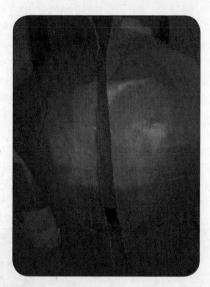

## Step 6: Seal the Back Up, Finish the Edges

Using several short fat strips, carefully join the cut line together. If you want to avoid excessive tape buildup along the back, you can also seal from the inside. NOTE: If you are making a hanging dress form using a rigid hanger, insert the hanger and affix it to the underside of the shoulders before sealing the back. The hanging hook sticks up through the neck hole. After the split line is sealed, finish the bottom and neck edges by folding strips of tape over from the outside to the inside. You can trim the sleeves off and do the same to those, or knot them and shove them inside the form.

## Step 7: Stuff the Inside and/or Decorate (Optional)

The form should be stiff enough to not collapse, but you can stuff the inside if you want to make it sturdier. Things that should work include: packing peanuts (in a bag, unless you seal off the bottom and armholes, fill through the neck, then seal), Poly-fil, old pillows, packing foam.

See the next step for details on how I stuffed and mounted mine. I am using a layer of insulation spray foam to coat about 1" on the inside (so pins will hold better). If you do this, just spray one section at a time, let it dry, and set for a few hours, then flip the form over and do the other section. You could also shellac the outside if you wanted to seal it, or decoupage, collage, paint, spray paint, whatever. It's not necessary, but if you are using this as a display mannequin decorating it could be really nice. I might decoupage some newspaper and lace onto mine. Alternately you can stretch and attach a sweater/knit shirt over the paper form to

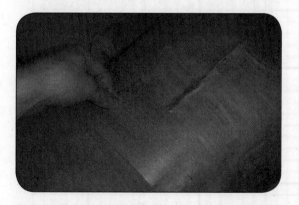

create a better surface for pinning fabric.

## Step 8: Mount the Form Onto a Base

I am going to hang mine on a collapsible music stand, but you could permanently mount your dress form on an old lamp base or music stand (probably easier to accomplish if the inside is stuffed). Or just hang it up. Or (if the bottom edge is straight enough) the form should be strong enough to stand upright by itself. Tada! You have cloned yourself a double.

# How to Sew an Envelope Pillow Cover!

By **jessyratfink** Jessy Ellenberger
{www.instructables.com/id/How-to-sew-an-envelope-pillow-cover/)

Pillows need updating? Don't buy new ones, just recover the old ones. I'm about to start recovering an entire couch and in the process of choosing fabrics I decided my pillows needed some updating as well. This is super easy and should take about a half hour per pillow once you get into the swing of things. Plus, the covers are washable. Yay!

## Before You Start

Some words of caution: If you plan to wash this pillow cover, wash the fabric beforehand in the way you normally wash. Otherwise, the unwashed sewn fabric can shrink in a hot wash or dryer later and cause the seam to rip. If you're in a hurry to get started, make sure to at least steam press your fabric. You'll just need to wash it normally and hang it out to dry later! This will keep your pillow cover in nice shape.

## What You'll Need

- ½ to 1 yard of fabric. I am estimating because I don't know how big your pillow is. We'll talk about that in a bit.
- matching thread
- scissors
- pen/pencil for marking
- ruler of some sort
- sewing machine
- iron & ironing board
- measuring tape

## Step 1: How to Measure Your Pillow!

This is dead easy if your pillow has a cover. Covered pillow: take cover off, measure across and down. Add an inch to each of these measurements. Uncovered pillow or pillow form: use your measuring tape to conform to the curve of the pillow and take the measurements. Add an inch to each of these measurements. In this example, I'm using a covered pillow, but the cover is awful bumpy thanks to the cording around the edges. So I took measurements both ways and compared. Better safe than sorry. My pillow is 18 × 18, so I'll be adding an inch to that.

## Step 2: Measure and Cut

Use the selvage (this is the "finished edge" of the fabric—it won't fray!) as a straight edge. It will make your life so much easier. I wanted to use my lovely clear ruler, but had to break out the yardstick instead. Since my pillow is 18 × 18, I'm cutting out one piece that is 19 × 19. The other two pieces, I'm taking six inches off the length. This way they overlap prettily. My other two pieces are 13 × 19. So, to summarize: cut one piece that is your length+1 and height+1, cut two pieces that are your length-6 and the same height.

### Step 3: Sewing the Small Panels to the Large

Sewing is my favorite bit; so much easier than cutting. We'll be using a ½ inch seam allowance. Take your main panel and place it right side up. Then, take one of the smaller panels and place it wrong side up at the edge of the large panel. Once your edges are aligned, pin down the side about an inch and a half in. Repeat on the other side. Helpful tip: On the left side, have the pointy bit of the pin facing away from you. On the right side, face the pointy bit toward you. This will keep you from stabbing yourself while sewing. Make sure to backstitch at the beginning and end of the cloth.

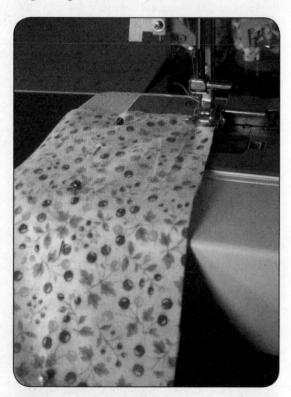

### Step 4: Hemming the Small Panels

Lay the cloth wrong side up on your ironing board. Go to the outside edge of one of the smaller panels and fold over the fabric so you're looking at a small strip of the right side. (Preferably ½ to an inch.) Press like a mad person, get it good and flat! Repeat this on the other small panel. Now, you'll sew these up using the same ½ inch seam allowance.

### Step 5: Sewing It All Together

Lay the fabric out wrong side up and press the inside seams flat. Then, flip the fabric over so the right side is facing you. Fold over one of the small panels and press. Fold the other small panel over and press. You should now be looking at the wrong side of the fabric. Pin the top and bottom of the fabric as we did before, about 1½ inches from the edge. Remember your left and right pinning rule. Make sure everything is pinned nice and flat. Sew the top and bottom seams using a ½ inch seam allowance and backstitching at the beginning and end of the fabric. Remove the pins! Cut diagonally across the corners as shown below.

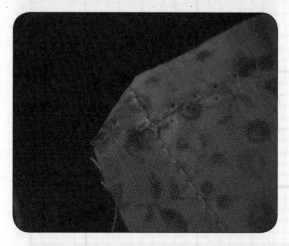

### Step 6: Turn It Right Side Out

Poke out the corners and stuff your pillow in it. Then show it off your friends. or cats, if that's all you have available.

## Fastest Recycled T-Shirt Tote Bag

By **sewmargaretsew**
(www.instructables.com/id/FASTEST-
RECYCLED-T-SHIRT-TOTE-BAG/)

Re-purpose an unwanted T-shirt today and easily turn the shirt into a re-usable tote bag. With just two quick seams and some fast cutting, you are finished! These T-shirt totes are strong and washable! Did You Know: Plastic shopping bags are typically used less than 30 minutes and only 1 percent are recycled. The average American adult uses approximately 288 bags a year, or 22,000* in an average lifetime. Make and use a recycled T-Shirt Tote bag today!

### Collect the Following Supplies

- Heavy-weight cotton T-shirt (heavy weight fabric & Youth size XL or Adult S or M work best)
- 3 to 5 straight pins
- pencil or pen
- dinner plate
- scissors
- sewing machine

*Source: 2008 Piedmont Environmental Alliance, NC.

### Step 1

Choose an old T-shirt and smooth it flat on a table. Use scissors to cut and remove the sleeves—make sure you leave the seam in place—this keeps your tote strong!

### Step 2

Position a plate about halfway over the neck opening of the shirt. Trace the plate with your pencil or pen. This will be your cutting line to create the opening for your tote bag. Cut along the traced line with the scissors. Turn the T-shirt inside out and pin the bottom of the T-shirt along the hem—closed.

### Step 3

Use the sewing machine to sew the bottom of T-shirt hem closed. Reinforce your tote bag by sewing over this seam a second time. Your bag is now sewn closed. As a variation you may consider adding a "gusset" at the bottom corners—as several commenters have—that's where you sew across the corner at a right angle so that the bottom of the bag has more depth and is not just flat—it "boxes" the corners of the tote bag. Another variation to consider; see the picture of the pink T-shirt tote bag below. My friend and I added pockets to the tote by using the cut away sleeve scraps and fashioning them into pockets. We added the three pockets onto the front of the tote.

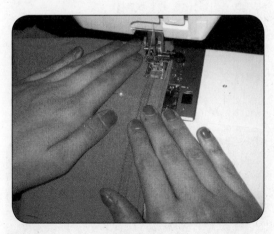

### Step 4

Turn the shirt right side out. YOU just made your own recycled tote bag. Fill it with groceries, gym clothes, pool supplies, library books, etc!

# Thick and Warm Crazy Rug

By CDandA
(www.instructables.com/id/Thick-
and-warm-crazy-rug/)

This is a super easy rug to make and it is a lot of fun! You will need about 5 yards of T-shirt material or something similar that coils up easily when stretched. You will also need a square (or any shape) of fabric for the base. The one I made is about 15" × 20" and it is super plush.

## Step 1: Base of Rug

Cut out a piece of fabric that measures 15" × 20" after you fold and hem in the sides.

## Step 2: Cut Strips of Fabric

Next cut long strips one inch wide of the T-shirt fabric.

## Step 3: Sew Rug

Take the long pieces of material and stretch them out so that they coil, then cut them into about 4 inch lengths. Line them up on the base and start sewing them right down the center, sewing each row close to the previous row. Each row should be separated by about an inch or inch and a half.

## Step 4: Great Time Saver!

Here is a great time saver! Line up a couple thin strips of tape (sticky side up) and place the fabric coils across them. Take the taped row and sew it down the center onto the base. Once you sew it down simply remove the tape.

## Step 5: That's All There Is To It

Keep sewing until you fill the base.

# How to Sew an Adjustable Chef's Apron

By **compwalla**

(www.instructables.com/id/How-to-sew-an-adjustable-chefs-apron/)

This tutorial teaches you how to sew a chef's apron. As far as aprons go, it's pretty basic.

What is different about it is the way the neck adjusts? Instead of strings that tie behind the neck or a neck that adjusts with a D-ring buckle, this one uses a single long tie that slides through casings at the armholes. You pull on the ends of the ties to slide the apron up or down as needed for each wearer.

Why this style? Because it's the style I like and it's easy for kids to adjust on their own. D-ring buckles have a way of coming undone when you least want them to. It's hard for a little kid to re-thread the end of the tie through them and a pain for their parents to do it for them. It's also easy to tie your hair inside the bow of tie-behind-the-neck aprons.

You can use cute fabric to make a hostess apron or use matching fabric to make a parent-child pair of aprons. Use denim or a masculine print and you've got a great Father's Day present for the dad in your life. Add a pocket if you want, add rick-rack or trim or a heart-shaped lace pocket. Be creative!

## Supply List

To make the apron, you'll need to gather up your supplies:

- Adult: 1½ yards of pre-washed and ironed fabric, give or take. You can get by with a little less if you make a shorter tie. I like the tie to be long enough to cross in the back and wrap back around to the front to tie so I can tuck a dishtowel in there for hand wiping and such. If you are ok with it tying in back, you'll only need about 1¼ yards.
- Kid: 1 yard of pre-washed and ironed fabric. A little less if you want a shorter tie.
- Paper to make your pattern
- pins
- thread,
- a big safety pin
- an iron
- optional: a 1" bias tape maker, rotary cutter, acrylic ruler, self-healing mat.

## Step 1: Make the Pattern

To make the pattern, you can use any kind of translucent paper or tissue. I like parchment paper. If you're making a bunch of these, parchment holds up well.

You're going to end up with two pattern pieces—one will be the apron, one will be for the casing. Start with the apron. Measure out the dimensions onto the paper and then draw in a nice curve for the armhole. Now you need to make the pattern for the casing. Measure in two inches from the arm curve and mark it with dots several places along the way. Connect the dots so you've got a consistent two inches all the way along the curve.

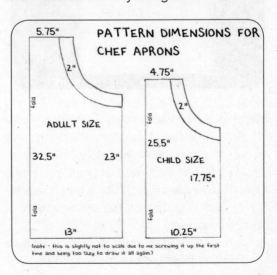

PATTERN DIMENSIONS FOR CHEF APRONS

5.75"  2"

fold

ADULT SIZE

32.5"  23"

fold

13"

4.75"  2"

fold

25.5"

CHILD SIZE

17.75"

fold

10.25"

(note - this is slightly not to scale due to me screwing it up the first time and being too lazy to draw it all again.)

If you're using parchment paper or other translucent paper for your pattern, place another sheet over your pattern and trace the curved boomerang shape. You can tape it to a big window or a sliding door during the day to make the lines more visible.

Now cut out the pattern pieces. You should have two pieces of pattern paper now, one apron piece and one casing piece. Make sure when you cut the apron out that you cut along the very outside edge. Do not cut off the piece with the casing drawn on it.

NOTE: If you really don't have a single piece of paper you can see through, using wrapping paper or other paper you can't see through, slip the second piece under the apron pattern, trace around the apron pattern, and the measure two inches in on the casing pattern piece. Make sure you cut along the OUTSIDE edge of the apron pattern.

## Step 2: Cut Out Your Fabric

Fold the fabric and pin the long end of your apron pattern along the fold. Depending on what width of fabric you have, it might save you fabric if don't fold it exactly in half. Play around with the arrangement to minimize waste.

Pin your casing piece down as close to the edge as possible but make sure you pin it where there are two layers of fabric since you're going to cut through both layers to make two casing pieces, a left and a right.

Cut around your pattern pieces through both layers of the fabric. Unpin the pattern paper. Unfold the apron piece. Now you should have three cut pieces of fabric: a left casing, a right casing, and the big apron piece.

## Step 3: You Want Me To What?

Take your curved casing pieces and move over to the iron. There are two sides to the curved piece, the short inside part and the long outside part. Just like at a racetrack. Fold the long outside part in about ¼ to ⅜ of an inch and press that down. It will be kind of tricky to get the fold an even width all the way along that curve but do your best. It's a whole lot trickier if you've already got it sewn to the apron and I managed to do it that way ten times already.

A note about pressing: for the love of FSM, don't skip any of it. If you don't have an iron, stop now and go get one. If you're going to do any sewing at all, an iron is as essential a tool as a needle. Pressing is the difference between something that looks hand-crafted and something that looks like it was made by your drunken auntie after her box of wine started running low.

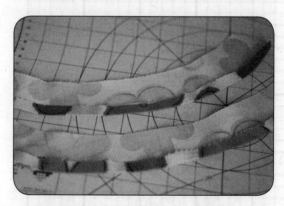

## Step 4: Sew on the Casing

Take your curved pieces back to the apron and line them up along the armholes, right sides together. Pin in place and sew them down along that inside curve. Fold them open press the seams just a little. It will be curving the wrong way, I know, but you want to flatten that bump out just a little before the next step.

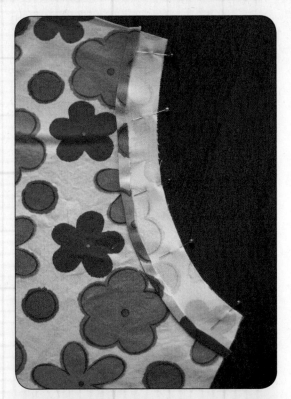

stitch but we're making an apron here, not a wedding dress.

## Step 6: Finish the Casing

Now to finish the casing. Now that the sides and top are hemmed, go back to the iron; fold the casing over to the wrong side of the apron, and press. You can see what's coming can't you? Imagine trying to press in that tiny fold on the outside curve of the casing now. It would be a major PITA, wouldn't it? Aren't you glad the fold is already pressed in there and all you have to do is pin it down? I know you are. So go do it.

Sew as close to the edge as you can. The space in between your inside and outside seams is the tunnel where the apron tie will slide so you want to ensure that space is at least ¾" wide because our tie is going to be ½" wide. The top of the apron should be completely done now. If it's not, you screwed it up. Go back and try to straighten that mess out.

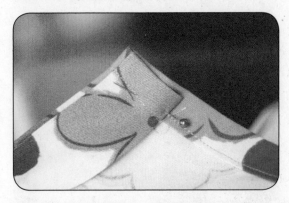

## Step 5: Hem the Top and Sides

Next we'll hem the top and sides of the apron. The top is the trickiest part so let's get that done first. The curved pieces will be sticking up like little horns but that is what we want since these will get folded in and sewn down and they won't stick up weird after that.

We're going to do a double fold along the top so head over to the iron. Fold over the raw edge once—about ⅜ to ½" ought to do it—and press it down. Just try to get it as smooth and even as possible.

Fold it over again and press it down. Do the same for the side seams. Pin those down and sew close to the inside of the fold. You could get all fancy and use a blind hem

## Step 7: Hem the Bottom

Fold up the bottom hem like we did the sides and top with a double fold to hide the raw edge. Clip the corners if you need to. Pin and sew that down. We're almost done!

## Step 8: Cut and Join the Strips to Make the Tie

Now we start the tie. Take what's left of your fabric and cut it into 2¼" strips along the longest length you've got. I use a rotary cutter and acrylic ruler to make this faster but you can use a regular ruler and scissors. Just try to make them as even as possible. Depending on how much fabric is left and how you laid out your pattern, your strips could be any length. Just figure out what length they are and cut enough of them to make the length

89

of tie you want. To make the longer tie that wraps back around front, you'll need 132" total of 2¼" strips. For a child size, you'll need 96" of strips. For a shorter tie which will tie in the back, measure around the waist of the intended owner and decrease the length needed by that many inches. I know it's math but it's just subtraction.

Take two strips and join them together by laying them at right angles, right sides together. Draw a little pencil line from corner to corner and sew along that line. Cut off the triangle to the right leaving a ¼" seam allowance. Go to the iron and press the seams open. You should now have a longer strip joined by a seam going across at a 45 degree angle. Really, the reason we do it this way is so the stress on the seam is spread out over the length of the bias tape and not concentrated in one spot. Once it's folded and sewn down, it's not going anywhere. Keep joining your strips this way until you get to the right length.

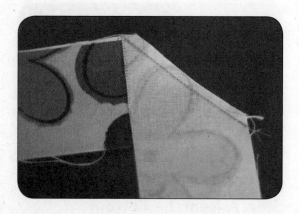

## Step 9: Make the Bias Tape

You've got one long strip of fabric now that we need to turn into bias tape. I use a handy little doohickey called a bias tape maker because I'm a modern person and I like using technology to make my life easier. But you can do it the hard way; it will just take a little more time.

Bias tape looks like a bent staple from the side. The sides are folded in to meet in the middle with a little space left down the center. You can follow the directions on the tape maker if you have one or you can fold the tape by hand which isn't really as hard as it sounds. You just need to give it a good start by folding

it in and pressing it down. Once you get it going, you can slide the iron along with your smart hand and use the fingers on your stupid hand to guide the folds.

To finish the tie, fold the bias tape in half again and iron it down. That's why you left the little space in the center, like in a side view of a spent staple. You needed the space to allow for the last fold. Now your bias tape should be four layers thick and about ½" wide. We need to sew it down but before we do that, unfold the ends, square them off, fold in about ¼" and sew the raw edge down. Clip the corners if you need to. Now take the long tape over to the sewing machine and sew pretty close to the edge. You may need to pin but I like to live dangerously and just guide the fabric under the presser foot with my fingers.

## Step 10: This One Goes to Eleven

Last step is to thread the tie through the casing. The safety pin is the star of this show. Poke the pin through the end of your tie and use it as a guide to thread it up one casing and down the other. Holy Cow! You're done!

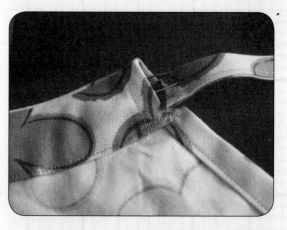

with your
# kids

Keep your kids occupied and entertained for hours with these great projects. Make science interactive by growing your own crystals and rock candy. Get outside with wizard's wands, water guns, duct tape swords, and homemade sidewalk chalk. Keep the little ones happy with crayon muffins and colorful works of art. Here you'll find great activities for kids of all ages.

# Make an Awesome Harry Potter Wand

By **KaptinScarlet** Chris Barnardo
(www.instructables.com/id/Make-an-awesome-Harry-Potter-wand-from-a-sheet-of-/)

With a sheet of paper, some glue and a bit of paint, and about 40 minutes to spare, this instructable will show you how you can make a Harry Potter type wand that would not look out of place in the film itself. For the first few stages I have drawn pictures of what you have to do and then for the painting part I have taken photos to show you exactly what to do. It's very simple but the effect is fantastic. For more projects like this visit www.dadcando.com where there are more Harry Potter type wizarding projects and a load of other craft printables and templates.

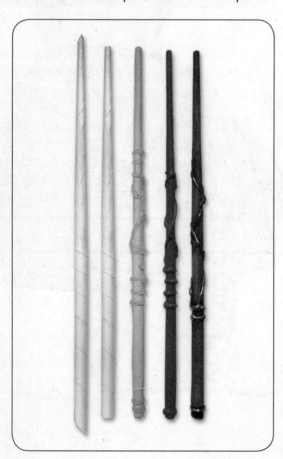

## Step 1: Prepare Your Paper

Stick a strip of double sided tape diagonally across a sheet of A4 or U.S. letter-sized paper.

## Step 2: Tightly Roll the Paper Starting in the Corner

Roll the paper starting in the corner and roll diagonally, rolling one end very slightly less than the other so that the thin paper roll is tapered. Roll until you get to the double sided tape, roll over this so that the tapered roll sticks to it

## Step 3: Glue the Last Third of the Roll

Smear the free corner of the paper with a little PVA glue (Elmer's Glue) so that whole surface is (or will be when it is rolled up) covered in glue.

Then continue to roll the wand tightly and hold (with fingers) till it's dry.

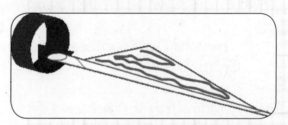

## Step 4: Trim the Wand

Wait about 20 to 30 minutes for the wand to dry. As the PVA (white glue/Elmer's) glue hardens, it should become much stiffer. When dry, trim a little bit off both ends of the wand to make the ends straight.

If you want to make a very stiff wand, roll another piece of paper and glue tighter than the first one and poke it down the inside of the first one after coating it in a bit of white glue.

I avoided using a chopstick for this because I didn't want the wand to become dangerous. I would rather the wand broke than someone got their eye poked out with it!

## Step 5: Plug the Ends of the Wand (and fill it)

Carefully dribble glue gun glue into both ends of the wand (one at a time, waiting till each end is set). For the bigger of the two ends, you can pack the end with a little rolled up tissue pushed down a bit with a pencil so that you don't have to use too much glue. For the bigger end you will probably need to have two goes. If you are careful you can achieve a rounded end, as the glue is setting make sure that you rotate the wand to stop it slumping to one side or dripping over the edge. The same goes for the little end, although if you have wound the wand tightly enough, you will not need to fill this twice.

NOTE if you want your wand to be stiff and very robust, then instead of using the tighter rolled up paper core, you can fill it with epoxy resin. Epoxy resin is that sort of glue that you use by mixing up two parts. It can be very runny when mixed up, so you will need to plug the smaller end. After plugging the little end, but before plugging the big end, fill the wand with quick setting, two part epoxy resin. Use the 5 minute setting version rather than the really fast 90 second version and carefully dribble the glue down the inside of the wand, making sure not to get it on the outside.

## Step 6: Create the Surface Detail

Holding the wand in one hand and the glue gun in the other slowly rotate the wand between finger and thumb as you gently squeeze out glue gun glue onto the surface of the wand. Try to keep it even and make a nice pattern. Start with one or two rings at the thicker end, leaving a space for the grip area, and then make a crisscross lattice effect lower down the wand by rotating and moving the glue gun along the wand at the same time.

As the glue sets rotate the wand in the air to make sure that no uneven drips build up. The glue gun glue should be set in about a minute or so, but might be tacky for a couple more minutes so be careful what you rest it on to set properly.

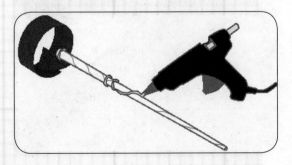

## Step 7: Spray with Base Coat

Apply a base coat to the wand to seal it, either you can use spray paint (more or less any color will do and spray paint is good because it dries hard), but you can use household emulsion instead if you haven't got any spray. (In the U.S., emulsion paint is called latex paint). If you use emulsion (latex) make sure that the wand is dry before going to the next step.

## Step 8: Paint on the Wand Main Color

Paint on the wand's main color. In this case I have chosen brown, but any color will do. I chose this because I wanted it to look like natural wood. But you could use black or an off-white for ivory or any other muted color. Paint the whole surface but don't worry if it isn't too even, in fact this will make it look more like a natural material.

IMPORTANT: you must use a type of paint that dries waterproof. Ideally use acrylic. The reason for this is that the next step uses a wash which you have to wipe off while it is wet and if you have used a paint that can wipe off for this stage, then when you apply the paint from the next stage it will rub this paint off as well (which is not what you want).

To mix brown use all the primary colors (red, blue and yellow) in varying proportions depending on what sort of brown you want, or one primary color with any secondary color (orange, purple or green). Mix in a little black (but not too much) for a darker brown and allow it to be streaky if you want.

## Step 9: Start Distressing the Wand

No this doesn't mean telling it upsetting news, distressing is the furniture-makers term for making something new, look old.

You do this by mixing up a wash of black. NOT too washy, but enough so that it remains wet long enough to be able to wipe it off. The best type of paint for this is acrylic. DO NOT paint the whole wand before starting to wipe the paint off otherwise it will dry and you won't be able to wipe it off.

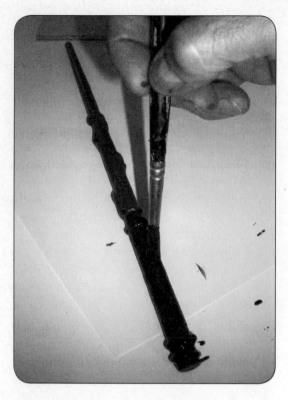

Work on the handle area, in real life handles get worn more so will be shinier and have less dark areas. Go with the flow, look at the work and wipe and paint until you are happy with the results.

Don't be afraid to go back a stage and add lighter colors and then repeat the distressing if you want to get the right effect. Always wait till the previous layer is dry. If you use acrylic you can do this as many times as you want. But you only need to really do it once.

## Step 11: Apply the Gold Detail

Using you finger tip apply some gold rubbing paste to the raised bits of the wand. You can use a gold marker or gold gel pen or gold modeling paint. The best stuff is the art store product that is designed to be rubbed on with the finger tip and then burnished a bit, but any gold paint will do.

For one of my kid's wands I used a bit of silver leaf to make some very highly reflective parts metallic looking. It was a brilliant effect. This is a bit more complicated in that you have to have gold or silver leaf and you have to paint a thin layer of gold size (a model makers' and artists' liquid glue that dries slightly tacky) on to the raised surface first and allow to dry for 2 hours and then apply the gold or silver leaf with great care (it is sooo thin) and then remover the excess with a very fine brush and burnish up with a soft cloth.

## Step 10: Finish Distressing the Wand

Wipe off the paint as you go along. Use a damp cloth or piece of kitchen towel. Dab and wipe, if you are not happy with the effect paint over and wipe more. What you are trying to achieve is the natural look of grim and aging that collects in the cracks and corners.

You won't be able to wipe all the paint off and some will collect in the corners round the glue gun glue and this will make it look really old.

If you found an ad for this instructable in the back of a comic book, it would read something like "Amaze your friends by growing a crystal tree out of common table salt and a few other ingredients available from the grocery store."

## Gather Your Materials

Gathering the ingredients is probably the most difficult step. To grow your Magic Crystal Tree, you'll need:

- Mrs. Stewart's Bluing
- table salt
- household ammonia (the kind with no soap added)
- cardboard (not corrugated)
- bowl
- water
- measuring spoon
- food coloring (optional)

The bluing is the hardest item to find but can be found in the cleaning section of many grocery stores. You can find the ammonia close by. The cardboard I used came as packing material from a new shirt, or the backing from a paper notepad. Cereal box cardboard might work, but it's thinner has printing on one side.

Depending on the temperature and humidity of your location, the ammonia is optional, but speeds up the crystal growth—the tree in this Instructable started "sprouting" in less than an hour. Without ammonia, it may take a couple of days to start.

## Step 1: Cardboard Shapes for the Crystals to Grow On

For this instructable, I made a tree formed out of two cardboard triangles, roughly 2" at the base and about 3.5" high. If you'd prefer some form of unspeakable tentacled beasty, send me a picture! Cut a slot from the top to the middle in one piece, and from the bottom to the middle in the other. The slots allow the two pieces to be assembled into a 3D shape. Make sure that whatever shape you create can stand up by itself.

## Step 2: (Optional) Color the Tree

If you like, you can add a little color to your shape by putting drops of food coloring on the edges. The food coloring will soak into the cardboard.

## Step 3: Adding the "Magic" Solution

The "Magic" Solution: Mix together:
- 1 tablespoon water
- 1 tablespoon salt
- 1 tablespoon bluing
- ½ tablespoon household ammonia

Put everything into a small bottle that could be shaken to mix the ingredients. Again, the ammonia is optional, but I'd recommend it. Find a place where you can watch your magic tree grow undisturbed for a few days. Put the tree into the bowl and add the solution.

## Step 4: Wait . . .

Wait . . . Wait a little longer . . . More waiting . . . (First sign of growth showed up at around the one hour mark.)

## Step 5: Time Passes

The tree after 12 hours. You can keep your crystal shape growing indefinitely by adding more water/salt solution to the bowl.

## Step 6: What's Going On?

The salt solution is wicked up into the cardboard tree via capillary action. Water evaporates from the surface of the tree, forcing the salt to crystallize out. Mrs. Stewart's Bluing is a colloid—tiny particles suspended in water (think of glitter in a snow globe, but much, much smaller). The tiny particles make it easier for the salt crystals to form. The ammonia helps speed up the evaporation process, which makes the crystals grow faster.

kids

# How to Remove Gum from Clothes

By **kqrpnb** Sean Duffy
{www.instructables.com/id/How-to-remove-gum-from-clothes/}

Kids will be kids! Even though mine are not allowed to chew gum, that did not stop my not-quite-youngest from getting gum on his NEW karate uniform! Actually, we do not know who got the gum on his pants, but that is not important for this instructable (anyone want to tackle "How to find out who really did it?"). This instructable will show you how to remove bubble gum from clothes. It is simple, easy, and involves no chemicals.

## Tools Required

- ice
- flat-edged butter knife
- sink or bowl
- clothes soap

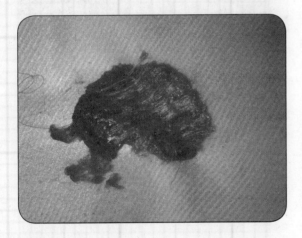

## Step 1: Prepare

Take your tools and the garment to a sink, or use some other bowl or container of appropriate size. Take out two ice cubes. I like to use the old-fashioned ice cube trays because they produce ice with a flat top and a flat bottom, but any ice will do if you can stack them. Place one cube under the gummed area, with as few layers of fabric as possible (i.e.in the pant leg). Situate the gum

spot in the center of the cube, and carefully balance the second cube on top.

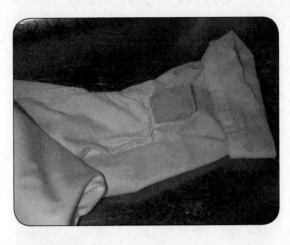

## Step 2: Wait

Wait for at least 30 minutes. You want the gum to get good and cold, through and through.

## Step 3: Scrape

You have waited long enough. Take the ice cubes off the fabric and find a flat surface. Grab the butter-knife and, using a non-serrated edge, scrape the frozen gum off. It should come right off in one big chunk. You may have to scrape off some small bits too; make sure there are none left on the fabric.

## Step 4: Wash

For best results, pre-treat the area with an enzyme detergent, or just regular clothes soap. Treat for as long as you see fit, then wash per garment instructions. That is all! I hope you have found the answer to the Burning Question, "How do I get this gum off my pants?"

# How to Make Boulder Candy

By **trebuchet03** Paul Jehein
(www.instructables.com/id/How-to-Make-Rock-Candy/)

## Materials
- sugar
- water
- large pot
- cotton string
- skewer stick
- spoon or something that covers the span of your jar

## Step 1: Preparation

Fill your jar with water leaving some empty space at the top. Pour this water into a pot. Place the pot on the stove over medium heat. Heat until you start to see steam rise off the surface of the water. Now, slowly stir in sugar. Keep adding sugar until vigorous stirring does not dissolve additional sugar. Next, pour the sugar syrup into a jar. Take care not to allow any sugar sediment to pour into the jar.

## Step 2: Make Candy!

Tie a long piece of cotton* string to a spoon, fork, skewer, etc. Then, measure the height of your jar and trim the string to this length. You may need to weigh your string down to keep it straight. For this, you can use anything that sinks in water—but avoid lead. Place your jar in a place that it won't be disturbed for about a week.

After about a week, pull out your candy! If you don't see any growth within the first few days—drain the sugar water into a pot, heat it and add more sugar. Also check that your string isn't super slippery. If ants are a problem, place your jar on a plate of water, and then add a few drops of detergent. This makes an ant moat. Here at instructables HQ ants are a problem when it comes to leaving food on the counter.

*Do not use nylon or other synthetic strings as these are too slippery for candy crystal growth.

## Step 3: Break Through

My rock candy was left in the jar for too long . . . So, to salvage, I had to break my jar for the full effect. Wear safety glasses.

## Step 4: How it Works

By heating and agitating water while adding sugar, a saturated liquid is formed. As the syrup cools and evaporates, the fluid becomes super saturated—meaning the water has more sugar than it can hold. When this happens, sugar looks for a place to escape—these places are called nucleation sites and sometimes called "seeds." The string provides the nucleation sites for crystal growth. As the water evaporates, more sugar crystallizes on the string, growing the rock candy.

## Make Your Own Sidewalk Chalk

By **scoochmaroo** Sarah James
(www.instructables.com/id/Make-
Your-Own-Sidewalk-Chalk/)

Sidewalk chalk is pretty darn easy to make, and by doing it at home, you can save money, create your own designs and colors, and have fun with the whole family.

### Materials

You can get everything you need for this project from a craft or art supply store and around the house. You'll need:

- plaster of paris
- water
- powdered tempera paint
- mixing bowl
- Molds: I used some fun molds that came with a plaster of paris kit, and some of the neat ice tube trays from IKEA. They even make tube-shaped ones if you want traditional chalk shapes. To make your own stick molds, try using toilet paper rolls. To make them thinner, just cut a seam, overlap the edges, and tape together.

### Step 1: Mix It Up

For every cup of plaster of paris, use ¾ cup of water. Add in as much powdered tempera as you like, and stir, stir, stir!

I found that the color of the chalk when using it on paper didn't come out as strong as it seemed like it would. So be prepared to do some experimenting.

### Step 2: Molds

Pour the mixture into your molds. For fun, mix up a few different colors, and swirl them together!

I used a wooden skewer to level off the tops of the molds so they'd have flat backs.

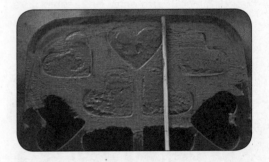

### Step 3: Clean-Up!

Clean up is very important and you don't want to rinse this stuff down your sink. See how it's setting up in those molds? It's going to do the same in your pipes!

Take a container like a small waste bin, and line it with a plastic bag. Pour in some water, and use this as a sink to rinse everything— all materials, your hands, everything! Let the plaster set up in the bottom, and the water will rise to the top. Once it's settled, you can pour off the water from the top, leaving the plaster undisturbed. Dispose of the bag.

### Step 4: Check out that Chalk!

Drying time will vary, depending on size of the molds you use. It's pretty easy to tell by look and feel when the chalk will be ready to de-mold. Even if you pop it out and it's not set yet, you can let it air dry a bit more without worrying about it losing its shape.

99

# How to Dye Noodles—the Crafting and Edible Version!

By **The Handmade Project**

Traci Ward

(www.instructables.com/id/How-to-Dye-Dry-Noodles/)

Dyeing dry noodles for art collages, stringing awesome necklaces, or sorting by color is a breeze! Go back to kindergarten with this easy project.

*Note: This recipe allows noodles to be used for craft projects, or technicolored meals!* Check out my blog, www.thehandmadeproject.com for more crafty tidbits.

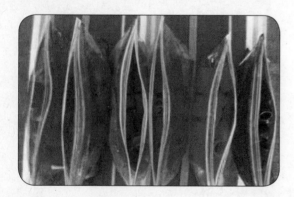

## Step 1

Take one willing two-year-old and post them next to you in the kitchen. Prep yourself with food coloring, white vinegar, baggies, and dry noodles.

## Step 2

Add one teaspoon (or less! Less is more in this step or else you will wind up with soggy noodles with unevenly distributed color) of vinegar to a baggie of dry noodles.

## Step 3

Squeeze in four to five drops of food coloring. Close baggie and distribute the color!

## Step 4

Open the newly colored baggie of noodles to let air dry. Enjoy just how easy it is to dye noodles!

## Step 5

Once noodles are dry, take out of baggie and get to stringing.

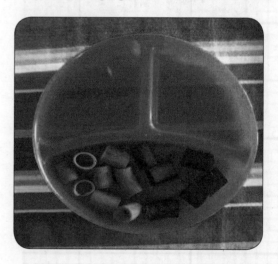

## Step 6

When finished working with your gem-hued noodles, and your gem-hued hands.

# Mini-Muffin Crayons: A New Life for Broken Crayons!

By **Always All The Time Craftng**
(www.instructables.com/id/MINI-MUFFIN-CRAYONS-A-New-Life-for-Broken-Crayo/)

Up-cycle your broken crayons into mini muffin-sized crayons. You will love the tie-dyed look and your young artists will love the mini disc-size—just right for small hands! Start the search—collect all your broken crayons from the bottom of the art drawer and from leftover boxes brought home from school.

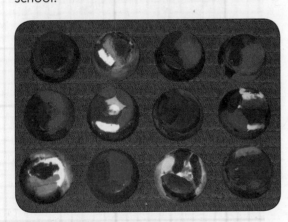

## Items You Will Need

- Preheat oven to 275°F
- mini-muffin pans
- as many broken/unwanted crayons you can find!
- oven mitt
- refrigerator (to cool melted crayons after "baking")
- dish towel

## Step1: Remove the Paper Crayon Labels

It may take several minutes to peel all the paper labels off the crayons. Many kids enjoy this activity. You may want to sort crayons by color as you remove the labels. This is also a good time to break any whole crayons into smaller pieces.

## Step 2: Arrange the Broken Crayons in a Mini Muffin Tin

Fill the mini muffin tin with the broken crayons. I suggest filling the cup up to the top since when the crayons melt, the volume will be less. Try mixing colors for a swirled "tie-dye" look or make solid colors if you seem to have 100s of broken orange crayons!

## Step 3: Melt the Crayons

Put on an oven mitt and place the mini muffin tin in your pre-heated 275°F oven. The crayons should be melted in about 10 to 13 minutes. Only an adult should remove the melted crayons from the oven!

Carefully place the hot muffin tin on a heat resistant surface and let cool for about 25 minutes. Then place tin in your refrigerator or freezer for about 5 to 10 minutes. If you place in the refrigerator/freezer before cooled, the muffins may crack from the extreme temperature change. Invert the muffin tin onto a dish towel covered surface and the chilled mini-muffin sized crayons should fall right out. The dish towel lessens the surface impact as the crayons fall from the tin.

*Great way to use dull and broken crayons brought home by students at the end of the school year! *Wrap the mini-muffin crayons in clear plastic bags and tie with a ribbon and use as birthday favors!

Oobleck is a classic science experiment that's perfect for entertaining both kids and adults. If you haven't seen it in action it's very fascinating stuff and before too long you'll have your hands covered with it, happily making a mess that can be washed away with water. Oobleck is a non-Newtonian fluid. That is, it acts like a liquid when being poured, but like a solid when a force is acting on it. You can grab it and then it will ooze out of your hands. Make enough Oobleck and you can even walk on it! Oobleck gets its name from the Dr. Seuss book *Bartholomew and the Oobleck*.

## Materials

All you need is corn starch and food coloring and the food coloring is optional.
- 1 cup water
- 1.5 to 2 cups corn starch
- a few drops of food coloring of your choice

## Step 1: Mix it Up!

Start with the water in a bowl and start adding the corn starch to it. You can use a spoon at first, but pretty quickly you'll be moving on to using your hand to stir it up. When you're getting close to adding 1.5 cups of the corn starch, start adding it in more slowly and mixing it in with your hand. The goal is to get a consistency where the Oobleck reaches a state that is the liquid and yet solid. Sometimes you will need more cornstarch. If so, keep adding more than the initial 1.5 cups. If you add too much, just add some water back into it. You will have to play with it to see what feels appropriately weird.

## Step 2: Add Food Coloring

Now that the Oobleck is just right, it's time to add some color. We save this step for later because it's a fun challenge to stir in the food coloring. You will have to slowly mix the Oobleck around to get it thoroughly mixed.

## Step 3: Play With It!

No go ahead and play with the Oobleck. That's the point of all this and you can find lots of tricks to try out. Here's a short list:
- Grab a handful, squeeze it, and let it ooze out your fingers.
- Make a puddle and quickly drag your fingers through it.
- Put it into a plastic container and shake it or quickly bump it against a table.
- Jab at the Oobleck and then slowly let your finger sink in.
- Put it on top of a subwoofer and play some low frequencies at high volume (tough to set up, but worth it).

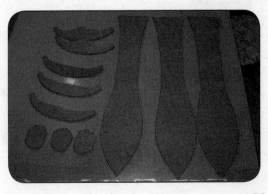
# How to Make a Duct Tape Sword

By **morfmir** Thomas Hansen
(www.instructables.com/id/
How-to-make-a-duct-tape-sword/)

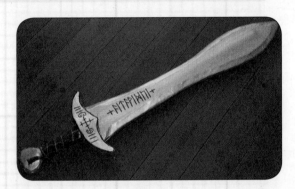

This is the second instructable in a series about how to make weapons and other equipment for LARP (Live Action Role Play). My main focus is that the weapons have to be safe, so kids can play with them without direct adult supervision, without getting hurt. Secondly, if you keep the design simple, big kids can make it themselves with a little bit of adult supervision. These weapons are perfect for a backyard battles or a game of LARP in the nearby forests.

## Materials

- sketch block
- a pencil
- a hobby knife, with interchangeable blades
- extra blades
- used dull blade
- a piece of cardboard or paper
- a black marker
- a cutting pad
- contact glue
- duct tape
- reinforcement tape
- double sided tape
- silver tape, for decorations
- a sleeping pad
- 10 cm of foam tube
- 2 strips of cotton cloth
- 3cm thick bamboo, fiberglass, or a broomstick

## Step 1: The Design and Research Phase

Start by finding some pictures of "real" swords by doing a search on Google.com for sting + sword, elf + sword, Viking + sword, or fantasy + sword. Now you have enough inspiration to make you own design. Just draw some quick sketches. They don't need to be beautiful; it is just so you will get the idea about how your sword will look like. My sword will be an elf sword, inspired by Frodo's Sting from Lord of the Rings.

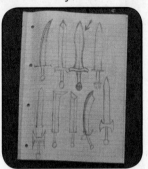

## Step 2: Template

Now draw the design of your choice on paper or cardboard. This will be your template so be careful and take your time to make it perfect. If you have problems with making the two sides of the swords identical, fold the paper in half and cut it folded. When you unfold the paper the template will be perfect, and the two sides identical.

## Step 3: Marking and Cutting the Foam

Draw the sword 3 times on the foam. Pay attention to the placing of the pieces so you don't waste too much of the sleeping pad. The small space between the sword pieces is ideal for cutting the cross guard. To be sure the pieces end at the right places I put numbers on them. In the middle piece I cut a hole for the bamboo stick. If the stick for the handle is too long, now is the time to cut it into length.

## Step 4: Putting it Together

I put a strip of reinforcement tape on pieces 1 and 3 of the crossguard. This will stabilize the crossguard to ensure that it will not break or be ripped apart.

Now apply glue to one side of pieces 1 and 3, and apply glue to both sides on piece 2.

Also apply glue to the handle. Let it dry for 10 to 15 minutes, and press the pieces hard together. Be careful the pieces glue together very quickly, so be sure that they are aligned, you will not be able to correct it. The only way to correct it is by cutting away on the outer side.

Safety note: If you're using the same glue I use you need to have good ventilation. If it's not too cold it's best to glue outside. It's possible to get water-based contact glue, and if you make this with kids, I recommend using that. But it takes a lot longer to dry.

## Step 5: Cutting and Shaping the Edges

To make the foam look like a real sword you need to cut the edge. If the layers got unaligned when gluing, this is the right time to cut that edge also.

## Step 6: Taping

Add strips of duct tape to the sword. Be careful when applying the tape special around the corners. Take the hobby knife and cut the tape into strips so it will not get wrinkled. When applying a new strip of tape, don't make the overlay more than 1cm. If you put on to much tape, the weapon gets hard and heavy, making it dangerous to play with.

## Step 7: Making the Handle

I found a old piece of cotton cloth and ripped it into strips. I covered the handle with double sided tape, and tied the cloth tight around it.

I use the black marker to draw some decoration and to highlight the edge to give the blade more depth. I cut some decorations of silver blank insulation tape and put them on the cross guard.

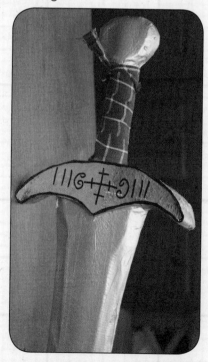

kids

# How to Make a Marshmallow Gun

By **ewilhelm** Eric Wilhelm
(www.instructables.com/id/
Marshmallow-gun/)

This marshmallow gun (marshmallow shooter) will completely surprise you with its accuracy, range, and ease of construction. Plus, it's tons of fun and a lot better than any store-bought toy because it encourages modifications.

Marshmallow shooter kits with all PVC pieces pre-cut are available in the Instructables store!

Instructions for Soda Bottle Safety Goggles are on www.instructables.com/id/Soda-Bottle-Safety-Goggles./.

## Step 1: Plans

Get the plans for the gun here (http://www.instructables.com/id/Marshmallow-Shooter/). You will need: 22 inches of ½ PVC pipe (½ is the nominal diameter, its actual outer diameter is closer to ⅞ inch), 2 end caps, 2 three way junctions, and 2 elbows.

## Step 2: Cut the PVC to Length

Cut 1 length of 7 inches and 5 lengths of 3 inches. Hacksawing is a good choice for this step; here is a How to Hacksaw tutorial: www.instructables.com/id/Hacksaw/.

## Step 3: Assembly

Layout your pieces and assemble them. Friction should hold them all together.

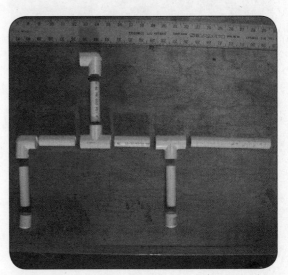

## Step 4: Test

Put on your safety glasses. Point the gun in a safe direction. Load a mini marshmallow into the mouth piece, seal your lips to the mouthpiece, and give the gun a quick burst of air. Yes, the marshmallow does go around all those curves. Pretty cool, huh?! Keep your ammunition sealed. Dry marshmallows don't work very well. Clean up your marshmallows when you're done. Especially, don't leave any around roads: they will attract animals to be hit by cars.

# Garden Hose Water Gun

By **bgepp1** Brent Geppert
(www.instructables.com/id/
Garden-Hose-Water-Gun-for-
Hero-Dads/)

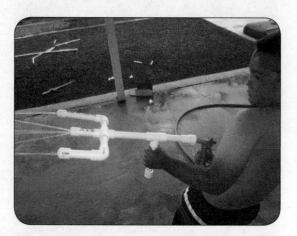

I love me some 40 schedule ½ PVC so when it got super hot today I decided to make one of those customizable PVC lawn sprinklers. Then I thought "hey, it would be fun to make a PV water gun that connects to the hose." I happened to have a sprayer attachment that had a threaded end so I tried my PVC hose connector on it and batta boom batta bing we were in business. This "ible" is not super detailed cuz it was a rush job but as all you hero dads know time is of the essence when you are trying to entertain and inspire your kids.

## Materials (this is for the triple barrel version)

- Approx 20 inches of schedule 40½ PVC (usually it comes pre-cut length of either 2 or 4 feet)
- 1 cross slip connector
- 1 "t" slip connector
- 4½ slip caps
- 1 garden hose
- ½" PVC connector (threaded one side and slip on the other. I got mine at Lowes next to the sprinkler heads)

106

- sprayer with a threaded end
- hacksaw for cutting the PVC
- drill with ⅛ bit

## Step 1: Drill the End Caps

Drill holes in the caps that will go on the end of the barrel. I experimented with several configurations. This came in handy because eventually we went from single barrel to the triple barrel.

## Step 2: Set up the Pieces

You'll have to cut these to the varying lengths (I did not show me cutting PVC cuz I am assuming everyone knows how to do that). None of this was glued together. I purposely just hand fitted all these pieces because it was fun making up new configurations with the various pieces.

One note with drilling: I used a fine drill bit (⅛ th) to make the holes. The smaller the bit the stronger the stream will be as well as the stronger the pressure.

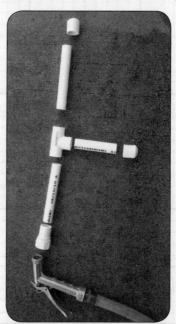

## Step 3: Slip all Pieces Together

Slip all the pieces together and screw it onto the sprayer gun. You'll have to be careful not to put the hose on full blast because most guns will come apart if you do (the pressure is too strong). If you really like a particular configuration you can always glue this baby together and then you'll really be able to crank up the water pressure.

Treat yourself with lavish bath salts, homemade soaps. Learn the best ways to get rid of sunburn, and how to clean your sinuses. Even make your own moisturizing sugar scrub! If there's something your body needs, you're sure to find it here.

# Home Made Soap the Easy Way

By **Babyshoes**
(www.instructables.com/id/Melt-and-Pour-Soap-Making---Home-Made-Soap-the-Eas/)

This is a great way to make "homemade" soap as presents for friends and family. I taught myself to do this about a year ago when I wanted to make presents for Christmas rather than simply buying them. I enjoyed it so much I continued learning and experimenting, and decided to share my techniques and tips in an instructable.

I will start with the absolute basics, and then include a few more ideas later on. If you already make soap and are just looking for new ideas, you might want to skim over the basics and head to the end!

## Ingredients and Equipment
- melt and pour soap base, either clear or opaque, or both (I tend to get mine in very big blocks on eBay). Beware, it must be M&P soap base as most ordinary soap won't melt. I learned this the hard way so you wouldn't have to!
- soap coloring—eBay again. Be sure to get the water soluble colors if you are using clear soap.

- cosmetic grade scent or essential oils: I buy essential oils from places like health food shops. Soap making sites stock special scents but essential oils are cheaper and more natural!
- surgical spirits—try your pharmacy. I got mine from Superdrug. I believe it is known as rubbing alcohol in the U.S. I have also read that you could substitute witch hazel, though I haven't tried it.

## Equipment
- microwave: You could do this in a double boiler on the stove if necessary, but that would be a nuisance.
- microwave safe container to melt the soap: I picked up a couple of microwave pots on sale in a local thrift store. A microwaveable plastic or glass jug works well too. You really want a pouring spout!
- something to stir with: I used some pieces of dowel rod we had lying around.
- a small spray bottle: Try the travel section of your pharmacy.
- a mould: This needn't be a specialist soap mould, though there are plenty of them available on eBay and soap making sites. Any reasonably flexible container will do, as long as it won't melt too easily. Think cream cheese tubs, yoghurt containers, silicone ice cube trays, etc.
- cling film (plastic wrap): This soap does not like being exposed to the air, so wrap it fairly soon after it has set.
- chopping board and knife, or a grater: Chopping or grating the soap base helps it melt .
- scale: This becomes less necessary as you learn to measure by eye.
- If you buy the powdered colorant, you will also need some small dropper bottles (pharmacy again) and other small containers such as plastic shot glasses to mix it all up in. Some people are fussy about not using the same piece of equipment for both craft and food, but this is soap for goodness sake!

**Optional**

Things you might want to add to your soap to make it look pretty include glass or plastic beads, children's novelty pencil rubbers (erasers), small soaps or pieces of commercially made soap, Buff Puff—those scrubby things made of plastic-y netting, small plastic or rubber toys, gold or silver glitter, powder, fake flowers, or any other non-organic, non-ferrous item you wish to embed in your soap. Don't be tempted to use anything that could react with water (e.g. dried flowers) as the soap has a high water content. It might look pretty now, but mould or rust in soap is not a nice idea!

The more expensive parts are the soap base, the coloring and special soap moulds. Everything else can be bought cheaply for a few pounds or less. If you keep your eyes open and shop around a bit you will find all sorts of things you can use, even if they are meant for something else entirely!

## Step 1: Preparation

Decide what mould, colour and scent you want to use and put them somewhere convenient near your microwave. Fill your spray bottle with surgical spirits, check it works by spraying somewhere like your sink or bath and have that handy too. If you are putting things in your soap, place the inserts into the mould and arrange them attractively before preparing the soap base.

Measure the volume of your mould in milliliters using water and a measuring jug if you have one. You will need a similar weight of soap base in grams. I tend to measure by eye and have a small mould (e.g. shaped ice cube trays) standing by for any excess, but it is initially difficult to guesstimate the amount of soap you will need.

Chop up your soap and weigh it, then place in your microwave proof container.

## Step 2: Nuke It!

Depending on the volume of soap, microwave it for 30 to 50 seconds before stirring well. Continue to microwave in 10 to 20 second blasts, stirring in between until the soap base is mostly melted. If you have just one or two small lumps left, stir until they melt rather than microwaving more. This stuff can get too hot and go funny, so be a bit careful here. You are aiming for just melted rather than very hot.

Add coloring and scent and stir it in. The amount of coloring will depend on the depth of color you are trying to achieve—if using clear soap in a white container the colour will seem deeper than it actually is. You will learn what works for you!

Be careful with strong essential oils like peppermint or tea tree, if you use too much they will sting when used on *ehem* sensitive areas. Start with a couple of drops and add more if needed. The soap will have a slightly stronger scent when it is used than when it is molten. Always add your color first so the soap has a chance to cool slightly before adding essential oils; if the soap is too hot you will simply evaporate them. This also goes for re-melting soap to which you have already added scent, you might need to add a little more.

**body**

**109**

## Step 3: Pour and Wait!

Pour your colored, scented soap into your mould and immediately spritz the top with surgical spirits—this reduces the surface tension and gets rid of any bubbles on the top. If you have some very small, foam-like bubbles around the edge that just won't go away, your soap was probably a little too hot. Don't worry, it will still work as soap, just try not to over-heat it next time!

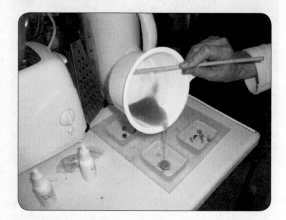

After pouring and spraying, leave the soap where it is to set. Try not to bump it for at least half an hour, as the soap forms a custard-like skin on top which will wrinkle if you bump it. Again, it will still work, but looks a bit odd.

## Step 4: Finishing Up

After about 30 to 60 minutes, depending on volume, your soap will have set enough to move it around. Do not try to take it out of the mould yet, it needs to be completely cool. This can take several hours at room temperature—ideally leave it overnight. Don't be tempted to put it in the fridge though, as condensation can be a problem. You can, however, put the soap in the freezer BRIEFLY once it is cool if you are having trouble getting it out of the mould.

To de-mould the soap, tip the mould upside down over a suitable surface, and gently flex your mould and push the base. If it is properly set, the soap should pop out quite easily. If not, leave it a while longer or try the freezer trick.

Admire your soap, then wrap it in plastic wrap. You don't need to do this immediately, but certainly within a day or two, as the soap

can "sweat" if left out for too long. If you like, you can make a fancy label for it.

## Step 5: Making it Look Good

When embedding anything, or making layers stick, spritz well with surgical spirits. The only limit is your imagination!

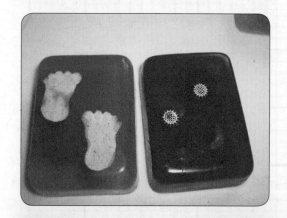

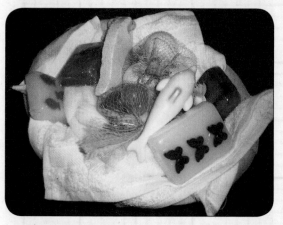

## Step 6: Presentation

I like to make up a basket of bath bits with homemade soaps. I usually line the basket with a face cloth, and add things like a novelty shaped nail brush, pumice stone, bath bombs, bags of mini-soaps, etc.

# Skin-Friendly Jelly Soap

## By ELF
(www.instructables.com/id/Skin-Friendly-Jelly-Soap/)

This is an instructable for making jelly-like soap that does not contain any unnatural additives that are bad for sensitive skin and which is easy for anyone to make.

The instructable is based on a recipe found at this blog: http://homemadebathproducts.blogspot.com/

## Ingredients and Tools

The ingredients have been somewhat adjusted for our recipe, as we didn't want to deal with melting soap.

**Ingredients**
- 1 cup clear liquid perfume-free soap
- 1 cup water (boiling hot)
- 1½ tablespoons vodka (prevents mold or fungus)
- soap color (fruit color MIGHT also work)
- essential oils
- 20 to 30g gelatin (1 to 2 envelopes, danish size)

**Tools**
- Molds, you can use anything that is not too rigid, like muffin shapes, small yogurt cups, etc.
- Measuring cup (½- or 1-cup size)
- tablespoon for measuring
- spoons for stirring
- 2 bowls

Suggestion: While normal soap can be kind of large without a problem, these can seem a little disgusting if they are too big. thin molds are also not recommended.

## Step 1: Preparing Gelatin

Place the gelatin in one of the bowls. Pour the water over (Make sure it is VERY hot, as it's hard to dissolve such a large amount of gelatin). Stir WELL, till the gelatin has been dissolved (almost) completely. Remove undissolved lumps.

## Step 2: Mix Soap and Other Ingredients

- Measure up the soap and vodka in the other bowl.
- Add color, a few drops at a time, and stir, till the color is to your liking (won't change much when mixed with gelatin). Suggestion: Keep the colors light, as this looks more "fresh" and fits better for a bathroom-type look
- Add essential oil. It should have a somewhat strong smell, as it will, unlike the color, be dampened when mixed with the gelatin.

111

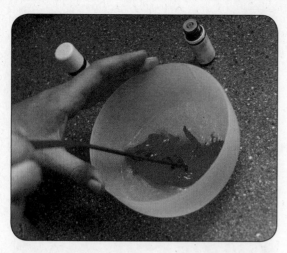

needed some support under, to avoid spilling.

And there you have it! Wobbly bubbly jelly fun for the whole family!

### Step 3: Mix It!

- Carefully pour the soap mix into the gelatin, and carefully stir it together.
- Optional: If there is too much foam on the mixture, remove it with a spoon.

### Step 4: Into the Molds and into the Fridge

- Pour the mixture into the molds.
- Place the molds in the fridge or cold place.
- Wait for an hour or two . . .
- Note: You are probably wondering why we put it on top of a big tray and placed that in the fridge.
- Well . . . The molds are not too rigid, and the mixture is very liquid-y, so we

# Make Your Own Moisturizing Sugar Scrub

By starshipminivan
(www.instructables.com/id/Pantry-Raid-Make-Your-Own-Moisturizing-Sugar-Scru/)

Make your own sugar scrub using ingredients you have at home. You control the ingredients and can customize it based on your own preferences and/or available materials. Not only does it exfoliate but it leaves the skin silky soft.

## Ingredients

- ¼ cup olive oil*
- ½ cup granulated or brown sugar
- essential oils for scent (optional)
- herbs (optional)**

---

*Optional Oils:
- sweet almond oil—replace olive oil entirely or use in place of part of the olive oil
- coconut oil—replace olive oil entirely or use in place of part of the olive oil
- jojoba oil—replace about 1 teaspoon to 1 tablespoon of the olive oil
- vitamin E oil—replace about 1 teaspoon of the olive oil

## Step 1: Creating Your Sugar Scrub

I suggest making a small batch of plain olive oil sugar scrub and trying it to see what kind of results you get before tinkering with added ingredients. I find that plain sugar and olive oil works well for me and that the lack of additional scents or herbs makes this scrub usable by the whole family. It's a fantastic product to use on the hands and arms when getting done working in the garden, shop, or art studio.

In a small bowl, combine oil(s) and sugar. If using essential oils, add a few drops. If using herbs, add about 1 teaspoon or so.

Using a spoon, stir together sugar, oils, and optional ingredients. Place in a small jar with a tight-fitting lid.

## Step 2: Using Your Sugar Scrub

If you find a layer of oil on the top of your scrub, just give the jar a shake to mix it in before opening.

**To use on Face or Hands**

After washing your face or hands, scoop out a marble-sized amount and rub the scrub onto the hands or face. Massage the scrub into the skin gently. If applying to face, be careful to avoid your eyes. Don't rub too vigorously. Allow the oil to sit for a minute or so and rinse off with warm water. If you find your skin seems oily after use, wash lightly with soap and water. If desired, follow-up with your favorite moisturizer for extra softness.

**Body Scrub**

While showering, scoop a gumball-sized amount out of the jar and gently massage into skin. Rinse well and use a moisturizing body wash to cleanse the skin.

---

**Optional Herbs: You can use whatever herbs you'd like or none at all. Suggestions include:
- mint
- lavender
- chamomile
- thyme
- rosemary

body

113

# The Single Most Effective Way to Get Rid of a Sunburn

By **drpepper8412**
David Pfeffer
(www.instructables.com/id/The-single-most-effective-way-to-get-rid-of-a-sunb/)

Well this is my first instructable, and is only going to be short because it's an extremely easy and effective method to removing a painful sunburn. This method was recommended to me by my friend's mother who is a nurse and therefore MUST know what she's talking about. Turns out she did. I hope this helps many a painful sunburn to recede or disappear.

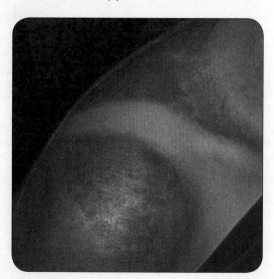

## Gathering Materials

You will need a total of five things:
- a bathtub to do this in (preferably ceramic, so it won't stain)
- a pitcher
- a rag that you don't mind getting stained
- water
- three bags of black tea (I use Earl Grey)

## Step 1: Fill the Pitcher

First things first, strip down, because you don't want to get any of your clothes wet. Fill the pitcher with warm water and soak the tea bags in it. When you have the water almost black, then move on to step 2.

## Step 2: Healing the Wound

Once the water has cooled to a warm/lukewarm temperature, dunk the rag into the tea, and dab it onto the sunburn. DO NOT WIPE IT OFF! Leave it on and let it be absorbed into your skin. Once its dry, re-apply as necessary, but never wash it off. If you do this process before bedtime, you can go to sleep and give it time to work its magic. In the morning you can wash it off in your shower. The sunburn should be substantially subsided or all gone, but remember: the sooner you can apply the tea after you get the burn, the quicker and more effective it will be.

Note: I had a severe sunburn and I also used the tea bags straight up, dabbing them directly onto my skin. You may use as many "coats" of tea as you want, but the more the better.

# How to Clean Your Sinuses

By noahw Noah Weinstein
(www.instructables.com/id/How-to-
Cean-Your-Sinuses/)

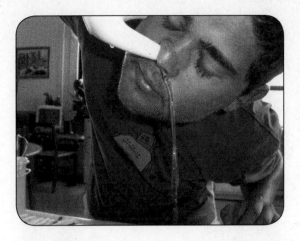

You can clean your sinuses really effectively just using warm water, salt, and something called a Neti Pot. I have done it a few times now and I have to say that it really works and feels good.

Many people suffer from some kind of nasal irritation, be it mucus, allergies, an infection, sinus pain, or even snoring. While a doctor may prescribe a steroid spray that costs a ton of money and never seems to work, there is a simpler and much more effective way to help your nose and nasal cavity. It's the ancient practice of nasal irrigation: the Neti Pot!

This is not an ad, it just happens to sound like one because I am excited about pouring salt water through my nose.

Using a Neti Pot to clean your nose seems to have all different kinds of effects on people. I felt clean, open and free of mucus after I did it, but since I didn't really have any severe allergies or irritations to begin with I can't report on the validity of those kinds of results.

(I used it because who doesn't want to pour water through their nose and see what comes out?)

The Neti Pot is reported to have many benefits:

- Removes mucus and pollution of the nasal passages and sinuses.
- Helps to prevent respiratory tract diseases.
- Daily use relieves allergies, colds and sinusitis.
- Cooling and soothing to the mind.
- Beneficial in the treatment of headaches and migraines.
- Alleviates anxiety, anger and depression.
- Removes drowsiness, making the head and sense organs feel light.

## Supplies

To use a Neti Pot all you need is:

- the Neti Pot itself (you can get one for about $10 at a drug or natural foods store. If you don't want to buy one look around the house because chances are, you already have something lying around that is perfect for sticking up your nose. Try a children's sippy cup or even a watering can with a narrow spout. Do you make gravy on Thanksgiving? The Neti Pot sure looks a lot like a fat drippings separator!)
- warm water
- non-iodized salt

## Step 1: Prepare the Neti Pot

Making the Neti Pot solution, which is really just saline/salt water couldn't be much easier.

Put a cup or two of water into a pot and warm it up on the stove. (I use cold water that I warm on the stove because the water heater in my apartment is old and I don't

115

really want to have water that has been in there all up in my brain.)

Once the water is warm, pour it into the Neti Pot and then grab your salt. Take about half a teaspoon of salt and put it into your water mixture. Stir it well.

Now you are ready to proceed. Find a sink, some privacy, and read on.

## Step 2: Insert the Neti Pot

Insert the Neti Pot into one of your nostrils.

It's not brain surgery, but it does feel a little funny at first.

Tilt your head to the side, and down elevating the nostril with the Neti Pot in it and lowering the empty one.

Once you feel like you have a good angle for the water to pour through one nostril and out of the other, slowly begin to pour the salt water from the Neti Pot into your upper nostril.

Water will begin to fill your upper nostril, flow into your sinuses, and then work its way out your empty nostril in a steady flow.

## Step 3: Pour Saline Through Your Sinus Cavity

Keep pouring water for about 10 seconds or so until you have got a good flow going and you feel the whole flow of the water going through your sinuses. Remember to breathe through your mouth—you won't choke.

The strange sensation may make you want to cough at first, but just stay with it, it becomes less awkward after the first second or two. Once you have done it once or twice it really is pretty easy and actually feels good!

As you come to the end, stop pouring the water through your sinuses and slowly bring your head upright again after all the water has drained out. Give some quick blows through your nose to clear things out and check out what's in the sink below. The first time I did this some big stuff came out, after that, I really have too much "nasal debris."

Take a second to compose yourself, refill your Neti Pot if you are running low on saline, and then switch nostrils and repeat the process. When you've finished pouring in the second nostril, blow air out through your nose in a few quick short breaths to clear out any water. You can also put your head down towards the ground to drain out any remaining water.

I don't think that it's possible to overdose on Neti potting, so do it as often as you like. I know lots of people who do this as a preventative activity every day. Enjoy your clean sinuses!

body

# Bathroom Scale Mod (For a Kinder, Gentler Morning)

By AlpineButterfly
(www.instructables.com/id/
Bathroom-Scale-Mod-for-a-kinder-
gentler-morning/)

I don't know about you all, but I hate getting on my bathroom scale. It only ever seems to tell me I'm getting bigger, and in such a mean way . . . even with decimal points, as if to say I can't dispute the scientific accuracy of it.

So I've decided to make friends with the scale . . . after I mod it of course, so it looks better & acts nicer. Luckily this turned easier to do than I anticipated.

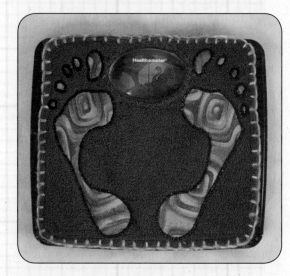

## What You'll Need

This project consists of 2 main parts: first modifying the scale.. so it doesn't have all that attitude, and then adding a fabric top, that is much more cheerful, and invites your feet to step on it in the morning.

## To Modify The Scale

- old mechanical scale (not the new fangled kind that shoots electricity through your body to tell you your body fat . . . and

doesn't seem to give you the same read out twice in 2 minutes . . . I have NO idea what to do with that one)
- metal spray paint & primer
- flathead screwdriver
- piece of wire
- crescent wrench . . . or whatever wrench is handy
- acrylic paints & Gesso (acrylic primer)
- enamel paints (like for model cars)
- small brushes
- tracing paper
- carbon paper was useful
- sandpaper

**Feet**
- fleece fabric (about ½ a yard should be more than enough)
- fabric scraps
- thread & yarn (colors of your choosing)
- needles: denim needle for your machine, large eye embroidery needle for the yarn.
- scissors
- double stick fusible web (You can find this in the findings sections of fabric stores, it makes life a little easier.)
- sewing machine (for appliqué)

## Step 1: Taking Apart your Scale

My Scale turned out quite easy to take apart . . . I hope yours is similar.

Flip the scale upside down.

On mine there was an attachment point for 2 springs.

Slide the springs off the attachment points. The springs were fairly strong, but you still want to be gentle not to warp them . . . you'll need them again later.

I could now lift off the bottom of the scale from the top.

## Step 2: Removing the Weight Indicator

Using your handy dandy wrench, go ahead and unscrew the nut holding on the disk with numbers indicating weights.

Remove this numbered disk . . . MAKING A NOTE OF THE POSITION THE ZERO IS IN!!

(It is likely not top dead center, because the springs you removed earlier were exerting some pressure already.)

Put the bottom assembly aside. (You can clean out dust bunnies, while paint is drying.)

## Step 3: Modifying the Weight Indicator; Prepping the Weight Indicator

Tape the weight indicating disk, on to a scrap piece of cardboard. This is so you can paint & trace it without it moving.

On the cardboard, indicate at least the zero position and across the circle from it.

Trace the indicator. This gives you a reference as to where you would like to draw things, and helps you line them up with an actual weight.

## Step 4: Prime the Indicator

Scratch up your disk with a little sandpaper to give it some tooth.

Using the metal paint primer, paint the disk . . . be careful not to go over your zero indicator on your cardboard.

After it was dry I went ahead and painted on a couple of coats of Gesso as well, to give my acrylic paints some tooth.

## Step 5: Sketch Up Your Design

On another piece of tracing paper sketch a design over top of the tracing you made of the weight indicator.

I used the web . . . and household objects to give me reference points for different weights. I tried to pick things that I like, and that inspire me & make me smile. So for example I used:

- for 10lbs—my cat
- for 30lbs—a bicycle
- for 75lbs—a canoe
- for 77lbs—a brick of gold
- for 100lbs—a sofa
- for 122lbs—Books (some on the web said that's what the encyclopedia weighed)
- for 140lbs—flowers start (this is the low end of my target weight limit)
- for 160lbs—a pair of pants on a line (This is when I had to buy new pants!)
- for 250lbs—a black bear.

Transfer your sketch on to the dry disk. (line it up with your reference points on the cardboard.) I used a piece of old fashioned carbon paper . . . useful stuff!

## Step 6: Paint! (This took some time . . . remember you may need a few coats.)

Paint with acrylic paints.
Set aside to dry

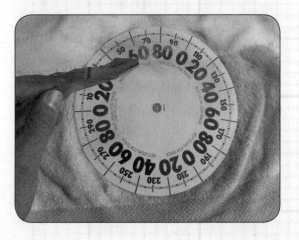

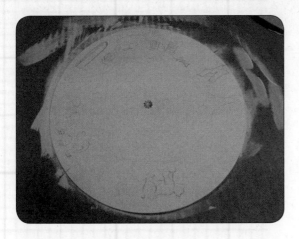

## Step 7: Painting the Top

I decided bathroom white was not so cheerful . . . so I painted the top of the scale as well.

I removed the plastic window and red line insert, cleaned and put them to the side.

Cleaned off old goo . . . from stuck on plastic stuff that's no longer there. This was done with the help of a screwdriver & Goo Be Gone.

With a household cleaner, wiped the surface clean after using the Goo Be Gone.

I traced the inside edge . . . where I would later be adding my mat including where the window hole was.

Took it outside . . . laid it out on some newspaper, and pray painted (a couple of coats).

## Step 8: Adding a Little More

When the spray paint dried . . . I grabbed a couple of enamel paints, and added some dots for fun . . . and a "Hi Sexy" 'cause we all need to hear that some times, and no matter what the numbers say, I'm still sexy right?!

## Step 9: Making the Inviting Mat

I thought It would probably look pretty cool the way it was. Only I felt like the metal would be a little cold on my feet in the morning. (I'm not good with cold). So I decided to make a mat that could go on top.

## Cutting out the Mat

I used fleece for this project, because it doesn't fray, and I figured it would hold up to bathroom humidity fairly well . . . and feel nice on my toes.

Using the pattern I traced on top of the scale, I cut out 2 pieces of fabric exactly the same size. I cut out the oval for the window as well.

## Step 10: Sewing

I sewed around the edge of the pieces (Good sides out) . . . to tack them together.

I then blanket stitched around the edges with some yarn. (See the image for the blanket stitch) This step was a little tough on my fingers . . . I think because my yarn was so fat.

I also blanket stitched around the window oval.

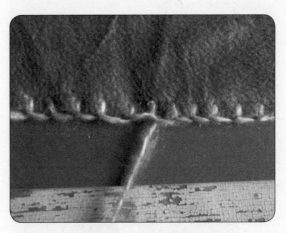

## Step 11: Adding my Footprint
**Easy Method: Trace Your Foot!**

Cat in the Hat/Make a mess all over your house, and watch the black spot grow method: (yup that's what I did): Get some water soluble ink, a roller, and some newspaper. Roller your feet with the ink . . . Step on newspaper. TA DA! (Now figure out how to get to the bathroom without making a mess.)

Grab a piece of fabric big enough for your foot prints. Fuse some of the double stick fusible web to it. (Keep paper on the one side, and don't iron long.)

When the ink has dried (and you've finished cleaning up) pin your foot print to the fabric you have fused.

Cut out your foot prints from the fabric and place them on your mat. Iron them on (using a damp cloth over top). You don't want to use a lot of heat because the fleece won't like that. Using a zig zag stitch and the thread of your choice (you'll need quite a bit), stitch around the footprint bits.

You will want your machine set to make stitch close together (#1 on my machine). I found closer, and the machine just sort of jammed up on the buildup of thread. I went around each piece 2 times to build up the color a little more.

Note . . . the toes were a pain in the butt; next time I'll do 1 large print.

## Step 12: Re-assembly! Putting it All Back Together
### The Disk

Once the paint has dried, put the disk back on, careful to place the zero spot where you made note of earlier.

Tighten the nut back on.

120

### Putting on the Top

Put the clean window piece back in the top, once the paint has dried. Place the top face down. (I put it on some scrap fabric, so my new paint job wouldn't get scratched.) Take the bottom part, with disk now attached, and place it back on the top part.

Using the wire, and a screw driver, go fishing for the spring! Once you have the spring, pull it up, and hook it back where it went originally. Do this for both springs.

### Accessorizing

Flip the scale over. Add your mat. Check to make sure the zero lines up in the right place.

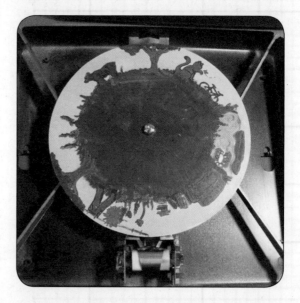

## Step 13: Ta Daa!!

Now you have a new, polite, even flattering scale! To help you remember to stay healthy and eat well, but also remind you you're wonderful everyday . . . even when you forget to feel like it!! I hope it brings a little brightness to your morning.

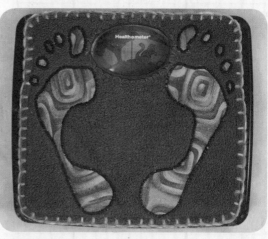

body

## with
# duct tape

You've heard of the duct tape wallet. Now learn what other crafty things you can make with duct tape—like a full-sized Batman mask, or some beautiful roses for your sweetheart. Caught in the rain? No problem, duct tape makes great gaiters, pants, jackets, and tents. These pages will show you how to exploit all of the amazing properties of duct tape.

# Duct Tape Chess Set

By **rabidsquire2**
(www.instructables.com/id/
Duct-Tape-Chess-Board-and-
Chess-Set/)

When I arrived at college, I realized that I was missing a chess board and chess set, the makings of which have kept me entertained for countless hours in the past. When I went to Target to remedy my lack, I realized that the prices of the chess sets exceeded what I wanted to spend for something I would only use once in a while, and were often far more extravagant than was necessary for a simple dorm room. Rather than invest in such a hefty item, I saw an opportunity to conduct a project that would provide me with a chess set while also being kind to my wallet. I purchased three rolls of colored duct tape, red, white, and black, my school's fight colors. The ability to personalize my set made the project all the more intriguing.

The following steps provide a simple and effective means of using supplies attainable on a college campus for little to no money to create a full, usable chess set. While these steps illustrate the means by which I conducted this project, they are in no way exclusive, and I urge you to customize the project based on your personal desires.

## Gathering the Materials

The first step in the process of creating this project is to gather the materials necessary to build the components of a chess set, including the chess pieces and the board itself.

This instructable will first address how to construct the board and then move on to the chess pieces.

## Materials for Constructing the Board
- three rolls of duct tape (two rolls for the board, one for looks and structure)
- USPS medium size standard rate box (or another box with at least one square side)
- scissors
- Sharpie marker
- ruler or meter stick

## Materials for Constructing the Chess Pieces
- remainder of the 3 rolls of duct tape
- two packs of different colored pipe cleaners
- 36 spare coins (mixture of quarters, nickels, and pennies . . . NO Dimes)
- scissors

## Step 1: Marking the Square Surface

The first step to creating the board that the game will be played on is to create a grid like pattern on the square bottom surface of the USPS box. To do this take the measuring implement, either a ruler or meter stick, and separate the length and width of the box into 8 even-sized boxed areas on each side. This means drawing seven lines across the width of the box at even intervals. Using the Sharpie, darken the lines to the point where they can be easily seen through a thin piece of white printer paper.

When you have finished this, you should have a grid like pattern across the bottom of the box.

## Step 2: Beginning the Alternating Chess Coloring

The next step is the process of repeatedly overlapping squares of different colored duct tape on top of one another to create a repeating pattern of alternating colors that correspond to the grid created in the previous step. To begin this pattern, cut a piece of white duct tape that is just slightly larger than a single square. Place it in one corner of the square grid, aiming to place it as close to the edge as possible. Next, cut an equal sized square of a different colored duct tape, and lay it along the grid line that you can see through the white tape. Both squares will slightly overlap the grid lines. This is fine, as the additional tape will ensure that none of the box shows through between the pieces. Continue this pattern along the rest of the grid until you have finished the row. Fold over the additional tape at the end of the row and then turn your attention back to where you began.

The second row will begin with a square that is the opposite color of the one you began the row above with. When repeated, this will create the alternating grip pattern that is evident in commercial chess boards. Finish the row, and repeat this process throughout the remainder of the rows.

## Step 3: Finishing the Grid

Continue overlapping the squares repeatedly until the entire surface is covered and appears as a red and white alternating grid. Because I used thinner duct tape, I decided that it was pertinent to add an additional layer of duct tape to the grid already down, mostly for appearances sake. This also ensured a more level playing ground, as the dual tape layers re-enforced the cardboard below it.

## Step 4: Taping the Sides

For appearances sake, as well as to protect the cardboard from spills/water/wear and tear, I felt it was necessary to wrap the sides that were not a part of the grid with a layer of duct tape. To do this, simply wrap layer after layer of duct tape (black in my case) around the edges and sides of the box. Repeat this process for the entirety of the uncovered box, making sure to overlap the edges of the long strips so that no cardboard shows. Also continue this process for the bottom of the box, using long strips lain in a single direction to ensure efficiency and appearance.

## Step 5: Gather Materials for the Pieces

For the pieces, you will need to gather the previously mentioned materials. For the duct tape requirement, use what remains of the previous duct tape rolls, as it should be more than necessary. Gather also the different colored pipe cleaner packs, as well as at least 36 spare coins, ensuring that they are a mixture of pennies, quarters, and nickels. You will also need a pair of scissors for the customization of each piece.

## Step 6: Creating a Basic Piece

Now that you have created an acceptable board, it is time to create a matching chess set out of coins, duct tape, and pipe cleaners. To begin, lay a piece of tape (which should be a rough square) out with the adhesive side facing up, away from the surface of the table. Next, lay one coin at the center of the square. Take a small length of pipe cleaner (roughly four inches in length) and bend it slightly at one end before placing it in the center of the coin on the table. Using the edges of the tape lying on the table, fold them inward and across the pipe cleaner bent section, effectively holding it in place. For the pawns, this was the extent of work, though I did bend the protruding length of pipe-cleaner, which was roughly three inches long in a spiral to give it dimension. For the more specialized pieces, I altered the means by which I added their unique characteristics. This will be discussed in following steps.

For the opposing series of chess pieces, I used white tape (as opposed to red) and white pipe cleaners (as opposed to black), but the steps were the same.

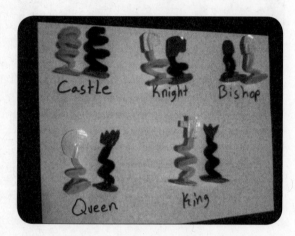

## Step 7: Customizing the Individual Pieces

In order to customize the pieces based on their specific purpose, I added a simple piece of tape to the top of the pipe cleaner and shaped it using scissors so that each piece was easily identifiable. I will not describe the process for each individual piece as, at this point, I encourage as much customization as possible.

The general shape of each piece is as follows:

- Castle: Twisted pipe cleaner upward in a cylinder like shape
- Knight: Slight bend meant to resemble the head of a horse after slight twist for dimension
- Bishop: Pope-like cap above curled pipe cleaner, like a bent staff

- Queen: (red: jagged to personify chaos; white: large circle to personify order)
- King: (Red: three pronged; chaos; white: cross; order)

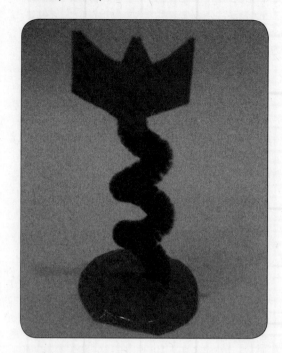

## Step 8: Finished Set

Following the customization of the pieces, continue with completing the set. A full set will include 16 pawns (8 white, 8 red), 4 castles (2 white, 2 red), 4 knights (2 white, 2 red), 4 bishops (2 white, 2 red), 2 queens (1 white, 1 red), 2 kings (1 white, 1 red) for a total of 32 pieces. Once you have filled in the blanks, simply place the pieces on the board and you are ready to play. The weighted bottoms will cause the pieces to tend towards the righted position, meaning that the chess set can be played even in places where you may be bumped or jostled.

Congratulations, you have now completed the dorm room chess set. I urge you to go into the customization aspect of this project far more in depth then I have, and I look forward to seeing what others have created. Let me know if you have any suggestions and I look forward to hearing from you soon.

As an additional note, a small cut can be made in the bottom of the box, allowing the pieces to be stored inside the hollow USPS box quite efficiently. In addition, spare duct tape and pipe cleaners can be stored inside for quick fixes and even more customization.

duct tape

# Duct Tape Hammock

By **Dadzilla**

(www.instructables.com/id/Duct-Tape-Hammock-1/)

This red, white, and blue hammock is the perfect place to relax on the 4th of July!

## The Pieces

- 3 × roll Scotch duct tape
- 2 × wooden dowel (48" × 1" diameter)

## Step 1: The Set-Up

Since this hammock is woven, and duct tape is as sticky as, well, duct tape, a rigid set-up is necessary. I used a wooden table I had built and screwed 2 × 4 scraps (12" long) to the sides then attached the dowel with another screw. The distance between the points of attachment of the dowel will be slightly more than your hammock width. My final width was about 34".

## Step 2: Long Loops

Roll tape out sticky-side up. Run under dowels on each end.

## Step 3: Folding Over

Press tape down onto itself on one side, then roll out enough tape to complete the loop and press the loop together.

## Step 4: Lots of Long Loops

Continue making loops, close but not touching, until full width is reached. Stagger tape joints.

## Step 5: Marking for Weaving

The important thing to remember before starting to weave is that the side facing up is the bottom. Take a ruler and mark where the tape edges go on the outer two loops of each side of the hammock. To duplicate my pattern, start on the outside with a mark about 2" from the end, then make a mark every 7.5". Move to the inside loop and make a mark 5.75" from the end, then make marks every 7.5" inches.

## Step 6: Weaving

I used a piece of ½" PVC (you could use a broom handle) to separate my loops then used the ruler as a shuttle to pass between them. Making these loops is the same as before, sticky side up then fold over. Be careful not to pull the outside loops in when you fold over.

## Step 7: Weave Set-up

Be careful when weaving duct tape, it will hang up given half a chance.

## Step 8: Bottom Side of the Weave

When weaving is finished it will look like this. Remember, at this point the bottom side is still up. Only the top side of the loop is woven. The bottom side (visible here) is stuck down all the way across. Also notice how the weaves shift up and down. This is because I have an even number of long loops. With an odd number it would shift inside and out.

## Step 9: Attach Rope

Make a triangular rope support for each end of the hammock. The length of the rope will be approximately 10' and tied to the hammock on either side.

## Step 10: Securing the Hangers

You wouldn't want the ropes to slip so secure them with . . . wait for it . . . duct tape! Tape over the dowel, the knot, and the dowel on the other side of the knot.

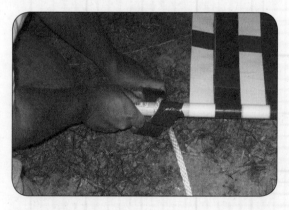

## Step 11: Enjoy!

Find some suitable trees, hang the hammock, and relax . . . or fake relaxing, like my son in the picture.

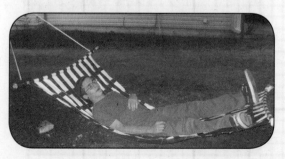

**duct tape**

# Duct Tape Typhoon Pants

By **ATTILAtheHUNgry**

Stuart Sweeney Smith

(www.instructables.com/id/Duct-tape-Typhoon-Pants/)

The rainy season has come early this year in Japan, and with it—typhoons. As a person who relies on my bike as my sole means of transportation, having a good set of rain gear is crucial to arriving dry. Unfortunately, my cheap-o $1.00 rain pants ripped open on my first ride out. Clearly it was time for me to step up my game.

And what better way to stay dry than with a pair of duct tape pants? And not just your everyday rain pants, theses puppies are full-on TYPHOON-pants, with a cinched waist, cinched legs, and a front pocket, all 100 percent duct tape.

Making these pants was a bit of a learning process (my largest duct tape project prior to this was my wallet), and my photos don't do a good job of showing the trial-and-error sequence of events. Anyone trying to make a pair of these will probably hit similar problems and find their own solutions, so this instructable will just give the basics, and I'll leave the particulars to you guys.

Here we go.

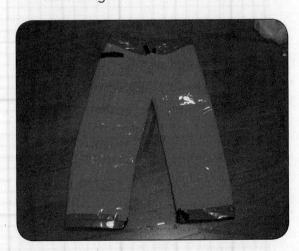

## Gather your Duct Tape

To make these pants I used 5 complete 50 ft rolls of duct tape, half of 3 more rolls, and a bit of a fourth, for a grand total of about 330 feet of tape—or a little over a football field.

I used 4 colors:
- Red—interior lining
- Yellow—exterior surface
- Silver— structural elements
- Black—trim
- I also used scissors, for clean cuts.

## Step 1: Ruin a Terrible Pair of Pants

This "ible" was inspired by the catastrophic failure of my original "dollar-store" rain pants a few weeks ago. But rather than throw them away, I decided to cut them open and use them as a template for my duct tape design. I drew a chalk outline (actually a duct tape outline) around the pants, and created a design template on the floor of my apartment.

## Step 2: I Make My Pants One Leg at a Time, Just Like Everybody Else

The next step is to begin putting your tape down over your template.

I did this starting with the interior layer. I began laying horizontal strips of the red duct tape from the waist down, proceeding until I reached the end of the first leg. (Obviously this is done with the sticky side up.) I only did one leg at a time, partly because I wanted to practice my technique before starting the second leg, and partly because it was easier to reach parts of the pants with only one leg getting in my way.

I added a few vertical strips in the seat of the pants, which is where I figured the most wear and stress would occur while biking.

The next step is to add your pockets. I had originally planned on having two or even four pockets, but they were so time consuming that I ended up leaving off at just one. In essence a pocket is just a square of duct tape, sealed on 3 sides, with the smooth side in and the sticky side out. Then you stick it to the rest of the pants.

This is also the step when you can begin planning where your cinch cord loops will be going.

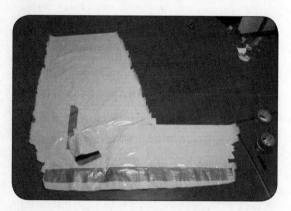

## Step 3: Weatherproofing (plus the second leg)

Next I added the exterior layer, the layer that will shield you from the elements. This layer doesn't have to be canary yellow, but honestly, why wouldn't it be?

I began layering strips of yellow tape vertically, to add structural support to the horizontal strips in the interior. This is also the step where I finished the cinch loop on the leg, and almost finished the loop at the waist.

Then I repeated the previous steps in making the second leg. Since the legs have a bit of overlap, I curled the edge of the first

leg and stuck it to itself temporarily, to keep them from getting tangled.

## Step 4: Roll It On Up

The final step is to roll your pant legs closed, followed by the waist, and seal them up.

For this, flip the pants over so the exterior (yellow) side is facing down, and begin by rolling just one leg closed. Use the excess tape at the edges to stick them together.

Repeat this process with the second leg, again sticking everything together (roughly at first) with the excess tape along the edges. It will still look rough.

Lastly, finish the pants by covering any excess stickiness and filling any gaps with nice yellow finishing tape. Cover the rim of the pocket, and the holes of your cinch bands with some black trim tape.

Now you've got a sweet pair of typhoon pants, ready to take you through the storm as dry as can be.

duct tape

I was inspired to make a duct tape jacket of some kind because of hat day at my school. Why hat day, you ask? Well . . . I didn't have any awesome hats, so I made a hex hat from duct tape. It was a hit with my friends, and a lot of people gave good feedback. I was excited to do something bigger. Something with some more "Wow" factor.

When first worn, this jacket is kind of stiff and pretty much a plastic tube. It keeps in a LOT of heat, and is great for wearing in the cold outside! It is also 100 percent waterproof and can be used as a rain jacket. The more you wear it, the more comfortable it gets.

So without any more delay, here is my Duct Tape Hoodie! I hope it has enough "Wow" factor for everyone.

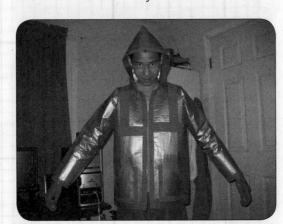

### Materials

First, you need the right tools:
- scissors
- razor
- Sharpie
- yard/meter stick

Now, gather your materials: duct tape. I used two 55 yard rolls and part of a 40 yard roll, along with fluorescent green tape for decorating. I probably spent around $15 for the duct tape. I didn't use professional tape . . . I used the cheapest I could find: masking tape.

You need a large flat surface that you can cut on. I have concrete floors, so it's no big deal. You may wish to use a large cutting board on a table if you need to (or improvise!).

### Step 1: Getting Started—Duct Tape Cloth

First, we must learn how to make duct tape cloth! Making the tape can be kind of tricky, but mostly when you are covering the first layer. If two sticky parts touch in the wrong place, problems can occur. Be careful when laying down the strips! There are variations on how to make duct tape cloth, but this method works well for me and lets me get the correct size duct tape sheets I need.

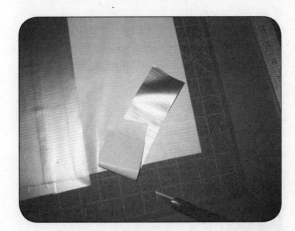

### Step 2: Wait—How Big Should It Be?

Well . . . I must admit—I stole my measurements from imrobot's instructable www.instructables.com/id/The-plastic-bag-hoodie-How-to-fuse-plastic-bags-a/#step5. On step 5 he has the measurements. Now, be careful! I used the medium measurements for the body, which is 68cm by 61cm. It turns out that it is WAY too wide and the jacket will be more like a tube. It is best to make the size measurement that is closest to your size, then tailor the jacket after you finish.

### Step 3: Sleeves

We need to make the sleeves. I started with the sleeves because they are the easiest. Make sure you make a plain rectangle the correct width (mine was 24cm × 39cm × 55cm. 55cm was a tad short for me. Adjust to your size).

inside seem of the sleeves. It is dark inside a plastic tunnel.

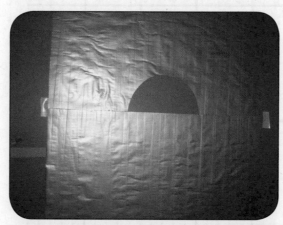

## Step 4: Starting the Body

The main body is large—so large, that it did not fit on my cutting board. I used my floor to make the body, and (using masking tape, a yard stick, and a sharpie) made a large measuring angle to get the right sized duct tape cloth. If you want a zipper or a cut down the middle, make sure to measure and mark off the middle of one of the duct tape sheets.

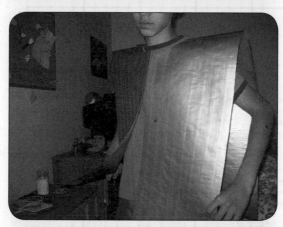

## Step 5: Attaching Things

We begin the end of the hoodie. The easiest way to go about attaching things it to first attach the two halves, then the sleeves, then the sides of the body. There could be another way, but I didn't see how I was going to get duct tape strips into the enclosed area of the hoodie. The hardest part of this step is adding duct tape to the

## Step 6: Tailoring and Pockets!

Morning. I wake up at 5:00 AM to get ready for school. I decided that since I was ready early, I would tailor the jacket and make it fit better. Afternoon. Home from school, time to work on some pockets! Because they are easy! Listen to remixes of the Tetris theme.

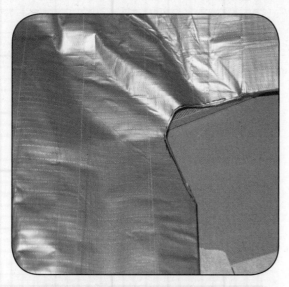

## Step 7: The Long Awaited Hood

Making the hood is pretty straight forward. All you need to do is conjoin two rectangles and attach them to the collar of the hoodie. Trim off the top corner of the hood and round it to make it look nicer.

## Step 8: Finishing Up!

The hoodie is technically done. But nothing like some color duct tape to make it look snazzy. You can put a bunch of stripes, checkered squares, or pictures and words with colored duct tape. I just did an easy choice and put one color of duct tape on what I consider to be borders of the jacket. After 5 days of work, it's finished! Don't be fooled—it takes a while but it really isn't hard. This jacket holds in a LOT of heat. I mean, while taking the pictures for this in my air-conditioned room, I

started sweating. It is pretty comfortable if it is cool outside with less sun.

This jacket is 100 percent waterproof also! So it is a bonus if it rains while you are outside in the cold. I tested this with a garden hose, and it repels very efficiently. The biggest issue is that the water drips directly onto your pants. Maybe future developments will fix this.

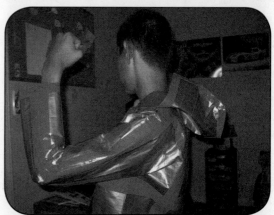

# Duct Tape R/C Plane

By **seamster**
(www.instructables.com/id/
Duct-Tape-RC-Plane/)

As a warning, this wing isn't very durable and won't make for a very good first experience in radio control. If you want to get into R/C airplanes, I recommend EPP flying wings as they are super-durable and fun to fly. I like traditional planes too, but I had a great experience entering the hobby through EPP flying wings, like slope gliders and combat wings.

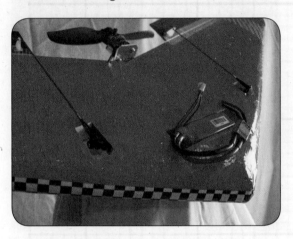

For the last few years I've been getting into radio controlled electric airplanes. I got the idea that it would be a fun challenge to try to make an R/C plane out of duct tape . . . just to see if it could be done.

## Step 1: Lay-Out

I made a frame for the plane out of foam core, and covered it with duct tape.

The wing is 40 inches wide, and the center of the wing is 8.5 inches across. I laid out each wing half separately on a single sheet of 20" by 30" foam core.

I have included a lay-out I drew up to give more details for those interested in making something similar. The rib patterns need to be printed out the correct size, however. Click the upper left corner of each photo online and grab a copy of the original size. You will have to do some resizing in your photo editor to make sure that the number 1 rib prints out at about 8 ½" (about 215 mm), and the number 6 rib prints out at about 6¾" (about 172 mm). This will ensure that all the rib patterns on both sheets are true to scale. The center lines on each rib pattern are used as a guide. This center strip is to be cut out and discarded when you cut out top and bottom half of each rib.

## Step 2: Wing Ribs

I examined the airfoil shape on a foam flying wing that I have, and drew out a similar airfoil shape on card stock that was the length of the center of my wing.

Using the biggest cross-section of the wing as a guide, I drew out each successively smaller pair of wing cross-sections based on the lengths that were already laid out on wing halves.

I made twelve unique airfoil shapes which were used as patterns to trace and cut out from foam core the top and bottom sections of each wing rib. All cuts were made with an X-ACTO blade.

## Step 3: Main Wing Piece

The two wing halves were glued together with white glue and reinforced with 3M Extreme Tape. It's a bi-directional filament tape that is incredibly strong and sticky. I ordered mine from Amazon, but I'm sure you could find it in some office supply stores.

I had an old 20" carbon fiber rod that I used to strengthen the wing. It was glued into a slot cut in the wing, and taped on both sides.

## Step 4: Ribs Glued to Main Wing

I used white glue to glue each rib in place, top and bottom. Pins were used to hold each piece in place while the glue dried.

## Step 5: Trailing Edge

The trailing edge needed a flat surface where I could attach the elevons (which are the steering flaps on a flying wing—a combination of elevator and ailerons). I added strips of balsa for this purpose, which also served to straighten out a little warp that was on each side of the wing.

## Step 6: Motor and Mount Assembly

The motor mount is actually a stud brace I found in the framing section at Home Depot. It worked very well for this purpose. The holes in the little bracket just needed to be reamed out a little so they would line up with the mounting holes on my motor. This was done with a drill bit of appropriate size.

A small piece of plywood was glued onto the wing to anchor the motor mount securely.

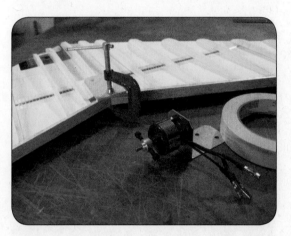

## Step 7: Onboard Radio Gear Placement

Many modifications were made to the wing to house the servos, receiver, speed control, and battery as seen here.

I knew the general location where everything needed to be based on past experience, but I just guessed where to put everything specifically. I knew if the battery was placed too far back, the plane would be really hard to have balanced without adding more weight to the nose, but if the battery was placed too far forward it wouldn't be protected in a crash.

This set-up worked well in the end, although I did need to add some additional weight to the nose before I felt it was ready to fly. If I was to build this again, I would put the battery just a little closer to the nose, although I would still probably need to add weight to get the center of gravity where it needs to be for stable flight. I found that the CG on the finished wing should be about 5 ½" to 6" back from the nose, which requires the adding of quite a bit of weight to the nose.

duct tape

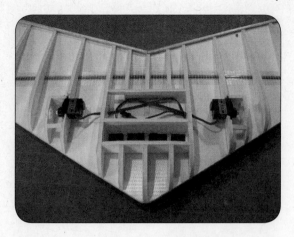

## Step 8: Duct Tape Covering

I weighed the wing before and after adding the duct tape. Based on my calculations, the duct tape covering came in at just over 4 ounces. That's a lot of unnecessary weight in just the covering alone, and wouldn't normally be tolerated!

## Step 9: Elevons

As I mentioned earlier, the elevons are what steer the wing. They were made out of ⅛" balsa, and covered with colored packing tape.

Hinges were made to attach the elevons to the wing with 1" strips of extreme tape. A strip was placed on both the top and bottom of each elevon.

## Step 10: Finishing Touches

The radio gear was installed and tested, with the transmitter programmed for delta wing mixing (which is the set-up for flying wings like this).

The servos were hooked up to the elevons, and I taped over the open areas to seal up the wing.

I added some foam pieces to either side of the battery hole to help cushion the battery and keep it from sliding around. A piece of tape is placed over the top of it when flying, which makes it easy to remove and swap out when it is dead.

Wing tips were also added, which are necessary to keep the wing stable in flight.

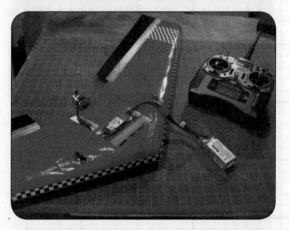

## Step 11: R/C Gear Info

The total cost of all the radio gear depends greatly on where and what you buy. I've learned that you can save a lot by shopping around. This is a partial list of what I used.
- Motor—CF 2812
- 18A Electronic Speed Control (ESC)
- 1350mAh Lipo battery (3S, 11.1V)
- Prop—7 × 6E
- 3mm prop saver
- MG90 micro servos
- Extreme Tape

duct tape

## Duct Tape and PVC Kayak

By **hyroc346**

(www.instructables.com/id/Duct-Tape-and-PVC-Kayak/)

This lightweight and easy to make kayak can be built in a few hours, weighs less than 20 pounds, and best of all, costs under $50. While I wouldn't recommend taking it out in any rapids, it works great for calm water, so get out there and explore!

## Materials

- five 10' long, ¾" Outer Diameter PVC pipes
- hacksaw
- scissors
- tape measure
- two or three large trash bags
- 2 × 4 wood plank between 3' and 4' in length (or similar) for the seat
- 3 rolls of Scotch Brand Tough duct tape (make sure it says waterproof on the label!)
- lighter (optional: used for easier PVC bending)
- 3 square feet of cardboard (optional: used to make paddle)

## Step 1: The First Cut

Cut two of the PVC pipes down to 8' with the hacksaw, making sure to save the 2' lengths.

Cut two 4" lengths of PVC from the same 2' pipe. Make a cut 2" deep into each of these pipes lengthwise, and bend the wings back until they create an angle approximately 60° with each other. These braces are essential to give the kayak its tapered shape. Note: Hold lighter under the area of the pipe you wish to bend in order to soften the PVC first.

## Step 2: Shape the Kayak

Place one brace between the ends of the 8' long PVC pipes and secure by taping each wing of the brace to the PVC pipe with Scotch Brand duct tape. Repeat at other end of kayak, ensuring the pipes have an even bend across their length and give you the shape you desire.

Take the whole 2' PVC pipe and the PVC pipe you cut the braces from and make similar cuts in both end of each pipe, approximately 2" deep. Bend the wings back perpendicular to the pipe so each end is "T" shaped. Press pipe against a flat surface to ensure all four wings are planar to each other.

Tape the longer cross-brace to the frame approximately 3' from one end (this will be the front), and tape the smaller cross-brace 2' from the opposite end (back). Note: Because the kayak is curved, the angle of the wings will have to be adjusted slightly in order to align properly with the frame. You have just completed the top of your kayak!

## Step 3: Finish the Frame

Cut two more 8' lengths of PVC pipe from the remaining pipes, again saving the 2' lengths for later. At the end of each pipe, cut out 3" wedges of PVC by sawing from the end of the pipe at an angle. Tape these pipes firmly to the braces at both ends of the kayak using Scotch Brand Duct Tape.

Cut two 10" segments of pipe from one of the 2' lengths. Create cross-braces similar to the ones created in the previous step. Tape these pieces between the top and the bottom of the kayak where the longer of the cross-braces is joined to the frame. Repeat this process at the other cross-brace using 8" lengths of PVC pipe cut from the remaining 2' PVC piece.

Add cross-braces to the bottom of the kayak by measuring the distance between the two cross-braces you just added. Cut these pieces from the remaining 10' length

of PVC. Don't forget to add 4" to each length to account for the wings that you will be folding back!

Congrats, you have now completed the frame!

## Step 4: Trash It

Now that your frame is complete, cover the kayak in trash bags using Scotch Brand Duct Tape to secure the bags to the pipes. Make sure to leave the top of the kayak between the cross-braces open, but seal the space between the top cross-braces and the bottom cross-braces.

To accomplish this, cut the bags open, and tape one edge to a piece of the frame. Wrap the bags around the frame, taping and trimming where necessary. The tighter you make it, the easier it will be to wrap the kayak in the next step. The plastic layer not only provides your kayak with an additional layer of waterproofing, but prevents things from sticking to the inside of the kayak once you add the duct tape skin.

making sure it is supported by both cross-braces. This step will involve cutting a slit in the trash bags. Tape firmly into place and apply duct tape around the opening in the trash bags to ensure a proper seal.

To create a paddle, take the remaining length of PVC pipe and cut it down to between 210 and 240 cm. Cut out the shape of your paddles from the cardboard and cover in duct tape. Tape paddles to PVC shaft. I made my paddles rectangles, but you can find other ideas and templates for paddle shape online.

That's it! Now don your life vest and get out there on the water!

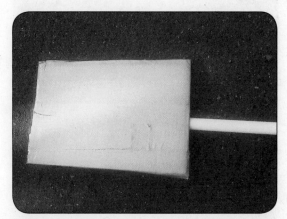

## Step 5: Tape It

Carefully add overlapping strips of Scotch Brand Tough duct tape to the outside of the kayak until the trash bags are fully covered (you don't need to tape the well where you will sit). I found it easiest to first add strips lengthwise on the bottom of the kayak and then vertical strips on the sides (from back to front) in order to minimize creasing of the tape. I then added an extra strip of duct tape on the bottom where the side panels ended for reinforcement and to ensure the side panels did not peel off. Lastly, I added duct tape to the top of the kayak.

Note: Carefully check your work here before advancing. Make sure there are no holes or gaps in your tape, and that the layers of duct tape overlap fully. This is very important if you want to stay afloat!

## Step 6: Accessorize

To add a seat, place 2 × 4 (or something softer if you desire) in bottom of kayak,

# Duct Tape Tool Tote

By fallental

(www.instructables.com/id/
Duct-Tape-Tool-Tote/)

How to make a versatile and TOUGH tool tote out of items around the house. This was inspired by an AWP tool bag that I purchased last year, and some Craftsman tool bags that I have seen at hardware stores.

## Materials Needed!

For this project you will need very few items, and it shouldn't cost much at all. I made mine with everything I had at home.

You will need:

- cardboard (and some paperboard for the pockets)
- scissors (optional)
- box cutter or razor blade
- LOTS OF DUCT TAPE!
- tape measure or ruler.
- tools to fill it with

## Step 1: Preparation

Before we start taping, some cutting is needed to be done.

Using cardboard, a ruler, and a box cutter, cut out three 12 in × 8 in cardboard pieces, and two 8 in × 8 in cardboard pieces. These will assemble to create the basic structure of your tool tote.

## Step 2: Taping the Structure

Lay the 3 12 inch × 8 inch slats together, with the 12 inch sides touching. Tape these sides together; the middle slat will be your bottom. Add the 8 × 8 inch sides and tape them together. Once there is a nice layer of tape, flip the cardboard over, and tape the other side.

## Step 3: Make the ends Flexible

Take the ends of the tool bag structure (8 × 8 inch sides) and work them with your hands to make them flexible. Make sure that they will be concave (hollowed inwards), and face inwards towards the tool bag, this will allow the tool bag to close fully.

## Step 4: Tape the Sides Together

Take each adjacent side of the boards and tape them together, making sure the ends that you just bent curve INWARDS. Once you see the structure taped, tape the inside seams together as well.

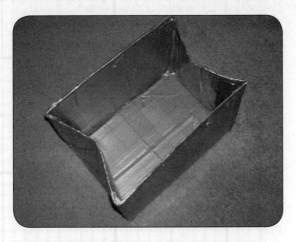

## Step 5: Creating Handles

Cut out 2 cardboard handles for your tool bag. Each handle should be roughly 1 × 7 inches. Once the handles are cut out, wrap them in duct tape to give them a nice duct tape layer.

## Step 6: Attaching the Handles

To attach the handles, use 5 inch strips of duct tape on both sides (8 strips total, 4 strips per side). Keep 1 inch of space between the handle and the tote, also make sure the handles are centered!

## Step 7: Making and Adding End Pockets

These are the pockets that will hold tools and go on the ends of the tool tote (the ends are the cardboard pieces you bent). Start by cutting out two 4 × 5 inch sections of paper board (to allow flexibility). Once the sections are cut, tape the pocket to the ends of the tool tote (making sure not to tape down the pocket opening).

## Step 8: Making and Adding Side Pockets

These are the pockets that hold your tools that are attached to the sides of the tool tote.

Cut out eight 3 × 4 inch paperboard sections, 4 sections will be taped on each side. Now tape each pocket to the side, being cautious not to close the pocket opening. You must tape the pockets individually so that they will be separate pockets, and not just 1 big side pocket (unless of course you want it that way!) Repeat for the opposite side.

## Step 9: Add Tools and Bask in Your Glory

Great for a gift for the handy man in the family! Take it anywhere you need basic tools, a water resistant bag for all your works needs.

and its . . . DUCT TAPE TOUGH!

duct tape

# Magic Duct Tape Wallet

By **Doctor What**
(www.instructables.com/id/Magic-Duct-Tape-Wallet/)

It's a magic wallet, made out of duct tape. The magic wallet has been done before, but I decided to make one, dirt cheap. This should last a while, and if it gets destroyed, just take another fifteen minutes and make another one.

The story behind it . . .

Well, I was watching QVC, and I saw that they were selling "Magic Wallets" for $20 for a set of two. I thought, OMG, who in their right mind would pay that much for something that they can make with stuff around their house? So, I decided to make one, on the cheap, with stuff in my bedroom. And I came up with this.

There is a magic wallet instructable out there already, and it is good, if you know how to sew.

## Crap You Need

Don't need much, but you do need:
- duct tape (for colors, go to Wal-Mart, they have every color imaginable)
- stiff cardboard (I used an old Converse shoebox)
- scissors
- pen

- Altoid tin (trace this for wallet shape) You don't need an Altoid box specifically, you could use a playing card, or anything wallet shaped that will fit cards into it.

## Step 1: Cut Your Cardboard

You need to trace the Altoid tin (the top, it's bigger), onto cardboard twice, then cut it out.

## Step 2: Cover Cardboard with Duct Tape

Cover each side of both pieces of cardboard with duct tape. Then trim the excess off of the sides. Sure, the wallet is not 100 percent duct tape, but if you don't use cardboard, it will be flimsy, and not work so well.

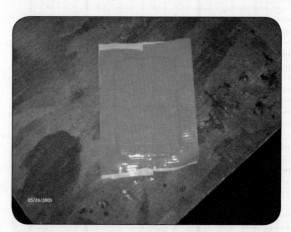

## Step 3: Create Straps

Put two pieces of foot long duct tape on top of each other to create one big strap. Then cut the big one in half, hotdog style. Then take the two strips, and cut them both hotdog style again to get four straps.

## Step 4: Attach Straps

You need to take two straps and attach them horizontally on one of the "cards." If you are using an Altoid tin, put them between one and two centimeters from the top and bottom. And then secure with a piece of tape.

Then, flip over the card so that the straps are on the left, under the card.

Next, fold the straps over the card, so that they go right.

Place the other card on top, so that the straps are sandwiched between the two cards. Then trim the straps so that they are one to two centimeters away from the edge.

Last, use a piece of tape to attach the strap ends to the back of the card on top.

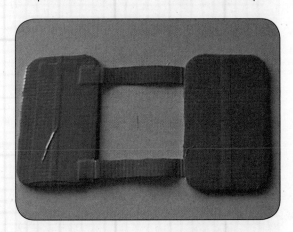

## Step 5: Attach Straps Part Deux

Now you need to attach the two other straps. Open the two cards and put the straps on the bottom card, in × formation. The two ends on the left need to go through the straps. Then place the top card on the bottom card again.

Trim the ends so that the straps are, once again, one centimeter away from the edges.

Make sure that the × straps do not overlap the horizontal straps, and that they are in-between the horizontal straps.

Then tape the ends to the back of the cards. For the right side, tape the ends to the back card. For the left side, tape the ends to the front.

## Step 6: Check Your Wallet

Get a dollar, and open up your wallet, and put it in, and close the wallet. Then open it from the other side. Then close it, and open it again from the side you started with.

## Step 7: Add Pockets

If you want pockets for your ID, credit card, etc. You need to put about three inches of tape sticky side up on your wallet. Then put another three inch strip on top of it, also sticky side up, so that you have a wide piece of tape. Make sure it is wider than your card. Then put some tape face down on it to cover the sticky stuff, and you have a pocket. You can make as many pockets as you want, on the front and on the back.

## Step 8: Hooray!!

You've now completed your geek wallet. Rejoice!!

# Duct Tape Flower
## By Wilcurt
### (www.instructables.com/id/ Simplifyed-Duct-Tape-Flower/)

Extra easy duct tape flower. Make one in less than 10 minutes!

## Preparation

You will need a few simple items before you can start:

- any color duct tape
- pliers
- some floral wire (or any wire but floral wire works best)
- scissors

And now you're ready to start!

## Step 1: The First Petal Part 1

To start your flower, first you must use the pliers (or scissors) to cut the wire in half. Next use the scissors (or your hand) to cut the duct tape into a 2 × 2 inch square.

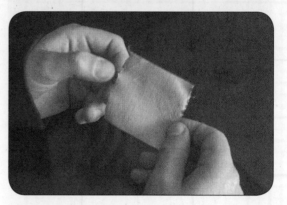

## Step 2: The First Petal Part 2

Next you will fold the square of duct tape over. Then you will fold it over again so it is like a little triangle on top.

## Step 3: The First Petal Part 3

Now the first petal can be hooked on. First get the wire and stick it onto the duct tape like so. Then flip the edge over so it won't come loose. Now you just twist it around and around and stick it on so it looks like a tube with a hole.

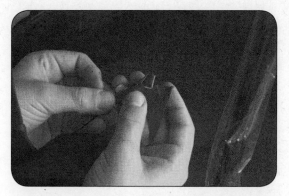

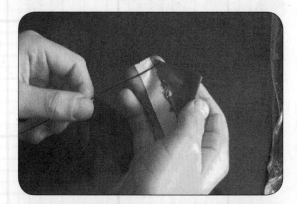

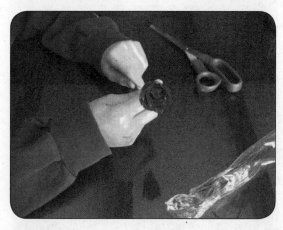

## Step 5: You're Almost Done!

The last step! *Ahhhhhhhhh.* You're finally there! Now you have the finished product!

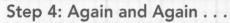

## Step 4: Again and Again . . .

Now that you have the first petal on it's going to get a lot easier. All you have to do now is repeat the previous steps over and over . . . sort of. You just make more petals and stick them on.

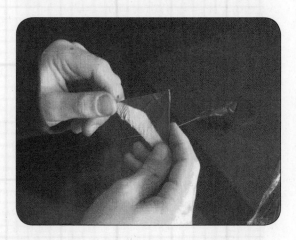

# Duct Duck
# (Duct Tape Duck
# Tub Stopper)

## By shesparticular

Kate Jackson
(www.instructables.com/id/Duct-
Duck-Duct-Tape-Duck-Tub-Stopper/)

duct tape

Duct tape is truly magical. It can be used for nearly everything, including creating an awesome little ducky which can then be attached to a tub stopper to make taking a bath super fun!

## You'll Need

- duct tape (I'm using yellow, but you can use whatever color you like)
- scissors
- grommet tool and grommet
- hole punch or leather punch
- tub stopper
- thin chain (approximately 10")
- two coins or other small weights (I used pennies)
- pliers (optional but suggested)

## Step 1: Making Duct Tape Sheets

Before we can get to the folding process to create a duck, we'll need to make some duct tape sheets.

Cut a piece of duct tape approximately 9" long and place it sticky side up on your work surface

Cut a two more pieces the same length and place them over the first so that they meet at its center

Flip the whole thing over and apply pieces to cover the outside edges

Repeat until you have roughly a square of duct tape sheet

Trim the sheet down to form a 8.5" × 8.5" square

## Step 2: Get Ready to Spread Your Wings

Fold in two sides of the sheet to the center to form a kite shape.

Fold the long point back to meet the shorter point.

Fold the long point back again so that the fold is even with the layers underneath.

Fold in the shorter point so that the tip meets the layers underneath.

Fold the long point under itself to form a beak.

Lift the entire thing up and fold in half to form two halves of a duck.

Pull the neck and head portions out slightly and crease them into place.

Fold the bottom portion on each side up to form the base of the body.

Fold the flaps at the back of the body inside to form the tail portion.

Position the coins under the body portion of the duck (on the inside) and cover each with a piece of tape. These will help ensure your ducky doesn't take a header when placed in water.

Cut a small pieces of tape and apply it to any areas that might need some help staying held together.

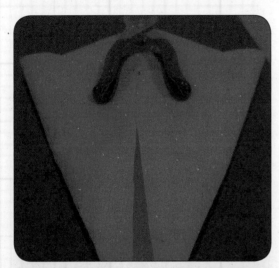

## Step 3: Duct Duck . . . Goose?

You can skip this step if you just want to make a duct tape ducky, but making it into a bath stopper is even more fun!

Punch a hole in the back portion of the duck using a leather punch or hole punch

Using a grommet tool, add a grommet to the hole

Connect the duck to the tub stopper using the chain

Fill your tub, add bubbles, and hop in!

duct tape

# How to Write Using Duct Tape

By **Poehis05** Gabe Poehls
(www.instructables.com/id/How-to-Write-using-Duct-Tape/)

After making a few other things out of duct tape, I wondered what else I could make from man's greatest invention. After some thinking, I came up with this. "How to Write Using Duct Tape." It may be pretty simple, but the final product can look very neat.

## Supplies

All the supplies needed to make this are:

- a small X-ACTO knife or any other craft knife
- a role of duct tape
- a binder: Now when you find a binder to use for this, try not to use one with the clear plastic screen on the front. If you do have one like this, cut off the clear plastic part. All it will do is screw things up.

Onto the construction.

## Step 1: Drawing the Pattern

Initially, rip your piece of duct tape off to whatever length you want. Lay it down and stick it there. Now you can use the craft knife to trim it down to the right length. After that's all done, use your pen to draw out what you want it to read. Make sure you do this in block letters, so all you'll have to do later is trace them. If you really want to, use a stencil to make it more professional. Once you've got your pattern, you can move on to cutting it out.

## Step 2: Cutting it Out and Peeling the Letters Off

This step may be self explanatory, but there are some tricks to getting it done

- Go slow. This may seem obvious, but it makes all the difference.
- Make sure to entirely cut the corners. This will reduce the amount of stringy things.
- Be careful on curves.

Once you have a letter cut out, you can peel it off. You'll probably want to use the tip of your craft knife to get it started before pulling it off the rest of the way. Even after all this hard work, you may still be left with strings. You will want to cut

duct tape

these off and trim down the edges to make it look nice.

Even though you will probably use this method mainly to do writing, you can also use it for doing pictures.

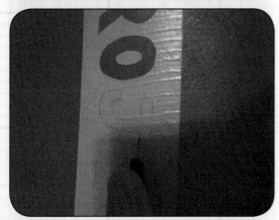

## Step 3: Doing Pictures

As I mentioned, you can also do pictures using this method. Depending on the size of your picture, you may need to lay down 2 to 3 strips of duct tape, side by side. Try not to overlap. After this, most of the steps will be the same as in the writing. Find your pattern, cut it out, and peel the pieces off. When you cut, try to cut out your picture in sections. This will reduce the amount of errors made. And in the end, you'll be left with one beautiful binder.

Give this project a chance, take your time and see what happens. Be creative and experiment with things a bit. I put writing on the side. Come up with your own unique twists. And most of all, have fun.

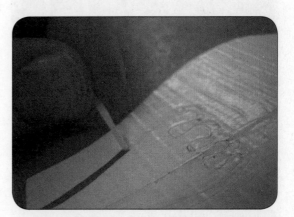

duct tape

# Duct Tape Batman Mask

By **seamster**
(www.instructables.com/id/
Duct-Tape-Batman-Mask/)

Here's a Dark Knight version Batman mask made of mostly duct tape. It was made to enter in a county fair "duct tape creations" contest. It won $15 dollars.

It's fairly rough, but maybe it'll inspire somebody.

## Step 1: Custom Fit for Your Head

To start, I laid out lots of strips of duct tape on my cutting mat and sliced them into various sized smaller strips. Using a plastic grocery bag to protect my head, I started putting tape all over my head to get my personal head-shape. I trimmed off extra plastic as I went. My head was sweating like crazy, as plastic and duct tape don't breathe very well.

## Step 2: The Lucha Libre Mask Phase

Added strips of tape to cover nose and cheeks, leaving eye holes.

## Step 3: Nose Piece

I drew on the mask with a sharpie (while it was still on) so I would know where to cut to make room for a nose piece. This was made through trial and error with triangular pieces of cardboard folded down the middle until I got one that fit comfortably over my nose. Another triangular piece was taped across the bottom to make it rigid. Then the nose piece was taped into place.

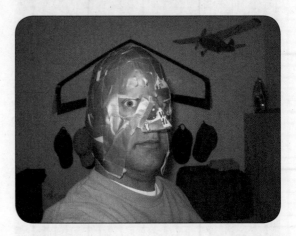

## Step 4: Let the Shaping Begin

Once the nose piece was in place, I stuffed the entire thing full of wadded grocery bags and put a few pieces of tape across the chin area to keep the whole thing in a solid, head shape.

At this point I had to just sculpt till I had results I could live with. I used wadded newspaper wrapped in masking tape to get the shapes I needed, and then taped them on. Using a snap-blade style utility knife with a sharp blade fully extended, I trimmed off extra bulk as needed.

I had to put about a six-inch slice in the back of the mask to get it on and off.

The antennae were made of cardboard with newspaper on the inside to add bulk.

Learn simple home repairs, how to paint perfect lines, and neat tricks for organization! From homemade cleaning solutions to managing pest invasions, this chapter has tips for making every room in your house a little easier to live in.

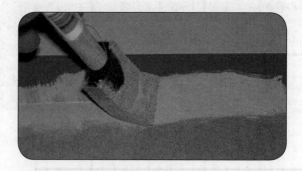

## How to Paint Clean Lines

By **starshipminivan**
(www.instructables.com/id/How-to-Paint-Clean-Lines/)

Making clean paint lines between two colors doesn't have to require a steady hand or special equipment. This technique is very simple and requires only paint, brushes, and masking tape. This time, however, you will be controlling the bleeding paint and using it to create crisp lines that precisely follow the edge of the tape.

### Step 1: First Color

Lay down the first color, extending past the area where the line will be. If you are using two layers per color, paint both layers.

### Step 2: Taping

Once the paint is dry, place your masking tape. In this case, the bottom of the masking tape marks the location where the edge between the two colors will appear.

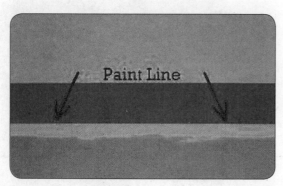

### Step 3: Bleed Line

Using the same color, paint along the tape edge. This seems strange but, there will always be some bleeding under the tape. By deliberately painting against the tape, you seal the edge with the first color, allowing it to bleed under the edge, so the second color can't do it. The edge of the tape becomes the edge of your line. Make sure the lower edge of the paint feathers softly away so you won't see a thick edge of paint later on.

### Step 4: Second Color

When the bleed-under layer has dried, paint the second color. Make sure your paint overlaps the location of the tape line.

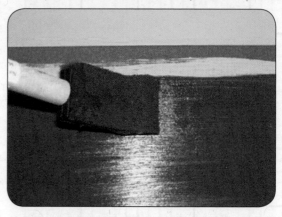

### Step 5: The Reveal

Remove the tape by pulling it at a 90 degree angle. Do this when the paint is wet, if possible. Tah-dah! Crisp, clean paint lines! (I haven't had any problems with the line when removing the tape after the second color has dried BUT other people I know have. It has to do with paint setting up and binding to itself. So, if you cannot pull the tape while it is still wet or at least soon after it dries, you might consider using a craft knife and a straight edge to score the line before pulling the tape.)

## DIY Magnetic Spice Rack

By **angelpeach838**
(www.instructables.com/id/DIY-Magnetic-Spice-Rack/)

I got tired of my plain, old, dumpy lazy susan spice rack taking up space on my kitchen counter, so I decided to make a wall mounted magnetic spice rack.

### Buy Materials

- sheet of steel (purchased at Lowes). There are many different sizes available, choose the one that best fits your need.
- toggle bolts (purchased at Lowes). The spice rack needs to be anchored to the wall if you're putting it into drywall. Mine were ⅜".
- super glue. I used E-6000 (purchased at Wal-Mart). The only thing I did not like about this was the drying time. At LEAST 16 hours.
- Neodymium magnets (purchased from eBay). I used ¼" × 1/16". Next time I would go larger in diameter because I ended up having to use two magnets in order to make a full jar stick to the steel.
- spice jars (purchased online). This is totally up to you. Personally, 4 ounces is PLENTY big enough. I probably would've gone for 2oz jars, but I couldn't find the shape I was really going for in 2oz (hex shape).

### Tools

- large drill bit and drill
- screwdriver.

### Step 1: Pre-drill Holes

In order for the toggle bolts (which are quite large) to get into the wall, you will need to pre-drill holes big enough for them to fit into. The holes were huge and quite scary, but anchoring is necessary!

### Step 2: Glue Magnets

This is pretty self-explanatory. Just follow the directions of whatever glue you choose.

### Step 3: Label

This step is optional, and since I can't tell the difference between chili powder and chipotle chili powder based on looks alone, I needed to do it. You can buy spice labels online pretty cheaply, but we just used a silver Sharpie.

# Best Way to Season Cast Iron Pans—Flax Seed Oil

By **noahw** Noah Weinstein
(www.instructables.com/id/Best-Way-to-Season-Cast-Iron-Pans-Flax-Seed-Oil/)

I try to use cast iron cookware whenever possible. It has excellent heat dispersion properties, lifelong build quality, and an inherent ability to cook foods with exceptional control at both high and low heats. It works on all kinds of stoves: electric, gas, induction—even a fire pit while camping.

The only snag about cast iron (if you can really call it that) is the seasoning process. "Seasoning" cast iron refers to a process of building up some amount of material, which I'll call a finish on the pan, that aids in cooking, creates a semi-nonstick surface on the pan, and protects the cast iron pan against any possible rust.

There are lots of theories on seasoning cast iron, from complex rounds of heating and oiling with different types of vegetable and animal fats, to doing nothing at all. Having tried many of these seasoning processes myself, I feel inspired to write about the flax seed oil method. It's the most durable and straight forward seasoning process that I've found, and the science behind the process agrees.

## Step 1: Flax Seed Oil

You can find flax seed oil in the refrigerator aisle at the grocery or health food store. Flax seed oil is the edible version of linseed oil, a very durable, hard drying finish that painters and woodworkers have been using for a very long time. As Cheryl Canter writes on her site: "The seasoning on cast iron is formed by fat polymerization, fat polymerization is maximized with a drying oil, and flaxseed oil is the only drying oil that's edible."

What that translates to in practical terms is a durable finish, that even after just a few coats and short term heating, results in a deep glassy black seasoning on the cast iron that has held up to months of my daily usage and cooking abuse.

As with any other cast iron pan seasoning, you don't want to use soap on the pan when cleaning it, but with this method, I've found that using a mildly abrasive sponge when doing the dishes doesn't seem to affect the finish at all.

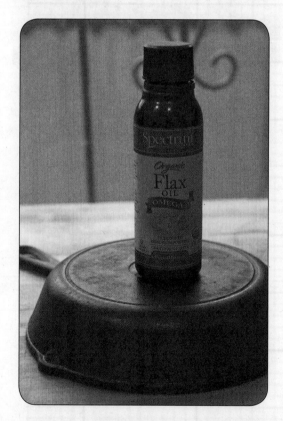

## Step 2: Oil the Pan

Pour a small amount of the flax seed oil into the pan. Less is more with this stuff, so shoot for more than just a few drops, but no more than a tablespoon. Start with a teaspoon and go from there. Then, using a paper towel or rag, spread the oil evenly throughout all the surfaces of the pan, including the bottom of the pan, the sides, and even the handle.

The pan should have a slight sheen to it, but no standing puddles of oil or thick areas of build up. If you're really feeling inspired, use your bare hands to spread the oil around and envision yourself back in the old world. Follow the rule of thumb for any other finish—shoot for a nice thin even coat. You can always apply more, and, as you'll soon see, you will.

## Step 3: Bake at 500°F for 30 Minutes

Place the oiled pan inside a 500°F degree oven for 30 minutes. Some sources say to heat the pan for longer, but, if you've put on a thin coat of oil I've found that 30 minutes is plenty long enough.

The pan will smoke a bit during this process. That is completely fine and natural; your oven will not catch fire.

The hot flax seed oil will smell a bit strange. That is also completely fine and natural, the smell will go away.

PRESS ON!

## Step 4: Repeat 4 to 7 Times

Once you've "cooked" the pan for 30 minutes, remove it from the oven and let the pan sit until it's cool enough to touch. When you're sure it's not still hot, reapply a thin coat of oil using the same method described in step 2, put it back into the oven, and cook it for another half an hour.

Keep repeating this process until you've gone through as many cycles as you'd like. I've found that 4 to 7 rounds was enough to result in a semi-gloss, beautifully smooth, tough, black finish that is ready for use.

## Step 5: Do All Your Cast Iron at Once

Final tip—do all your cast iron pans at once. In my opinion, if you're gonna crank the oven up to 500°F for several hours and make the house smell a little funny, you might as well make good use of it and season all your cast iron cookware at once. The good part is that you won't have to repeat the process very often. I've been going on the same seasoning session for several months now and they still look great. Also, if you want to avoid making your house smell like smoking oil, use a grill if you have one.

home

## Homemade Green Cleaning Recipes

By **jessyratfink**

Jessy Ellenberger
(www.instructables.com/id/
Homemade-Green-Cleaning-
Recipes/)

Clean nearly everything in your house with simple and non-toxic ingredients.

### Ingredients Used In These Recipes

The recipes use very few ingredients, most of which you should have around the house!

- water
- baking soda
- rubbing alcohol or vodka
- castile soap
- white vinegar
- essential oils
- unflavored gelatin
- salt

- In addition, you'll need spray bottles and glass containers, depending on the recipe. You can reuse bottles from old cleaners—just make sure to clean them thoroughly!

### Step 1: All Purpose Cleaner

**What You'll Need**

- a large spray bottle
- 24 ounces (3 cups) water
- ⅛ to ¼ cup liquid castile soap
- 2 tablespoons white vinegar
- essential oils, like lemon, lavender or tea tree

Fill your spray bottle with 3 cups of water. Add the tablespoons of vinegar and the castile soap. (Make sure you add the soap AFTER the water, or it will get very sudsy and exciting.)

Now you'll add the essential oils. I like adding 10 drops of lemon and 10 drops of tea tree.

I use this in my kitchen and my bathroom with great success! It's amazing at getting the stove top clean, and I love how clean it gets my counters and tabletops. Also great for cleaning the fridge.

I recently started scaling down the soap and adding more vinegar. I like it a lot. I'm using closer to ⅛ cup of castile soap now. The extra vinegar cuts down on soap scum/residue, and using less soap has been just as effective, but with less bubbles to clean up.

### Step 2: Ghetto Febreze

This is a very easy Febreze alternative—I've seen a ton of recipes using fabric softener . . . but those aren't very "green."

**What You'll Need**

- a small spray bottle
- ½ cup rubbing alcohol or vodka
- essential oil
- 1 cup water

Fill the spray bottle with 1 cup water and ½ cup rubbing alcohol or vodka.

You'll now add the essential oils. I typically start with 30 drops and then work my way up. You can also mix oils to create custom scents. I also like using The Body Shop home fragrance oils in this mix and I've had no problems with them.

Note that you will be able to smell the alcohol, but only for a minute or so . . . after that things will just smell lovely. Rubbing alcohol has a stronger smell than vodka!

I use this on my couch, bed, curtains, dog bed, towels, etc. and the smell lingers for quite a while.

## Step 3: Gel Air Freshener

Very simple to make and very, very cheap! Perfect for bathrooms or closets. Will last around a month.

The instructions for this will depend on the type of gelatin or pectin you use.

**What You'll Need**

- plain, unflavored gelatin or pectin
- water for preparing gelatin
- food coloring (optional, just for added flair)
- essential oils
- small glass jars or bowls (I filled three with 2 cups of finished gelatin)
- 1 tablespoon salt (prevents mold)

To make this, place 1 to 2 drops of food coloring in each of your glass jars or bowls, and then prepare the gelatin according to the package directions, adding the salt during boiling. Once the gelatin has dissolved in the water and it's ready to set, add 20 to 30 drops of essential oil and mix. Then pour into your individual containers and mix with the food coloring.

Check the strength of the smell at this time and add more oil if necessary.

This will firm up at room temperature, but if you want it to set quicker you can place it in the fridge.

You can cover these with thin cloth or perforated paper if you like, but I keep mine up high enough that anything that sticks to the surface is out of sight.

## Step 4: Window and Gloss Surface Cleaner

This one is easy, though a little smelly, but don't worry, the smell goes away pretty quickly and you'll have nice clean windows!

**What You'll Need**

- small spray bottle
- 1 cup water
- 1 cup vinegar
- squirt of castile soap (this is optional, but helps reduce streaks)

Pour the water and vinegar in the bottle, and add a tiny squirt of the castile soap. Shake it up and you're ready to clean!

Many people recommend using newspaper to clean your windows, but as I don't get it delivered, I use flour sack towels or old cut up T-shirts. This solution takes a little longer to dry than your typical glass cleaner, but don't worry, it'll look very nice when totally dry.

You can also use this solution to clean appliances and countertops.

## Step 5: Drain Cleaner

This is very simple—just baking soda and white vinegar. You can also use lemon juice if you have that on hand! This works best on drains that are running very slow, but not those with standing water. If your problem is soap scum or other build up, this will break it up and get things moving again. It also works as a good deodorizer for kitchen drains.

Shake a bit of baking soda over the drain—I'd say a ¼ of a cup or so. Push it into and around the drain, and then pour a bit of vinegar over it until you get a good bit of

**home**

bubbling and the vinegar begins to pool in the sink.

Let this drain and set for 15 to 20 minutes and then flush with hot water.

And as a bonus, you can also clean your sink with the little bit of mixture that'll be left at the top of the drain.

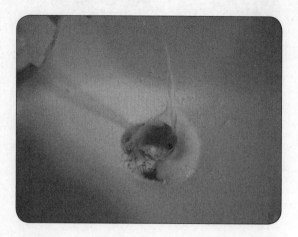

## Step 6: Extra Cleaning for Pots and Pans

If you've burned food to a pan, or if you've made yourself a nice hardened, stuck-on food mess along with your dinner, there's an easy way to get it out.

Add about ¼ cup baking soda to a couple of cups of water in your pan and bring to a boil on the stove for 5 to 10 minutes. While this is going, it helps to scrape the bottom of the pan with a wooden spoon.

After you take it off the heat, give it a good scrub. You should have a nice clean pan! If not, rinse and repeat with a little more baking soda. This will also help remove stains for things like tomato sauces.

## Step 7: Additional Green Cleaning Tips

Try to use cloth towels for nearly everything. If you can't afford towels, a good way to save money is to cut up old T-shirts into rags. Just clean with them, rinse in hot water, and hang to dry. I tend to hang mine on the sides of my recycling bin.

Once you've used them a few times (or for a really gross mess) they're easily thrown in the washer.

Also, here are some other uses for the ingredients used to make the cleaners in this instructable:

- use water and baking soda to make a paste to clean especially nasty messes—a greasy stove top, a spill in the oven, your toilet bowl.
- vinegar and baking soda can be left overnight in the toilet bowl and then scrubbed in the morning to get rid of stains and odors.
- baking soda sprinkled in litter boxes and mixed in helps control all those urine odors . . . I've been doing this for years with both plant-based and clay- litter.
- straight vinegar is awesome at getting rid of hard water stains in showers . . . simply put it in a spray bottle, spray down the walls and let them soak for a few minutes, and then grab a brush and get scrubbing! I cleaned my mom's shower this way—it was all orange streaks before and the normal cream color after!
- you can use castile soap as a cheap but effective hand wash—just fill an old soap dispenser with half water and half soap.

home

# Cleaning Your Oven without Poisonous, Earth-Destroying Chemicals

By ejarrell
(www.instructables.com/id/Cleaning-your-oven-without-poisonous-earth-destro/)

## Things You Will Need

- baking soda
- vinegar
- a bowl or a squirt bottle (preferably a squirt bottle)
- a dirty oven
- a spatula

## Step 1: First Things First

Remove the racks. Using a spatula, scrape up as much of the debris as you can and throw it away. Most of the big stuff should come up pretty easy. Tip: Move the trash can closer to the oven.

**Then**

Using about a cup of baking soda, more or less depending on the size of your oven, sprinkle it all over the floor of your oven.

**Then**

This is where a squirt bottle comes in handy. Spray vinegar all over the baking soda. Use your fingers or a rubber spatula to spread the baking soda around so that

it comes into contact with the vinegar and every dirty part of your oven floor. Let sit for 10 to 20 minutes.

(alternative: Mix vinegar and baking soda in a bowl to form a paste, and then spread that over your oven floor. Make sure to pour the vinegar slowly because it fizzes up pretty high.)

## Step 2: Scrub a dub dub

Get a scrubbing pad (I used one of those metal curly wiry ones) and scrub in a CIRCULAR motion, rather than back and forth. This will make your job go by so much more quickly. Grime should come off pretty easily.

When you can slide the pad gently all over the oven floor and no longer feel any rough patches, you are ready to clean up the excess baking soda/vinegar mixture. Use a damp sponge and get it all out of there! You will have to keep rinsing off the sponge.

## Step 3: Before and After

157

# Reusable Swiffer Mop Pad

By **kibblesknits**
(www.instructables.com/id/Swiffer-
Mop-Pad-a-reusable-one!/)

Sew a reusable pad out of old T-shirts and a wool blanket for your Swiffer-type mop. I do not like using disposable cleaning products. I use cloth diapers on my kids and I use washcloths instead of paper towels. But my Swiffer mop is so convenient! It seemed to me that it was time to stop using disposable mop pads. It will save the environment and save money. I decided to make this pad out of discarded clothes and a wool blanket I never use. Cleaning with this pad takes a little more elbow grease than the disposable pads but it cleans great. I recommend making at least two so you have a clean one while the other is in the laundry.

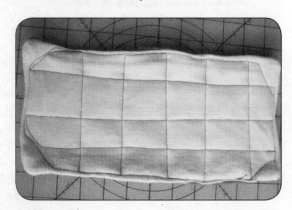

## Materials List
- an old t-shirt
- woven wool blanket (or anything you have on hand that will stick to your mop head)
- disposable pad that comes with your mop
- pencil
- freezer paper
- iron & ironing board
- scissors or rotary cutter
- pins

- sewing machine
- thread

## Step 1: Trace Your Pattern
Trace your disposable pad twice onto the paper side of a piece of freezer paper. Trace your disposable pad once onto another piece of freezer paper.

## Step 2: Adhere Freezer Paper to Fabrics
Place the freezer paper plastic-side-down onto the fabric. Iron the paper to the fabric using a low heat and no steam. It will only take a couple seconds. Iron the freezer paper with two tracings to the T-shirt. Iron the paper with one tracing to the blanket. You could also pin the paper to the fabrics. I just find this to be much easier.

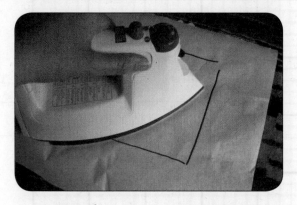

## Step 3: Cut Out Your Fabric
Cut along the lines. Remove the freezer paper after you have finished cutting. Remove all the paper. You should have four pieces of T-shirt fabric and one piece of blanket.

## Step 4: Layer and Pin the Fabric

Layer them as such: 3 pieces of T-shirt, 1 piece of wool blanket, 1 piece of T-shirt. Pin along all of the edges leaving a 3-inch gap. You will not be sewing this gap at first. You need a spot to turn the fabric out-side-in.

## Step 5: Sew It: Take 1

Line the fabric up to the edge of the foot of your sewing machine. Sew along all the edges leaving a 3-inch gap of unsewn fabric (this is the hole you will turn the fabric through).

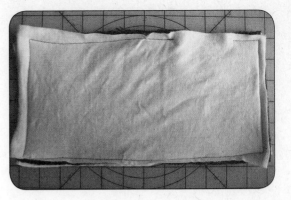

## Step 6: Turn the Piece Out-Side-In

Turn the single piece of t-shirt fabric over, pushing all the fabric through the gap and using your finger to poke out the corners. You should now have four layers of T-shirt fabric all stacked on top of one another with a piece of blanket fabric on top.

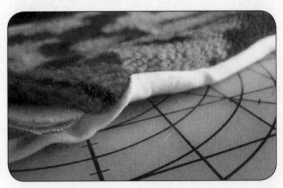

## Step 7: Sew It: Take 2

Pin the gap and sew once along all of the edges of the piece, making sure you close the gap. Then, sew vertical lines approximately 1 to 2 inches apart. Now, sew horizontal lines approximately 1 to 2 inches apart.

## Step 8: You're Done!

Now, go save the environment!

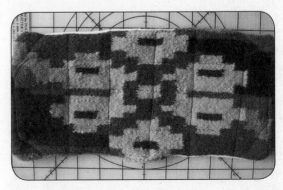

# Homemade Laundry Detergent

By **gowithflo**
(www.instructables.com/id/
Homemade-Laundry-Detergent/)

I wanted to
A. Save money
B. Be ecologically phosphate free
In addition to my clothes coming out "so fresh and so clean," it was a very satisfying and aesthetic creating process!

## Gather Materials

- food processor
- 1 bar laundry soap like Fels Naptha or Zote, or Ivory—Zote can be found in Hispanic grocery stores
- 1 box Borax—found in the laundry aisle
- 1 box washing soda or OxiClean, or baking soda
- OPTIONAL: essential oil of your choice, I didn't do it but I think tea tree might be nice.

**Powdered Laundry Detergent**

- 1 cup grated Fels Naptha soap
- ½ cup washing soda
- ½ cup Borax

For a light load, use 1 tablespoon. For heavy or heavily-soiled load, use 2 tablespoons.

## Step 1: Grate Your Bar

I used the ultra pink Zote laundry bar, this is where I wonder if it's actually phosphate free, but look at the color! yummy pink shreds!

160

you may want to cut the bar down a bit before stuffing it in and using the grating disk attachment.

## Step 2: Add Other Ingredients

The big shreds of the bar soap might not dissolve as is, so you will need to change to the chopping blade of your processor. Now is the time to add the powder to the bowl of the food processor and blend it till it is fine, and don't huff the particulates.

## Step 3: Conclusion

Clothes came out great! The total came out to be $10.09. I estimate one or two little scoops is enough, which makes about 75 washes, equaling out to around $.12 per wash.

# Add a Shower to Your Toilet

By **jeff-o** Jeff Schmidt
(www.instructables.com/id/Add-a-Shower-to-your-Toilet/)

Disposable diapers are very hard on the environment. That's why my wife and I use cloth diapers. Instead of sending pounds and pounds of soiled diapers to the dump every week, we simply wash the diapers in the washing machine. However, you can't just dump the dirty diaper directly into the machine! That would be . . . truly nasty. You have to clean off the majority of the solid waste before it goes into the laundry.

So why not spray it off—directly into the toilet? Commercial units that do the same thing cost $40 to $60, but you can make one for $30 or less if you have the parts lying around.

Some sort of backflow prevention would be a Really Good Idea for this installation. In Canada, either a vacuum breaker or an RPZ (Reverse Pressure Zone) valve may be used, and the sprayer will then be completely up to code. Unfortunately, these are somewhat expensive and complicated to install. If you use this sprayer, I suggest shutting off the water at the valve before releasing the sprayer trigger, just in case.

## Parts and Tools

What we're going to do is splice a hand-held kitchen sprayer into the water line that feeds the toilet.

The sprayer can be used to wash the larger chunks of poop into the toilet, where they can be flushed away. The diaper can then be put into the wash.

- 1 T-junction with one male ⅜" compression joint and two female ⅜" compression joints
- 1 valve with ⅜" compression joints (optional)
- 1⅜" compression to ¼" threaded pipe joint adapter
- 1 kitchen sprayer wand with a ¼" connector
- 1 2" long piece of ⅜" OD plastic tubing
- 1 stick-on hook (optional)
- 1 vacuum breaker or RPZ valve plumber's tape and adjustable wrench rags

## Step 1: Assembly—Part 1

I had a heck of a time trying to find an adapter that converted a compression fitting to a regular threaded pipe. In the end I had to settle with using a short piece of tubing.

The first few pieces can be put together "on the bench." Take the T junction and remove the nut from both the long and short ends. Set them aside for later. Compression fittings don't need plumber's tape, so screw the valve directly on to the short end of the T junction. Tighten it with a wrench.

Take one of the nuts and slide it onto the end of the short piece of tubing. Tighten the nut onto the output of the valve using a wrench. Remove the nut from the compression fitting to ¼" adapter, and slide it onto the free end of the tube. Then tighten the nut onto the adapter. You may need to use two wrenches, turned in opposite directions, to properly tighten the nut.

Now it's time to use the plumber's tape. Wrap a few layers onto the free end of the adapter, and screw on the kitchen sprayer hose.

Finally, screw the sprayer head onto the other end of the sprayer hose.

## Step 2: Assembly—Part 2

It's time to move things to the bathroom. Locate the short piece of flexible hose that carries water from the valve to the toilet. Turn off the valve (turn it fully clockwise), then flush the toilet. This will drain the water in the tank.

With a rag under the valve, unscrew the hose from the valve and allow any remaining water in the hose to drain out. Grab the splice you created in the previous step, and screw it onto the output of the valve. Make sure it's good and tight. Since this is a compression fitting, you won't need to use plumber's tape.

Now screw the hose from the toilet onto the top of the T junction. That's it! You'll probably want to add a hook somewhere for the sprayer.

Now, turn on the valve for the sprayer and again check for leaks.

Using the sprayer is pretty straight-forward. Simply hold the poopy diaper inside the toilet bowl and spray it off. Always aim downward, and work from the top to the bottom. You may want to wear gloves.

When the diaper is rinsed off, plop it in a bucket with all the other rinsed diapers. Flush the poops down the toilet, and rinse off the sprayer head in the sink. Close the valve* for the sprayer each time you're finished using it. And there you have it! No wiping, no scrubbing and no garbage bins filled with guacamole poop.

Once the diapers are washed in the laundry machine, hang them outside to dry on a clothes line. The UV light from the sun helps disinfect them further, and the fresh air makes them smell fresher. When your kids have outgrown diapers, simply remove the sprayer and donate it to a friend!

My wife has informed me that the sprayer is also great for cleaning out the catch bowl from our daughter's training potty, and for rinsing out the sink after it's been washed.

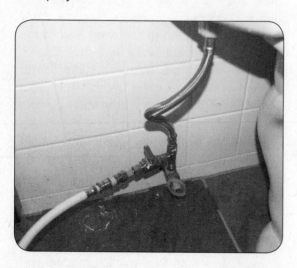

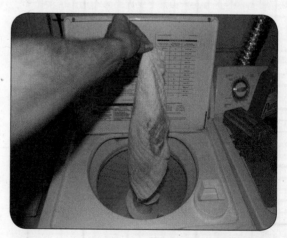

## Step 3: Using the Toilet Sprayer

With everything hooked up, turn on the main valve that comes out of the wall. Check to make sure there aren't any leaks.

*The valve is technically optional, though I do recommend it. If you have a toddler, they will almost definitely find the hose and try to use it. The valve will hopefully prevent them from filling the bathroom with a foot of water.

# How to Get Rid of Fruit Flies

By **Tim Anderson**
(www.instructables.com/id/Fruit-Fly-Trap-1/)

Fruit flies—yuck! Catch them in four different easy-to-make traps. Got an infestation? Control it right now! I compare the effectiveness of four different types of traps.

## Step 1: Inverted Cone Fly Trap

This is the only trap here that can catch other types of flies besides fruit flies. To make it, cut off the top of a soda bottle and insert it into the remaining part inverted. Tape or hot glue it in place. Put some liquid bait in the bottom. The flies will fly in and will follow the walls back up, not finding the way out. Instead of the plastic cone some people use a paper cone, a plastic bag with the corner cut off, or a piece of Saran wrap with a small hole in it. Some people use these Alternative Baits: juice or sugar water, sugar water with yeast, apple cider vinegar, or pickle juice, for other types of flies use meat, fish, canned cat food, or whatever the flies seem to like.

## Step 2: Soap Bubble Trap

The flies are attracted by the bait and get stuck in the soap bubbles. I used red wine as bait and added some dish soap.

Put your hand over the top and shake it up to make the bubbles. Then put it near your infestation.

## Step 3: Soapy Bait Trap

This one is even easier. Put a dab of soap on your fingertip and touch that to the surface of your liquid bait. The soap breaks the surface tension and the flies fall into the liquid when they touch it.

## Step 4: Wine Bottle Trap

This one is just a wine bottle with wine left in the bottom.

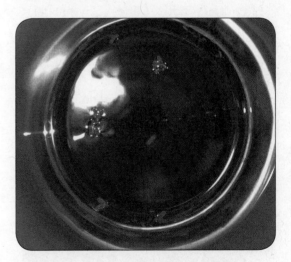

## Step 5: Which is the Best?

I caught one or two flies in each of the first three traps. The wine bottle wasn't supposed to be a trap. I left it out by accident at the other end of the counter. All the flies flew in there and died. Now I can't do any more experiments. Fermentation of wine releases carbon dioxide which is heavier than air. I suppose they flew down into the $CO_2$ and suffocated. And that's it! After having a fruit fly infestation for almost a year, an accidental trap wipes them out!

163

## No More Roaches

By **Ninzerbean** Nina Davis
(www.instructables.com/id/No-More-
Roaches/)

This is the story of how I got rid of the roaches in my home and they have stayed gone for 10 months now after just the initial treatment.

### What You Will Need

- boric acid powder*
- Karo syrup—you may substitute honey or maple syrup or pancake syrup
- rice flour—you may substitute any flour you have on hand
- 1 popsicle stick
- 1 mixing bowl

Amounts as follows: 2 parts boric acid, 1 part rice flour, enough Karo syrup to make a peanut butter like consistency mixture.

Important note: Boric acid powder is not something you want to inhale, get into your eyes, or swallow, so mix this up outside. Wear a dust mask too until it is mixed up. It has no odor.

For a 2800 square foot home with 4 bathrooms, I mixed 2 cups of boric acid with 1 cup rice powder and about ¾ cup of Karo syrup. I used a plastic bowl to mix it in and stuck the bowl and left over bait up into the attic/crawl space when I was done baiting.

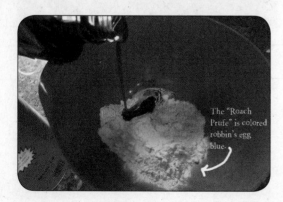

The "Roach Prufe" is colored robbin's egg blue.

---

*(available in hardware stores in the US as "Roach Prufe," this was the only way I was able to buy it, the canister is 98 percent boric acid and 2 percent blue coloring).

### Step 1: Once Upon a Time . . .

About 16 years ago I rented a house that was infested with roaches. I called an exterminator who declared it was the worst infestation he had ever seen (in case you don't want to take my word). His company used a bait that had the consistency of peanut butter and he put a little dab of it behind all the drawers (out of reach of pets or children), under the sinks, on the pipes coming out from the wall, and he even took off all the outlet and switch plate covers to put the bait inside the walls. It was a miracle; I never saw a roach again. In that house. When I moved I used the same service and the same guy (let's call him John because that was his name) did the same thing, but this time it was a new house that I had bought. Once a year John would come back and do the same thing and in 14 years I never saw a you know what. Alive that is. Once in a while there would be a dead one. Back then I had a husband so the dead ones were not so much a problem.

### Step 2: Then . . .

The husband left, I had to move and buy a new house and guess what? I took John with me, but this time John wasn't using the bait. In fact I was calling John every week for help with the roaches. My new house was new to me but really very old, and it had a lot of roaches. A week would not go by when I did not see one or two or . . . . more. It was so bad I could not get out of bed at night and turn on a light for fear of what I would see. I implored John to use his magic peanut butter but he just told me "We don't do that anymore." What was a poor girl to do? The Internet to the rescue!

### Step 3: And This is What I Found Out!

The magic peanut butter that John's company had been using was so successful that clients started canceling their contracts. Oh. Gosh, why hadn't I thought of that! Who's going to hire a pest control company if they don't have pests? John wasn't using the stuff that WORKED because if he did his company wouldn't have any business. It has been 10 months since I ended my contract with the pest control company and I baited my house with my home made poison, and (drum roll please) I have found one dead roach in all that time.

## Step 4: How and Where to Use It

Using the popsicle stick, put a dab of the bait where roaches like to go—up high and near water. They also like to live in your home's walls so undo all of your switch plate covers and outlet covers and smear some on the back of the outlet cover itself. The bait is not sticky so I find it easier to put it in areas where it can sit so it won't fall off. After it dries out it becomes hard and stuck to where you stuck it.

Roaches like to bring food back to their colony and when they bring this food back it will kill lots and lots of roaches, roaches who never even scurried over to your house.

It took me most of a day to go all around my home looking for out-of-the-way places to place the bait, undoing all the switch plate covers took the longest. Pulling out the drawers in the kitchen was really easy because most of the time you can access the back of the drawer from the cabinet underneath.

The most important places are the pipes coming into your home either for your sinks or your washing machine and dishwasher. Attics and crawl spaces are prime roach habitat. Roaches have no bones so they can slip through the smallest sliver of space. It's gross.

Bait

Bait

Place bait on top of door frames.

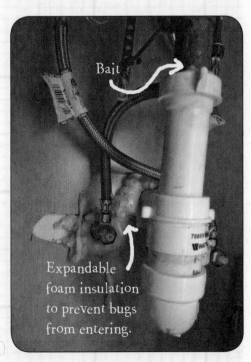

Bait

Expandable foam insulation to prevent bugs from entering.

Pocket doors are a great place to place bait because basically they go back into your wall - I put bait on top of the door - here

## Step 5: Why this Works

Boric acid powder is a proven roach killer, what I am presenting here is a way to get the roaches attracted to it (sweet smelling Karo syrup) and to eat it (flour and Karo syrup). Making it into a paste enables you to place it in areas where powder alone would not stay.

home

165

# How to Re-Cover Chairs

By **canida** Christy Canida
(www.instructables.com/id/How-to-
Re-Cover-chairs/)

An easy way to fix up old or used furniture. Why didn't we do this earlier?

## Step 1: Before

We got an old chair with a ratty seat cover from Craig's List about three years ago. The seats had been re-covered in a neat red silk that looked good but didn't wear well. After months of ignoring the shredded red silk, we finally yanked it off to discover the original black fabric, which also looked pretty bad.

Since we were planning to have 40 people over for Thanksgiving the next day, it was the perfect time to start a new project. Right.

## Step 2: Find Your Fabric

We headed off to the local fabric store to find some nice, thick upholstery fabric. This will wear better than that thin silk, and hopefully stand up to years of daily abuse at our kitchen table. I chose some nice swirly blue stuff that would look good with the dark brown wood of the chairs.

You don't need much fabric—just the size of the seat plus a couple of inches around each edge of the seat. Remember to measure your seats before running off to the fabric store, or else you'll have lots of extra fabric, or worse, not quite enough. (I'm planning to make cloth napkins from my leftovers. Eventually.)

Remove the chair seat and place it upside-down against the back of the fabric. (Remember the good stuff should be facing up when you're done.) Make sure it's properly aligned with your fabric's pattern, especially if there are stripes involved. Trim around the edge to leave enough fabric to fold over on all sides. Depending on the thickness of your cushion, this could be 2-5 inches.

## Step 3: STAPLE!

This is the fun part—an excuse to use a staple gun. Ours is a sweet electric version that can punch through most anything. In any case, be careful—don't staple your fingers, your eyes, your leg, or anything else but the fabric and the seat back.

Start with the flat front side, and staple from the center out towards the edges. You want to make sure the fabric is smooth and tight, without bunches between your staples. This is much like wrapping a present—if you can do that, you can re-cover a chair.

Now spin the seat, and tug the back of the fabric into position. Pull firmly against the front row of staples to be sure you've gotten rid of any wrinkles or bunches. Again, start stapling at the center and spread outwards.

When the seat back starts to curve, take folds/tucks in your fabric. The goal is to have all the bunching UNDER the seat, not on top. Try a few different things, and see how it works. Remember, you can always pull the staples out and try again until you get it right.

Staple the sides, again tugging firmly to make sure the fabric is tight over the top of the seat.

Do the corners last. I found it best to take a fold on each side of the corner, and then make a pleat along the diagonal. Again, yank staples and re-do anything you don't like.

### Things to Think About

1. How many staples to use? My staples were kind of small, and I love stapling, so I used more than absolutely necessary. Scale as appropriate for your fabric, staple size, and entertainment, but make sure you use enough to share the strain across your fabric.

2. Where do the screws go? If you have to screw your seat back on, take care not to block the screw holes with lots of fabric or staples. You can go through one layer of fabric easily, but staples are a problem.

3. Is it tidy? Be sure to hammer down any staples that aren't flush, and trim any extraneous blobs of fabric.

## Step 4: Stain Protect

We sprayed the new seat covers down with Scotch Guard.

Set up some milk crates or other support structure, and spray the seats according to package directions. Be sure to do this OUTSIDE, as the vapors are pretty foul and probably carcinogenic.

Let them dry overnight in a protected but well-ventilated area. If you can put them in a porch or garage this will protect you from the vapors while also protecting your shiny new seats from dangerously well-fed birds.

## Step 5: Reassemble and Use

When the seats are dry, reassemble your chairs.

Use and enjoy your newly-refreshed seating, and wonder why you didn't do this earlier. Start checking out the rest of your furniture, and wonder whether recovering a couch is really that much harder.

**home**

for your
# pets

Pamper your pets with healthy treats, comfy beds, and homemade toys. Learn the best methods for grooming, training, and entertaining your little loved ones with these great ideas.

## "Indestructible" Dog Toy

By **shesparticular** Kate Jackson
(www.instructables.com/id/
Indestructible-Dog-Toy/)

My mom's dog, Molly, loves to play—an activity that for her usually involves rounding up all her toys and ripping them to shreds. In an effort to make some kind of indestructible toy or at least something that she could play with that might last longer than a half hour, I rounded up a few things and gave it a shot.

While she was able to dismantle this awesome rope and dried sweet potato contraption, it at least took her a little longer, and she seemed to really love it. Molly was probably able to obliterate this because she is so tough but it would be awesome (and probably last a little longer) for dogs who don't shred toys up in record time, as well as for puppies.

### You'll Need

- hemp or jute rope (I used 9 pieces of a thin-ish diameter braided together to make a larger rope. Approximately 2½ feet works well for medium dogs, less is needed for a toy for a smaller dog and more for a larger dog). Hemp and jute rope are used here because they're super strong and durable, and also because if Molly managed to eat some of it, it was much less likely to cause any of the issues that ingesting a synthetic rope would.
- sweet potatoes or yams (2 for a medium-sized dog toy, one for a smaller one and 3 or 4 for a larger-sized toy.) Sweet potatoes and yams are awesome for dogs as well as people. Dogs seem to love to chew them, and when they eat them they're also getting a big dose of nutrients
- sheet pan and parchment or foil
- sharp knife
- round cookie cutter a bit larger than the diameter of your rope
- vegetable peeler (optional)

### Step 1: Potato Prep!

Preheat your oven to 250°Fahrenheit.

Wash your sweet potatoes really well (you can peel them if you want, but I just leave the peel on).

Slice the sweet potato into rounds approximately ½" thick.

Using the cookie cutter, remove the center of each round. Give your pup some extra love by boiling these little cutout portions up and mashing them—this is a great and easy way to get your dog to take medicines they might otherwise refuse (or you can add a little maple syrup and a dash of cinnamon and gobble them up yourself!). You can also dry these bits alongside the rings and give them to your canine friend as treats.

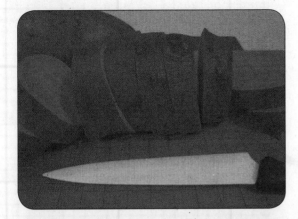

## Step 2: Bake 'Em Up

Place on cookie sheet and bake for 2½ hours

Flip and bake for another 2½ hours

When they're done they should be totally dried out and hard—if there are any squishy bits, bake longer and keep checking every 30 minutes or so

Once they're totally dry, allow to cool fully

## Step 3: Lots of Knots

Make a knot in the end of your hemp rope.

If using multiple thinner pieces, braid them together to make stringing the pieces on easier.

String on two sweet potato rings and make a knot above them.

Add two more rings and knot.

Repeat until you reach the end of your rope.

Give this awesome new toy to your canine companion!

pets

171

# How to Brush Your Dog's Teeth

By **Beastbunny** Jenna Ziedler
(www.instructables.com/id/How-to-brush-your-dog-s-teeth/)

pets

While dogs rarely get cavities, plaque and tartar on your dog's teeth can lead to serious problems. Gum disease can be painful and cause tooth loss, bone loss, bad breath, and infection. The bacteria that grow in an infected gum can also spread to other parts of a dog's body and cause endocarditis (heart valve infection), kidney and liver damage.

Before starting an at-home oral care regime for your dog, I suggest you have a vet look at her teeth and determine what level of build-up is present. If there is tartar build-up, they might remove it with a scaler, usually while your pet is anesthetized. It is important that you never try this at home as the vet removes plaque from both above and below the gum line while at home you can only reach what they eye can see.

After you are given the OK by your vet, you are ready to start getting your dog accustomed to brushing.

It's worth noting that some dogs are predisposed to extreme tartar production due to hereditary traits passed on through generations. If your dog seems to have recurring tartar issues, discuss with your vet how best to proceed.

## Supplies You'll Need
- dog toothpaste, see note below
- gauze pads (optional)
- soft finger toothbrush or soft small-head toothbrush
- treats: commercial dog treats, string cheese, hot dogs, or anything else your dog likes and that you can dole out in small portions.
- toothpaste: it is very important to only use a toothpaste made especially for pets. There are many different flavors and varieties available at pet supply stores. However, I highly recommend the CET brand pet toothpaste as it works enzymatically rather than with an abrasive cleanser like some other brands.

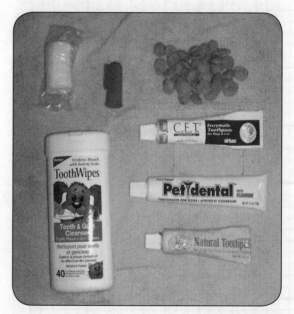

## Step 1: Acclimate Your Dog to a Finger in His Mouth

Using just your finger, touch/rub the outside of your dog's lips, praising him and stopping to give him a treat. Proceed to rubbing your dog's gums and teeth with only your finger. If you'd like, you can wrap a gauze pad around your finger to lightly clean the teeth and gums during this step or use a pet tooth wipe. Be sure to praise and treat your dog after each step. Do this once a day for a week or so or until your dog is comfortable with your fingers in his mouth, then proceed on.

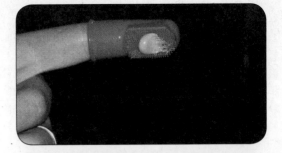

## Step 2: Acclimate Your Dog to Toothbrush in His Mouth

Using a dry brush, lightly touch your dogs lips and teeth. Treat and praise your dog while he is calm. If this step goes well, move on to the next step: adding toothpaste. If at any time your dog gets agitated, take a step back and get him used to the previous step.

## Step 3: Add Toothpaste and Increase Duration

Using a small amount of toothpaste on your brush, lightly brush your dog's teeth, paying special attention to the back molars where tartar builds up readily. The teeth do not accumulate as much tartar on the inside, so it is most important to brush the outside surfaces. Work up to brushing for 30 seconds on each side of the mouth.

## Step 4: Other Options

If your dog simply hates this activity even after the acclimation period (give it at least a month before giving up), there are other options though they are not as good as daily brushing at keeping plaque at bay.

There are food and treats designed to keep plaque from accumulating.

You may have heard as long as your dog eats crunchy food then they're fine. This is not true as most foods are not crunchy enough or in the mouth long enough to have any effect. There are a few foods and treats, however, that carry the Veterinary Oral Health's Council seal of acceptance which have been shown to reduce the accumulation of tartar and plaque. Check for this seal before believing your dog's teeth are being protected.

### Dental Toys

Chew toys that are billed as dental care devices may or may not work. But if you truly can't brush your dog's teeth, anything is better than nothing.

### Water Additives

There are also solutions that you add to your pet's drinking water. These reduce the bacterial growth within the mouth which reduces tartar buildup. I know some people who have had great results using this kind of product. One brand is AquaDent.

pets

# How to Make Healthy Homemade Apple Cinnamon Dog Treats

## By aelbert
(www.instructables.com/id/How-To-Make-Healthy-Homemade-Apple-Cinnamon-Dog-Tr/)

The following tutorial will guide you through the simple task of preparing a batch of homemade apple cinnamon dog treats. From start to finish, it only takes an hour or two to make roughly 50 treats.

## Supplies and Ingredients

Common kitchen supplies you will need include the following:

- a set of standard measuring cups
- a set of standard measuring spoons
- two medium-sized or large stirring bowls
- a plastic or wooden stirring spoon
- a standard butter knife, fork, or other straight edge
- a grater
- a rolling pin
- a small cookie cutter
- cooking spray
- a large cookie sheet
- an oven
- a kitchen timer or clock
- an oven mitt
- a cooling rack
- a large storage container with a lid

Ingredients

- 4 cups of whole wheat flour (as well as a handful or two of some white flour which will not be added to the actual dough, but used for non-stick purposes)
- ½ of a cup of cornmeal
- 1 egg
- 2 tablespoons of vegetable oil
- 1 teaspoon of cinnamon
- 1 small apple
- 1½ cups of water

Health Benefits of these Ingredients to Your Dog

- Cornmeal is used for both its nutrient and fiber content, and helps a dog's digestive system run smoothly.
- Eggs are an excellent source of complete protein and provide many of the essential amino acids that dogs need.
- Fats (like the kind in vegetable oil) deliver certain vitamins to a dog's system and are utilized as a primary source of energy. They can also keep his/her skin, paw pads, and nose in good condition.
- Cinnamon is an excellent source of antioxidants, which are a basic component of canine nutrition. One teaspoon of cinnamon contains as many antioxidants as a full cup of pomegranate juice.
- Complex carbohydrates include fruits (such as apples), whole grains (such as wheat flour), and vegetables. Although they take longer to digest, they supply a dog with a slow, steady stream of energy.

## Step 1: Mixing the Ingredients

Measure out all of your dry ingredients and their respective amounts using your measuring cups and spoons (Dry ingredients include the whole wheat flour, cornmeal, and cinnamon.) Use a straight edge if necessary to level off the contents. Combine it all into one of the large bowls, mix with a spoon, and set aside.

Grate the apple using the grater. Toss the grated apple bits into the other large bowl, being careful not to get any seeds in with it. Add the water and vegetable oil to the grated apple, as well as the egg. (Be careful not to get any part of the shell in the mixture!) Stir well.

Carefully pour the dry ingredients in with the wet ingredients. Stir well until the mixture becomes a thick dough.

## Step 2: Rolling and Cutting the Dough

Turn out the dough on a lightly floured surface such as a counter or tabletop.

Spread a small handful of flour on the rolling pin so the dough does not stick to it, and roll it out until it is approximately ¼ to ½ of an inch thick. Add more flour as needed to prevent any unwanted sticking of the dough to the surface or rolling pin.

At this point, it is recommended you preheat your oven for 325°F.

Using your cookie cutter, punch the dough and set the slices onto a lightly greased cookie sheet. These treats do not rise or expand during baking, so they can be placed fairly close together. (Just as long as they aren't touching.) Also, depending on how large your slices are, you may need to use a second cookie sheet if you run out of room on

the first one, or you can simply use the same cookie sheet after the first batch is finished baking and cooling.

## Step 3: Baking the Treats

Carefully place the cookie sheet in the oven, using an oven mitt if necessary, and set a timer for 15 to 20 minutes.

After the timer sounds, carefully remove the treats from the oven using an oven mitt. CAUTION: The cookie sheet will be very hot!

## Step 4: Completing the Process

Let the treats cool down completely on a cooling rack for another half-hour or so.

At this point, you can either call your dog over for a taste test (as I do with my beagle, Jiggsey), or simply store the treats in a sealed plastic container. You can also freeze them. This is especially recommended if you know they won't all be eaten within a week after baking.

**Sources Used**

Mehus-Roe, Kristin. *Dog Bible: The Definitive Source for All Things Dog. 1st ed.* Irvine, CA: BowTie, Inc., 2005. 499-501. Print.

There are many things every dog should know, but sadly as we all know there are a lot of things (that are very important) that most dogs don't know. What it all comes down to is the trust and bond you have with your dog. Remember, a good dog doesn't do tricks, a good dog listens and obeys out of respect, not fear or dominance.

## Step 1: "No" & "Yes!"

The first "No" is not "NO!" and the first "Yes" should be "YES!!"

When we first get our dogs, we like to make sure they know who is boss. "No!" This word is thrown around very loosely around dogs.

My belief is "NO!" should be "No." Firm and calm, not controlling and angry.

Don't be fooled into thinking, "My dog is an ancestor of the wolf therefore I need to dominate him."

We want domesticated dogs to work with us, so why are we so convinced that they don't want to respect us and listen to us? Dogs were created to do work on our behalf, any dog that is misbehaving is crying out for you to pay attention and to listen.

Once you begin to work with your dog you must give the right responses. For example, let's say you are trying to teach your dog the "Down" command. Instead of down, your dog sits.

Do not ever use "No." EVER! "No" is for when your dog has had accident on your carpet, not for a wrong command.

Once your dog does the command right it's not. "Yes." You need to freak out (positively) with praise. "Yes" needs to be "YESS!! WHAT A GOOD DOG!!!!" and then a thousand kisses.

That way your dog is extremely sure of what it is you want him to do.

## Step 2: "Listen to Me/Watch Me"

When your dog hears this his ears should go up, and his eyes should be on you; waiting for a command.

Most people will use their dog's call name for this. I think the call name is for getting your dog to come to you and this command is for getting your dog's attention. This command is easily taught with a small reward. Give the dog the command to "Watch me," "Listen up," "Listen to me."

Then once the command is given, put the reward to your eyes until your dog makes eye contact, even if it's just for a moment.

Then reward with dog with a big "YES!"

## Step 3: Let's Walk

While walking on a leash is a very difficult task for some dogs, for others it's as natural as eating. I do not condone the usage of prong collars, harnesses, choke chains, or flat collars. I use no collar or leash unless I am required to, in which case I use a flat collar or depending on the dog's training level or bond with me, a chain collar.

**Steps For an Easy Walk**

1. Make sure the collar is properly fitted and safe for your dog. If you are using a dominance collar (chain collar or prong collar) make sure the collar is high on the neck.
2. Make sure you do not walk with a retractable leash, you will have little to no control over your dog.
3. Place your dog beside you, allow him some room to walk, don't attach him to your hip. If your dog pulls put a small reward in front of their face, this is known as baiting.
4. After baiting your dog for a while, reward the dog with the treat. Do not become over excited because you will excite the dog and the unwanted behavior of pulling will return.

### Step 4: "It's Nothing/Leave it/ Doesn't Matter"

I like to use this command when I'm walking my dogs. Let's say I'm walking my dogs in the dog park (off lead) and their favorite thing comes up, a large gross puddle of murky water. I can quickly give the command of "Leave it!" and my pack will walk around it.

Now don't expect your dog to completely leave any object alone after this command. They will usually continue to try to sniff and look interested in the object (they're a lot like kids). Don't get upset when this happens as long as they aren't trying to bite, chew, or pick up the object, they listened to your command.

This also works well if you have small children and your dog tries to sniff their faces.

1. Put a toy in front of the dog.
2. As soon as your dog attempts to sniff it; brush his nose away with your hand while giving the command.
3. Once your dog's eyes leave the object and look at you or somewhere else give the dog a reward. (This may take a while depending on how determined and play driven your dog is. Be patient.)

### Step 5: "Stay Back!"

This command is often used to keep a dog from bolting out the door.

1. Grab the handle of your door, if your dog runs in front of you, his nose against the door. Or he is right at your heels; toss back your foot gently, and tell him to "Stay back."
2. Your dog may simply ignore you and keep trying to push his way out. So don't open the door, just grab the handle and give it a twist, if he remains calm and keeps his distance, reward him.
3. Whenever you go to your door give this command even if you are going on a walk, repetition is key.

pets

# Best Cat Scratching Post Ever and Cat Weight-loss Device

By **weiblen.c**
(www.instructables.com/id/Best-
Cat-Scratching-Post-Ever-AND-Cat-
Weight-loss-/)

Watching cat behavior over the years, I have noticed that they scratch not only to flex their feet and claws, they actually like to stretch their shoulders and back, using their claws as leverage. This stretching behavior will tip over a commercially available "normal" sized scratching post.

Whenever I have observed one of my cats try to get a good stretch out of a standard cat post, it has moved or tipped and the cat has immediately given up and gone to find a more suitable object for an anchor—usually my sofa.

I have noticed that when my cats start scratching at the furniture, the pieces they choose to destroy have a few things in common:

1. They are stable and heavy.
2. They are wider than any standard cat posts.
3. They are taller than any standard cat posts.

Merely disciplining a cat for using the furniture as a scratching post, but not providing them with an alternative that meets their needs is not likely to be a successful method of training. A post that serves a cat's needs better than the furniture will be naturally preferred for scratching, and it should make training the cats much easier, since they will not be deprived of stretching out and getting a good scratch in when their physiology demands it.

## Supplies
- 10 × wide elbows
- 2 × narrow elbows
- 22 × .5 inch washers
- 26 × .75 inch screws
- 44 × 1 inch screws
- 2 × scrap lumber (½" inch thick, by 3.5 inches wide, by 36 inches long)
- 1 × concrete tube (10 inches in diameter, by 48 inches tall)
- 1 × edge-glued wood panel .75 inches thick, by 20 inches wide, by 36 inches long
- ½ bucket of plaster (about 6 lbs)
- a few feet of duct tape
- 5 × rolls of sisal (.25 inches thick, by 100 feet long, for a total of 500 ft)
- 1 × plywood circle (12 inch diameter or 18 inch if you have two or more cats)
- 1 × circle of foam (12 inch diameter or 18 inch if you have two or more cats)
- 1 × circle of cloth batting (12 inch diameter or 18 inch if you have two or more cats)
- 1 × large bottle of fast-drying wood glue (16 oz)
- 1 × piece of cloth or carpet to cover the top platform (I used a cotton bath mat.)

## Tools
- pencil
- handsaw
- screwdriver

pets

178

- drill with ⅛" bit and ½" bit
- bucket
- stirring stick for plaster
- mixing bucket for plaster
- scissors
- magnet on a string (for fishing out tools and screws that you drop into the tube)

## Step 1: Prepare the Post

Carve a notch out of two sides of the cardboard tube on the top and bottom edges, to accommodate the depth of the metal elbow brackets.

## Step 2: Reinforce the Cardboard Post with Wood

Saw the scrap lumber into two small pieces, about five inches long, and two longish pieces, about 31" long.

To attach each wood support inside of the cardboard tube, first screw the long side of a wide bracket to the end of the wood. Leave a ½ inch space to one side of the wood, which will be used later by a second, narrower bracket.

Line up the bracket on the end of the piece of wood with a notch in the tube end. Place one of the narrow brackets on the outside of the tube, where the screws will be able to reach into the wood. Screw through the cardboard and into the wood from the outside of the tube, using long screws.

Add several more screws and washers along the length of the wood. Fasten it to the tube as securely as possible.

These wood supports will be the structural strength of the post, and will bear the weight and force of your cat jumping on and off of the post, climbing up and down, clawing at it, and generally trying to wreck it. If your cats are anywhere near as rambunctious as

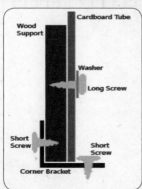

mine, without this wood support, I think the cardboard would give out pretty quickly.

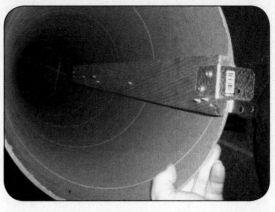

## Step 3: Attach the Base

Screw the post as-is to the large wood panel. I lined mine up a little towards the back of the rectangle, so that it will be closer to the wall and it hopefully won't bang around too much when my cats jump against it.

## Step 4: Add Plaster for Weight and Stability

Use duct tape to seal around the edges of the base.

Mix about three pounds (¼ bucket) of plaster and pour it in. Wait a few minutes until the plaster sets, then mix another three pounds and add it. (By adding the plaster a little at a time, you preserve the weak seal made by the duct tape. If you add too much weight of liquid plaster at one time, the duct tape will give way and leak all over.)

Wait a couple of hours for the plaster to cure and the cardboard tube to dry completely before proceeding.

## Step 5: Reinforce the Base Joint

Add the remaining wide brackets around the bottom of the post, to secure it to the wood. Use short screws to fasten the brackets to the wood base and longer screws to go deeply into the plaster.

## Step 6: Add the Platform Top

Using the same technique as before, add the short pieces of wood to the inside of the top of the post. Secure them from the outside using washers and long screws.

pets

179

Set the ½" diameter plywood circle on top of the post, lining it up so that the brackets do not protrude past the edges. If you're drilling pilot holes, as I did, it is helpful to trace the outline of the brackets, as well as the location of the screw holes.

Secure the plywood using short screws, so they don't protrude from the top of the wood.

**Note**

Four months later I added an 18 inch circle for the top platform because my two cats were fighting over it too much. If you have only one cat, 12" will probably be fine. If you have two or more cats, I suggest using an 18" or larger platform from the very beginning, now that I've seen how my cats squabbled over it.

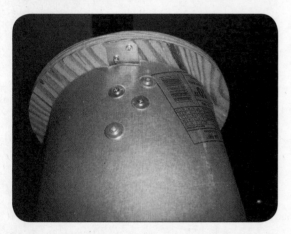

## Step 7: Add Handles to the Base

At this point, I found that the post was becoming too awkward to move easily.

To solve the problem, I propped up the base and drilled two pairs of ½" holes. Then, I knotted sisal through them, to make simple handles.

## Step 8: Wrap the Sisal

Starting at the base and working your way up in a spiral, wrap and glue the sisal to the post. I glued three sides of the post, leaving one side densely packed but unglued.

You have to glue at least half way around the post, all the way up, or the sisal will slide and pull into big gaps after the cats get their claws into it.

Be sure to cover up the screws and washers all the way around the post. They have a tendency to grab the sisal and prevent it from lining up snug with the other layers.

Use a couple of rows of sisal to cover the brackets at the base.

## Step 9: Finish the Top

Use a small amount of glue to tack the foam to the top of the plywood platform. If it ever wears out, you can replace it easily if you don't over-glue it.

Put the batting on top of the foam. Cover with whatever fabric or carpet you like. I used a cotton bath mat that my cats already adopted to sleep on.

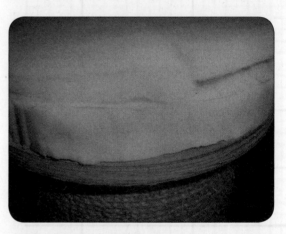

## Step 10: Cat Reactions

# Automated Cat Feeder

By merjinvw Merijn
van Wouden
(www.instructables.com/id/
Automated-Cat-Feeder/)

Somedays no one can stay at home to feed the cat at the right times. This is especially annoying if you have a cat with a weak stomach, so he needs to eat several smaller meals a day, because with one big meal he will puke it out. For such days I made this device. It has a round feed with four segments, in which you can put four meals in the morning. During the day, a disc on top will rotate, leaving a gap for one segment. The disc rotates on the hour point of a clock motor, giving it one revolution per twelve hours, so the cat gets access to another meal after every three hours. On top there is a cap with an image of a cat, which is connected to the second pointer of the clock motor, so you can see it moving. It is not only an indication that the cat feeder is working, it also holds the disc below in place, because the cat could push it off (the cap is connected more firmly than the disc). With a little power you can pull the cap out, and remove the disc. Then you can fill all the segments at once, wash them, or replace the battery if needed.

The things I used for this are easy to get. The main piece is a clock motor. I used the most common clock motor there is; almost all clocks have it (a square black one saying QUARTZ). You might have many of these in your house.

In the next steps I'll explain how to build this. If you start building it, keep in mind that you need to make the rotating parts move smoothly over each other, because these clock motors are built to rotate very light pointers, and they do not have a lot of power. If the parts can't slide smoothly over each other the mechanism will stop.

It is uncertain if it's harmful to let polymer clay get in contact with food. I recommend that if you use polymer clay, add a layer of harmless varnish (I don't know if that exists). You can also make the feed segments out of river clay, or completely out of wood.

The cat feeder I made seems to stagnate sometimes; this is because the disc is too heavy for the motor. You don't want it to suddenly stop when you're gone, so make the disc as light as possible! I made a new disc out of a thin sheet of plastic, it works better. You can also look for a stronger clock motor.

You could also make a small version of this, hang it upside down above the aquarium and use it as a fish feeder.

## What You Need

You'll need:
- clay (I used FIMO, which is a polymer clay and expensive if you use a lot. If you can get a cheaper clay that works just as well, use that)
- an oven to bake the clay
- thin wood: this is for the cap on top, for the disc, and for a little block under the clock motor
- from a clock: the motor, the second pointer, and the hour pointer
- a wide round cookie can you don't use anymore
- two nails
- cutting pliers

## Step 1: Getting the Motor

I bought the cheapest clock I could for the motor. On the back was this motor. Almost all clocks have these, except the small clocks where they don't fit. Get the motor out of it, DON'T THROW AWAY THE SECOND POINTER AND HOUR POINTER! But you can throw away the rest. There are two white tubes in the middle around each other, for the hour- and minute pointers; the pin in them is for the second pointer.

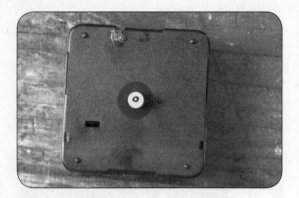

## Step 2: The Lowest Part with the Segments

Get a wide cookie can. Draw a line all around it about 3.5 cm from the bottom. Cut the above part off. You can do this with a cutting pliers. Make a layer of clay on the side of it, and make it round on top. Try to make it flat, so the whole side is on one height. Then bake it. You can later paint this side.

Get a piece of wood about the size of the clock motor. If you lie the motor on top of it on the middle of the can, the black part of the motor should be below the sides of the can. But not too far below, best is about 1 mm, so the white thing in the middle is higher than the sides. This piece of wood is actually just to save clay.

Now make this with clay. Take the color of clay you want it to be in the end because you shouldn't paint this part as your cat could eat the paint. Also, with clay you can just wash it out with water. I made the motor holder in the middle square-shaped on bottom to match the shape of the motor and round on top to match the shape of the disc.

Fit in the motor. If it doesn't fit, you can dull the corners a bit out with a dremel, and you can later soften it with a polish bit. You can use a polish bit on all of the clay to make it smooth so that it looks better. You probably had some fingerprints in it somewhere; you can wash them away.

## Step 3: The Disc

Take the hour pointer. Bend it in half and put tape around it. This makes it stronger but it needed to be shortened anyway. If your hour pointer is still too long you can cut a part off.

Mount it to the motor. Also, make things on the sides that can hold the motor in place (don't glue the motor to the clay, because later you may want to replace the battery). I used metal wires inserted in a hole in the clay. Bend inside.

pets

Make this disc out of thin wood. There should be a hole in the middle that fits around the white thing on the motor. (Also cut a quarter out that can be covered until we come to the motor part.)

Take two nails and smash them into the wood near the hole, so that on the other side the hour pointer can fit between them. Make the heads as flat as possible, to make the surface flat.

Cut the nails off so they don't touch the motor, but leave them as long as possible. Put the disc on the cat feeder, with the nails around the hour pointer.

## Step 4: The Cap

Take the second pointer and place in around the second pin. It should tick. If it doesn't reach the second pin (so when it doesn't tick), you should make the hole in the disc bigger, and follow the instructions in this step, then you make something between the second pointer and the cap, so it goes deeper and reaches the second pin.

Cut the sides of the second pointer off. Make a cap from wood about this size. Put the second pointer upside down on it. I had to make a little pit in the middle of the wood with a drill to make it fit.

Connect it to the wood. Mount it back to the second pin. It should again tick.

## Step 5

You can now add paint and varnish. Only paint the feed segments if you have paint that doesn't dissolve in water and that's hard to get off. I glued an instructions manual (*handleiding*) on bottom because I'm giving this as a present. And four mats so it stands more stable and the bottom keeps clean.

# Deliver Kittens

## By leahculver
(www.instructables.com/id/Deliver-Kittens/)

Listen to Bob Barker and have your pet spayed or neutered. However, if a stray pregnant cat decides to live with you, here's how to help her give birth to her kittens.

## Materials
You will need:
- some old towels
- wide box (1.5 ft × 3 ft or larger)
- scissors
- sewing thread or dental floss
- kitten food (for the mom cat)
- microwave (for the towels)

## Step 1: Wait for It
The mom cat will have her kittens whenever she is ready, so you'll just have to wait. I found my cat, Reyka, wandering around downtown San Jose, CA looking awfully round. She lived with me for about a week before she had her kittens.

As soon as you know your cat is pregnant, start feeding her crunchy kitten food with a high amount of calcium and phosphorus. The kittens will be using a lot of calcium to develop, so it is important for the mom cat to have plenty extra in her system to help birth the kittens.

Place the kittening box (the large cardboard box) in an area that is warm and

dark. Place some old towels in the bottom. Cats seem to do whatever they please, so it is highly unlikely that your cat will actually give birth in the box. Closing off areas of your house or confining your cat to one room is the probably the best way to keep her from giving birth on your bed or on top of your laundry. Reyka was very considerate in choosing my bathroom as the place she wanted to have kittens in.

At this time it is helpful to read all sorts of internet articles on the subject and learn all about birthing kittens. Some facts about kittens:
- they are born with fur and their eyes closed;
- kittens look a lot like sleeping hamsters when they are born;
- newborn kittens are really boring—all they do is eat, sleep, and whine (softly);
- each kitten comes from a separate egg so . . . each one has its own umbilical cord and placenta;
- one litter of kittens can have multiple fathers (scandalous!)

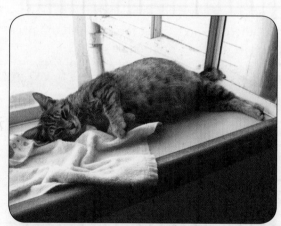

## Step 2: Birthing the Kitten
Reyka had her first kitten at 11:30 AM on a Saturday. I had just gotten out of bed and saw her in the bathroom with what looked like a black water balloon coming out of her.

Kittens are born in a sac that looks just like a water balloon (only with fluid and a kitten inside). Since the smaller the object, the easier it is to push out a small hole, it is nice to the mom cat if you gently pop the sac. I carefully pinched each with my thumb and pointer finger, being careful not to pinch the kitten.

Kittens can be born either head or rear feet first so don't worry if the kitten's legs are the first part out. The mom cat will have about 4 to 6 contractions about 10 minutes apart as she is birthing the kittens. I am not sure if cats have contractions much before giving birth because I was asleep all Saturday morning.

To help birth the kitten, gently ease it out of the mom cat as she is contracting. It also helps to stroke downward on her belly to encourage her to push the kitten out. The kitten should be fully out of her mom within about 15 minutes (about 2 to 6 sets of contractions). If it seems to be taking longer, contact a vet.

New mom cats can get very frightened by having kittens and enjoy being petted and comforted during delivery. Reyka purred while delivering her kittens, which seemed a bit odd.

## Step 3: Immediately After Delivery

When the kitten is first born she will often have trouble breathing. As soon as possible, start wiping off the kitten with a towel that has been slightly warmed in the microwave. Make sure to wipe off the nose and mouth well.

If the kitten's breathing is raspy, she may have fluid in her airways. You can help clear the fluid by holding the kitten between your hands with its entire body and neck supported. Then hold the kitten above your head and swing it down rapidly. Repeat this a couple times, and then wipe her nose and mouth again.

Keep stimulating and cleaning the kitten by rubbing her with the towel until she is breathing or mewing regularly. Then return her to her mom so she can feed.

## Step 4: The Placenta

The placenta is usually delivered right after the kitten. The kitten is attached to the placenta by its umbilical cord. You should begin the process of rubbing the kitten as soon as possible, even if the placenta is still inside her mom.

Some websites recommended breaking the umbilical cord immediately after the kitten is born, while the placenta is still inside the mom cat. I would highly recommend against this because the kitten's blood flows between the placenta and the kitten. Cutting or breaking the cord too early can result in excessive bleeding and may harm the kitten. It is best to care for the kitten with the placenta still attached.

In nature the cat will eat her kitten's placentas. You can let your cat do this if you want. Reyka only ate the first placenta and left the others. I don't really blame her.

For any placentas that your cat doesn't eat, you will want to eventually remove them. Blood flowing through the umbilical cord is bluish in color and is fairly obvious. Soon after the kitten is born, the blood should stop flowing through the placenta and the umbilical cord will turn white. At this point you can simply cut the umbilical cord about 1.5 inches from the kitten's belly and throw away the placenta.

If the placenta really grosses you out and you want to remove it sooner, tie the umbilical cord with the thread or dental floss about 1.5 inches from the kitten's belly. Then, using your thumb and forefinger, pinch and rub the cord until it breaks (this helps cut off the flow of blood).

Cutting the umbilical cord and removing the placenta should only be done when the kitten is breathing or mewing regularly and is in stable condition.

## Step 5: Repeat

Cats normally have 3 to 6 kittens so you may have to repeat this process a bit. Reyka had 4 kittens within 2 hours then had two more about an hour apart after that. You can put your hand on the mom's belly and try to feel for more kittens in between births.

After all the kittens have been born and are done feeding, you can move them into the kitten box. I moved all the kittens into the box and Reyka just followed them there.

## Step 6: Enjoy Your Kittens

Congratulations! You helped deliver kittens. Hopefully they were all born healthy and alive.

The mom cat still needs to eat kitten food until she is done nursing the kittens. The kittens don't really require any work on your part anymore and their mom can take care of them. The kittens are ready to adopt between 6 and 12 weeks depending on when they learn to eat solid food and use the litter.

REMEMBER: there are currently more cats and kittens than good homes for them. Please spay or neuter your cat! Reyka will get spayed and immunized after weaning the kittens.

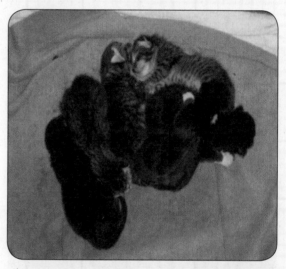

pets

pets

### Step 1: You've Found a Nest!

Rabbits' nests are generally well hidden and can turn up anywhere. The most common places are near bushes, trees, and tall grass. A rabbit's nest can be identified by its common construction of grass and fur. Tall grass is tightly woven into clumps of the mother's fur, providing insulation and camouflage. This covers the burrow underneath.

If you come across a nest under no special circumstances, the best thing to do is leave it be. Don't lift the cover to see the cute bunnies inside. Yes, baby rabbits are incredibly cute and fun to watch, but don't let that be a risk to their survival. If nothing looks out of the ordinary, do not disturb the nest.

### Step 2: Your Dog Found a Nest!

This is the most common occurrence in my experience. There are several identifying factors indicating your dog has discovered a nest:

She or he is very excited, running to the same spot over and over again.

Abnormally heavy panting. Loud screeching noises, often confused for a squeaker toy. (Baby rabbits sure have a major set of lungs, I once heard this cry for help when I was inside at the computer.)

Your dog has something in its mouth that seems odd, and is acting strangely about it.

You see an adult rabbit (the mother) frantically dashing about.

I will walk you through several scenarios.
**Your Dog has Something in its Mouth**

Immediately order your dog to drop it. Put force into your voice to tell the dog you mean business. If your dog is well trained, he or she will comply. If not, grab hold of your dog's nose and lower jaw. Gently force the mouth open and retrieve the rabbit. If someone else is present, have them take the dog inside. Walk over to the rabbit and check for any obvious signs of injury. This includes blood, broken bones, and intense squirming. If the rabbit is injured, immediately call the local vet or humane society. Unless you are a professional, any attempts to care for the wounded rabbit are futile.

### The Rabbit is Uninjured

I know what you're thinking. This cute, helpless baby rabbit is spooked, confused, and "homeless". I know, I'll raise it myself! Whatever you do, DO NOT TAKE THEM INSIDE! Any care you think you're giving could, and probably will, kill the rabbit. In fact, it is illegal to take in a young wild rabbit in most states. This will also cause the mother and captive baby to become frantic. This often results in the baby injuring itself.

Gently pick up the young rabbit. If you can, wrap it in a small towel. Don't be startled if the rabbit begins to rub and push its head against your fingers. It won't bite, it is simply trying to burrow into a less traumatic environment. The rabbit will probably be wet in places from your dog's saliva. Don't worry about this too much. The nest cannot be too far, you should find it within a few minutes. Gently place the rabbit back into its burrow and replace the cover.

### The Nest is Destroyed

If your dog found the nest, it is likely in disarray. Do your best to reconstruct the nest, it is vital to the rabbit's survival. If it is absolutely necessary, you can move the nest up to ten feet away. To do this, dig a shallow hole about as deep and wide as the original burrow. Gently pick up the rabbits and transfer them to the new nest. If possible, surround the nest with a bunny accessible fence to keep your dog away. Be sure to leave a gap large enough for the mother. Fences aren't foolproof, you will still need to keep an eye on your dog. Mine managed to trap itself inside the fence. Be extra cautious when the rabbits enter their exploring stage.

Do not worry, the mother will not abandon her young if your or your dog's scent is on it.

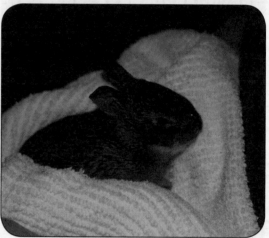

## Step 3: The Mother is Nowhere in Sight

Don't worry this is completely normal, mother rabbits are known to be absentee parents. During the day, the mother leaves the nest to feed and conceal the location to predators. At night or in the early morning, the mother will visit the nest for up to five minutes. The mother's milk is very nutritious and among the richest of all mammals. This provides enough energy to last the young all day. When she is finished nursing, the mother will leave the nest again.

There are several ways to check if the mother is returning to the nest. The first is to make a crisscross or tick-tac-toe pattern on the nest with grass. If this is disturbed in the morning, the mother has visited the nest. This doesn't always work though, the rabbits can enter and exit the nest without

pets

disturbing it much. It's best if you place it near the area you think is the entrance.

You can also place unscented baking soda near the nest and check for disturbances the next day. Also, once a day carefully remove the cover of the burrow. Look inside and check the condition of the rabbits. If they seem skinny, dehydrated, cold (no body heat), or are whining often, the mother is not returning. A sign of dehydration is a lack of "springiness" in the skin. If you gently pull on the skin around the back of the neck and it does not spring back, the rabbit is dehydrated. You should call your local vet or Humane Society if any of these signs apply. If the rabbits seem healthy, replace the cover and leave them be.

## Step 4: Lost Rabbit

On one occasion I came across a lost rabbit. This was back when the rabbits were inhabiting the fern. If you notice a young rabbit at least ten feet from the nest, take note of its location. If it hasn't moved in an hour or more, it is probably lost and confused. Gently pick it up and place it near the nest, not directly in it. Not too far though, place it directly on the edge or within an inch of the burrow. Make sure the nest is uncovered when you do so. If the rabbit runs into the burrow and snuggles in with its buddies, you've found the right nest. If not, it's best to place the rabbit back where you found it.

## Step 5: Truly Orphaned Rabbits

As I've had no experience in this field, I'll direct you to my resource. Again, make sure you KNOW for sure the mom was killed and the bunnies are abandoned (not warm, etc). You will not see the mom. Remember, the mom will only come back in the middle of the night to feed her babies. If the mom was killed, the best thing you can do for a wild orphaned baby bunny is to get in touch with a skilled rehabilitator. In the meantime, call your local humane society or animal control.

pets

# Turn Your Old CRT Computer Monitor into a Fish Tank!

By manderson76

Mike Anderson

(www.instructables.com/id/Turn-Your-Old-CRT-Computer-Moniter-Into-A-Fish-Tan/)

Talk about a great screen saver! I've been wanting to do this build for a while now. Just about every time I see an old CRT computer monitor by the side of the road on trash day I think to myself . . . that would sure make a cool looking fish tank. So here is my first attempt at turning an old computer monitor into a fish tank.

## Gather Your Materials
- an old CRT (Cathode Ray Tube) computer monitor
- Plexiglas (I use ⅛ inch)
- two part epoxy
- clear bathroom/kitchen grade silicone caulk
- paint for the background of the tank
- duct tape
- hot glue
- permanent markers
- expanding insulation foam
- safety glasses or face shield
- thick work gloves
- Hammer screwdrivers

190

- Utility knife
- rotary tool with cutting bit
- pliers
- speed square
- measuring tape, etc. . . . whatever works

## Step 1: Removing the CRT

I began by removing the old speakers attached to the side of the monitor by unscrewing two bolts on each side. I then promptly plugged them into my iPod. They worked great giving me amplified music to work by.

Next I removed four screws that held together the plastic housing, opened it up, and removed the monitors guts . . . very interesting stuff. The Cathode Ray Tube itself was attached to the very front of the plastic housing with four more metal screws that I, of course, removed (make sure you save all the mounting screws as you will need them later).

pets

## Step 2: Keeping the Curve

WARNING—the Cathode Ray Tube is in vacuum. Breaking the tube can be VERY DANGEROUS. If you are to attempt this please be sure to wear proper safety gear (eye protection/face shield, gloves, etc.).

When I began this I was really hoping to be able to simply cut/drill a hole in the top part of the CRT, clean out the inside, caulk the back where the cathode is, and then fill it with water. BOY WAS I WRONG. Long story short, there is a big metal screen inside the CRT and I cracked the glass beyond repair, but who knows, maybe I will try again sometime now that I have gotten a better look at the inside of the CRT.

Luckily, after my failed attempt at putting a fairly large hole in the CRT, the front of the tube was still not cracked. So it was up to me and Mr. Hammer to get rid of the excess glass.

Once the excess glass has been removed you will need to remove the metal screen. The metal screen can be removed by pressing down and over on the screen support clips.

Now that the metal screen is out the screen needs to be cleaned. I used some WD40 and an old T-shirt rag and it seemed to do the trick. Be careful; the stuff on the screen flakes off a lot and is probably not very good to breath in, so wear a mask and turn your shop-vac on to catch as much of the flake/dust as possible.

Next I went ahead and put some duct tape around the edge of the glass to soften the edge and keep it from biting me.

## Step 3: Plexiglas is Your Friend

Okay, so I decided to use the front of the glass CRT as the front of the fish tank and make the rest out of Plexiglas. Begin by measuring, measuring, and some more measuring. See what will fit inside your monitor. (Chances are that you will change these as you build, but you need to start somewhere right?)

When cutting Plexi you can score it deeply with a utility knife and then snap off the pieces. On the other hand, if you are fortunate enough to have a band saw, you can just measure, mark, and cut. In my experience, using other saws requires a special blade because otherwise the Plexi will splinter or crack. Anywho, measure, and cut out your pieces, then lay them out. I used some small pieces of duct tape and taped them together to see what it was going to look like. Remember, the front of your tank will be curved so the front of your Plexi should also have a curve to it. Try as best you can to match the curve of the glass. Once I had all the Plexi pieces cut and ready, I laid all the pieces flat, mixed up a batch of two part epoxy for plastics, and glued the three sides and the bottom together using a little duct tape to hold them in place while the glue set up.

191

## Step 4: Painting a Background

I did not want to look at the dull gray plastic of the inside of a computer monitor, so the next step I did was to paint on the OUTSIDE of the Plexi fish tank. I began by taking a silver Sharpie permanent marker and a speed square and I drew out some circuit board lines (again on the outside). I then took a green Sharpie to add some shadows under those lines. Finally I masked off the edges and spray painted the OUTSIDE with some cheap green spray paint (of course you could paint whatever you would like).

epoxy, spread it on the front edges of the plastic tank, as well as on the glass front, and then maneuvered the tank into place. I then put a few pieces of scrap wood inside to push against the plastic in order to bow the edges. This effectively curved the edges out to the edges of the monitor and then let it cure. While the epoxy was setting up I added some hot glue around the outside of the tank in an effort to fill gaps and to create a better fit.

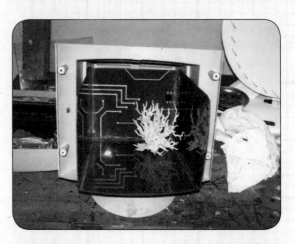

## Step 5: Access Panel

To make the access panel I used a rotary tool with cutting bit and carefully cut along the top edge of the top of the tank. This allowed it to be secured by slipping the already present tabs under the front part of the plastic monitor housing.

## Step 6: Attaching Plastic to Glass

After many test fits, I went ahead and mixed up a batch of two part multipurpose

## Step 7: Fill-er-up!

I felt it wise at this point to test fill the tank. Good thing too because it leaked! So

pets

now what? Well I first tried hot glue. . . It still leaked. Then, after searching my workshop, I found a partial tube of clear bathroom/kitchen grade silicone caulk. This seemed to do the trick, of course if you happen to have a tube of aquarium sealant that would probably work better. After a few more test fills and leak checks the tank was ready to be returned to the monitor housing.

## Step 8: Lighting

For lighting I picked up a small fluorescent bulb that fits into a regular light bulb socket. Also, after searching the basement I found an old heat lamp that I could use for the fixture. To keep the light bulb from falling in the water I cut a small piece of 2 inch PVC pipe, cut a groove in it for the light switch to fit, sanded one side, and then used some super glue to glue it to the underside of the access panel. The power cord for the light goes out the back of the computer just like the monitor power cord normally would. The tube for the bubbler worked in much the same way, with the tube coming out the back.

## Step 9: Water Support

Begin by returning the tank to the monitor housing and securing it with the screws you originally removed. Next make sure your lighting and air lines are in place. At this time it would be a good idea to fill the rest of the computer housing outside the tank with expanding insulation foam. When it cures this will not only insulate your new tank, but more importantly, it will support the weight of the water that the Plexi is attempting to contain. My concern here is that if there is no support under the plastic tank it may rip away from the glass front.

## Step 10: Finishing Up

Fill your new tank up with water, add gravel, rocks, fish, etc., plug in and enjoy. Extension ideas: Make a clear plastic hood to keep any water from splashing up to the light. Connect the light switch to the on button on the monitor.

# How to Build a Hermit Crab (or other small critter) Cage

By **samfelis** Sam Felis
(www.instructables.com/id/How-to-Build-a-Hermit-Crab-or-other-small-critter/)

This instructable will provide you with the details on how to build a hermit crab cage. If you're not a fan of hermit crabs, you could use it for hamsters. Or lizards. Or mice. Or . . . well, you get the idea.

The kids decided they wanted to get hermit crabs this summer, but when I saw the price of new cages at the boardwalk sea shell shops, I knew I could make them a larger cage much cheaper.

Hermit crabs require an environment with high humidity (70 to 80 percent). Although this mesh cage will not provide that environment, it will serve as temporary housing until a more suitable, permanent home can be found.

If you're interested in learning more about caring for your hermit crabs, take a look at one of the following sites:

http://hermit-crabs.com/
http://www.hermitcrabassociation.com/
http://www.crabstreetjournal.com/

## Ingredients

Here's what you'll need to build one like I did. If you want a bigger (or smaller) cage, adjust the size of your dimensions as necessary.

First and foremost, you need a plan. The old adage of "fail to plan, plan to fail" will bite you otherwise. Sketch out your cage from a couple of angles, labeling the pieces that you'll need to build. Be sure to use sizes that are mass produced and easily available at your local lumber yard, otherwise you'll be back at the drawing board.

The measurements below are based on standard size wood stock (but real measurements). For instance, the board that makes up the floor and back was sold as 1" × 12" even though it really measures ¾" × 11¼". I don't know why that is . . . maybe it's a vast wood industry conspiracy to confuse us or something.

Here's the list of materials (and the dimensions) for the cage I made:

### Materials

- ⅜" × 1½" × 18" (4) wood trim (2 front, 2 top)
- ⅜" × 1½" × 12" (2) wood trim (2 top sides)
- ⅜" × 1½" × 10 ¾ (4) wood trim (sides)
- ¾" × 1½" × 10" (4) wood vertical supports
- ¾" × 11¼" × 18" (2) wood floor, back
- 10" × 18" (2) wire mesh top, front
- 10" × 8¾ (2) wire mesh sides
- 2" hinges (2) (comes w/ screws)
- Hook and Eye (1 each)
- 6" length of chain (need a ¾" screw)

*The wire mesh was sold in a roll 72" long and 24" wide. This worked out perfectly as I was able to get the four pieces I needed cut with a minimum of waste.

### Tools

- jigsaw (a table saw could be used instead)
- miter sawdrill/bits
- wood glue staple gun (loaded with ¼" staples)
- sandpaper (fine grit)
- wire snips
- corner frame clamp (optional, but comes in handy when gluing the top frame)
- primer paint

## Step 1: Cut/Sand the Wood

Measure and mark the pieces you'll need before making your cuts. For the front and side trim pieces, as well as the vertical supports, you simply need to make a horizontal cut.

For the top frame pieces, however, you'll need to make angle cuts. Since the frame will be a rectangle, set your miter saw to cut 45 degree angles (or 135 degrees). Place all four boards in a stack and make a single angled cut on one end of the stack. This will ensure that the angles are complementary once you're done cutting. (Of course since all the cuts should be 45 degrees, they should be complementary by default, but just in case your miter saw isn't 100 percent accurate, making the cuts this way will ensure they'll fit together nicely.) This will make them fit much better than if you cut each one separately.

After the first cut, rotate the wood and cut the opposite end from the other side of the blade (e.g., if the majority of the wood was to the left of the blade for the first cut, place the majority of the wood to the right side of the blade for the second cut). Once you make the second cut, you'll have four pieces of wood that will fit together nicely.

After you've got all your pieces cut to length, use fine grit sand paper on the ends to remove any loose bits. Also, you might want to go over the rest of the wood with the fine grit sand paper as well to make it nice and smooth. This will help later when you paint your cage. (Sanding isn't required, but helps make a better looking end result.)

Cut the floor and back panel to length using your miter or table saw. If you're using a jigsaw, it's recommended that you clamp a straight edge to the wood so that the jigsaw has something to use as a guide. It's very hard to cut a straight line freehand and having the edge removes the need to straighten it later with a rasp and sandpaper.

Don't forget your safety goggles and hearing protection around power tools!

## Step 2: Glue the Wood

Once all the pieces have been cut, it's time to glue them together.

Lay a bead of glue along the back of the floorboard and press it against the piece of wood making up the back panel. If you have large enough clamps, go ahead and clamp the two pieces of wood together to get a solid seal. You should now have an L that, once dry, will stand on its own.

Before it dries all the way, you'll want to glue the four supports on. Glue the back two supports ⅜" from the side of the floorboard and abut against the back panel. Glue the two front supports ⅜" from the side and

³/₈" from the front of the floorboard. (The supports are offset by the thickness of the framing strips.)

Before the back, floor, and supports dry, glue the framing strips (so that you can ensure the framing strips are flush with the floor and back—not required but it gives a neater finished appearance). Glue the bottom strips first (in order to get a better bond, clamp the strips to the supports using your clamp of choice). Once the bottom strips are dry, repeat the process with the top strips. I found that by turning the cage over, the strips wouldn't slide down the supports.

For the top frame, you can either glue the pieces and hope for a tight seal or use a corner frame clamp. The downside of using a corner clamp is you need to wait for the pieces to dry before moving on to the next one. The upside is that you're going to get a better bond and a stronger overall frame.

While you could strengthen the bonds by adding some wood screws to the joints, I don't think it's necessary for hermit crabs. They're not going to be rocking the cage like other critters might.

## Step 3: Paint the Cage

Now that the glue has dried, it's time to paint the cage. Pick out a color scheme that you think your critters will enjoy. Or that you (or your kids) will enjoy. Or both. You can either use spray paint or a paint brush, although using spray paint will result in a smoother finish.

Prior to painting the cage, you should prime the wood so that it won't soak up the paint and require you to put on more than two coats.

Once the primer is dry, follow the instructions on the paint and paint the cage.

After the paint has dried, you may want to add a coat of shellac to seal the paint from any moisture sources you'll be adding to the cage (unless you're using high-gloss paint, which should be somewhat moisture resistant already).

## Step 4: Cut/Install Wire Mesh

After you've finished painting the cage, it's time to cut and install the wire mesh.

Measure the opening on the left side of the cage (or the right side, it doesn't matter) from top to bottom and front to back. If you followed my plan, it will be about 8" × 10" or so. You'll bend the wire so that you can staple it against the vertical supports, so make sure you add another ¼" to ½" on either side (so that it's ~9" × 10"). (The wire mesh in the materials list is sized correctly. If you're following this plan, simply cut them to size as listed in materials.)

Bend the mesh along the long side so that there is a row of squares making up the right angle.

This can be easily done if you place the wire mesh under a board (except for the edge to be bent) and then fold the wire up (using your hands—the wire is pretty malleable).

Do the same for the opposite side and then slide the mesh, with the bent portions touching each of the vertical supports so that the wire completely covers the opening.

pets

You may need to adjust it a little if the bend was too big (or too small).

Staple the mesh into place using your staple gun (remember eye protection!).

Repeat this process for the front and opposite side.

For the top frame, simply measure the interior of the frame, add ½" to the length and width and cut the mesh to size. Staple in place and you're ready to go. No bending is required for the top mesh.

I found it easier to deal with the wire mesh when it was cut as close as possible to each square (e.g., there were no "orphan" wires sticking out). This also makes for a cleaner finished product.

## Step 5: Add the Hardware

Once the mesh has been installed, you're ready to add the hardware. In this case it's a pair of hinges, a hook and eye latch, and a chain (to keep the top from opening too far).

For the hinges, it's important that you add them so that they'll support the frame evenly. I found it easier to put one side of the hinges on the cage first and then screw the frame onto the other side. You may have other ways of doing this, but, regardless of which way you do it, be sure to drill pilot holes

first! If you don't you run the risk of splitting the wood (especially on the top frame, which in my case was only ⅜" inch thick).

For the hook and eye, position the eye in the center of the front of the top trim and the hook in the center of the front of the front of the top frame. After drilling pilot holes, screw both the hook and eye into their appropriate places. You may need to bend the hook a bit to make the connection a little tighter.

Finally, attach the chain so that the lid will open to 120 degrees or so. This will allow you to open the cage and reach into it without having to use one hand to keep the lid open. Using a screw that's a tad bit shorter than the vertical support is deep (~¾"), attach one end of the chain into one of the vertical supports and connect the other end to the wire mesh on the lid.

## Step 6: Add the Critters and Decorate as Necessary

Now that you've finished your cage, it's time to add your critters and decorate their home to your heart's desire.

Watch out for the claws on the hermit crabs, though, they've been known to pinch!

Here I'll show you how to make a fake rock cave/basking spot for your reptile cage. This is one I've made for my Bearded Dragon, Viggo.

## Step 1: Design!

I made my original design months ago. The design has changed since then by the basic concept was a large cave, with a door allowing access to it from the outside, a basking spot above, and a ramp going up. PLAN AHEAD. I can't stress this enough. It will make things much easier for you. I used Google SketchUp to render a 3-D model, something I highly recommend for this project. Google SketchUp (or a similar program that might not be free) is an essential tool for any craftsman/

designer/builder and can be downloaded easily.

## Materials

- Styrofoam—free (this is trash, you can find it for free. It's used to pack all sorts of things. Try going to the back of an electronics store and asking if they've got any you can save from the landfills. I used a broken Styrofoam cooler and some odd packing bits.)
- Grout mix—$8.98 (I got a carton of sanded grout mix in HEMP color. The sanded leaves a rougher texture than unsanded. The hemp is a kinda dark gray color that already looks like rock. It gives a nice dark base color and could be used without coloration if you want)
- Cement Color—$4.96 (I used Terra Cotta. Mixed with the Hemp grout it gave a nice red rock color. This is a liquid color mix. You can also use powdered grout color mix. It's about a buck cheaper, but they were out of the color I wanted.)
- Great Stuff Expanding Foam Insulator—$5.00 (Trust me, this stuff will make things much easier and is well worth it)
- Water (To mix the grout)

pets

- Water Based Polycrylic Satin Sealer (Go for Satin, not as shiny as gloss and gives a more natural look. You'll need enough for 3 coats. A small can will probably suffice.)

## Tools

- Knives and hand saws (to cut Styrofoam and shape your cave)
- Hot Glue Gun and glue sticks (works great for gluing pieces together and it's safe. DO NOT USE SUPERGLUE. Superglue, or other such chemical glues will melt/eat through Styrofoam and give off toxic fumes)
- Bucket (for mixing grout in)
- 2 cheap bristle paint brushes (one for applying grout, one for sealer)

## Step 3: Start Building!

The best advice I can give you here is to actually work inside your viv. This helps you make sure it will fit, as well as gives you an idea of proportions. You wouldn't want to accidentally make it too large. Remember to leave some extra room around the edges. You don't want it to be a tight fit now because you still have to grout it. Start with a real rough cut, just laying things out. Don't glue anything down yet. It also helps if you can draw on the floors and wall of the viv to give yourself reference points for shape. If you don't actually want to mark your floor, lay down some newspaper you can draw on. Get your basic shape together. Don't worry about leaving holes and don't do any detail carving yet.

## Step 4: Glue

In order to get everything back the way you have it now, it really helps if you draw marks and lines onto your shape. Trace the outline of a piece onto the piece below it. Trace the bottom footprint onto the bottom of your viv or newspaper. Take off each layer and start gluing things down working from the bottom up. (Don't glue it to the floor!)

## Step 5: Expanding Foam!

This stuff is truly great. I guess that's why they call it "GREAT STUFF." Spray it in to fill in all those little holes and gaps. Use a little more in places you want it to build up. Leave it to expand and dry overnight.

## Step 6: CARVING!

Pull out your knife and saw and go to town! Time to get creative and let your artistic side show. What you're carving now will be the shape of the final piece. Remember, don't go into too fine detail. The layers of grout will fill in a lot of the small stuff completely. If you want it to show up, cut it deeper!

## Step 8: Paint!

I didn't paint mine, just used the cement color, but if you're gonna do that, now would be the time. Acrylic works best I hear.

## Step 9: Seal it

This is a very important step. Use a safe, low fume sealer such as water based polycrylic sealer if possible. Shellac also works well but will leave it shiny. I actually ran out of polycrylic so I used shellac inside the cave and on the bottom where it wouldn't be seen. Use your other brush and apply 3 coats of sealant, once again, making sure to get into every crack and crevasse. Once you've finished, let it air out for a few days, preferably with a fan blowing on it.

## Step 7: Grout!

Ok now, time to make this look like a rock, and not a big chunk of foam. Mix your grout. Don't mix it all at once. Leftovers will dry out while you're waiting between coats. Try using about ¼ of your grout per coat. I don't really have a set measurement for water, but you want it to be kinda thin and soupy. It will brush on easier that way. If you're using coloration, this would be the time to mix it in. Once you've got your soupy grout, start brushing it on. Make sure you get in all the cracks and crevasses, including the bottom. Let it dry overnight between coats. Apply 3 coats! This will ensure everything is covered and it will be nice and strong.

## Step 10: Enjoy!

Well, this step isn't so much for you as it is for your dragon, but hey, you can still sit back and enjoy looking at your handiwork.

pets

## in the
# garden

The garden is one place where you get out of it exactly as much as you put in. Take your skills to the next level with self-watering planters, recycled seed starters, and useful techniques for getting the most out of your green thumb.

# Hydroponics for Beginners

By **trebuchert03** Paul Jehlen
(www.instructables.com/id/
Hydroponics---at-Home-and-for-
Beginners/)

## Basic Intro

### What is Hydroponics?

Basically, growing plants without the use of a traditional dirt medium and using a nutrient rich water solution. Those mediums range from fiberglass to sand and from fired clay balls to nothing at all.

### How do I Get Started?

Well, you can buy a kit—but it's going to cost you . . . a lot. Or, you can improvise and create your own kit to suite your needs.

### What are my Options?

There are many different methods. NFT (nutrient film technique—stream a thin layer of nutrient solution over the roots) is common among professional kits along with ebb and flow (temporarily flood your root system and allow to drain). The most interesting method involves suspending your plants in mid-air and spraying the root system very frequently (a.k.a. aeroponics). Drip systems are also common and have its own advantages. There are MANY methods—all of which do not use dirt.

### What Method is Used Here?

By far the simplest and cheapest is a bubbler system. That is, keep your pots filled with your choice of medium just barely above your nutrient solution level—then keep the solution well aerated. The popping of the air bubbles will keep your medium moist.

### What Medium is Used Here?

I have used several different mediums in the past. Chopped rockwool, rockwool cubes/blocks/slabs, fired clay, and a combination of rockwool and fired clay. This system will work best with chopped rockwool (cubed) or fired clay (extra attention is needed if starting from seed with this medium).

### Cost?

I'm in college, so cost is very important to me. This can be a very cheap project if you collect parts slowly. I believe I have spent a total of $30 for new materials.

### Lastly, WHY HYDROPONICS?

Hydroponically grown foods not only taste better and are more nutritional, you can change the properties of your food, monitor what goes into your food, and pollute less. You can also grow more in less space.

## BOM—Bill of Materials

**Parts and Supplies**

- Opaque container that can hold water with lid (I am using an old 18 gallon storage bin)
- Mesh Pots (how many depends on what you're growing and the size of your container; I am using 6 5.25" pots, $9.90 for 6 heavy duty)
- Rockwool Growcube (chopped rockwool) $5.95 for three gallons
- Growing Solution (I have used Dyna-Grow brand 7-9-5 with excellent results, $12.95)

garden

- Aquarium air Pump (nothing special; already have/not using)
- Air Stone(s) and air hose ($3). See the start growing step for additional instruction
- Recommended but optional: Syringe, for making more precise measurements of growing solution ($2.60 for 60mL); construction tools: razor, knife, pencil, a compass would be nice.

### Step 1: Make a Home for Your Pots

Place your pots upside down on the top of your container lid. Now trace around each pot with a pencil making sure that no lines overlap. Now, if you have a compass, set it to the radius of the BASE of your pot. Eyeball the center of each circle (or measure if you prefer) and trace another circle inside the larger ones. Next, cut away the SMALL circle and cut perpendicular relief cuts up towards the larger circle. The idea is to push the pot down into the hole and the container lid will hold on tight making a better seal.

### Step 2: Aeration

My container has breather holes in the handles, so I plan on running my airline through there. You may wish to cut a hole in the top, side, or other location. It is not imperative where the hole is as much as it is functional. Keep in mind that you want to keep sunlight out of the container and keep rainwater OUT. Prep your air stone(s) as per the instructions on the packaging (typically rinsing and a water soak). Please use new stones to avoid introducing contaminates.

Connect your air stone(s) to your air line and connect to your aquarium pump.

### Step 3: Sterilization

Now, fill your container with water. I am assuming your container is clean and free of debris. Fill to the brim and then ADD 1 TABLESPOON of CHLORINE BLEACH. This is very important as it will kill most intruders you don't want hanging around to cause trouble. Begin aeration to mix your sterilization solution—put your pots in the container too. After about 20 to 30 minutes, dump all the water and then allow to air dry completely to get rid of the chlorine.

### Step 4: Initial Fill

Follow the directions on your nutrient solution bottle. My directions call for 2 to 3 teaspoons per gallon for RECIRCULATING systems and 1 teaspoon/gallon for bag systems. The reason is nutrient toxicity (more on that later). I will treat this as a bag system with a little more.

When filled to the proper level, my container will be holding about 15 gallons of water. So that requires 15 teaspoons of concentrate. Converting to CCs (the graduation on my syringe), that's about 73cc. I will be adding 80cc of concentrate solution.

So, fill your container with water, begin aerating, and then add the proper MEASURED amount of nutrient concentration. At this point, your garden should be where you want it as water is pretty heavy, this goes double for larger systems.

of nutrient solution. Completely soak the medium.

While the medium is soaking, wash off all of the dirt from your plants. ALL of it—but take care not to damage the root system. Place a little bit of growing medium in the bottom of a pot, then place the plant in and fill the pot with your medium.

Put the lid on your container, and press the pot into an open hole. Repeat for the rest of your plants.

## Step 5: Introducing Plants and Prepping Medium

I will be buying plants that have already started. I want to grow herbs to start off as I love having them fresh for cooking. So obtain your plants. If you will be starting from seeds, read the next step.

### A Special Note about Rockwool

Rockwool is made from fiberglass . . . so precaution must be taken. Wear a dust mask while handling and, as instructed, soak the medium in water. Water keeps the fibers bound together which further reduces any inhalation risk. The risks involved are no more than handling fiberglass insulation or accessing an attic with fiberglass insulation—just wear a mask.

Using a pot, scoop out pots of growing medium. Rockwool will shrink a little, so add a little more—you do not need this for fired clay. If you have 6 pots, take 6 potfulls of medium and put it into a large bucket, bowl, etc. Fill this bowl with water and estimate how many gallons you added. Then measure off the appropriate amount

## Step 6: Starting From Seed

If the last step applied to you, you can skip this step or just read it for your information. This requires extra materials—mainly rockwool seed cubes and a method to germinate. But basically, you're going to soak the cubes, drop in a few seeds, and then place in your pots with the main media. Be sure that you can see the top of the seed cube. NEVER put a seed into a dry cube as the dry glass could damage your seed(s). You're going to need to

garden

water by hand to ensure the seed gets the loving it needs. You may want to place a hood over the pot to make the conditions better.

## Step 7: Maintenance

Every other week, you need to replace your nutrient solution. Otherwise, the water will become toxic to the plant and it will stunt its growth or cause death. Larger operations don't do this as they have adequate filtering and methods of removing toxins generated by the plants; we don't have this. Besides, the plant is going to soak in those nutrients thus removing it from the water anyway.

Monitor your fluid levels in between water changes. If the water gets too low, go ahead and top it off.

When you first start, you want to keep the water level just above the base of the pot. The root system will works its way down into the container (out of the pot) and into the water. When this happens, lower the water level slightly (about an inch below the pots) and make sure to keep aeration going. Aeration prevents the root system from becoming "too wet" and having some of the root system exposed to air helps.

## Step 8: Options

### So What Else Can You Add On or Do?

Well, when you're ready, I recommend adding a water level gauge—basically just a clear hose that connects at the bottom of the container and goes vertical to show the maximum level.

Want to grow indoors? You're going to need a grow light—this adds a considerable amount of cost but it may be the only option for those of you in very cold regions.

A simple valve placed at the bottom of the reservoir can make draining much easier. If you can drain into a bucket, you can use this on other plants in your area.

It is a good idea to monitor pH levels and conductivity of your water solution.

## Step 9: Lighting

I do not own a lighting system. I wish I did, but they can be quite expensive as these are very specialized systems. Regurgitating. . . .

What kinds of lighting are used for growing plants?

Most applications use HID (High Intensity Discharge) lights. All HID systems require both a ballast and a bulb in addition to the socket and reflector. You can also use a T5 High output fluorescent bulb which blends the light spectrum. You can use regular T12 fluorescent bulbs for smaller seedlings and cuttings.

**T5?**

There are two types of T5 bulbs—one for blooming and one for growing. Compared to their HID counterparts, they use less heat and all of the spectrum output is used by the plant. The ballast works for both types of bulbs.

**HID?**

There are three main types of HID: Metal Halide (MH), Mercury Vapor, and High Pressure Sodium (HPS). For growing, only MH and HPS are used.

**What do I Need for HID?**

If you're growing leaf/bushy plants (lettuce, greens, herbs), you want MH all the time. For plants with a vegetative and bloom phase (i.e. tomato, flowering annuals, fruits), you want to start with a MH and then switch to HPS while the plant flowers and starts producing fruit. If all you're doing is supplementing natural light, use HPS.

**What if I Can only Afford One Light System?**

Here are a few options:

1. Use a MH system for growth and then an HPS conversion bulb for flowering.
2. Use HPS for flowering and a MH for growth.
3. Buy a standard system and upgrade to an enhanced color corrected bulb. Most go for an HPS system because of the higher lumen output per watt compared to its MH counterpart.
4. Buy a switchable system where the ballast can support either type of bulb
5. Use a T5 system with cool spectrum lamps and warm spectrum for flowering.

*garden*

# Vertical Vegetables

By **pippa5** Phillippa Temple
(www.instructables.com/id/
VERTICAL-VEGETABLES-quotGrow-
upquot-in-a-smal/ )

This Instructable explains how to solve the problem of cats digging and toileting in the vegetable patch so that you can grow veggies in a very small garden. I needed a solution and the answer occurred to me after watching The Chelsea Flower Show on TV and seeing walls of flowers and herbs. The only thing I had to hand was a hanging pocket shoe organizer and I decided to use it to grow my plants in.

## Materials Needed
- Hanging pocket shoe organizer
- Pole and attachments (curtain pole or pipe fittings, screws)
- Strong metal saucepan or utensil hanging hooks
- Compost of a good quality moisture holding type.

- Selection of plants or seeds. (e.g. mixed leaf salad, herbs, sorrel, peas, mini tomatoes.
- Piece of wood 2" x 2" as long as the width of the pocket store to keep the base of pockets away from the wall.
- Trough planter to catch drips.

## Step 1: Attach Pole to Shed or Wall

I attached a strong chrome pole with metal fittings to the shed.

You could use a curtain pole.

Make sure it is at the correct height especially if you want to grow plants in a trough below (see step 7). This uses the surplus water from the pockets above.

## Step 2: Attach Hanging Shoe Organizer

Use strong hooks or wire to attach the shoe organizer. They must be strong enough to support the weight of the compost, plants, and water.

## Step 3: Test Drainage

Pour water into the pockets to check the drainage, if they don't drain then make a few small holes in each of the pockets.

## Step 4: Fill Each Pocket with Compost

Add a good moisture retaining compost, fill to 1" below the rim so that water does not pour out over the rim.

garden

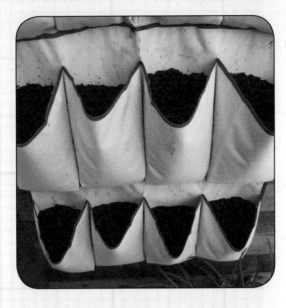

## Step 5: Add Plants or Seeds

Sow seeds or add seedlings. I suggest herbs like thyme, sorrel, chives; salad lettuce like leaf, mustard, cut and come again, or spinach; minibel tomatoes; and petit pois peas.

## Step 6: "Drip Aid"

Use a piece of wood to make sure the excess water drips into the trough below.

## Step 7: Maintaining a Healthy Hanging Veggie Plot

- Water slowly with a gentle flow, or you could wash soil and plants out of the pocket, dirtying the crop below. Add water retaining crystals to the compost. Hint: Add water to some crystals in a container and allow them to swell then add that to the compost and fill your containers. Otherwise when the crystals swell they can grow so much that they push the compost, seeds, and plants out!
- Plants like tomatoes will need regular tomato fertilizer (and slow release granules) as the fertility of the compost will soon get exhausted. Do not over pick salad leaves, so the plant re-grows. It is important to keep a look out for aphids, slugs, caterpillars, and other pests. Remove diseased, infected, or damaged leaves and compost them. Remove unproductive plants and compost them. When reusing pockets add some fresh compost.

**garden**

207

## Growing Avocado Plants from Seed

By AlissaSueK

(www.instructables.com/id/Growing-Avocado-Plants-From-Seed/)

You'll need: avocado seeds, toothpicks and jars for the water method, dirt, gravel, and pots (or the ground).

### Step 1: The Seed—Water Planting

The particular seed I worked with had sprouted inside of the avocado before I had even eaten it. Be careful to not cut any deep gouges when removing the seed.

If you are using the toothpick method, stick three toothpicks in the side of the seed about halfway down. You want half of the avocado to be under water. Set it on the rim of a glass or jar and fill it up.

Refill the water as it evaporates and keep the avocados in a bright window or outside. They will begin to sprout anywhere from a few days to several months. One avocado seed took three months to get going, but I've never had a seed not sprout eventually. When roots begin to fill the glass, transplant the whole deal carefully in a pot.

### Step 2: The Seed—Dirt Method

The dirt method is just as simple. If you are using a pot, put a little gravel or some pebbles in the bottom for excellent drainage. Avocados love water but they do not like soggy soil. Leave the top of the seed a little above the soil.

Soon enough your plant will be sprouting.

### Step 3: To Prune, Or Not to Prune

As they grow, some people recommend pruning the top bunch off to create a bushier plant. If you plan on keeping the plant inside (avocados make great houseplants!) you may want to do this to keep the size reasonable and to have a more attractive plant.

### Step 4: Watering & Enjoying

I was lucky enough to come across three Fuerte avocados (the most delicious, in my opinion). Although they can take several years to produce fruit, IF they ever do. I am keeping a watchful eye on these three plants in hopes they someday will. Avocados need a good watering, but do not like being watered small amounts daily. It is best to thoroughly soak the soil and then only water it again when it is beginning to dry. I've stuck to watering them every other day (or less). Watch your leaves carefully!.

# Eggshell Seed Starters

By NaturalCulture
(www.instructables.com/id/Eggshell-Seed-Starters/)

These biodegradable eggshell planters are perfect for starting seeds! When the plants get too big for the shells, you can transplant them straight to the soil, shell and all.

## Materials

You will need:

- Eggshells
- Egg carton
- Potting soil & spoon
- Awl/needle/pin—anything long and sharp
- Knife
- Seeds
- Optional: Pot & stove, spray bottle, egg cups/miniature clay pots for display

## Step 1: Prepare the Eggshells

If you eat eggs, then save the eggshells when you use them. If you don't eat eggs, ask a friend to save the shells and carton for you.

Carefully crack the top third of the egg. You can do this by tapping the egg on the edge of a bowl, or tapping with a sharp knife.

Empty out the eggshells completely.

Wash the eggshells out well. Optional step: If you are concerned about salmonella on the eggshells, put the empty eggshells in a pot of boiling water for a few minutes.

## Step 2: Add Drainage

Take the empty eggshell, and poke a hole in the very bottom with your sharp object. If you are using a thin needle or pin, widen the hole a bit with a pushpin or small nail. This hole provides drainage, so the roots of your plant don't drown. You only need to poke one small hole; more than one might crack the shell.

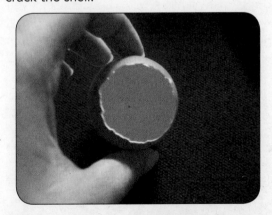

## Step 3: Add Potting Soil

Using a small spoon, fill the eggshell with moist potting soil. Optional: If the potting soil is dry, spray it with water from a spray bottle as you fill the eggshell.

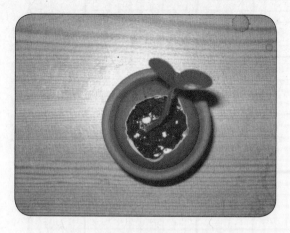

## Step 4: Add Seeds

Think about the amount of light you have available in your home and garden, and use seeds that will thrive in these conditions. Plant your seeds according to directions. The seed package will tell you how deep to plant the seeds, or you can find this information online. If you want quick results, try beans or cucumbers, they usually sprout in a few days. For bonus points, use seeds that you saved from last year's crop instead of buying seeds. Oh my goodness, seeds are AMAZING!

## Step 5: Display Your Green Treasures!

Carton: After you have planted the seeds, you can simply put the eggshell planters back into the carton. The carton provides a stable base with room for drainage, is freecycled and looks cute. Clay pots: You can get miniature clay pots, or use eggcups to display the planters. Mini Greenhouse: If you want to keep your seedlings extra snug and promote faster growth, you can make them a greenhouse out of a pop bottle.

## Step 6: Care for Your Plants

Put your completed planters in a sunny spot, and mist them daily with water so that the soil stays moist. For easier care, you can build a simple greenhouse out of a plastic bottle. I did this with mine and it worked amazingly well. When the plants grow too big for the shells, gently crack the shells and plant them straight into the garden or a bigger pot. The shell will eventually biodegrade, and the roots will grow out of the shell. The shell also supplements the calcium in the soil.

garden

# How to Grow Pineapples

By woofboy111

(www.instructables.com/id/How-to-Grow-Pineapples/)

Pineapples are wonderful fruit. Not only are they delicious, but they are also very easy to grow. All you really need to start growing your own pineapple farm is a pineapple and some dirt (and a pot if you live in a colder climate).

## Step 1: Obtain a Pineapple . . .

Go to wherever you like buying fruit from whether it be a supermarket, farmers' market, or from a guy selling fruit on the side of the road. Buy a nice looking pineapple. Make sure it's nice and ripe. Take the fruit home, and move on to the next step.

## Step 2: Cut and Eat

Take your pineapple home with you. Rinse the fruit off, and then place it on its side on a cutting board. Take a knife and cut off the leafy top part of the pineapple, along with an inch or two of the pineapple's meat. Set this aside while you proceed to eat the rest of the pineapple.

## Step 3: Figure Out Where to Plant Pineapple . . .

Your leftover pineapple top from the previous step is all you need to grow a pineapple. A pineapple is a fruit, so therefore it can produce seeds, but from what I understand seeds are rare in domesticated pineapples. I've personally never gotten any seeds in any of my store bought or home grown pineapples. Because of the lack of an overflowing supply of seeds, using the cutting from the top of an eaten pineapple is the ideal way to go.

For the planting itself, I have found that putting the pineapple top directly into the ground works best.

If you live in a warmer climate, you can plant your pineapple directly into the ground. Where I live, there is an occasional frost each winter, but that's about the worst of the cold weather. My pineapple plants handle that just fine. If your winter weather is any worse than the occasional freeze, plant your pineapple in a pot where you can take it inside.

When you pick out a spot (or pot) for your pineapple, make sure it has room. The plants grow to about five feet across and get spiny leaves, so take that into consideration when deciding where you plant your pineapple.

## Step 4: Plant Your Pineapple

Once you have decided where to plant your pineapple, dig a hole in the dirt. The hole only needs to be deep enough to cover the fruit still attached to the pineapple's leaves. Place the pineapple in the hole, and cover with dirt, leaving the pineapple leaves exposed above ground. If you're planting in a pot rather than the ground, the same applies with the only difference being that your dirt is contained within the pots walls.

garden

211

### Step 5: Water and Forget . . .

Once your pineapple is in the dirt, water the plant. If you are growing your pineapple in the ground, you can basically forget about it for a while. Pineapples are very low maintenance plants. After the initial plantings, I never go out of my way to purposely water my pineapple plants. It can't hurt if you do water your pineapple plants more often than when it rains, but the plants definitely won't die if you forget to water them every few days. My plants have lived several years with this let-them-be attitude and are now on the third season of producing fruit.

### Step 6: Wait . . .

Pineapple plants grow slowly. After about a year, you will definitely notice the growth in your plants. It took somewhere between 2 to 3 years for my plants to start producing fruit. The fruit will start forming in the center of the pineapple plant. It starts out looking like a large bright red and yellow flower. The flower eventually transforms into the normal looking pineapple fruit that everyone is familiar with.

### Step 7: Harvest

Let your pineapples get ripe on the plant. They taste better that way, rather than the store bought pineapples that get ripe on the shelves. When the outside skin of the pineapple starts changing from brown to yellow, go outside with a saw and cut through the stalk supporting the pineapple. Take the pineapple inside and enjoy eating your home grown fruit. Enjoy it, and save the top so when you're finished you can make your pineapple plants multiply.

If you are out of town frequently or have your hands too full to keep up with plant watering, this is an easy solution. Make your own Self Watering Window Boxes.

## Gather your Supplies

You will need:
- 24" plastic window box liner
- 24" galvanized cage wire
- a small submersible water pump
- 4' of vinyl hose sized to match the diameter of your water pump nozzle
- Potting Soil
- Plants
- Plumbers Putty
- Two pieces of felt
- a Dremel with your smallest drill bit
- Scissors
- Wire Cutters
- Automatic Timer

A note about the water pump: Water pumps are rated based on how high they can lift the water and how many gallons per hour they can pump. This water pump will only need to lift the water a few inches and won't be required to cycle lots of gallons of water. The tiniest water pump you can find will probably suffice.

## Step 1: Cut and Fold the Cage Wire to Create the Support

CAUTION: Cutting the wire can result in some sharp edges. You may wish to wear leather gloves and safety glasses for this step.

Using your wire cutters, cut a piece off the spool of cage wire that is 12" wide. Then trim this piece down lengthwise so it is 12" × 21". Gently press the cage wire until it is flat. Fold the edges down 3" from edge. Once folded, the piece of cage wire should sit nicely in the bottom of the window box liner. Test fit it in place and keep shaping the wire as needed. If you are planting a plant that needs a trellis support, cut your cage wire piece to be 25" × 21". Fold the extra 13" vertically.

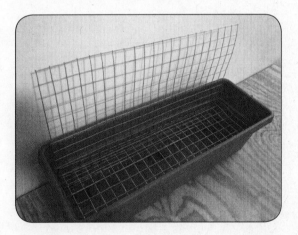

## Step 2: Drill Holes in the Tubing for Water Circulation

Time for some Dremel action! Layout your tubing and drill holes with the Dremel about every inch or so. Once the holes are in place, plug one end of the tubing with Plumbers Putty. Attach the hose to the water pump.

## Step 3: Set up the Pump

The pump has four little suction cup feet on the bottom. Wet them and adhere the pump to the bottom of the window box liner. Once the pump is in place, replace the cage wire support and run the tubing up through it.

## Step 4: Lay in the Felt and Set up the Tubing

Lay the two felt pieces on top of the cage wire support. Cut a hole for the tubing and the power cord to come through. The tubing will lie on top of the felt. The felt will act as a support for the soil. It will allow excess water to drain back into the reservoir without letting the soil pass through.

## Step 5: Test out Your Handiwork

The area under the felt and cage wire support will act as a large water reservoir. Fill the bottom of the window box liner with water. Testing out your water circulation system could get a little wet, so protect your workspace.

Be careful not to get the power cord plug wet while you are adding the water. Make sure there is nothing around that would be damaged if it gets wet accidentally. Plug in your pump to test out your new system!

If the water is circulating nicely, Congrats!

If some of the holes aren't letting water through, unplug the pump, and re-drill the holes a little bigger.

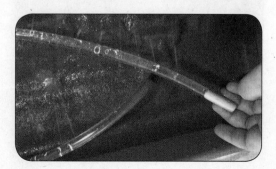

## Step 6: Add Dirt and Plants

Once you know your water pump and water line are circulating water, it's time to add dirt and plants.

The tubing will get buried in the dirt so it delivers water directly to the roots of your plants.

## Step 7: Next Steps . . .

Once every week or so add a gallon of water to keep the water reservoir filled. Pour the water into a corner so it won't drown your plants and will just drain down into the reservoir. You may wish to add some fertilizer to the water supply to give your plants a boost. There are lots of liquid fertilizers available at www.hydrofarm.com. For super easy plant maintenance, consider plugging your water pump in with a automatic timer.

Set the timer to come on for fifteen minutes once each day. This should be enough to water the plants, while allowing the excess water to drain back into the water reservoir. If it's not warm enough for your window box to go outside yet, add a grow light. Set it on a timer to come on for 16 hours each day.

garden

# How to Keep a House Plant Alive

By **growerman**
(www.instructables.com/id/How-to-keep-a-house-plant-alive/ )

Keeping plants alive indoors can prove next to impossible to some, but it really isn't all that hard to do. Plants need light, water, support, nutrients, and an adequate air supply. Like anything in this world, an excessive amount of any one thing is often a bad thing, even if that substance is necessary for survival. Just because you think your plant might want more of something, doesn't mean you are doing your plant any good.

## Step 1: Try to Figure Out What Your Plant is Called

Each plant will have a common name, and a Latin name. For the most part, knowing the common name should allow you to find the growing requirements of your plant. Latin names are often better, as they are universal. These names will only help you find extra information on how to grow each specific plant, and how to correct any problems that may occur.

## Step 2: Give it the Light it Needs

The amount of light a plant receives inside a home is almost always the single greatest reason why a plant does not grow.

Various plants will need various levels of light. They have grown accustomed to differing levels of light through evolution. Plants receive the energy they need to survive from light—mainly the red and blue wavelengths of light (the reason why plant lights give off a bluish-purplish light).

For those of us in the northern hemisphere, the sun is always to the south. This means that south-facing windows will let the most sunlight into the home. Most plants will appreciate being placed right in front of a window (A south-facing window is best).

It is not just light intensity that matters—the duration of light is also important. Try to give your plants a whole day's worth of sunlight. That being said, if you have no windows facing somewhat-south, you are at a clear disadvantage. You should get them as close to their light source as possible. Interior plants that receive light through a north-facing window may need supplemental light. Turn on a fluorescent light bulb to simulate day time. Get the bulb as close to the plant as possible, without the plant being overheated by it or touching it directly.

Plants also need darkness to survive. This is how they have evolved. Give them at least a couple hours of darkness every night if possible. If you aren't using a room at night, turn the lights off to give the plants some darkness. This is better for the environment anyway. 12-hours light, 12 hours darkness, is a good rule of thumb to follow. One does not have to follow this exactly. Plants tend to flower and produce fruit when a certain day length is met, and held constant for a period of time. Each plant will be different.

Leaves that develop under any particular lighting condition will contain a particular amount of chlorophyll that will be most beneficial in that light intensity. If a plant is moved from a low-light situation to a high light situation, the leaves that developed under low light will soon become burned, and or bleached out.

On the other hand, if the plant is moved into a darker area, any dark green leaves that developed under high light intensities will be sacrificed by the plant, only to be replaced by leaves better suited for the plant's new environment.

A plant must be acclimatized to its new environment. Simply put, ease the plant into any dramatic change in its environment. Increase the light levels gradually, and not all at once.

## Step 3: Watering

Plants need water, just as every other discovered organism on earth does. Drowning a plant isn't a good thing, and leaving it high-and-dry isn't all that good for it either.

A good way to accurately and efficiently find out when your plant needs more water is to keep an eye on the soil. When the soil looks dry, just stick your finger in it. If the soil is dry in the first couple centimeters, is it probably time to give the plant more water. If your finger comes up with a little water on it, your plant is probably fine.

Try not to water your plants while the sun is shining on them. Any water droplets on the leaves will act like tiny magnifying glasses. If the light hitting the water droplets is strong enough, the leaves may actually be burned.

Some plants like their soil to be continually damp, and some plants like the soil they grow in to dry out a little in between watering.

How much water do you give it?

Saturate the soil. Pour water into the soil slowly, so that water is moved throughout the soil before exiting the bottom of the pot. If you do this correctly, the soil will be thoroughly and adequately watered by the time water comes out the bottom of the pot. Keep watering (slowly) until a little water comes out the bottom of the pot. A good rule of thumb is about $\frac{1}{10}$ of the water you put in should flow out the bottom of the pot.

Water quality is very important! If you have a lot of dissolved minerals and salts in your water, the soil will eventually absorb these minerals and salts, and will be injured by them.

Rain water is an excellent source of water for your plants. Any rain that flows off the roof will be fine. A rain barrel is a worthy investment!

## Step 4: The Kind of Soil

Soil from out in the natural environment will not be a good potting soil. The moment the soil is ripped out of the landscape, the natural soil profile is destroyed, and water will not flow through it as it did out in the natural environment. Soil from outside will often compact too much when used as a potting soil, and it will hold water too tightly, leading to overwatering, among other things.

garden

Potting soil found in bags at the store will suffice for most plants.

You can make your own soil-less potting soil as well. Sphagnum peat moss, coconut coir, perlite, vermiculite, and concrete-grade sand, and bits of pine bark are all good to use as ingredients for a potting mix. If you want to make some of your own, you are going to want to buy the ingredients in bulk, as it is a lot cheaper than way.

A Few Recipes Include:

- 1 part Sphagnum peat moss, 1 part vermiculite
- 1 part coconut coir, 1 part sphagnum peat moss, ½ part perlite, and ½ part vermiculite
- 3 parts pine bark, 1 part sand, and 1 part sphagnum peat moss
- 1 part soil, 1 part sand, and one part sphagnum peat moss.

Each one of these formulations provide different growing conditions for your plant.

Dry sphagnum peat moss is notoriously difficult to get wet. To combat this problem, just put the sphagnum peat moss, or sphagnum peat moss containing mix in a water-proof container with some water. Shake the container around a while. Warm water will speed up the process.

You can also microwave the container as long as the container is glass, or recyclable number 5. The steam will quickly infiltrate the moss. Just remember to let the mix cool before you put a plant in it.

The soil provides the plant with support, while giving it access to adequate amounts of air, water, and nutrients.

## Step 5: Fertilizer

If your plant is actually growing, it will eventually need fertilizer. It is hard to judge whether your plant needs fertilizer or not, but there are certain things that remain constant.

For the most part, your plant won't need as much fertilizer (if any) during the winter months, as the temperature indoors is most likely cooler, and the light source isn't as bright. Cooler temperatures and dimmer light sources lead to slower growth rates. Plants don't need as much nutrients when their growth has slowed down to a crawl.

There are 17+ elements that are utilized in the plant—17+ elements that are required for normal growth and development.

89% of a plant's weight is made out of elements supplied by water and $CO_2$.

The other 11% of a plant's weight is supplied by elements supplied by fertilizer, organic matter, or elements already in the soil.

There is almost always a set of three numbers written on any fertilizer package. The first number is the percent of nitrogen in the fertilizer. The second number is the precent of P205 (a compound containing Phosphorous) in the fertilizer. The third number is the percent of K20 (a compound containing Potassium) in the fertilizer. Nitrogen, phosphorous, and potassium are 3 macronutrients (elements needed in high quantities by the plant). Nitrogen and potassium are needed in much larger quantities than phosphorous. There are benefits and downfalls of each form of nitrogen commonly used in fertilizers.

garden

The other three elements that are needed in large quantities (besides carbon, oxygen, and hydrogen) are magnesium, calcium, and sulfur. These may or may not be supplied by the fertilizer. It is generally good to use a fertilizer containing these three elements as well (don't look too hard. . . .) Epsom salts found at almost every grocery or drug store will supply magnesium and sulfur.

Fertilizers are sold either as slow-release fertilizers, or quick-release fertilizers.

Slow release fertilizers are generally coated in a material of varying thickness that breaks down over time to release the tiny fertilizer pellets inside over a period of a few months.

Quick-release fertilizers are water soluble fertilizers that are immediately available to the plant. These fertilizers can easily damage the plant if over-applied. If you are unsure of how much fertilizer to use, it is better to apply a weak fertilizer solution than one that is too strong. If one chooses to use quick-release fertilizers, I would recommend diluting the fertilizer and adding the diluted fertilizer to the water normally used to water the plant, thereby fertilizing the plant every time it is watered. This is called fertigation (fertilization plus irrigation).

Organic matter is the alternative to commercial fertilizer.

This is one way you can easily supply all the elements (besides the input of $CO_2$ and water) a plant will need to grow. Compost or grind up plant scraps, weeds, or lawn clippings. These plants gathered all the necessary nutrients in the correct quantities for you!!!

Do not use plants as fertilizer that have been sprayed with herbicides. They may still contain residues of these herbicides, leading to the death of anything you that you fertilize with these herbicide-sprayed plants.

You may have heard of and/or bought the fancy organic fertilizers that contain kelp or seaweed. Well, if you live anywhere near the water, pick your own—it's free! Wash the plants off though, especially if they grew in salt water.

The cooled water left over from cooking vegetables is also a safe source of a number of different nutrients. Water the plants as you would otherwise.

## Step 6: Potting/Repotting

Actively growing plants will need to be repotted eventually.

If you want to check if they do or not, gently slip/shake/wiggle the plant out of its pot (soil still on roots). If the roots are wrapping around the pot, it is most likely time to repot. If the pot is literally deformed by the roots, it is also time to repot.

Roots have little single-celled hairs that grow on them. These are called root hairs. The root hairs suck up most of the water and nutrients that the plant needs. They are extremely delicate. Disturb the roots as little as you can. Trying to find these root hairs will most likely rip them all off. Don't do this.

Choose a pot that is slightly larger than the original root ball or pot. Do not double the size of the pot each time you repot, as most potted plants do not like this. Plants react differently when they are potted as compared to outside in the soil.

A good pot must have drainage holes. The size of the drainage hole isn't really all that important of an issue. As long as the pot has a hole that is large enough to let excess water exit, without vast amounts of potting soil falling out with it, it is fine.

Always wet the potting soil before you add the plant to it, and also after the plant is potted up again. This will reduce the shock of having some root hairs ripped off during the potting process.

garden

The original soil surface should remain the soil surface after repotting. Do not bury the plant any further down than it was originally—keep it level with the original soil surface.

Placing a little soil on the bottom of the pot before placing the plant into its new container is always a good idea. Make sure the soil in the pot and the bottom of the soil/root ball make good contact. Large air bubbles in the soil should be avoided.

Also, do not fill the entire pot full to the brim with soil/plant. Leaving a little space will make it easier to water the plant (less overflow).

Tall pots drain better than short pots. This is due to gravity, and the weight of the water on itself. Try holding a wet sponge vertically as compared to horizontally.

Anything semi-rigid to rigid will do for a pot, keeping in mind the depth of the container. All the pot needs is a few small holes in the bottom. Try digging through the recycling.

## Step 7: Air Supply

Plants need air. They take in $CO_2$, and spit back out oxygen, but they need both in order to remain healthy. One reason why terrarium plants seem to decline over time is the $CO_2$ content in the air. After a certain amount of time, the $CO_2$ in the terrarium will be exhausted unless proper ventilation is supplied.

If you happen to be growing plants in a large soda bottle (hopefully clear plastic, not green), the plants growing inside it will appreciate it if you unscrew the cap for a while. Breathing into it will replenish the $CO_2$ levels inside the terrarium as well. You should unscrew the cap at least once every couple of days.

Air flow will also help reduce disease. If you want a terrarium plant to last a while, try installing a small computer fan into the wall of the terrarium, or even inside the terrarium (be aware that humidity might reduce the life of the fan). It does not need to run on high, but just enough to circulate the air.

Plants in windy conditions will grow more compact, and sturdier than plants grown in a complete absence of wind.

garden

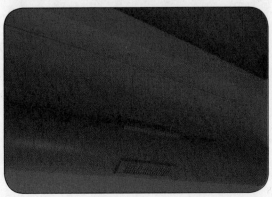

I use the tray watering system for my carnivorous plants, but had lots of trays and pots all over the place. It was tricky to get the amount of water in every tray right, and the rate of evaporation was different, so it required frequent monitoring. Also, larger trays gave better humidity around the plants than smaller trays. I was at the lumber store and spotted some free wooden pallets, and hit on the idea of using a pallet to make a tray for my carnivorous plants. With some pond liner to seal it, I made a nice wide tray with a consistent depth, humidity, and easy maintenance, and it looks tidy too.

## Materials
- wood pallet—free from lumber store
- saw
- hammer
- pond liner from pet shop. See step 5 for size.
- extra boards (optional)
- extra nails (optional)

## Step 1: Take the Boards and Nails from the Pallet

We'll only be using half of the pallet in this tutorial, so start by taking off all the boards

you don't need. Try to keep the slats intact, because we'll use them later on to make the bottom of the tray. Keep the nails you pull out as well, unless you have some that you plan to use. I pulled off all the slats except for two, which will be the start of the tray.

## Step 2: Saw the Pallet in Half

Pretty self-explanatory—cut off half of the pallet. I picked the nicest half to keep, and cut off the more broken side. I kept the 2 × 4 in the middle so that the tray would have extra stability if I had to move it around.

## Step 3: Put Boards on the Side and Bottom of Your Tray

Use the nails and boards that you have from step 1, and put 4 boards on the bottom of your tray. If you don't have enough boards or nails you'll just have to go out and buy some. I used a couple of slats to make sides for the tray.

## Step 4: Finishing the Bottom of the Box

Use a few lengths of 1×1 board to tie the bottom of the box together. This also keeps the box a little off the ground to prevent rot. None of this needs to be pretty because it's all going to disappear in the next step.

## Step 5: Line the Tray with Pond Liner

This holds the water. The tray liner should be large enough to wrap around all the sides. Since the tray is six inches tall, an extra foot and a half all the way around is good. Don't forget the 2 × 4 in the center of the tray is going to use of a foot of length. Tuck it in, and make neat folds in the corners. If you want the corners to be perfect, leaving the liner in the sun for a while or heating it with a hair dryer will make it easier to mold to the shape of the tray. You can glue the liner if you want, but gravity, the water, and the plants will hold everything in place.

## Step 6: Fill the Trays with Water and put Your Plants Inside

Fill the trays with water and put your plants inside. Duckweed on the top of the water reflects heat and helps prevent evaporation, and looks nice too. I've tucked the extra pond liner under the tray to keep the wind from lifting it, and it looks tidy that way.

garden

This instructable will show how I made a cheap, all-purpose organic pesticide for my herb & vegetable garden. It can be used on a variety of insects that live in the dirt or on the plants including worms, mites, and other parasites. This entire pesticide will eventually break down and be reduced to nothing, so it is OK to eat any herbs or vegetables that are growing.

## Materials

The materials used to make the pesticide should be easy to obtain. You will need:
- an empty & clean gallon jug (such as a milk jug)
- a spray bottle with spray nozzle
- a funnel
- a piece of cloth such as a shirt or bandanna
- a pot that can hold 1 gallon
- 2 small onions
- a jalapeño pepper
- a clove of garlic
- some dish soap.

Take 1 gallon of warm water, dump it in a pot and you're ready to begin making the pesticide.

## Step 1: Killer Salad

Take the vegetables and begin cutting them up. It doesn't have to be pretty, since nobody's going to eat it! Chop up the 2 onions, the garlic and half or ¾ of the jalapeño pepper. The seeds can be left in, since they're hot too. Blend all the veggies together until pasty in a blender. The killer salad is now a killer paste. ***Take care not to rub your eyes or face after handling the liquid or the vegetables. The pepper especially can really burn if it gets in the eye!***

## Step 2: Making the Killer Soup

After everything has been blended, dump the paste into the pot of warm water and let it sit for 20 minutes. The ground up vegetables and water will make the killer soup or tea. It's going to be mighty fragrant at this point. Just let all those offensive tastes and odors seep out into the water.

garden

## Step 3: Straining Out the Veggies

Once the soup has been allowed to sit and a lot of the flavor and odor has mixed with the water, the liquid needs to be strained. I used a funnel and bandanna to catch the vegetable particles as I strained the liquid into the gallon jug. I tried using a coffee filter at first to strain the liquid, but it clogged easily. Cloth seems to work best. The mush that collects in the cloth can be squeezed out into the jug and the leftover can simply be thrown out or put into a compost bin.

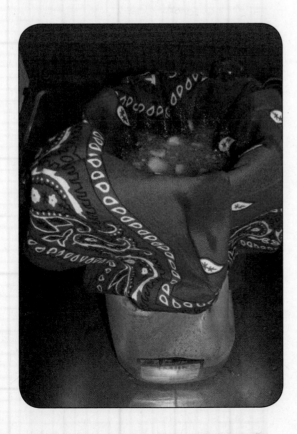

## Step 4: Add Some Dish Soap

After all the straining was complete I added 2 tablespoons of dish soap to the liquid. Keeping with the spirit of this being an organic, plant-friendly pesticide, I used a vegetable-based dish soap. It is free of petroleum-based chemicals, dyes, and perfumes and biodegrades naturally. If you are using a soap that is petroleum-based or has dyes or perfumes, try adding half of what I used. The soap makes the already bad-tasting, stinky liquid soapy and even less palatable to the insects that inhabit the plants.

## Step 5: Using the Pesticide

Using the funnel, fill the spray bottle up and set the nozzle to a light mist. At this point, the rest of the liquid can be capped and stored in the refrigerator for up to 2 weeks. Simply shake it up before it is used. Take the spray bottle and spray the plants first. Try to get all over the plant including the stem and under the leaves. Spray the soil as well so that the top of it is wet. What this liquid does is make every part of the plant that it touches unpalatable to the insect. The water evaporates and leaves behind the odor and flavor. It smells and tastes gross and they won't eat it. When they won't eat anymore, they eventually starve. The liquid will not kill the insects on contact, so do not get upset if you see increased activity after the application. They're simply struggling to find something to eat. Treat every 4 or 5 days to kill off the pests and prevent newly-hatched babies from feeding. It may take 3 or 4 treatments, but the numbers should gradually decrease.

garden

223

This is really, really easy to do. (Note: you may be able to use this technique to grow other stuff in the form of a square (actually in the form of a cube) and apply the general idea to other shapes.)

## Materials and Tools

- (6) 8" square, $^3/_{10}$" thick (or thicker) sheets of polycarbonate plastic. (Lexan)
- 4 gate hinges
- 2 hinged clasps with flat head machine screws and hex nuts plus at least 8 or more 1" to 1½" long, thin wood screws
- possibly a 36" length of angle iron or aluminum angle (cut to 8" lengths to yield four pieces) if you have thinner polycarbonate
- a power drill and hole saw
- a hand saw or power saw such as a jigsaw.

## Step 1: Cut the Stem Pass Through

In the first sheet drill a 1" diameter hole in the center with the drill and hole saw. Then, using a hand or power saw, cut 2 parallel lines from the hole perpendicular to one edge of the sheet and remove the material between.

## Step 2: Add First Set of Hinges

Use a box to rest the left side sheet, place the top sheet left edge over the left side sheet edge and fasten the sheets together.

## Step 3: Trim the Inset Sides

Measure the width of the sheets and trim each side of the inset sides by this width.

## Step 4: Fasten Sides

The edges of the inset sides will have to be trimmed the thickness of the poly you use so they can be inset and still keep the box square. Drill pilot holes through the edge of the left and right sheets into side sheets between them to accept the wood screws. Use 2 or more screws per joined edge. A piece of angle iron or aluminum can be used to beef up the corners if the polycarbonate you have is too thin.

garden

## Step 5: Do the Bottom

Place the box on its top, add the last sheet for the bottom, and secure with hinges as you did the top.

## Step 6: Add the Clasps

Clasps go opposite the hinges on the top and bottom sheets.

## Step 7: Usage

Plant watermelons. As soon they begin to grow large enough to place them in the box with the stem through the slit and hole, do so. Remove when ripe.

## Step 8: Addendum: How to Grow a Watermelon

How to plant your watermelon:

Watermelons come in about 1,200 varieties worldwide, divided according to season and seed production. China is by far the world's largest grower of watermelon. Growing time is from 70 to 85 days for all varieties and growing season begins when all danger of frost has past. Watermelons can be grown indoors any time of year but require extra amounts of space and constant temperature between 80° and 85°F. Seeds for seedlings to be transplanted outdoors may be started indoors 3 weeks before transplanting outdoors. Seeds are planted one inch deep in groups of 3 and seedlings are thinned to the best 1 or 2 for planting.

You can use this method with peat or potting soil to start seeds indoors. Seedless varieties must be planted alongside seed producing varieties in order to pollinate and set the fruit. Hills for single transplants are spaced 2 to 3 feet apart while double transplants are spaced 4 to 5 feet apart. Rows are spaced 7 to 10 feet apart. Use black plastic to cover the hills and rows and plant through the plastic. Drip irrigation is sometimes used sparingly in cooler climates.

How to tell when your watermelon is ripe:

1. light green, curly tendrils on the stem near the point of attachment of the melon usually turn brown and dry;
2. the surface color of the fruit turns dull;
3. the skin becomes resistant to penetration by the thumbnail and is rough to the touch; and
4. the bottom of the melon (where it lies on the soil) turns from light green to a yellowish color. Many watermelons do not emit the proverbial "dull thud" when ripe. For these, the dull thud may indicate an over-ripe, mushy melon. The above indicators for choosing a ripe watermelon are therefore much more reliable than "thumping" the melon with a knuckle. *Source: University of Illinois Extension Service*

garden

# Rolling Compost Tumbler from Trash

By **ManMan.inc**

Logan Mackey

(www.instructables.com/id/Rolling-Compost-Tumbler-From-Trash/)

garden

I needed a compost tumbler and did not want to pay up to $100 for a plastic barrel!.

## Materials

- some hinges (from old cupboard)
- a plastic barrel (found on side of the road)
- a rolling garden hose stand (had one rusting out in the yard)
- some kind of lock (replaced deadbolt on door; used old one)
- a handle (this was in the garage, no idea)
- a hodgepodge of miscellaneous nuts and bolts (had jars of these)
- two pieces of PVC tubing the same length of the barrel (I have tons of miscellaneous PVC my grandfather collected)
- four really long screws
- some wire (clothes hanger)
- two really long bolts for the reattachment of the wheels
- dark colored spray paint

## Tools Needed

- drill
- screw driver
- wrench
- socket wrench
- pliers
- your own two hands
- hacksaw

## Step 1: Disassemble the Rolling Garden Hose Stand

Pretty much everyone has one of these rusting in their yard. Take all the screws out. Keep the two sides of the wheels and the handle and the "gear" parts with the crank.

Keep the sides of the wheels, the hose guard, and much all the plastic pieces; I recycled all the metal parts and used the small hose for a floor sink.

## Step 2: Cut a Big Square in the Barrel

This is pretty easy to explain, just make a big square less than half the circumference of the barrel.

With a hack saw, make it wide enough to be able to dump it all out, leaving 2 to 4 inches on the sides for support.

## Step 3: Attaching the Sides of the Compost tumbler

Turn the barrel on its top, and put on one of the "wheels" (this is the center part that the hose winds up on, check out the picture you will understand) from the rolling garden hose stand.

I had to hack off the center part with a hack saw on the side you're attaching to the barrel to make it level, and then drilled a hole in each "spoke" and threaded a bolt through, then did the same on the bottom of the barrel.

226

## Step 4: Adding the Hinges and Hardware

Now that the hole is cut get out your hinges and place them on the barrel, marking the holes where you're going to drill.

Do the same with the holes in the dead bolt and the handle. Drill the holes, and thread the nuts and bolts into place. I tried to use pop rivets but the plastic was too thick, though one of the hinges held on with them. Make sure to line it all up before bolting it together.

## Step 5: Attaching the Sides/legs and Crank

OK now attach the plastic triangles that act as the stand for your compost tumbler. Take one of the triangles and attach it to the top.

One side will be attached with the "hub cap." This is where the hose part came from; mine had 2 screws I just reused those. On the other side, attach the triangle using a crank. I also had two old screws that I used for this part. Now your compost tumbler has a stand and a hand crank.

## Step 6: Attaching the Wheels, Braces, and Handle

I lucked out and found two almost perfect sized bolts. I had to cut a small length of pipe to secure to fill the space.

So securing each wheel back into its place on the triangle frame: Attaching the braces, take your 2 PVC pipes and secure them in the bottom corners of each plastic triangle. I used a long screw and drove it though the plastic on the one side through the PVC and into the plastic on the other side; these held pretty well.

Attaching the handle: Get the handle for the wheeled garden hose parts, mark and drill four holes through the PVC pipe in the center on the one side. Take your wire and wind it though all the holes on the handle and through the pipe.

## Step 7: Paint and Compost

I spray painted it green, darker the color the better. Then I added some yard clipping and my lunch scraps. And since it has wheels I can roll it right to where I want to lay my compost and open the door.

garden

227

# How to Make a Seed Bomb

By **treesneedtobehugged**
(www.instructables.com/id/How-to-Make-a-Seed-Bomb/)

Do you hate those blank vacant lots on the side of road and city streets? Have you wanted to put a flower garden in one of those lots but have been afraid of being arrested? Is the lot just too hard to get into? And think of how many times you have seen a bare plot with nothing in it or a neglected flower bed that you just wished you could plant on? Well the seed bomb is just right for you. The seed bomb is cheap compared to buying transplants, is natural and organic, easy to make, pocket sized, and you can easily cover a large area with seed bombs in a very short time.

## Materials

All materials in this instructable are cheap or free, easy to find, and are natural and organic.

- clay from your area (if clay is unavailable in your area, you can use Crayola air dry clay, found at Wal-Mart for about $5.00 and is used to portect seeds from insects, birds, etc. that might eat them)
- water (for forming clay, do not water seed bomb when finished)
- seeds native to your area (check with your local nature conservancy or your state's department of natural resources for which seeds/plants are native to your area; buy seed mixtures of native flowers and plants. Not only will they grow well, they will not crowd out other plants, disrupt bird and insect populations, or do other environmental damage)
- compost or worm castings
- yogurt container top or any large flat surface

For the dried red clay: mix 5 parts clay with 1 part compost and 1 part flower seeds, put some careful drops of water into the mixture (make sure not to make it into a goopy sloppy mess!). Knead with hands into a ball, flatten it out and cut to desired size. Now just make into a small ball and let it dry in the sun. Now you have a red clay seed bomb.

## Step 1: Cutting

Cut a very thin piece of the clay

Tip: (The thinner you make it the easier you can press it down and shape it into a ball.)

## Step 2: Cutting (Continued)

Press down on a large flat surface (making it not paper thin but not as thick as a book). Cut to about 2 and a half inches wide and 2 inches high.

## Step 3: Adding the Compost

Sprinkle the finest compost onto the clay; the more compost you put on the better the chance the seeds will germinate.

## Step 4: Adding Seeds

Add about 2 seeds to the mixture (depending on the quality you think the seeds are).

## Step 5: Adding the Water

BE CAREFUL HOW MUCH WATER YOU ADD! Add just a few drops or it will become a sloppy mess that's almost impossible to take off! The water will also help the compost stay inside the seed bomb.

## Step 6: Making into a Seed Bomb

THIS IS GOING TO BE DIRTY! Scrape off with your fingers the clay and roll into a ball and make sure you don't let the seeds go out of the seed bomb!

## Step 7: Adding More Compost

To have a better chance of your plant in your seed bomb of growing, put your seed bomb into a pot of compost and rub the compost in, then take it out and rub it in again. You can keep repeating this process till about the 5th rubbing when you have most likely covered the seed bomb with the compost.

## Step 8: You're Finished

Now just let your seed bomb air dry and you're finished. Now throw your seed bombs of change into any vacant lot, neglected flower bed, or bare lot and don't forget to water your new brand new guerrilla garden!

garden

# Superhero Garden Gnome Mod

By **The Papier Boy**
Kristopher Sebring
(www.instructables.com/id/
Superhero-Garden-Gnome-Mod/)

Evil lurks in the shadows of our backyards. Rogue snails. Radioactive skunks. My yard has a maniacal possum that will stop at nothing until he controls the entire area behind the compost pile. That's why every backyard needs a hero. One who can clean up the garden and make it safe for all law abiding neighborhood critters.

Batman and Robin: One gnome is in a proud, alert stance. The other is sitting with his head resting on his hands. This gnome pair struck me as a great duo. To me, the obvious choice was the classic Dynamic Duo of Batman and Robin. But I thought I'd change it up a bit and make the standing gnome be the Boy Wonder and the sitting gnome be the Dark Knight. I thought this was more unexpected.

Spiderman: I also had a crawling gnome. As I was holding it and positioning it in different orientations, I noticed that if I held it vertically it looked like it was crawling up a wall, and the knee area had a hole in it to use as a place from which to hang it. So to me Spiderman seemed like a no-brainer. I could position the gnome so that it looked like Spiderman clinging to a wall.

## Step 1: Choose your Hero

The first thing you'll need to do is determine your gnome's alter ego. Spend time with the gnome. Sleep with it if you have to. Look into its eyes . . . its soul. Look around your yard too. What type of issues are the yard inhabitants facing? Are there other-worldly invaders? Common street thugs? Neighbor's dog? This will help you determine if you need a dark vigilante type or a hulking all-powerful brute.

## Step 2: Supplies

- ceramic garden gnomes
- Sculpey (Super Sculpey is my preference but Sculpey III is good too)
- Bondo body filler
- craft paint (any type that is rated for ceramics . . . some aren't. Read the label)
- paint brushes (artist's and/or craft brushes)
- spray paint (clear, outdoor enamel)
- imagination
- razor knife (or XACTO knife)
- oven (to bake the Sculpey, silly)
- aluminum foil
- baking sheet

garden

- rolling pin (or piece of PVC pipe)
- a smooth, hard surface (such as a sheet of glass or countertop)
- sand paper (120 grit and 200 grit)
- wooden spatulas or tongue depressors
- construction adhesive
- accessories: such as little buttons, buckles, twine, etc.

You'll also want to have a blank canvas. So if you are not using a brand new gnome you should take the time to prime it. That way all of the colors will be vibrant and uniform.

## Step 3: Sculpting

First thing to do is sculpt the masks. For Robin's mask and Spiderman's eyes make a paper template. Next roll the Sculpey out into a thin sheet on a very smooth surface using a PVC pipe or rolling pin. A piece of glass makes a great surface. Use the template to cut out the masks using a razor knife. For Batman's mask just make a large rectangle; no template needed. Place the masks on the gnome faces and press them tightly into place. For Batman, drape the rectangular sheet of Sculpey over the gnomes face and cut away the excess. Pinch the nose between your thumb and index finger to create the pointed nose. Use your pinky to make the indentations for the eyes.

Make a little ball of Sculpey and squish it into a circle. Use it to decorate Robin's belt buckle.

For Batman's ears roll two Sculpey balls and shape them into pointy cones. Use your thumb to smoosh them into place on the side of the gnome's head. They'll probably stick there in place and hold on their own.

You should have excess Sculpey rolled out. You can use a razor knife to cut out a Bat-a-rang. Make a paper template if needed.

## Step 4: Baking

Once the gnomes are decorated it is time to bake them. Sculpey is an oven-bake polymer clay. So it is soft and pliable until it's baked. First, heat the oven to 275 degrees Fahrenheit. While waiting for the oven to pre-heat, put some foil on a cookie baking sheet. Then carefully put the gnomes on the cookie sheet being very careful not to let the Sculpey touch the sheet or the rack. Put the entire gnome in the oven and bake for 15 minutes. Put the bat-a-rang on the sheet too. Since the gnome is ceramic it's safe to put it in the oven. The kiln that it was fired in was a lot hotter than your kitchen oven. When the 15 minutes is up take them out and let them cool completely to room temperature. Note: If your Sculpey pieces are thicker than about 6mm then you can bake it a few minutes longer than 15 minutes.

Remember, there is nothing holding the Sculpey onto the gnome (no glue or anything). But the Sculpey will probably stick to the ceramic really tightly anyway. I doubt that the Sculpey will stick to the gnome long term so you should carefully pry the Sculpey piece off and glue it back on with construction adhesive. This will hold pretty well outside.

## Step 5: More Sculpting

There were a couple of areas on the Batman gnome where you'll really want the Sculpey to blend in seamlessly with the ceramic. So you can mix up some Bondo to fill in the gaps.

garden

### Step 6: Sanding

Once the Bondo is dry, sand it with 100 or 120 grit sandpaper. Feather it in really well so that the seam is invisible. Then clean all of the dust off of the gnome with a damp rag.

### Step 7: Painting

At this point it is ready to paint. But first you have to choose the colors. There is a process for color selection. You want to select "gnomey" colors—colors that you could imagine a gnome wearing. You want earthy colors and not bright colors. So you do not want to pick literal interpretations of the comic hero. So, for instance, don't use black . . . use burnt umber brown. Don't use red . . . use maroon. Not white . . . parchment. Etc.

There is no need to prime. Just start painting. Another thing to consider is the costume. It's better to roughly follow the gnomes existing clothes than to crowbar in an exact interpretation of the comic book costume.

### Step 8: Sealing

Once all of the paint dries you need to seal the gnome. This will protect it from the weather and make all of the colors pop. An enamel clear spray paint works nicely. Spray on 3 even coats of a satin clear coat and let it dry overnight.

### Step 9: Accessorizing

Remember that bat-a-rang you made earlier in step 3? Use your acrylics to paint it "black" and spray it with clear spray paint. Then wrap the hemp twine around it in an x pattern and use construction adhesive to glue it in place on Batman's shoulder bag.

For Robin, take 24 inches of hemp twine and neatly coil it up. Then use construction adhesive to glue it onto Robin's shoulder bag.

Take some of the buttons and buckles that you gathered and glue them to the gnome's shoulder bags and jacket cuffs.

### Step 10: Displaying

You can display the gnomes anywhere in your yard, but it is best to place them in an area where they can get a good view of the entire yard and any particular trouble areas. If you've modified your gnomes correctly, your garden should be in order within a few weeks. Any new threats can be handled with additional super gnomes or by forming a super gnome league or justice guild.

Take your gnomes inside during winter. The crime rate drops dramatically during the colder months anyway.

garden

This berry picker is made out of PVC pipe. Heat is used to shape the plastic. Two "fingers" at the working end do the picking. The berry then falls through the pipe and lands in a plastic bag tied to the other end.

## Step 1: Safety

We love plastics for what they do for us, but plastic manufacture and decay tend to pollute the environment and negatively affect our health.

Vinyl Chloride, one of the components of PVC, is carcinogenic. When it is locked up in the polymer, however, it is much safer to be around. In my years of experience working with PVC, I have not noticed any adverse effects on my health from being around it.

Always work in areas with good ventilation. If you do get caught in a cloud of smoke, hold your breath and move to clean air.

When heating PVC with a gas stove or propane torch, try not to let it burn. Smoke from burning PVC is bad. With experience one burns it less and less. Don't panic the first time you do burn some. It scorches, but doesn't immediately burst into flame. Move the material away from the flame and try again.

While heating PVC over a gas flame, keep the plastic an appropriate distance from the flame. Avoid scorching the surface before the inside can warm up. It takes time for heat to travel to the center of the material being heated.

Keep the plastic moving, and keep an eye on the state of the plastic. When heated, the PVC material is flexible, like leather. Beyond this stage, you risk scorching it.

## Step 2: The First Cut

I used 1¼ inch PVC for this berry picker. A smaller version, using 1 inch pipe turned out to be too small for the berries I was after, but might be good for smaller berries.

The first cut is made at quite a sharp angle. This gives you plenty of material to cut the two "fingers" out of. Use a pencil to sketch out the cuts you are going to make.

## Step 3: Cut out the Pattern

This pipe was thin-walled and easy to cut with snips. I cut a center line with the saw, and did the rest with snips.

## Step 4: Smoothing the Edges

Sometimes a file does the job, but one of my favorite tools for smoothing edges is a scraper made from a broken knife blade.

Notice the PVC handle on the scraper. It was heated and then just squeezed over the knife fragment to hold it firmly.

garden

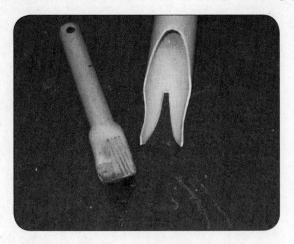

## Step 6: The Bottom End

The bottom end of the berry picker is flared out so that a bag tied to the end will not slip off. The berries travel down through the pipe and collect in the bag.

You could use something conical, or rounded to make the flared end, but I thought it would be appropriate for the project to be flared over a glass hand juicer. It gave the end an interesting hexagonal shape.

I tied the plastic bag on with a piece of string.

The final step is to go pick some berries!

## Step 5: Heat and Form the Fingers"

Heat the end carefully over the stove to soften it. Keep it moving and at an adequate distance from the flame to keep the plastic from burning.

Bend the fingers into the hook shape by pressing them against something, such as a wall. You can always do touch-up heating with a propane torch to modify the shape.

Make sure the slot between the two fingers is open enough to accommodate the berry stem. If it is not, you may have to open it up more with a saw, or file.

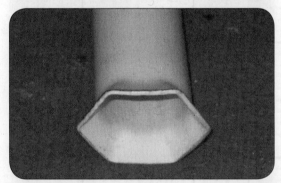

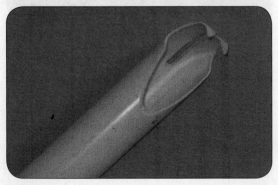

**garden**

234

Have more fun in the water! Perfect your swimming form, learn how to water ski, and build a floating dock from barrels. In this chapter, you'll learn skills to improve your boating, diving, and fishing techniques. You'll even learn how to carve a pumpkin under water!

# Low Tech Lap Counting

By **cleversomeday**
(www.instructables.com/id/Low-Tech-Lap-Counting/)

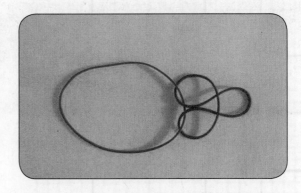

I swim for exercise but hate keeping track of how many laps I've completed. I searched for a lap counting solution and found waterproof sports watches and dedicated counters at $30 and up. Those were overkill for what I needed, so I developed my own counting system that works great and costs pennies. Now I can spend my swim time thinking or unwinding instead of counting.

## What You Will Need
- 4 rubber bands that fit comfortably around your wrist. You can even hijack the kids' sillybandz for this.

## Step 1: Connect the Bands

Loop one band around another and back through itself so that they interlock and form a figure eight. Do the same for the second pair. Nothing tricky here, you are just making two standard rubber band chains with two bands each.

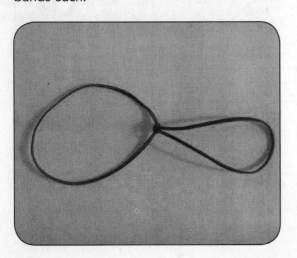

## Step 2: Put the Bands On

Put one of the bands around your wrist with the knot towards the inside and so that its attached band hangs free. Do the same for the other wrist. This is the zero position from which you will start the count.

## Step 3: Get Acquainted with the Counting System

Here's how it works: one hand counts by ones and the other hand counts by fives using rubber bands resting in the "slots" between your fingers and/or thumb to keep track of laps you have swum. You may recognize this as similar to the 4-sticks-and-a-slash tally system commonly used to count things, unless you are the studious type who will recognize it as base 5.

I use my left hand for the ones, my right hand for the fives and start at my thumbs as shown in the sketch. It really isn't important which hands/starting points you use as long as you can remember it and be comfortable with it.

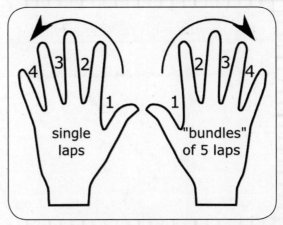

single laps

"bundles" of 5 laps

## Step 4: Begin Counting

After you complete your first lap, take the dangling band on your left wrist and loop it around your left thumb. (Front and back views shown below.) After the second, third and fourth laps, increase the count by moving the rubber band over by one finger (each further away from the thumb). After 4 laps the rubber band will be between your pinky and ring finger.

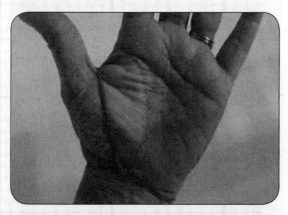

## Step 5: Continue Counting

After the 5th lap, return the band on your left hand to the starting position (dangling) and place the dangling band on your right wrist around your right thumb.

Continue after each additional lap moving the band on your left hand away from the thumb one slot at a time until you run out of slots, (indicating a multiple of 5 has been reached). Return the left hand band to the starting position and move the right hand band over one finger. Continue in the same manner until you reach 25 laps, and then start over.

I find it easiest to place one hand on the wall and move the band with the other hand.

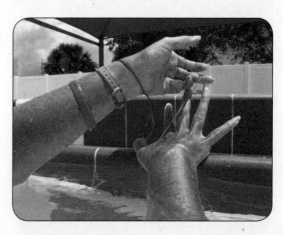

## Step 6: Where am I?

To tell how many laps you've completed, count by fives on your right hand until you reach the band and add the remaining laps shown on your left hand. (If you've gone around more than once, add any multiples of 25 you have completed.)

Hey, I've done a kilometer already (22 laps × 50 yards per lap)!

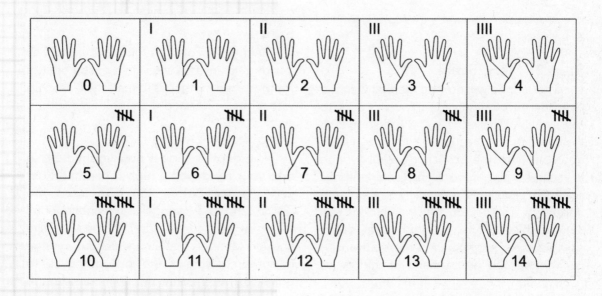

# Diving Depth Gauge

By **Aleksi**

(www.instructables.com/id/Diving-Depth-Gauge/)

Make a simple depth gauge for free diving out of a syringe. This is also an experiment with Boyle's law which states that the product of the pressure and the volume of an ideal gas is constant.

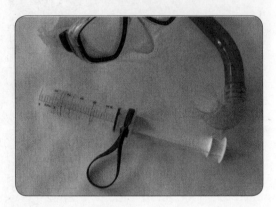

## Materials
- 1 syringe (preferably the syringe should be large and have a scale with divisions to sixty)
- 1 zip tie
- a marker pen
- a knife

## Step 1: Mark Scale

The syringe will now be marked with the pen but unfortunately the ink won't stick to the syringe. Therefore we will first scratch the plastic with the tip of a knife and then apply ink into the scratch. A 60ml syringe is most suitable for making a logarithmic scale. The scale is practically readable to depths of 15 to 20m which I think is still comfortable. More extreme free divers going deeper might want a more advanced instrument. The depth marks should be as follows: 0m = 60ml, 5m = 40ml, 10m = 30ml, 15m = 24m, l20m = 20ml, 30m = 15ml, 40m = 12ml, 50m = 10ml, 172m = 3.3ml (World record 2005/10, totally insane!)

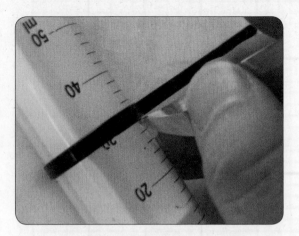

## Step 2: Make a Hole at the Surface Mark

Make a hole in the side of the syringe to always allow 60ml of air into it at surface level. You can make the hole by pushing a soldering iron through the plastic.

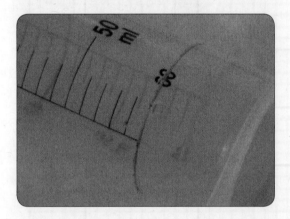

## Step 3: Seal the Tip of the Syringe

Seal the tip of the syringe. You could fill it with glue, insert a screw in it or something. My preferred method is to melt the plastic tip with a gas lighter and then mold it together.

## Step 4: Go Diving!

The depth gauge is now finished. Strap it to your hand with a rubber band and get under water. Before you dive insert the piston and the syringe will contain 60ml of air (at surface pressure). When you dive and go deeper the air inside the syringe is compressed and the piston moves to equalize the pressure difference inside and outside the syringe. When you return to the surface the air in the depth gauge will expand and the piston moves back.

water

# Make Your Own Prescription Swimming Goggles

By **engineerable**
(www.instructables.com/id/
Prescription-Swimming-Goggles-for-
12-See-Underw/)

Wearing your glasses in the water is a sure way to end up having to buy a new pair, and contacts tend to pop out when swimming. I have seen many a pair of expensive glasses lost into the deep blue yonder or the murky abyss.

Cindy came up with this simple and great idea to make her own prescription goggles for only $12 (the cost of the goggles), saving $$ compared to buying a pair from the optometrist or dive shop. If you have an old pair of prescription glasses, you can probably make a pair of these for cheap, and in only a few minutes.

Not only do these work well for swimming, but they are especially useful if you're doing a water sport, like surfing, kayaking, body boarding, kite surfing, etc, where, if you're like me, will end up doing a face plant.

Okay, okay, so you're not going to look like a rock star wearing these, but if they are carefully made, no one else will notice that the lenses are glued on. Only with thicker lenses do you notice because of the distortion, which is visible with regular glasses anyways. Although, who wears swimming goggles to look cool? They're all about functionality, and what's more functional than not only keeping water out of your eyes, but also being able to see clearly.

## Materials

The materials you will need to make the prescription swimming goggles are:

- pair of old prescription glasses that you don't use anymore. The prescription just has to be good enough to see, not read.
- pair of swimming goggles. The Boomerang Goggle from Speedo worked the best of any goggle I found.
- 5 minute epoxy. As many people have suggested, use SILICONE adhesive instead. It remains more flexible, seals better, and makes a stronger bond.
- fine grit sandpaper

I said it was simple, right?

## Step 1: Remove Lenses From Your Old Glasses

Use an eyeglass screwdriver (usually a small flathead screwdriver) to remove the screw that clamps the frame around your lenses. If the lenses are held in the frame without screws, they may just be popped out by hand.

water

239

## Step 2: Test Fit the Lenses onto the Goggle Frames

First, put the goggles on, and hold the lenses up to the goggles to check if you can see well with them. Ideally the lenses should be close to the same distance away from your eye as the eyeglass frames that originally held them, and this quick test will determine if you will be able to see well with them once they are glued on.

The lenses should at least overlap the frame of the goggles on the left and right sides. This is the minimum amount of glue area that you will need. In this case, the top and the bottom edge will be open, allowing water to flow freely between the glasses lens and the goggle lens. This is probably the easiest and most reliable solution.

If the lenses overlap the frame all the way around, then the glue can be applied all the way around. This will created a sealed space between the glasses lens and the goggle lens. There needs to be as little moisture trapped in the space as possible to prevent fogging, so this should be done in a dry place, or you can apply some anti-fog to the lenses on the inside of the space. Also, the glue needs to be properly applied to prevent leaks.

If you are going to buy a pair of goggles, you may want to remove the lenses from your old glases first, take them with you to the store, and see if they would fit well over the goggles.

If the lenses are very curved, then you should only apply glue at the edges where the lenses touch the goggle frames. This is the preferred method, because you don't have to worry about leaks.

If the lenses are flat, and they fully overlap the goggle frames, then you can apply glue all the way around. This is risky, because you may end up with leaks. I therefore highly recommend putting a temporary spacer between the lenses and the goggles to allow for a 1 to 2mm gap, and only applying glue to the edges, leaving a space at the top and bottom to allow water to flow through.

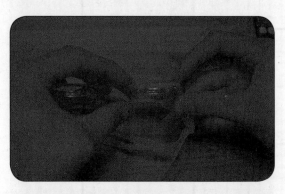

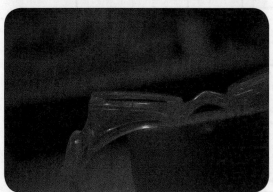

## Step 4: Sanding the Surfaces in Preparation for Gluing

The edges of the prescription glass lenses that overlap the goggle frames need to be sanded for better glue adhesion, if you are using plastic lenses. Using the fine grit sandpaper, lightly sand around the edge of the lenses (on the inside surface) where they will be glued to the goggles. You should also lightly sand/ roughen the goggle frames to which the sanded edges of the lenses will touch. This will help the glue adhere to the goggles.

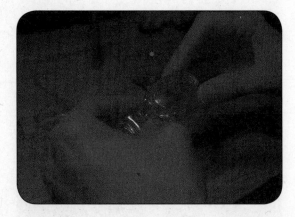

## Step 3: Note: Curved vs. Flat Lenses

You may have to glue the lenses on differently depending on whether they are very curved, or flat.

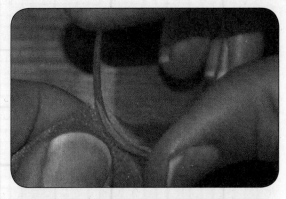

## Step 6: Glue the Lenses to the Goggles (Flat Lenses)

Follow these instructions if your lenses are almost flat, or overlap all the way around the frames:

1. Mix the epoxy very well.
2. If the epoxy is very runny at first, you may want to wait till it thickens a little. Just don't wait too long, because when it begins to harden, it will harden quickly!
3. Apply the glue all the way around the edges of the frame where the lenses overlap. Put just enough so that there will be a good bond between the frame and the lens. I made the mistake of putting a little bit too much the first time and making a mess.
4. Position the lenses onto the frames, and fill in any gaps with epoxy. Make sure that there is a watertight seal between the lenses and the goggles.
5. Hold the lenses in place until the glue hardens. It should only take a few minutes.

## Step 5: Glue the Lenses to the Goggles (Very Curved Lenses)

Follow these instructions if your lenses are very curved.

1. Mix the epoxy very well.
2. If the epoxy is very runny at first, you may want to wait till it thickens a little. Just don't wait too long, because when it begins to harden, it will harden quickly!
3. Apply the glue on the edges of the frame where the lenses will overlap the goggles. The top and bottom is left open for water to flow through. Put just enough so that there will be a good bond between the frame and the lens
4. Position the lenses onto the frames, and hold in place until the glue hardens. It should only take a few minutes.

## Step 7: Finished, Now Go for a Swim!

After leaving the goggles alone overnight so that the epoxy can fully cure, you are ready to go for a swim and test them out.

water

241

## How to Clean and Re-Wax a Surfboard

By **kinawera** Fiona Whitelaw
(www.instructables.com/id/How-to-clean-and-re-wax-a-surfboard/)

What's the matter? Got sand in your wax? The main problem with surfing, apart from the fact that it is almost impossible, is that you get sand in your wax, which turns your board into a manually operated belt sander, especially as you duck dive under waves. This is not such a problem in cold places, because you wear a nice long wetsuit. But in warmer spots, your legs/knees with soon resemble a raw souvlaki column. This instructable tells you how to clean the old wax off, and put new stuff on!

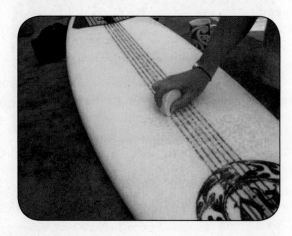

### Step 1: Start with Clean Board

This board has just been cleaned. There are a number of different ways you can clean the old wax off, but the best way, I think, is to leave it in the sun to let the wax soften, then scrape off with a board scraper (that I lost) or your driver's license (that I haven't lost). The license works better. You can remove the last of the wax by rubbing the board with a rag soaked in turps (turpentine). I've heard that Vaseline also works well for removing wax, but it's not as instant as turps and the fumes don't make you giggle as much.

### Step 2: Waxing

If you are doing this on concrete, put something like a towel under your board...

Choosing your wax!

There are all different kinds of board wax to suit different water temperatures. Where I live, the water is about 22C at the moment, so I use Sexwax 3× cold water soft "Quick Humps". I'll leave that there. There's a big difference in types of wax, in warm water you want thicker wax, in California you can just about dip your board in diesel and have it wax up. Ask the surly guy with his pants halfway round his arse in the surfshop what to use for your local area.

Now, rub the block of wax across your board, and then lengthways over the same area. Pay special attention to the rails—it's not considered 'cool' to have lots of wax on your rails because in theory it cuts down your speed on the wave. However, this is like worrying about the wall paper on the space shuttle. The only people who are good enough to notice a reduction in board speed have an army of groupies to wax their board for them. For regular surfing mortals, wax on the rails means you can hold and push the board down for duck diving—if your hands slip off during this process you cop a board in the face, 'Sticky rails to you, till we meet again' etc. So: sticky rails is nice rails.

### Step 3: The End

So this is what it should look like—you should have lumps of wax all over your board. It should resemble bad 70s wallpaper, but sticky. More lumpy is better. Right, now go get wet!

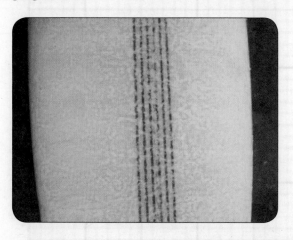

water

## Step 1: Clean the Wound

Pick which side the patch will go on. Cut

that top surface with the cloth layer (if any) away so it tapers down to the hole. Wetsuits are made of neoprene rubber foam. The little bubbles in the rubber foam make it a good insulator. Old-style wetsuit material like this has thin knitted nylon cloth laminated on both sides. It's a lot more durable than the newer suits with cloth on one or neither side. It's also heavier, less elastic, and less warm because the outside cloth stays wet when you get out of the water, and then your body heat has to evaporate this water. Modern suits are a compromise between durability, elasticity, and warmth.

## Step 2: Clean Wound, Prepare Skin Graft

You'll have plenty of surface area to make the patch stick. The tapering means you won't get stress concentrations for rips to start. Isn't it great being a nerd?

Find a donor wetsuit with a compatible type of tissue. Cut a patch big enough to cover the whole wound. Cut all the fabric off one side of the patch and taper the thickness of the patch down to the edges. If you want to get fancy leave an area of fabric in the middle the same size as the hole. I'm not getting fancy today.

## Step 3: Daub Glue on the Patch

I use DAP Weldwood brand Original Contact Cement. Follow the directions. Don't breathe the harmful fumes. Put it on thick enough to be glossy. Let it dry long

enough. Longer is better than shorter. I made an instant foam paintbrush by ripping a chunk of foam rubber and gripping it with the pliers of my leatherman. If you ever want to glue neoprene cloth to cloth, you need to apply several thick coats.

## Step 4: Brush Glue on the Wound

Same as the patch. Smear it on a larger area than you think is necessary. Be extra generous with the fabric areas. Let it dry well before sticking the patch to it.

## Step 5: Affix the Patch

Press it down hard. Make sure all the glue molecules on both surfaces get really intimate with each other. You're done. Enjoy your non-perforated wetsuit. If the patch is in

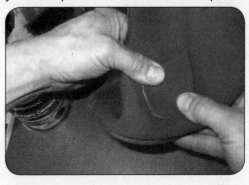

a really hardworking area like the wrist, ankle, or crotch, you can sew the fabric edge of the patch to the fabric edge of the hole. Don't poke all the way through the wetsuit. Just sew the surface cloth together.

243

# Buoy

### By Samuel Bernier
### (www.instructables.com/id/BUOY/)

My parent's cabin does not have drinkable tap water, so we use a lot of water bottles, juice bottles and all kind of bottles (my father prefers beer bottles). There is also no recycling system in this area, so we have to bring all these containers back home. I found a way to reuse them (using only my father's tool box) by turning them into a useful, good looking, and entertaining buoy for the lake. They can be used as seats for exhausted swimmers, anchor for your kayak, or rock warning . . . It is also really fun to try to run on them like in a Japanese game show . . .

## What you Need
- board of wood or plastic at least 0.5 inch thick (no fiberboard)
- saw
- plastic rope
- lighter
- knife
- 16 pan head screws
- 16 water bottles and their caps
- paint (the color you want)
- piece of flexible foam (½ inch thick and more)
- Teflon tape or silicone tube (optional)
- drill
- hot glue gun

## Step 1
With a drill or a punch, make a hole (the size of your screw in the middle of the HDPE caps. Note: Do not use a nail, it would stretch the plastic.

## Step 2
Cut a circle in your board. The diameter should be about the size of your foot. If you don't have feet, (sorry) make that 12 inches. You can sand or cut 16 equal flat surfaces around the circumference. Drill a hole in the middle, the size of your rope.

## Step 3: Be Precise
Make sure to mark your board correctly

## Step 4
Drill 16 holes at equal distance. Make sure the drill is in line with the center of the circle.

## Step 5
Screw the caps to the center piece. (Adding a drop of silicone in the middle of the hole will make it water tight longer.)

water

## Step 6

Paint it!

## Step 7

Cut an 11 inch circle in the foam. Make a hole in the middle (two times the size of your rope).

Glue the foam on the board (perfectly centered please).

## Step 8

Make a tight knot in the rope after passing it through the hole. Melt the strings together (do NOT breathe the fumes).

## Step 9

Adjust the length of the rope depending on where you decided to anchor the buoy.

Tie the other end to something heavy but easy to carry (like a bike lock that lost its key).

## Step 10

Screw the 16 bottles to the center piece, adding silicone or Teflon tape if you notice any leak, and you've got a wonderful multipurpose BUOY. Once you've finished and tested the first one, you can keep saving your bottles to make new ones varying in size, shape, and color.

## Step 11: Make a Lot of Them!

water

245

# Floating Dock with Barrels

By **pilx** Mike Cohen
(www.instructables.com /id/
Floating-Dock-with-
Barrels/)

This is a floating dock that's easy to make and works beautifully.

## Here is a quick parts list of everything I used

- (4) 2" × 8" pressure treated lumber, 8 feet long.
- (7) 2" × 4" pressure treated lumber, 8 feet long.
- (17) 1" × 6" pressure treated lumber 8 feet long.
- (4) 4" × 4" pressure treated posts, 8 inches long.
- (4) 55 gallon plastic barrels
- 100' of rope
- (16) screw-in eye hooks
- 10 to 20 "L" shape braces
- galvanized screws and nails
- drill/screwdriver
- hammer
- silicone caulking
  Here are the parts for the ramp/walkway I added (step 7)
- 55 gallon plastic barrel
- (2) 2" × 8" pressure treated lumber, 12 feet long.
- (2) 2" × 8" pressure treated lumber, 3 feet long.
- (2) 2" × 4" pressure treated lumber, 12 feet long.
- (3) 2" × 4" pressure treated lumber, 33 inches long.
- (4) screw-in eye hooks
- (6) "L" shaped corner braces
- 1" steel pipe . . . length depends on water depth.
- Rope, screws, hammer

## Step 1: Build the Frame

So once you have your parts head out to the body of water you want to place the dock in. Get as close as you can as your final product will be quite heavy and you don't want to have to move it too far.

Lay your 2×8 boards out in a square and screw them together. Make sure and keep two sides of the square on the inside of the square, effectively making an 8'×8'×4" square. I used the pieces of 4"×4" posts in the corners as a right angle. I didn't screw these in yet in case I needed to make adjustments.

At this point you can also ready your barrels. Make sure the plugs are tightened and then apply a layer of silicone caulking over the plug to ensure a good seal and prevent leaking. I did not fill the barrels with any sort of ballast but some people suggest doing so for stability. But my final product was quite stable so no worries.

## Step 2: Support the Frame

Now that you have the basic shape we need to add supports.

Measure out the middle of the square and place a 2" × 4" support there.

The remaining bottom layer pieces are playing two roles. They are supporting the frame as well as holding the barrels against the dock and preventing them from pushing up against the decking. Place two of the boards in a way that allows you to lay a barrel on top. Shift the boards around until you get the barrel sitting nicely in between the boards without touching the ground but also fitting nicely around the curve in the barrel. Mark that point, screw them in, and do the same to the other side.

Now the top layer of supports that run perpendicular to the rest also have two jobs. They provide the cross support and keep the barrels from moving back and forth while in the water. So once again place your barrels on the bottom supports and measure where the barrels end. Place your top layer supports here and screw them in.

## Step 3: Add the Barrels

After screwing in the 4" × 4" post pieces in the corner to solidify the structure, you can make things a little more stable with L braces placed at each of the support intersections. This will make sure that everything stays where it is and really tightens up the frame. Now, place eye hooks in the bottom layer of supports where your barrels lay. Two on each side the barrel. Lay your barrels in their slots and tie them up! After you do all 4 barrels you are ready to flip.

## Step 4: Flip It

I did everything up to this part alone. Now I recruited some friends to come and help me move the beast. With only 3 of us total we easily got it up on its side and slid it in to the lake. I'd say we might have been able to do it with just 2 of us but 3 worked nicely. Flip it in to the water and tie it down to something. You don't want it floating away while you go inside to get the beer.

## Step 5: Deck It

Now that you have a friend or two . . . and your beer, this part is a breeze. Lay out the 1" × 4" boards and make sure everything fits nicely. Leave a little spacing between each board. Drink your beer and hammer in the boards along each support. Once you get a few in you can jump on top and finish from there. Feels nice and stable doesn't it!

## Step 6: Float

One thing that is nice about a floating dock is that you can untie it and float out in to the middle of a lake or pond for a nice swimming platform or just a nice place to hang out.

water

247

## Step 7: A Ramp Begins . . .

So now with the floating platform/dock I needed a way to easily get on to it without stepping in the water first, so here is the walkway/ramp. Frame the entire ramp with the 2" × 8" boards. Screw them together and level. Add the 2" × 4" boards down the middle as support for the barrel as well as the walkway area when you flip it over. Throw in the 33" pieces of 2" × 4" board for support every 3 feet. Add the eye hooks for the barrel, rope it down and you are ready to flip it. I did this in about an hour and a half. Most of that time was spent making sure it was level . . . and it still wasn't perfect.

they are more like ¾" × 5½" . . . . so I came up short.

## Step 8: Flip it and Float it

Once again, bribe a friend with beer (or in my case my friend actually brought the beer) and flip the ramp over and walk it in to the water.

Now, this is where this could easily not work for some people depending on their shoreline. Mine has a nice little hill the ramp can sit on while on land. So I set that end down and the other side floated nicely out by the platform. I had to add some dirt underneath the land side just to get everything straight but it wasn't too bad.

Now put the decking on just like before . . . thanks to those 2 "× 4"s running long ways you have plenty of support for the deck boards.

I actually ran out of boards for decking because I wasn't really thinking . . . remember, after wood gets milled and sent to the store it is no longer it's original dimensions . . . I calculated for 1" × 6" boards, when it reality

## Step 9: Attach and Secure

Now it's all finished but the platform is floating free and the ramp is somewhat unstable. So I placed poles on the corners of the platform and sunk them as far as I could in to the lake bed. I also placed a few on the ramp to keep it from getting pushed to the side. Just don't make anything too tight, everything needs to be able to move by wind, people walking, water level changes. I've already found the poles make great places to lauch bottle rockets from as well as place tiki torches!

I also attached the platform to the ramp with rope, carabiners, and eye hooks. Now it can still be easily detached to float out if need be.

It's not as stable over all as I hoped . . . if you walk to the far corner of the ramp it dips pretty low in the water and actually rolled the ramp before I added the poles. I guess I could just add 4" × 4" pillars and take out the barrel . . . maybe once the water level goes back down to winter levels.

# Dried Kelp

By **Tim Anderson**

(www.instructables.com/id/Dried-Kelp/)

Here's how to gather and dry kelp. Kelp is rich in iodine, something many people don't get enough of. Instead we ingest large quantities of nitrates and perchlorates, which can cause thyroid problems, especially in people with an iodine deficiency. The nitrates mostly come from preservatives in meat. The perchlorates mostly come from solid-fuel rockets and runoff from military installations, and are concentrated in the leaves of irrigated salad crops.

## Step 1: Gather Kelp

Don't pick living kelp that's still anchored by its stem. Only gather kelp that's either drifting freely or has washed up on the beach. If there's current, here's how to tell if kelp is anchored without even touching it: If the "head" is pointing upstream, the kelp is anchored. If the "head" is pointing downstream, it's drifting freely. If you still see a lot of the stem floating at high tide, the kelp is drifting. At low tide you'll see a lot of stem even on anchored kelp.

## Step 2: Rinse the Kelp

If you pick your kelp up off the beach, you'll need to rinse the sand off. The best place to do this is in the sea, right where you gather it. Fresh water makes the kelp really slimy so the sand sticks to it. It's easier to wash the sand off in salt water than it is in fresh water. If you want your dried kelp not to be so salty, rinsing in fresh water will do that. I like mine salty.

## Step 3: Dry the Kelp

Drying kelp is easy. Just hang it anywhere there's some airflow and it will dry out. You might think of hanging it on a clothesline, but...

## Step 4: Built in Clothesline

Kelp has a built in clothesline! If you find a long piece of kelp, you can just string the whole stem from tree to tree. The Northwest Coast Natives used to use dried kelp stems as fishing line. If you need to tie two stems together, use a "granny knot". The "granny knot" looks like a square knot done wrong. It's usually a weak and unsafe knot, but is good for tying roots, vines, bark, and other stiff materials that will break if you bend them too far.

## Step 5: Dried!

Before long your kelp will be dried. It's amazing how thin and crispy it gets. Even the heads can shrink and turn into something you can bite and chew. The white stuff on these heads is crystals of salt from the interior. There are some spots on these leaves, they're eggs from some small sea animal; I eat those too.

In this instructable I will be showing you some of the basics that you need to know to catch the big one. You have to understand there are many different techniques that are used to catch certain species of fish and it would be nearly impossible to fit them all in one Instructable. Before you start, remember that fishing can be a very frustrating sport, so if you fail just get up and try again.

## Gear

No matter who you talk to about fishing, they will always agree on one thing: you need the right gear to catch fish. No matter what kind of fish you plan on catching you are going to have to have these essentials:

- fishing rod and reel (strongly recommended)
- fishing line
- fishing regulations (if you plan on keeping your catch)
- landing net
- pliers/de-hooking device
- hooks
- weights
- other fishing lures or bait
- tape measure or ruler
- other useful items: fishing buddy, a boat, GPS device, depth finder, maps.

Before you go fishing make sure you check with your state laws to see what kind of weights or hooks are legal to use in your state, because some states strongly enforce laws that keep you from using barbed hooks or lead weights.

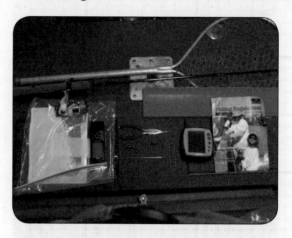

## Step 1: Location, Location, Location

Many people that I talk to say that whenever they go fishing they don't catch a single fish. Then, I ask them where they went and they say someplace I've fished and didn't catch a single thing. This area of fishing is one of the most over looked areas, because most people think that they can just walk out to some random spot and start fishing. I'm about to tell you different.

When fishing inshore it's good to look for areas with a lot of bait and rocky bottom. Also, sometimes if you see fish hitting the surface that usually means that the fish are feeding. Grassy points are good spots when the tide is high and the water is rushing past them, because as the water moves past these points the bait fish move with the water and the bigger fish eat them as they go by.

Another good place when fishing in shore are oyster bars. These places harvest baby crabs, which are eaten by many different species of fish.

Fishing offshore is totally different from fishing inshore, because the fish that you catch are usually a lot bigger. One approach that I like to do is to troll or drag lures behind the boat until we find a rock to fish on. Rocks show up on your depth finder as large mounds, and they usually have dark

water

arcs over them, which are fish. When you locate the fish you can either: 1. continue to troll or 2. bottom fish the rock by anchoring over it or drifting over it. We seem to catch more fish trolling, but in my opinion its more fun and challenging to catch the fish while bottom fishing.

Freshwater fishing is a little different from saltwater fishing, because the behavior of the fish is a little different. One difference is that in the Summer the bass make beds under tree limbs, which is an ideal time to use top waters to try and get a bite out of aggression. Also, trolling for Lake trout is a good way to catch big fish.

## Step 2: Fishing Lures

There are many different fishing lures on the market today. Some are better than others. Choosing your lure comes down to a few key things: type, action, hook quality, and design.

The type of lure that you want to use all depends on where in the water you want to fish. For example, when you want to fish on the bottom I suggest you use a jig head and plastic jig or worm. When you want to fish in the middle of the water you may want to use a swim bait or unweighted jerk bait. Fishing the top of the water requires a floating lure that makes a lot of sound.

The action of the lure mostly depends on the type and design of the lure. Most top water lures and swim baits have a long plastic lip, which controls the swimming action of the lure. Gold spoons are shaped with a curve so that they spin or rock back and forth through the water.

When choosing a fishing lure the most important thing to remember is hook quality. The shape of the hook and sharpness are key to getting the fish hooked and keeping it hooked. The point of a hook should be very sharp to the touch, and the hook should not be bent to far in.

The final thing to consider when picking out a lure is the design. Most fishing lures that you want to use should either be very flashy or admit a lot of sound to attract the fish. Also, you must remember that the design of the lure affects the lures action, so don't pick a lure that doesn't run right.

## Step 3: Technique

In this final step I will go over the basic procedures and techniques that you will want to do when you get a bite.

1. OK you feel a fish bump your lure. Now set the hook by yanking up on the rod, but not so hard that you break the line. The fish is on so now what you want to do is pull up slowly and reel on the way down. Make sure you keep the line tight or your fish will get away. When the fish pulls out line make sure you let it pull some line; don't reel against it or you'll break the line.

2. Now that you have him near the boat get the net ready and scoop him up head first. When you have him in the boat, put him on the measuring board and check if he's eatin' size. If he's right on the line, make a decision. Maybe it's too close to call. Take the hook out and throw him back. Try to catch a bigger one next time.

# Water-Resistant, Upcycled Camcorder Case

By **Susanrm** Susan Midlarsky
(www.instructables.com/id/Digicam-
Water-Resistant-Upcycled-Protective-
Case/)

I recently bought a digital camcorder that came without a case. I wanted to make one that would be pretty, provide everyday protection, and also be water resistant so I could use it on a boat. I also wanted to keep the cost low.

## Tools and Materials

You will need:

- duct tape
- clear packing tape
- pouch made from packing material, or similar stuff you can make into a pouch
- a plastic sheet cover
- a Ziploc or other brand bag with as high-quality a closure as you can get. Not the kind with the zipper, though
- sticky-back Velcro
- a D-ring
- cord or lanyard
- Sharpie
- scissors
- knife
- camera (for measuring)
- ruler, preferably metal

## Step 1: Make the Inner Pouch

First, place the camera inside the transparency so it is in a corner with two sides sealed. My camera has a lens that pops out (it has an optical zoom), so I had to add extra space in the case to allow the lens to pop out. In any case, it's a good idea to overestimate how wide it will need to be by a little. Draw lines where you plan to cut with a Sharpie and the ruler, then cut the pouch out.

Next, place the Ziploc back inside the pouch to see how wide you will need to cut that. The zipper will be the way your pouch seals. Again, mark lines and cut it out.

Finally, using packing tape, tape the zip closure to the inside of your transparency pouch. Take your time with this step. It took me a few tries to get the packing tape in the right spot and to get it to stick in the right area of the top of the sheet protector pouch.

Once you have achieved this, tape up the remaining side of the pouch. You now have a water-resistant, transparent pouch through which you can take video.

water

## Step 2: Add the Padded Pouch

Place the camera inside the padded pouch. Draw a rectangle on the front a bit larger than the lens will need. Do the same on the back for the LCD screen, or make it large enough to see the controls as well. I found seeing the LCD screen was adequate, as I could feel the buttons through the case.

## Step 3: Duct Tape, Part One

Insert the inner pouch into the padded pouch. Tape over the body of the case. Where the opening is on the side, add a bit of extra tape to overlap and stick to itself. It should not look neat at this point.

When you finish duct-taping the body, unstick the side pieces from each other and re-open the side of the case. Using your knife and the cutting board, cut a flap using the rectangle as a guide. Cut only the top and sides, leaving the bottom of the flap intact. Do this for both sides of the case.

## Step 4: Add Velcro & D-ring

Cut small pieces of Velcro to hold the flap open. Stick on the top of the flap and where the flap meets the outside of the case, on both sides.

Tape the side cleanly. I used extra tape to compensate for the part of the pouch I mistakenly cut off. Add tape to the bottom. Insert the baggie case into the outer case.

I thought hard about a solution for wearing the camera around my neck. Eventually I decided to cannibalize a belt I bought from the thrift store for one of its D-rings. I taped this in really well, using various layers and directions of tape, and going under the top of the back window with some of the tape.

The neck thing it hangs from is a giveaway from a trade show—another good way to upcycle junk lying around.

## Step 5: More Duct Tape & Finishing touches

Tape over the top flap, and add contrasting tape (if desired) to the undersides of the top flap and window flaps.

Add Velcro to the top flap, making sure you are using the right type (soft or hard) so that both the top and window flaps can attach to the same piece of Velcro.

Create a flap to hold down Velcro that holds the back flap closed. I also used the duct tape to secure the D-ring further. Add narrow strips of tape (clear or duct, your choice; I used clear) around the edges of the windows to seal up that opening. Attach a neck cord to the D-ring.

The resulting video has a slight haze from the plastic, but nothing too bad. I'm very happy with my case, and I hope you are too, if you try it!

# Underwater Pumpkin Carving

By **sk8ter20art** Michael Cohen
(www.instructables.com/id/
UNDERWATER-pumpkin-carving/)

In this instructable I will show you how to carve a pumpkin underwater. Although it seems like a simple task there are a few tricks to make it easier.

## What You Will Need

For carving a pumpkin underwater you will need:
- a pumpkin
- pen, or marker
- knife or pumpkin carving kit
- 1 to 2 bricks or extra lead weights
- (optional) collection bag
- and of course scuba gear, unless you can hold your breath for over 2 minutes.

I thought about using my dive knife but it's not really suited for cutting out details or curves.

## Step 1: Getting Prepared

Planning ahead makes this task much easier. Go ahead and cut open the top of your pumpkin and clean out the insides.

Draw your design on the pumpkin with a ballpoint pen or sharpie (use a red sharpie if you're worried about not following the lines exactly).

Once you have prepared your pumpkin. Go ahead and start putting on your scuba gear.

This is where the brick or lead weights come into play. Even with the top of the pumpkin cut open and filled with water, IT STILL FLOATS. So place your brick or lead weights inside the pumpkin. I used 1 regular red house brick. This made my pumpkin neutrally Buoyant, you may have to play around with the weight depending on your pumpkin size.

Also when you get ready to enter the water it's a good idea to leave the lid you cut out at your prep station. It will float away if you try to keep it with you. For the pumpkin carving knife I just stuck it into the rim of the pumpkin so I wouldn't lose it.

## Step 2: Start Hacking away

Once you're in the water and settled on the bottom you can start carving your pumpkin. The pieces you cut out will float away. So if you don't want to leave them floating around put them in a collection bag.

The mouthpiece I cut out also floated away ( I did retrieve it). The fish are interested in the pumpkin, but don't really care for the taste.

## Step 3: Enjoy Your Pumpkin

Take your carved pumpkin on a night dive. Put your brick or weights back in, tie in some glow sticks, attach the top somehow with nails or staples. Take your pumpkin to the bottom. You will want to add a few extra pounds of weight than you did before so that it will stay on the bottom where you place it. Turn off your dive light and enjoy Halloween underwater.

Some reefs are erroneously constructed from car tires (a bad idea due to the toxicity of rubber disintegrating in salt water), and some are built using broken-down cars, old boats, and scrap metal. Our goal was to ensure that fish and other marine animals, such as crabs, octopus, and eels, looking for a place to live and reproduce had the best environment available. The reef project chose cinder block because the block was much easier to handle than cars and other heavy industrial items and the calcium content of concrete bolsters the growth of various plant and invertebrate life forms. Also, logistically it made more sense because block is readily available. The fish habitats are formed into an "igloo" and "caterpillar" shapes, which offer the best environment to live, breed and find protection.

### Step 1: Choose Location

The very first step is to choose a low current location that is conducive to undersea life, reproduction, and feeding.

In 1985, a 60-foot tuna-fishing vessel of Mexican origin was anchored close to the beach in Playa Hermosa. A fire broke out aboard causing considerable damage and the boat sank. In 2002, fishermen living in Playa Hermosa discovered the location of boat and helped discover the wreck and the remains of the fishing vessel. The wreck has a N-S direction. To the south is a drum with nets and ropes completely covered with vegetation and corals, at the center is the engine and various mechanical parts of the arms. At the other end, the north, one can see a metal cube of about 100 cubic feet that is most likely a fuel tank. The wreck lies about 400 meters west from the beach, facing the parking lot of the first entrance to Playa Hermosa. It sits at a depth roughly 20 to 30 feet depending on the tide. 12 fish habitats consisting of the igloo block structure are located around the wreck.

While the CondoFish project in Playa Hermosa Costa Rica obtained full government approval for the project, this may or may not be relevant in other international locations. Costa Rica is a very ecologically conscious country and anything regarding natural resources or wildlife requires approval and constant surveillance.

### Step 2: Test Reef Design Outside of Water

While you may have a good idea of what your design will be. We highly suggest testing your design outside of the water. This will save valuable building time underwater.

The following steps will show the design that the Playa Hermosa Artificial Reef Project used. It seems to be good design to start with.

water

## Step 3: Move Materials to Site

Move your materials to your building site. We chose a clean patch of ocean floor and dropped the cinder blocks one by one. Then we built the Reef structures by moving the blocks from the pile to the building site.

## Step 4: Build Base, First Levels

Build your base on level sea floor. Anchoring should not be needed if the location chosen is calm enough.

Build the sides up to the 4th level.

## Step 5: Add the 5th Level and the Center Support

Add the 5th level and the center support.

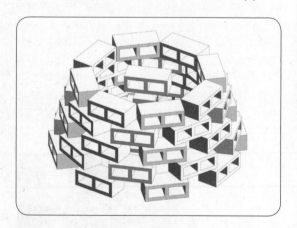

## Step 6: Monitor, Maintain, and Protect

Now, monitor, maintain, and protect. We make weekly visits to the site and constantly think of way to make things better. Pending approval, we'll be building more structures and requiring more and more support.

## Step 7: Progress After 1 Year

It's been nearly a year since we dropped the first blocks in the water. What was once a bare sand bottom, is now teaming with life. The blocks are covered with calcium based creatures, soft corals, crabs, fish eggs, and school of fish frequent the area. Add to that the life in the Benthic zone under and around the structures is doing very well.

water

### in the
# garage

Tune up that old clunker, fix up your bike, or turn your gas-guzzler into an environment-loving hybrid. Or just trick out your car with a push button ignition! From simple repairs to custom mods, you'll find some great projects to inspire your inner grease monkey.

# Paint Your Car With RustOleum

## By DrSimons

(www.instructables.com/id/Paint-Your-Car-With-Rustoleum/)

Do you have a fun car that you just KNOW will go faster with a brand new paint job?

This method is based on the idea of using a foam paint roller to put many layers of RustOleum on your car. Except, I used a professional airgun and only 2 coats. The result? Pretty dang good, for the money.

Why?

So why RustOleum? Well, on the internet you can find people who rolled it on, and the cars look pretty good. But most of all, you can get a quart for under $5 at any hardware store, whereas automotive paint can be 20-50 times that much.

I have a neighbor who has a paint shop in his garage, so I got to use his spray gun. You will need a spray gun and air compressor, but if you don't you can still try rolling on the paint.

## Preparation

First, you'll need some items:

- a car you're willing to ruin the paint job on
- 2 to 4 quarts (depending on size of car) of gloss RustOleum, color of your choice
- 4 or more cans of RustOleum auto primer spray paint
- 1 quart of acetone
- 1 can of Bondo (optional)
- sandpaper—120, 400, 800 grit (or the closest you can get)
- mixing can/bottle/whatever
- stir stick
- masking tape and paper
- 4" super-fine foam paint roller (optional)
- spray gun—bigger nozzle seems to work better
- air compressor—big enough for the spray gun's requirements
- dry, well-ventilated area to paint in
- a bunch of miscellaneous tools—these may include screwdrivers, ratchet sets, Allen wrenches, a can of Liquid Wrench, 2 gallons of diligence.
- You'll do well to make sure the primer is RustOleum, to ensure compatibility (paint can act stupidly if it doesn't like the primer). Also, use dark primer if your car color is dark (blue, green, black, etc.) and lighter primer if the paint is lighter. This way you won't have to spray on 20 coats to cover it up.
- It's also a good idea to handle any bodywork your car needs. If you don't want to do this, get a professional to do it but see if you can have him skip painting it to save money. However, for small dents Bondo (or any number of superior, more expensive fillers) is really quite easy to use. I had to replace a destroyed fender and Bondo a big dent on the hood before painting, but it was a lot easier than you'd think.

## Step 1: Remove Trim

Look at your car. Especially in the door jambs. Imagine masking all those little parts off, one by one . . . sound like fun? No. Remove them (this may be a long process, but most trim comes off pretty easily with the right tools).

### What Exactly Should you Remove?

- Hood, trunk, gas tank lid (if removable) - these are a lot easier to paint separately
- Rubber gaskets/trim
- Lights
- Reflectors

- License plates
- Door latching stuff

Stash all the parts somewhere they won't get lost, stolen, rained on, etc. A nice empty work table is great, then you can lay them out in an organized way.

## Step 2: Sand!

Sanding the car before painting it is like opening a bank account before making a deposit. Ya just gotta do it. First, use strong soap, wax, and grease remover, or whatever you have lying around to clean the heck out of the paint. Then sand it with 300 or 400 grit paper. For difficult areas, you may want to get some abrasive foam or scouring material that conforms better than regular sand paper. The point is to completely eliminate the shininess of the finish, and get past the clear coat. You don't want to sand down to bare metal, there's no point.

## Step 3: Bondo!

In case you do have some dents you'd like to make go away, it's nice and easy. Ask yourself: is this dent really big, like over an inch deep and 6 inches wide? If so, get a dent puller or something (not my area of expertise). For small dents, sand 2 inches all around the dent down to bare metal (use really rough sandpaper, maybe 120 grit). Make sure the metal part is really rough. Then get a can of Bondo—you can find it everywhere—and mix it up on a clean, non-porous surface. Slap it on the dent, cover the whole area past flush. Try not to get bubbles mixed in, these look terrible. Then you sand the Bondo back down to flush, using really big sanding strokes to make it even with the whole surface. Use progressively finer sand paper to get a nice smooth end product. You shouldn't be able to feel where the Bondo blends into the car.

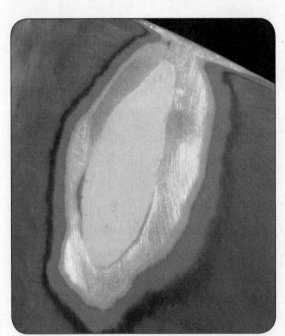

## Step 4: Mask!

You don't want to paint your window now do you? No . . . that wouldn't be very smart. But never fear, masking tape is here! You'll need painters tape (blue) or extra strong auto masking tape (green) to cover all the areas that are already the right color.

Some things to mask:
- Windshield
- Side windows
- Rear window

garage

- Mirrors
- Rubber gaskets that you weren't able to remove in step 2
- Door handles
- The inside of the car (you'll have the doors open when you paint)
- Tail pipe
- Engine bay
- Radiator (believe me, it looks quite ridiculous if paint gets on there when you paint the front of the car)
- Tires
- Any important-looking labels inside the door that have important car information

Again, things like tail lights, head lights, rubber gaskets, car logos, etc. should really be removed before you paint, or it will end up looking like a noob did it with finger paint.

For big areas use quality masking paper or cardboard, and garbage bags work well for tires. The quality of the mask job is immeasurably important. If you do super crisp accurate masking, your paint job will look like the car was always that color. Spend as much time on this step as possible.

## Step 5: Prime!

You put primer on the car so the regular paint stays on. Pretty straight forward. I used spray paint, since this doesn't really affect the final finish. RustOleum makes "automotive primer" so I figured that was appropriate. I'm not qualified to give any advice on spraying, other than do it outside and wear a mask so you don't get cancer.

Prepare the surface. Use some tack cloth and clean off all the loose paint and dust on the car.

Paint! The coat doesn't need to be thick, but it has to cover everything. Spray it on, have fun. Let the stuff dry . . . maybe an hour or 2 before you paint a second coat (if it needs it). Let it dry for a day or two.

Sand it!

According to my professional car painter neighbor, you should sand the primer before painting on the top coat. Since fresh primer is extremely "soft", you can use 800 or so grit and get a really smooth surface. Be very careful not to sand through the primer though, or you'll have to spray on some more.

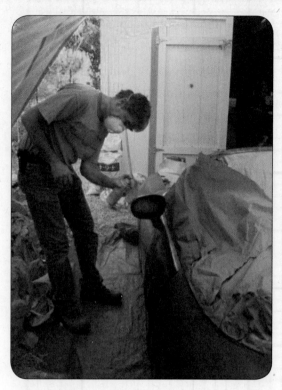

## Step 6: Paint!!!

This is the big showdown. You'll have spent many hours preparing by now, and this is the moment you've all been waiting for! If you want to try rolling on the RustOleum, be my guest. People have had success with that in the past, but I have a feeling that doing the door jams would be hell compared to spraying it on.

You may want to re-mask everything, because dust and paint on the used masking paper can find its way onto your new finish. And remember to clean off all dust on the car by hitting it with compressed air or using tack cloth.

**For Rolling on Paint**

Get a foam paint roller (4" wide should do) and make sure it's as fine as possible. This creates a very smooth finish if the paint is thin enough.

Mix acetone into the RustOleum in a mixing can. I've read that you want something around the consistency of water, which means a LOT of acetone. You'll probably need more than 1 quart to do the whole car. When mixing paint, stir it with a stick, DON'T shake it or bubbles will happen.

**Note**

This method requires a lot more patience than spraying, as you're supposed to do

garage

8 or 10 coats, sanding in between each one if orange peel starts happening.

### For Spraying it on

To spray on paint, mix a little acetone into the paint. The can recommends no more than 5%, but don't worry about that since the thinner the paint, the smoother it goes on. However, it is also more likely to run on vertical surfaces so be careful.

This process is somewhat risky, but has great potential. Hard to get areas like door jambs, cracks, etc will look amazing when the paint is sprayed on. On the other hand, the entire car may turn out looking like an orange. If that happens, you probably need to mix in more acetone.

If you get lots of orange peel, fish eyes, or other demonic paint problems, you can always sand them away and try again, and in hard to get to areas it won't matter anyway. Spraying on multiple coats also makes for a smoother finish. Wait a few hours between coats to allow drying.

Leave the paint to dry peacefully for at least a few days. I let my car sit in a dry garage for over a week before putting any of the trim back.

## Step 7: Finish the Job

After your paint is nice and dry (it should be invulnerable to you pressing your fingernail into it), you can put all the trim back on. Admire your work, and make sure not to scratch it! I did while carrying the hood, and got rather upset.

All in all this was very fun, very experimental, but also quite satisfying. The

trick is to have a positive attitude about it. Because you don't know if it's going to turn out well, you have to just assume it will. If the finish looks bad, sand it and try again. The forces of good will prevail.

## Step 8: Long-Term Results

After almost 2 years, I have finally washed the car for the first time! On America's birthday I washed off a thick layer of dust to find that . . . it looks as good as new! When compared to the when it was first done, the paint looks as bright, shiny, and clean as ever.

For a while I kept the car under a UV-shielded car cover, and for the last 6 months it's been under a carport, to minimize the UV exposure (a good practice for regular automotive paint too). Note that there are a few issues . . . in one or two locations the paint has cracked from impacts, but more noticeably there are a few spots where bird droppings dissolved the paint. This happened because I neglected to wash off said droppings for several weeks. I will probably touch up these spots with the spray-paint version of RustOleum.

# Awesome Push Button Ignition

By **HAL9000** Vance Langer
(www.instructables.com/id/Push-Button-Ignition-for-your-Car/)

I really wanted a sweet push button ignition and an engine kill switch, like a rocket or a race car or something cooler than an early nineties economy car.

It should take between one and two hours, depending on how fast you can take apart your dashboard, but could take considerably longer. This project cost me $25 for a soldering iron, wire, one relay, two momentary buttons, and a switch.

## Gather Materials

- One Single Pole Double Throw Relay (a SPST normally open will work as well)
- One Momentary switch, Normally open (toggle or button)
- One Single Pole Single Throw Switch (toggle or button)
- Soldering Equipment/Knowledge
- Wire (I used 18 g)
- Screwdriver
- Wire Cutter
- Other various tools

Be sure that whatever momentary switch or button you get is a normally open, momentary switch.

## Step 1: Open Up the Dash

Here you will need to get inside your dashboard to where your ignition harness is. This is near the keyhole. Once you get to this bundle of wires you will need to cut the ignition wire and the starter wire, so probably disconnect the battery first. You will have to find a wiring diagram for your car to know what wires do what. I can tell you that for Hondas the ignition wire is black and yellow, and the starter wire is black and white.

Cut these wires and strip the end enough that you can solder it or splice it well.

As long as you cut the wires such that you can splice or solder them back together you should be OK, but be aware that cutting wires to your ignition could become a problem.

## Step 2: Assemble the Hardware

Now we will solder together the chain of switches and wires and buttons and relays to make this all work.

Basically the way this all works is that the ignition wire, which needs to remain a closed circuit as long as the engine is going, is connected to the relay, and we will borrow some of the current going through it to switch the relay and start the engine.

## Step 3: Put it All Under the Dash

Now that your parts and wires are all wired in its time to test it. Turn the key to the "Engine On" position. Flip the switch on. Push the button. If you have wired everything all correctly you will start the engine. Now put your dash back together and put your buttons and switches wherever you like.

# How to Fix Rust Spots on a Car

By **intoon**
(www.instructables.com/id/How-to-Fix-Rust-Spots-On-a-Car/)

I drive a 1985 VW Golf (diesel), and it's in pretty good condition for being 21 years old. There are three spots on the front left fender that have rust on them. These spots are not only an eye sore, but they are sure to spread in the salty Nebraska winters. My goal in fixing these was function, and not so much glamour. As long as the rust was gone, it would look better, and I wouldn't lose a fender.

## Step 1: Assess the Situation/ Remove Wheel

Having never done this, or any other body work on a car, it took me a little longer to figure out what exactly I was going to do. My original plan was to take the entire fender off, but after inspecting it, that would be too much of a hassle and would require me to disassemble a lot of the front of the car. Instead, I jacked the car up then I pulled the wheel. I unscrewed the plastic thing protecting the wheel well and set it off to the side. That gave me really good access to see up behind the sheet metal on the car. I was originally going to pound out the dent on the upper part of the fender, but space was tight and I couldn't easily do it. Having the wheel well open will help when I'm grinding and painting.

## Step 2: Remove Paint

The first thing I did was remove the paint around the rust. I used a 4½" grinder with a 120 grit 3M Sandblaster wheel. It worked really well for taking off the thick layers of primer and paint. I carefully worked my way around the rust spots and removed paint until I could see clean metal surrounding the rust. I also used that wheel for removing all of the light rust that hadn't pitted the metal. Note: Before grinding, cover up anything that you don't want to get dusty. The paint dust is super fine and covers everything. I had my hood open to help access some rust, so I got a tarp to cover up the engine. Having your windows rolled down here would be a bad idea.

## Step 3: Grind Some More

After I got all I could with the sanding wheel, I changed over to a metal grinding wheel. When using this, be super careful because these can do a lot of damage. I worked really slowly so that I could get a nice finish on the metal. It was really good

garage

for taking the thick rust off and getting into those pits. After 99.9 percent of the rust was removed, I sanded by hand (with 120 grit 3M Sandblaster sandpaper) to get a nice smooth metal surface. If I wanted, I could have used Bondo to even out some of the dents, and fill the space where the paint is gone.

## Step 4: Prep for Painting

I found some really good primer that is ideal for painting on bare metal: Dupli-Color Self-Etching Primer. Then I found some auto spray that matched the color of my car: Dupli-Color Auto Spray in Sunburst Gold Metallic. I followed all of the instructions on the back of the primer: I mixed up a little bit of car wash soap and water and washed the areas that I was going to paint. Then I got a 400 grit wet sandpaper and sanded the areas, then wiped clean. I then masked off the areas with tape, and then taped newspapers on all the surrounding areas within at least three feet. Paint spray can get everywhere because it gets suspended in the air and blown around and settles somewhere. Once everything was masked off, I was ready to prime.

## Step 5: Prime, Paint

When applying paint, it is important to spray thin coats and keep it even. The paint that I was using was really nice, and went on very smoothly. I ended up spraying three coats of primer, waiting about two minutes between each coat for it to tack up. I let that sit all night and sprayed the paint in the morning. I had to spray the paint on even thinner, because it really wanted to run and sag. I ended up having five coats

of paint on top of the primer. That gave me a nice color and a nice finish. I let it set at least 24 hours before I pulled off the tape. The paint turned out pretty well, and it just looked like little patches over the old rust. The color wasn't quite the same as the old, but it was pretty close. It also had no clear coat on it, so it had a little different finish. I didn't bother buffing the edge of the paint so that it blended with the old paint.

## Step 6: Wash and Wax

After the paint had cured a good 48 hours, I washed and waxed the car to bring back the shine. It ended up looking fairly good. It cost me less than $15 and 4 to 6 hours of labor. I spent an additional 4 hours washing and waxing. If I had taken it to a body shop, it could have cost me $200. So I saved a lot of money and got the satisfaction of doing it myself, which is the best part.

garage

# Windshield Deicer and Ice Prevention Spray

By sunshine
(www.instructables.com/id/
Windshield-De-Icer-And-Ice-
Prevention-Spray/)

I have been making all of my own cleaning supplies. I needed a windshield deicer and found these recipes. Making your own is much more economical and it will ease the task of removing ice from the windshield. Use these applications at your own risk and own choice. Keep all products out of the reach of anyone or anything that could be at risk of injury.

## Ingredients for Ice and Frost Prevention

- 3 parts white vinegar/1 part water. I added the food coloring to the water to help distinguish the different products.

## Utensils for Ice and Frost Prevention

- spray bottle
- liquid measuring cup
- funnel
- marker

### Step 1: Measure

Measure ingredients for ice and frost prevention: 3 parts vinegar/1 part water

### Step 2: Mix and Label

Mix all ingredients and label. Please note: The ice and frost prevention is sprayed on the windows the night before to help prevent the ice from sticking. The wipers should easily remove the snow and ice so you don't have to.

## Deicer Ingredients and Utensils

This is what you need:

- 1 part water to 2 parts 70 percent Isopropyl Alcohol
  Same utensils as before.

### Step 1: Measure, Mix, and Label

Measure alcohol and water. Pour into spray bottle, label. Please notice the directions call for 70 percent Isopropyl alcohol. I used colored water in the bottles for picture purposes only. The deicer is used to spray on the ice to allow for easy scraping.

## Washer Fluid Line (Ice Prevention)

This is what you need:

- Same utensils as before except you don't need a sprayer just a lid and bottle.

### Step 1: Measure, Mix, and Label

Fill a bottle with ONE HALF 70 percent alcohol and ONE HALF windshield wiper fluid.

Add a few drops of dish soap. Label. This is used to fill your washer fluid reservoir to keep the lines free from freezing.

# Hack Your Hood Ornament

By **reno_dakota** Robin Ivester
(www.instructables.com/id/Hack-
Your-Hood-Ornament/)

Make a unique hood ornament out of a recycled trophy! Instead of the standard hood ornament, I've installed a chromed angel off of a thrift-store trophy. It's cheap, easy, makes me smile, and gets noticed everywhere. I once had a park ranger in Utah ask me for bolt-cutters so that she could steal it. I figure that counts as a compliment.

## What You Need

Check the hood ornament fitting on your car. On mine (1985 Crown Victoria), the hood ornament sits in a base that's bolted in front of the hood and fastens by means of a wire threaded through a spring. The spring gives the ornament a little wiggle room and serves as a break-point when the ornament is struck. If your hood ornament is removable, has a base with a ~½" center hole, and uses this kind of spring attachment, you're in luck. Go out and get yourself a new hood ornament! What you're looking for is the figure from the top of an old trophy—a winged-lady-with-torch, a bowler, a diver, a soccer player, whatever. What you need:

- car with an appropriate hood ornament fitting
- metal figure from a trophy, with a base larger than your hood ornament fitting

- ~¼" base screw long enough to extend through the fitting and the hood of the car
- good strong ~⅛" diam. Wire
- very stiff spring ~1" long, either from the original hood ornament apparatus or scrounged up elsewhere
- silicone adhesive
- chrome spray paint
- adjustable wrench
- small pliers
- wire snips

## Step 1: Dismantle Your Hood Ornament

On the Crown Vic, there's a bolt to unscrew fastening the fitting to the underside of the hood. Once this is loosened, the hood ornament (with spring and wires attached) slides out, and the fitting can be detached from the hood. Note: The new hood ornament setup requires the spring and wires to be a bit larger; they have to be removed before the fitting can be separated from the hood. I just left the fitting bolted on. I picked up a replacement factory-model hood ornament at a pic and pull yard recently.

## Step 2: Drill Through the Base-Screw

Drill through the base-screw of the trophy figure. Clamp the figure in a vise if possible to hold it stable and drill a perpendicular ~⅛" hole through the center of the screw.

## Step 3: Make it Shiny!

Time for painting! Prop the trophy figure up so that you can spray paint all sides of it evenly, give it a solid coat of chrome paint, and leave it to dry. I'd suggest looping some wire

garage

through the hole you drilled in the base-screw and hanging it upside-down to paint and dry.

## Step 4: Adapt the Trophy-Figure Base to the Top of the Hood Fitting

Obviously, the base of the trophy and the top of the hood fitting aren't matched. On mine, the trophy base is round and ~2" across; the hood fitting is rectangular and smaller. I needed some way to fit the two together so that the figure had a stable base that could deal with vibration and wind on the road. To solve this problem, I used a silicone adhesive to fill in the hollow base of the trophy and essentially mold it to the hood fitting. It's waterproof and flexible, and seems to work well enough so far. I filled in the base of the trophy figure with silicone adhesive, then slipped the base screw through the hole in the hood fitting, pressed the two pieces together, fixed them in place so that the figure would stand vertical when on the hood, and let the two pieces dry together. This took a day to dry, and probably could have used another 24 to 48 hours to fully cure.

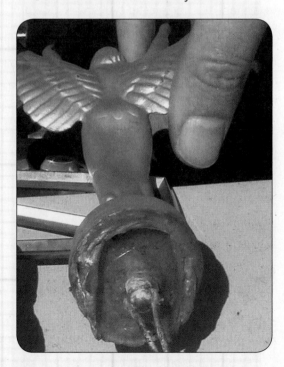

## Step 5: Installation

First, bolt the hood fitting back onto the car, tightly. Next, thread the wire through the hole in the figure's base-screw. Make a loop such that you have two 4" lengths of wire extending down from the base-screw. Then thread the ends of the wire down through the hole in the hood fitting and set the figure upright, matching its base to the hood fitting. It helps to have a friend around to hold the figure upright while you finish the attachment. Under the hood, fit your spring over the two lengths of wire that extend down out of the bottom of the hood fitting. Mash the spring down tightly and bend the ends of both wires up, fastening the figure tightly down to the hood ornament. You should have a little bit of flex, but not too much; you don't want the hood ornament to be flopping around in the wind on the highway.

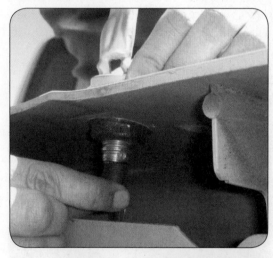

For the original story, go to PopularMechanics.com. We've all been there—hastily putting the car in reverse, failing to check the blind spot, and cringing at the crunch of bumper meeting barricade. Fortunately for your bruised bumper, plastic repair and refinishing materials are widely available and reasonably simple to use. Fixing damaged plastic bumpers involves grinding, sanding, sculpting, and painting, but it's worth the effort for repairs that would cost less than your deductible.

### Step 1: Choose an Adhesive and Prep the Fascia

After you remove the plastic piece from your bumper (the screws connecting the plastic covering can be tricky to locate: try under the tail lights, behind the wheel wells, and below the trunk latch where we found our Honda Civic's), you'll need a warm, dry place to work in so that the repair adhesives can cure properly. But which adhesives you need will depend on the type of plastic in your bumper. Thus, the first step is to find a stamp on the inside of your bumper labeling it as PP, PPO, TPE, PUR, or TPUR. When you purchase your repair products, be sure to consult with the counterman at the auto parts store to determine which recipe is right for your bumper's plastic. Be sure to stick to the same brand for all of your products to ensure compatibility. To prep, begin by slightly scuffing the damaged area and cleaning it with plastic surface cleaner. If the bumper is cut or torn through completely, make sure to scrub the inner and outer surfaces. After rinsing and letting the surface dry, wipe the area with prep solvent, moving in only one direction.

### Step 2: Grind a "V"

After the solvent has dried, sand the area by hand with 80-grit paper. Next, you'll need to form a "V" groove in the damaged area on the front and back sides of the fascia. The grooves allow you to align the two edges more easily. They also provide more surface area for the repair material to adhere to. For plastic types that powder when sanded (PUR, TPUR), cut the grooves with a 24-grit disc on a sander. For plastics that smear when sanded (PP, PPO, TPE), make the grooves using a cordless drill and a rotary file.

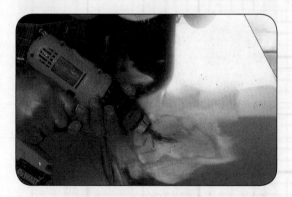

### Step 3: Mix the Adhesive and Repair Tears

Repair tears and cuts from the back side of the fascia. If the cut or tear is large, you might have to align and then hold the edges of the repair with masking tape on the front of the fascia. Use self-stick fiberglass-repair

garage

268

tape to add structure to the cut or tear. Next, thoroughly mix equal amounts of hardener and repair adhesive on a piece of cardboard or paper and apply it over the tape with a body-filler squeegee. When the first layer of tape is in place, apply a second layer so the threads run at a 90-degree angle to the first layer.

## Step 4: Spread the Plastic Filler

Once the material has hardened (in about 20 minutes), move to the front of the fascia and remove any tape (if applied). Next, using 80-grit sandpaper, remove any material that has squeezed through, and sand any spots that are above the finished level of the fascia. Fill the cut or tear and any low spots in the front of the fascia with the appropriate repair material, and squeegee it level.

## Step 5: Sand and Contour

After it has hardened, sand everything level, first with 80-grit, then 120-grit, and then apply a light skim coat of repair material to fill pits and surface imperfections, and to restore the original contour. Then finish sand with wet 400-grit paper.

## Step 6: Paint

When the repair is completed, apply two wet coats of flexible part sealer. After drying for 30 minutes, the fascia is ready for priming and painting. Prime the fender with two coats of any two-part primer-surfacer, making sure to let the primer dry between coats. Once the primer has hardened, dry sand the repaired areas with 400-grit paper to level it and remove any imperfections. Before spraying the bumper with basecoat, wet sand it and gently wipe the area with a tack rag to remove dust, then spray according to the manufacturer's instructions. You may need to repeat this process two or three times to cover completely. Once the base coat is dry (usually about 30 minutes), mix the clear coat with hardener. Apply two medium clear coats, allowing each to dry in between. After drying overnight, the fascia is ready to be reinstalled.

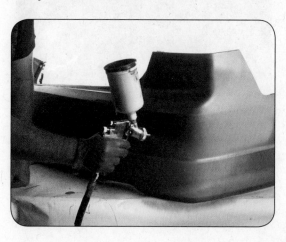

garage

269

# Cargo Area Platform Slider for SUVs, Trucks, and Station Wagons

### By galadriel

Galadriel Billington
(www.instructables.com/id/Cargo-area-platform-slider-for-SUV-truck-station/)

I wanted to be able to slide out the "bed" of my cargo area in my Chevy Tahoe. I primarily wanted a work surface (leaning over the bumper was killing my back), but this should make it easier to access items stored in the cargo area as well. There are really nice products made that will do this, but they're quite expensive and the majority of them are not made for anything smaller than a Suburban. I didn't want to spend $1000; I wanted to spend less than $150 (and I was successful). I have a '99 Chevy Tahoe, and those are the measurements I'll give. This concept should be easily adaptable to any SUV, maybe a station wagon, possibly even a pickup truck but the platform would have to be much longer and well-secured.

## Supplies

The "bed" of my Tahoe is 48" by 48", so this is sized for my Tahoe. I will include descriptions so that you can alter it for your own vehicle width (side to side, measure at the narrowest part of your cargo area) and depth (back of the seats to the lip of the cargo area—leave enough room to close your doors or tailgate).

- (2) ¾" plywood sheet, 48" (width) by 48" (depth)—I was able to buy one 4' by 8' sheet and cut it in half.
- (4) 48" (depth) 2.25" × 1.5" slotted angle iron
- (2) sets of "Appliance Rollers"
- 30 × #8 × ⅝" screws—you may need more or fewer depending on the length of your cargo area
- (10) washers to fit the #8 screws—you may need more or fewer
- (10) ½" long bolts, with rounded heads, not hex, each with washer and lock nut—you may need more or fewer
- (1) 2" long bolt; ¼" or ⅜" diameter.
- You're probably also going to want some sand paper, possibly some wood finish or paint. If you're going to put this in an area exposed to the elements (like a pickup truck bed) you should certainly paint or finish it.

## Tools

- Eye protection and gloves,
- sensible clothing
- pencil for marking measurements and screw hole locations
- measuring tape
- Philips head screwdriver
- socket wrench with socket to fit the lock nuts
- circular saw
- table saw, or other wood saw with a blade to cut plywood
- drill with ½" bit for "stop" hole
- ⁵⁄₆₄" bit for screw pilot hole, and Phillips screwdriver bit
- metal cutting saw
- hacksaw—possibly optional
- angle grinder—possibly optional, but I strongly recommend it
- a pair of clamps if you're going to be using an angle grinder or if you're going to be making any precise circular saw cuts, or for many other uses.
- router if you've got access to one (lucky you)

## Step 1: Build the Base

Make sure you use eye protection. Cut your plywood so you have two pieces, each the size of your "bed." This is a good place to stop and make sure that you have the measurements correct. Try to slide the board into your "bed," oriented properly, and make sure it goes in without a fight. When you're finished, the whole thing will be just a touch wider than the base. Put one board (the top board) to the side. You'll only be working on the base at first.

On the base plywood board, measure 3 straight lines from forward to backward, making sure you're orienting it as it will be in the "bed." Take several measurements from the side of the board, at each end, in the middle, etc, so that you know you have a very straight line. Use a line 4" over from each side and at the center line. Trace these straight lines—I used the angle iron because it was handy.

Attaching the rollers: Take out your "appliance rollers" and unscrew the screw/wing nut that holds the two pieces together. You now have 8 individual rollers, each with a long tail. You will put these in place by lining up the tail with the line you have drawn. Line up the tail, and put a mark for a screw hole at each extreme end of the slots (one at the close end of the close slot, one at the far end of the far slot), and a mark at the middle of the middle slot. Mark screw holes to put one roller in each corner, and three rollers along the center line (that's a total of 7). Once you have carefully marked the screw holes, (use eye protection) carefully drill a pilot hole at each mark. Now line your appliance rollers back up in their places, and use a screw per pilot hole. Your rollers are in place.

## Step 2: Put in the Retaining Angle Irons on Each Side

Make sure you use eye protection, and for power tools on metal protect your hands (gloves), arms (long durable sleeves), legs (long pants), surrounding area, etc., from flying sparks. Make sure you securely clamp anything you will grind. Cut your angle iron so that it is the length of your "bed" (angle grinder, hacksaw, other metal saw); you may also want to round the edges with an angle grinder or other metal saw. I certainly did; I know I'll scrape myself on the edges if they're left sharp.

Fit one slotted angle iron up against each side (left and right) of the plywood base, with the short side of the angle iron up against the bottom of the base. Clamp the iron in place, and use a screw with a washer about every foot to screw it down. Your base now has vertical edges.

Again on each side (left and right), fit a second slotted angle iron up against the first; bolt them together such that the vertical side is about 3" tall. Use your short hex bolts, a washer, and a lock nut about every foot. I put the top angle iron on the inside on each side, as I ended up sanding/rounding the top board such that it is slightly more narrow than the bottom board.

## Step 3: Finish the Top Board

Next I rounded the front and side edges of my top board and sanded the top surface. I abused my angle iron to get the rounded edges, but a router would do that much more easily, and it's also possible to do by sanding it down (lots of work). I'll probably leave it bare wood, but I may try to find a scrape-resistant finish (looking around, seems like my best choice is penetrating resin).

## Step 4: Finishing Touches

### Making a "Stop"

Slide your top board between the rollers and the retaining angle iron. Situate it such that the top and bottom boards are parallel. Mark the top of the board under the first circular hole.

Slide the board out to a few convenient lengths, and mark the top board under the first circular hole for each one.

Pull your top board back out and drill a ½" hole at each mark.

Slide the top board back in all the way, and drop the 2" bolt through the first round hole into the ½" hole underneath. It's finished!

If you can manage to align the drilled holes, the "stop" will be even more secure if it goes through the base as well as the top board. You'll want a 2½" or 3" bolt. Be careful not to drill all the way through the base and into the angle iron, as the drill may kickback and injure you.

### Tweaking

If you find that you have too much leeway sliding it in and out (it wobbles), you may wish to consider attaching a very thin wood strip to the inside vertical edge side or underside of the top edge of the retaining angle iron, so that it holds the top board more snugly. Both surfaces will need to be polished very smooth or otherwise allowed to slide against each other. I've read that UHMW (ultra-high molecular weight) tape is good for such applications.

### "Installing" it in Your Vehicle

Slide the whole thing into the "bed" of your vehicle with the rounded front edge facing out. To use the slide, pull up the bolt, roll the top board out and drop the bolt back down into another hole to lock it until you're done.

### Bolting it Down

If you will be putting a lot of weight on the extended slide, you will probably want to find a way to bolt it down. In the back of my Tahoe, there are rings bolted to the "bed." I could use a U-bolt through each of those rings and then bolted to the base, or I could simply remove the ring itself and bolt the base down to that hole. I also considered attaching a strap to the front edge, and wrapping that strap around the seat hinges directly in front of it. You'll need to examine your cargo area to see what is feasible for your vehicle.

### Automatic Stop

I'd also like a mechanism to keep the platform from extending too far. It would need to be easily disconnected so that I can dismantle the sliding platform without too much hassle.

# how to do absolutely everything

## with
# trash

Don't throw it away—turn that trash into treasure! In these pages you'll find great projects to reuse old paper, plastic bags, egg cartons, and more. Make your life simpler, cleaner, and more creative with these great ideas!

# Egg Carton Flower Lights

By mcco4371
(www.instructables.com/id/Egg-Carton-Flower-Lights/)

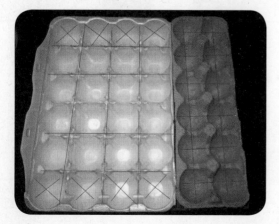

## Gather Your Materials
- Egg Cartons (Cardboard or Styrofoam)
- Acrylic Craft Paint
- Sharp Utility Knife
- Foam Paintbrush
- Hot Glue Gun
- String of Christmas Lights
- Cutting Mat

## Steps 1 and 2: Cut Your Cartons and Shape Your Flowers

Using the utility knife cut the egg cartons along the red lines in this picture. With a Styrofoam carton, not every cup will make a good flower shape, because the first and last row will not turn not well.

## Step 3: Paint Your Flowers

Now it's time to paint your blossoms! I've found that sponge paint brushes work best to cover the irregular surfaces and works the paint into the little creases and dimples well. Styrofoam will show your brush strokes. This gives the flowers a water colored look. The cardboard will paint up nice and evenly. I recommend painting the insides of all the flowers first. By the time you've painted the last flower, the first should be dry and you can then begin painting the outsides.

## Step 4: Assemble Lights

Once all the paint has thoroughly dried, use the utility knife to cut a small X shaped slit in the bottom of your flower.

Insert one of the light bulbs through one of the flowers just far enough that you can remove the bulb and change it if it burns out.

On the back side of the flower, hot glue the flower in place. It helps to hold the flower in position until the glues is set. Repeat this step for each flower, making sure the glue is cool before moving onto the next light.

# Make a Basket Out of Plastic Bags!

By **jessyratfink** Jessy Ellenberger
www.instructables.com/id/Make-a-basket-out-of-plastic-bags/)

No knitting or crochet required, just some sewing and braiding. It's not the quickest project—it'll probably take you a couple days to make one, but the results are well worth it, I think!

## What You'll Need

- sewing needles (just regular old sharps—nothing small like quilting needles or big like embroidery)
- white thread (I chose polyester for added strength)
- plastic bags of all types—grocery bags are easiest, but you can mix and match. The thicker, more opaque bags will produce a thicker braid, while thin, more transparent bags will produce thinner ones. Try to get as many colors as you can—my basket is made almost entirely of white bags with very small amounts of color, and I think it would look even

nicer with some full color bags mixed in. It took me 51 plastic bags to get 60 feet. Not too shabby. I completed my latest rope in less than 8 hours of work, too!

## Step 1: Cutting Your Bags into Strips

It is very important to cut these strips pretty wide. For most normal sized bags, it is possible to get three continuous strips about 4 inches wide. I never got out a ruler, but it's very useful to size up the side seam of the bag before you start cutting to determine how many strips you'll be able to cut.

Lay out a plastic bag, and fold in the sides. Snip off the very top/handles and the very bottom. Then open the bag to its full width.

Turn the bag so a side seam is facing you, and cut up and to the right in a sweeping motion until you get at least four inches in, and then begin cutting in a straight line. When you get near the side seam, slip a hand in the bag and turn it so that the side seam is flat and you can start on the second strip.

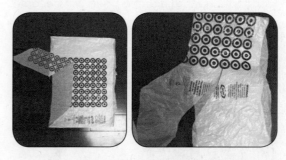

Cut up and to the right again, mirroring the first time you did it, and then cut straight until you reach a point where you have one closed strip left. You're going to make another diagonal cut to the right, this time cutting to the very edge of the bag.

So essentially, just keep cutting towards the right and mirroring the original diagonal cut.

You will need to do this to three bags to start your braid, though I suggest doing this whole process as you were a one person factory line—flatten all the bags you have, cut off the tops and bottoms, and then cut them all into strips, hanging the strips somewhere they won't get too tangled.

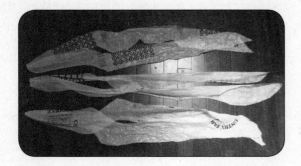

## Step 2: How to Get Braidin'

The strip from each bag will be doubled over, and the two parts will count as one part of the braid. You will have six strands, but each will have a mate.

It is easiest to secure the looped ends of your strips over something small and sturdy, like a nail. I happened to have one sticking out of my desk. I assume you could also tape the ends to a table with decent results.

Once your strips are looped over the nail, make sure they're divided properly into their pairs and get braiding.

It's important to not braid too loose or too tight—too tight will make you lose all the wonderful texture and the braid will become quite small, and if your braid is too loose you'll have problems sewing it into a basket later as the foundation will be pretty floppy.

## Step 3: Braiding Methods

There are two ways to do this, and one of them is undoubtedly more efficient. I'll give you both options, though . . . just in case you like repetition.

Process only three bags at a time, resulting in one 3 to 4 foot length of braid. You'll fold the strips in half so the ends are even, braid them together, and then trim and sew the ends. You will end up with lots of lengths of

braid that you have to sew together . . . so lots of extra work and you probably won't be able to feel your fingers after.

Process tons of bags at a time by knotting new strips to the ends of the initial braid—no sewing required except for the very beginning and end of the braid. This does require more patience and a bigger work area, but goes very quick once you get the hang of it.

## Step 4: The Wrong Way to do This

If you would like to take the hard road, do it this way:

- cut three bags into strips.
- double those strips in half, and braid as suggested in step 2.
- sew both ends of the finished braid closed.
- trim off the excess.
- sew together multiple braids by folding the ends in and sewing around the edges.
- repeat, repeat, repeat.
- curse your needle.
- curse your thread.
- curse the plastic bag gods.
- begin using your teeth to pull the needle through the doubled-over-already-sewn-braid-meeting-lumps.
- call your dentist.

As you can see nothing good comes of this. Move along to a happier place by checking out the right way to do this!

## Step 5: The Right Way, and the Best Way

This will significantly cut down on your sewing time. Not only will you be a happy camper, you will be a sultan of efficiency!

(That's possibly not a real thing.)

trash

- Fold over three strips, so the ends are slightly off center and don't meet exactly. (You'll see why in a moment.)
- Loop these over a nail or tape them to a surface and begin the braid.
- Continue braiding until you near the ends of the strips.
- Make sure your strips all end at slightly different lengths, trimming if necessary.
- Now you'll tie on additional strips to each of the six original strands.
- Make sure not to pull too hard while knotting, or you could rip the bags.
- Also make sure not to knot too many times—two knots is more than sufficient.
- Once you have all six strands extended, match them up into their proper pairs and keep braiding, trying to tuck the recently created knots into the braid, untangling your work every once in a while.
- Once you get past the first round of bag extensions, you will most likely need to find a new place to braid. It works best to find somewhere to tie it off so that you can stand and do it comfortably.
- If you sit and try to braid, you'll find yourself being very tangled very quickly.
- Once you have 20 to 30 feet worth of braided plastic bag, you should have enough to start your basket. Sew and trim the ends as shown in step 4.

## Step 6: Starting the Basket

Coil the rope tightly, skinny side up, until you reach a base size you're happy with. Secure this with a pin or another sewing needle. Now, pick the uglier side of the round—it'll be side you sew through to secure it.

You're going sew to four separate lines into the bottom—one vertically, one horizontally, and two diagonals going through the center.

Here's the protocol for each line:

- Thread your needle with doubled thread, and make sure the knot at the end is quite large or it could pull through.
- Anchor the thread at one edge by pushing through the first round, and then going back over and through it again.
- Push your needle through every other round, pulling/keeping the thread taut as you go.
- Once you reach the other side, make sure the thread is nice and taut, and that your base is good and flat, and then anchor the thread in the outside round and knot a few times.
- Once you've finished all your lines, bend the base a bit to see how stable it is. There will be shifting, but none of the rounds should fall totally out of place. Larger bases might require additional lines . . . so keep that in mind!

## Step 7: Building Up!

Get yourself another looooooooooooong length of doubled over thread and knot it several times.

Grab the tail of the braid that you pinned into the base, and bring it up diagonally to form the bottom row of the basket. Push your needle down through the base, and then bring it over the braid and back down through the base to secure the bottom row. Do this every 1 to 2 inches, keeping the thread diagonal and tight and the braids upright and straight, until you're left with 3 to 4 inches of thread.

Then, anchor the two layers of braids together, and knot on the inside of the basket.

You'll keep repeating this process until you get close to the end of the braid, or until you reach a size you like.

## Step 9: You're Done!

At this point I double checked the strength of the bottom, added a few stitches through the. outside two rounds for extra stability, and then decided I was finished.

## Step 10: Additional Hints and Tips

A thimble will probably be your best friend through this project. Pushing the needle through the plastic bags can sometimes get tricky. If you don't have a thimble, try to vary the fingers you use to push/pull the needle through the braids.

If you're not excited about the plastic bags, I'm sure braided T-shirts or other fabric would work just as well. I'm thinking about trying that next. Make sure that you're always pulling the thread tight when building the basket—it'll keep the braids in the right position and keep them from shifting as you add extra layers. Depending on how tight/loose you pull the braids as you sew, you can create curves in your basket.

## Step 8: Finishing the Basket

Keep doing those diagonal up and over stitches until you come to the end of the braid.

Then, tuck the very end of the braid behind the top row and stitch into place. You can trim or fold over the end of the braid to make it look neater if you like.

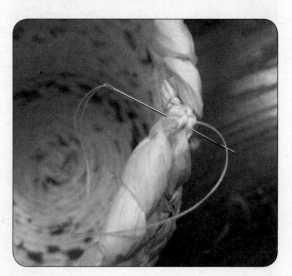

This instructable shows you how to make a newspaper log in less than two minutes.

To get a solid log, you must change the structure of the newspaper from sheets to pulp. Usually there's no shortcuts in papier-mâché, but you'll learn how to make these logs very quickly using a rubber mallet.

The paper logs burn best when combined with wood. They will create more ash than wood. The hole through the middle will help it to burn and make the drying out process quicker.

## Step 1: Prepare the Newspapers

You will need newspapers, a strong bucket, a rubber mallet, and a dowel about an inch thick. You will also need a concreted/cemented area to work on. Fold the newspapers and put 3 or 4 into the bucket and cover with water. The newspapers will probably float to the top so put a piece of wood on the papers.

If you have a leaky gutter with a bucket under the drip or collect rainwater in a tank it would be a great idea to use rain water for the logs.

The newspapers in this instructable were soaked for two days. One day is enough. If you want to speed up the softening process put a squirt of cheap detergent in the water.

You could also add flour, which is a really good way of helping everything bind together.

## Step 2: It's Hittin' Time

If you ever feel the need to hit something instead of somebody, now is the time. Get a wet newspaper out of the bucket, letting some water drain off it first. Lay it out on a hard surface like cement. Starting at the top of the newspaper, hit it with the mallet and work your way down until you've done it all. Not too hard or the newspaper will fall apart. Now carefully lift the mashed newspaper from one side and flip it over. Now hit the other side with the rubber mallet. If you hit the first side too hard you will find it hard to flip the newspaper over. Just turn what you can and piece it back together.

trash

## Step 3: Rolling and Squeezing

Your dowel should be longer than the width of the newspaper. Place it at the end of the newspaper nearest to you. Curl the paper around it and start to roll it on. As you roll you need to squeeze at the same time. This compresses everything into a log. When you finish, you'll need to make sure that you press the end of the newspaper into the log so that it doesn't unravel.

## Step 4: Tidy up the Ends

When the log is complete, spend a few seconds squeezing and shaping it with your hands to get it as solid as possible. When you have finished rolling and squeezing the log turn it up on its end. Slide the log down to the end of the dowel so that it is resting on the ground. Use your thumbs to press in on the ends of the log to make it neat. Repeat at other end. Remove the dowel

## Step 5: Finished/Dirty Hands

There's your finished newspaper log. Now look at your hands. If you make about eight in one session your hands will be really black.

Put the logs in the sun to dry. It depends on the weather how long they'll take to dry. The logs I made for this instructable dried in one day. But it was a hot day (30°C/86°F). If you're making them in cool weather it could take two weeks if there's no sun. Once the fire season starts you can get your logs dry

within a few days by stacking them on top of the wood heater or in front of an open fire.

If the weather is lousy, but you haven't yet had any fires you can make use of a well aired spot. If you keep your firewood under cover, it would also be a good place to dry your paper logs. In cool cloudy weather I make a space for the logs to sit for as long as it takes. I put an old screen door on some boxes and use that as a drying rack. Air can get to the logs from underneath. Any area that gets the wind but is protected from the rain will do fine if you can afford to wait a couple of weeks for them to dry.

You really need to make a whole lot of them before winter. Otherwise it will be too cloudy and cold. At the beginning you will probably love making them, so take advantage of this and make as many as you can. After a while your enthusiasm will wear off and it will turn into a chore, especially if you're out in the cold and your hands are freezing while you play around with cold wet newspaper.

But anyway . . . good luck if you decide to make them. Your firewood will last a lot longer.

## Step 6: Paper Log Tweaks

Here are some last minute tips. Adding coffee grounds to the logs could make them give off more heat. The grounds could be sprinkled on top of the paper after it's been mashed on both sides. Then roll the logs up with the coffee grounds inside.

Also, pine needles could be added for some crackling. The pine needles could make them burn hotter, too. You can improve the appearance of the logs by wrapping them in soaked brown paper from a paper bag; the addition of coffee grounds or related coffee/tea products into the soaking water would give a nice brown tinge to the logs to make them look nicer as well.

trash

# Grocery Bag Shoes

By **neeebs** Alex Niebur
(www.instructables.com/id/Grocery-Bag-Shoes/)

This is my first instructable! I came up with this idea of making shoes after I learned how to fuse plastic bags. I don't really explain in detail how to do it in this but you can look it up and its pretty straight forward. I wanted to make something but I didn't want to make a big dress or anything like I've seen so I made some shoes! It's so easy if I had more time and more plastic bags I would do it all day long!

## Step 1: Begin Taking Apart the Shoe

So first I bought these pair of Converse at a market for really cheap near where I live. I got Converse because I thought they would just be the easiest pattern. I took out the insole then I started with the stitching right next to the toe and cut them with a tiny pair of scissors. If I had a seam ripper that would have been much easier.

## Step 2: Take Apart the Shoe Even More

I may have had lower quality shoes because I'm in China and there is never a guarantee you're getting the real thing, but for me, it was really easy to pull the rubber away from the fabric sides. I did this all the way around and it ended up being just one piece that came off. I

left the tongue on the shoe because I really like that orange color. There were extra stitches that kept the side fabric sewed to the inside-bottom of the shoe so I had to cut those also before the sides could be taken off.

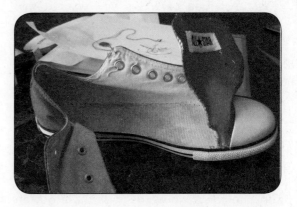

## Step 3: Remove the Heel Piece

That seam ripper would have been helpful removing the heel piece too. I took it off because I wanted to keep it for the final product to make sure the heel was still supported and strong.

## Step 4: Make a Pattern

I traced the piece I would be replacing with plastic onto paper to use as a pattern later. The sides ARE NOT IDENTICAL. It may seem so, but they're just slightly different and it actually matters. Label the sides and which shoe, Left or Right, the pattern is for.

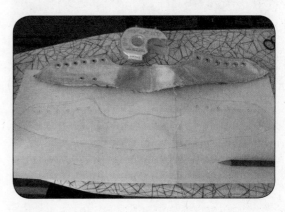

## Step 5: Plastic Bag Fusing

I'm not describing how to fuse the bags, but basically you iron a bunch together and make a big piece of fused plastic.

I used my pattern to help me put together my design for about where I wanted the words and colors to be. I used a bunch of bags from our local grocery store Jenny Lou's and they do shrink just barely when they're fused together so don't trace the pattern directly to the plastic, then iron it, THEN cut it out or it will be wrong. Get a general idea of where you want items, pictures, or certain colors to be and then fuse it together. Make sure its long enough to cut out the final shape or else you'll be in some trouble. After its fused, then you can trace the pattern and cut it out.

Make sure you have enough layers or you might melt through and ruin the plastic.

I almost forgot to put a clear layer over the colors too. Without the extra layer on top, the color and words might have gotten all warped or not turned out as neatly.

I punched the holes using a toothpick, then a pencil to widen the holes. A real hole-puncher might have been convenient as well. This was all being invented as I went along, I didn't really plan out all my supplies in the beginning.

## Step 6: Reconstruct the Shoe!

So now we put it back together! To get it out of the way, I tucked the tongue into the shoe so it wasn't flapping around. I used double sided tape all around the inside edge of the rubber and then just stuck the plastic on there. I superglued the inside seam then duct taped over it. I would not suggest double sided tape . . . Maybe a hot glue gun or pretty much any other kind of adhesive would work. But I liked the duct tape just for extra security. So the walls are

up, and it's beginning to look more like a shoe again. For the heel, I just taped and superglued it into the new shoe and it was fine.

I also had a bit of trouble getting the fabric off the second shoe, so some of it was stuck behind making the heel not stick to the rubber. Whatevs, you can hardly tell.

## Step 7: Finish!

Stick in the insole and then lace 'em up! Pretty cool and pretty easy! Use the plastic bags you have in your house to be green!

Do the same thing with the other shoe. They don't have to match, that'd be cool if they didn't. It was just easier for me.

Woot! Hope ya like em!

trash

# Cozy Slippers from Your Old Woolly Jumper

## By ThePrintPlace

(www.instructables.com/id/Cosy-slippers-from-your-old-woolly-jumper/)

Whoops . . . . Shrunk your favorite woolly in the wash? Never mind, try making these cozy slippers and you should have plenty left to make other goodies.

These lovely warm slippers can be made in an evening if you are stitching by hand. If you have a sewing machine you could whip up a few more pairs!

I have made a padded leather sole for mine because we have freezing cold floors, but this embellishment can easily be left out.

## Materials

- An old pure wool jumper that has felted (wash it in a hot wash and tumble dry), alternatively you could use thick synthetic fleece.
- Strong tissue paper but newspaper or kitchen roll would do.
- Some strong darning wool or thread in either a matching or contrasting color to your jumper.

### Optional

- Leather ( I used the sleeve of an old jacket)
- Padding material (I used insulation wool that we get as packaging in our meat box delivery from Riverford (www.riverford.co.uk), which is naughty as we are supposed to give it back—perhaps they ought to sell it!)
- Extra strong thread

### Tools

- Darning needle, pins
- Tape measure
- Scissors
- Pen

### Optional

- Sewing machine with size 16 needle
- Set square

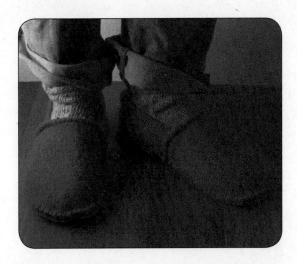

## Step 1: Making the Pattern

This is the most time-consuming bit . . . it helps to be patient. I cut my original pattern by copying an old espadrille shoe. You could do that too or follow these next few steps if you don't have an espadrille. It helps to draw a little table like this before you start.

| Example (my measurements) | |
| --- | --- |
| A = Height of arch | 16 cm |
| T = Arch to toe | 13½ cm |
| H = Under ankle to arch | 25 cm |
| A/4 = &frac14; height of arch | 4 cm |
| A/4 plus 3 cm | 7 cm |

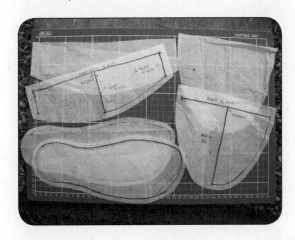

## Step 2: The Sole Pattern

Put your foot on the tissue paper (about a centimeter from the edge) and draw around it.

283

Take your foot off the paper and smooth the lines out, make the heel slightly wider and the toe end slightly flatter.

Cut it out leaving 1 cm seam allowance all round. Use this shape to cut an identical one for the other foot

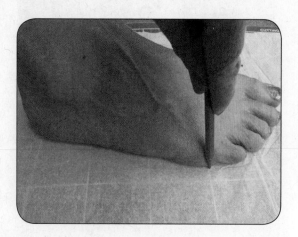

## Step 3: The Toe Piece Pattern

Locate the "arch" of your foot. Mark this point with a pen.

Measure the distance from the ground, over the mark on the top of your foot to the ground on the other side. This is the height of your arch (Line A). It helps to draw this line on your foot.

Now measure from this line to the end of your longest toe. This is the "arch to toe" (Line T) length.

On your paper, draw a line the length of your "height of arch (A)" and mark its midpoint.

From the midpoint, draw another line at right angles to the first one, the length of arch to toe (T).

Fold the paper in half along the arch to toe (T) line and draw a smooth curve between the end of the lines. Cut out the shape with a 1 cm seam allowance all round.

Use this shape to cut an identical one for the other foot.

Tip

Locating the arch: This is on the uppermost surface of your foot, about half way between your inward facing ankle bone and the joint at the beginning of your big toe (lift your big toe up and this joint is where the crease is).

## Step 4: The Heel Piece Pattern

Measure from the arch line on the inside of your foot, under the inner ankle bone, round your heel and just over the outer ankle bone to the arch line on the outer side of your foot. This is the under ankle to arch (H) length.

Draw a line this long on the paper and mark its midpoint.

At both ends of the under ankle to arch (H) line draw a short line at right angles, which is ¼ of the height of the arch (A/4) (i.e. divide the measurement you took for height of arch when you made the toe piece and divide by 4, e.g. if the height of the arch is 16 cm, this will be 16/4 = 4 cm).

From the midpoint of the under ankle to arch (H) line, draw another line at right angles, which is the length of A/4 plus 3 cm. e.g. 7 cm in my case.

Fold the paper in half along this midway line and draw a very slightly curved line from the end of A/4 + 3 line to the end of A/4. When you open it out you should not have a point at the fold line- this needs to be a gently curving line.

Leaving a seam allowance of 1 cm all round, cut out the shape and an identical one for the other foot.

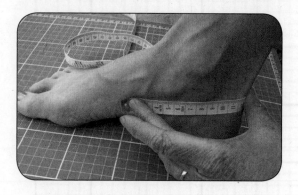

## Step 5: Yay—Your Pattern!

You should now have 6 pieces of paper.
Well done, that bit was hard work!

Tips

The circumference of the sole seam line should be the same as the curved sides of the toe and heel piece added together. You can test this using wool to measure the curves.

If you are nervous about your pattern or have very precious fabric, you may want to assemble the pattern to check that it works. Follow the "assembly" step but just use a running stitch because it's much quicker.

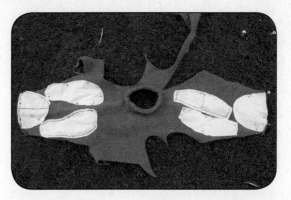

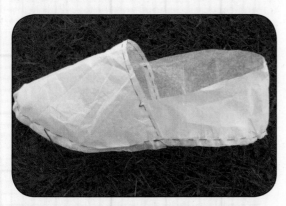

## Step 6: Cutting Out Your Fabric Pieces

Cut up the side seams and under the arm seams of your old woolly jumper

Lay out your tissue paper pieces on your fabric and cut them out. I managed to get them all out of two sleeves.

### Leather Sole Option

Cut one of each sole piece from leather and one of each from padding.

### Tips

- Remember to turn one of your sole pieces so that you have a right and left, not two lefts.
- If possible align the straight edge of the toe piece along a cuff or bottom hem as this will save you some sewing later. If you can do this you will not need the seam allowance on the straight edge because your seam is already finished, so align the drawn line with the edge of the fabric you are using rather than the cut edge of your pattern.
- If you are not using leather and padding as a sole, you may want to cut two pieces for each sole to give you more padding/insulation.
- I used the shiny side of the leather as the outside surface and the suede on the inside. They are a little slippery on wooden floors so you may want to try suede side out.

## Step 7: Assembly: The Upper

Hem the straight edge of the toe piece (line A) by folding the seam allowance to the right (top) side of the fabric and stitching by hand (overedge stitch/ running stitch or back stitch) using the darning wool or you could use a machine. I did not need to do this as I used the cuff so the seam was already finished. (See next step for how to do the stitches).

With right/top sides up, align the short seam line of the heel piece (A/4) with the straight edge seamline (A) of the toe piece so that the toe piece overlaps the heel piece and the straight sides form an L and the curved seams are aligned.

Starting at the bottom (the curved side) secure the thread by stitching over the edge a couple of times then backstitch the two pieces together (see the next step for how to backstitch) or machine stitch them together.

Turn the pieces over and overcast/ oversew the flap of heel piece to the toe piece (wrong side).

Curve the other end of the heel piece round to meet the other end of the toe piece (seam A) and repeat.

Hem the straight side of the heel piece in a similar way to the toe piece (you could easily do this before you attach the two bits together instead).

Hooray, you've finished the upper-lip; It's looking more shoe-like now.

**Tip**

Mark the midpoint of both your pieces with a pin. This will simplify things later when you come to attach the sole.

## Step 8: Tip: How to Backstitch and Overedge Stitch

**Backstitch**

This produces a continuous line of neat straight stitches on the right side and an overlapping row of straight stitches on the wrong side. It is a strong stitch worked from right to left.

Basically, with the right side up, bring the needle up through the fabric one stitch length ahead of where you want to start (A). Next push your needle down at the start point (B) (i.e. back a stitch) and then bring it back up one stitch ahead of where your thread currently comes out of the fabric (C). Pull the thread tight and you should have done your first stitch.

Put your needle in exactly where your first stitch began (A) and come up one stitch ahead (D) of where your thread currently comes out which should now be C. Pull tight and keep going!

**Overedge Stitch**

This is a way of securing a free edge of fabric that can be quite invisible. I have adapted this stitch to use it to secure the hem too.

Secure the thread by stitching a couple of times in the same place, then bring the needle up through the hem about half way between the fold and the edge.

Push the needle through the fabric just below the free edge at an angle so that you come back through slightly further to the left halfway between the fold and the free edge again.

Continue all the way to the end and secure the thread by stitching two or three times over the same stitch.

## Step 9: Assembling the Sole

**Leather/Padding Options**

For the sole you can keep it really simple by just using one or two layers of woolen fabric. I wanted more cushioning so I added some padding and some leather.

If you are using a single layer of wool you can leave this section out

Make a sandwich of sole pieces, remembering to have a right and left, not two of one side.

Hand stitch (backstitch) together around the seam line. If you are using leather this will be MUCH easier by machine.

## Step 10: Putting the Sole and Upper Together

With the sole piece sole down mark the midpoint of the heel and the toe end with pins. Place the upper (right side out) on the sole, aligning the midpoint of the heel piece and toe piece to the sole first and then pinning all the other edges.

Blanket stitch together the edges (see tip in next step). I just blanket stitched the two fabric edges together, and left out the leather, as I thought the leather may protect the stitches from wear a little bit.

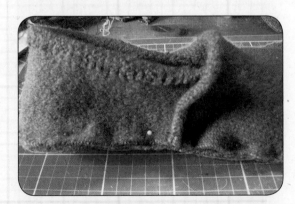

## Step 11: Tip: How to Blanket Stitch

This stitch holds two edges of fabric together and protects them from fraying a little. It is also quite decorative if done neatly.

It is similar to overedge/oversew/overcast stitch except that you push the needle through the loop you create before you pull it tight. It is easiest worked from left to right and uses LOTS of thread.

Secure your thread as before and squashing both layers of fabric between thumb and forefinger, bring the needle up in the gap between the layers (so it comes out at the top of your seam).

With your thumb hold the thread down and push the needle through from the back about ½cm to the right and about 1cm in from the edge (or as close as the sole seam will allow) so that the needle comes through a loop you have just created.

As you lift your thumb up to release the thread, and pull the stitch tight, you can see the loop you have made. If you forgot to go through the loop you can always pop your needle through at this stage.

Pull tight and your thread should then cause your loop to right angle over it creating the "bar" over the space between the two pieces of fabric and your thread is in the right place for the next stitch.

Continue round and finish by securing threads as before.

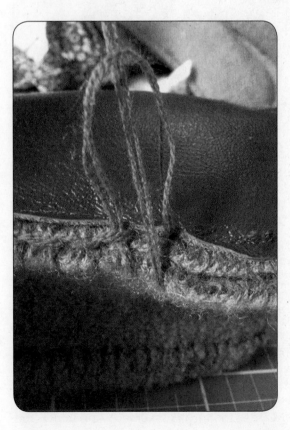

trash

287

# Coffee Cup Packaging

By **AlpineButterfly**
(www.instructables.com/id/Coffee-Cup-Packaging/)

I tote around my plastic refillable mug, and get 10 cents off (Dutch people like to be cheap) so I hadn't thought about it much. Until I got yet another box in the mail. I hate getting all those new boxes in the mail, I wish they would re-use other boxes (I like the stuff inside, don't get me wrong)! So I figured I'd mash up 2 problems and maybe get a solution: Coffee Cup packaging is born. (This could change the world you know!)

## Materials

OK; so first step, I needed a coffee cup; headed down to the local coffee shop, to see if I could snag a few. Had a grown-up hot chocolate, a.k.a. "Mocha" (in my plastic cup) and went dumpster diving.

Yes, I'm admitting it; sorry guys, I am using other people's trash in this project. I figure with the plastic things on top it's not like their mouth gets to the cup anyways. Lucky for you, if that seems squeamish, you can always just enjoy a coffee yourself, and use that.

Mind you acquiring a paper cup was harder than it first seemed. Apparently this paper trash doesn't seem to get left in the shop, but follows all these coffee drinking souls to work. Dope! So I waited.

Paper cups acquired; I also needed:
- The cup sleeve
- A knife, or other sharp object
- Scissors
- Something to poke holes (my Swiss army knife served well)
- Scrap cardboard
- A piece of ribbon
- A bit of String
- Glue
- Tape
- Painting supplies

## Step 1: Clean Out the Cup

I rinsed the cup right away, to get the syrup out. Then cleaned it more thoroughly at home.

## Step 2: Constructing a Top

Trace around the top of the cup on your scrap piece of cardboard.

Find a circular object that fits inside the circle you've drawn, with a little room to spare. About 1/8 of an inch on all sides should do it. You want the top you're making to be smaller than the top of your cup so that it fits insides.

Trace around your new circular object. Cut out the smaller of the 2 circles.

Using a knife or X-acto cut a small slit in the center of your cardboard circle. Make it just big enough to accommodate your ribbon, or string.

Fold your ribbon in half, and push it through the cut you just made. Cut your ribbon, with enough extra that you have something to glue down. Glue your ribbon down with white glue. Allow time to dry.

## Step 3: Painting the Top

Get out the paints. Mostly you need some browns, and maybe a cream color.

**On One Top**

I used a lighter brown paint to paint a circular blob type shape. Then, using the cream color, painted another smaller blob shape over the top of the light brown. And a small cream blob got painted on the other side. I was trying to create some "reflections."

**On the Other Top**

I tried to create that effect some coffee houses do, where they make shapes in the coffee froth. (I love that! ). So to make the froth, I used a sponge to stipple a lighter color brown on, and then I stippled the cream color over that (each time leaving a bit of the color below show through). I then used the lighter brown, to paint the coffee design in, and finally went back and stippled over that with the cream color (really lightly).

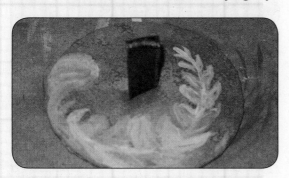

## Step 4: Assembly

Make a note, or small present, put it inside, and put the lid on. I added some coffee beans for fun, and to fill it out for stability.

**Easy Version**

If you're just going to hand it to someone, this is probably, all you need to do. The cardboard will stay in place if you push down on all sides snuggly (not too much; just snug). Your recipient can pull on the tab, and ta daa!!

**Secure Version**

I was trying to make a slightly more secure version, but I didn't want to use glue so that it could be re-used. So I poked holes around the top (just above when the lid fits in securely). An odd number of holes work best. I then sewed around the top of the lid (going around 2 times, to make it look solid on the outside). The string on the inside helps to keep the lid in place. You only need about 7 to 9 holes; too many more makes the cup weak. You could do fewer holes, but your string will cross over closer to the center.

**trash**

# Gift Box from a Cereal Box

## By blightdesign
(www.instructables.com/id/Gift-Box-from-a-Cereal-Box/)

After watching J.J. Abrams's TED talk, I was fascinated that he was interested in box design. I was inspired and figured I'd give box making a shot. I eat a lot of cereal, and had a lot of almost empty boxes lying around.

## Tools/Materials

You'll need the following tools and materials:

- Hot glue gun with glue
- Scissors
- One cereal box—that's it!

## Step 1: Cut and Flatten the Box

Cut the box down the middle. I like to cut down the side that doesn't have the tab on it.

## Step 2: Three Folds

Fold the box in half. All of the folds don't have to be exact.

Fold the bottom half in half. At the bottom of the box, cut up to this fold on the right and left. From the top of the box, cut down to the first fold on the right and left.

Fold only the middle section of the top half in half.

## Step 3: Cut Away What You Don't Need

Cut the box so it looks like the picture below. The cuts don't have to be exact.

290

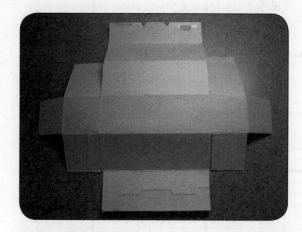

## Step 4: Glue Down the Front Flap

Flip the box over. Use hot glue to secure the front flap down.

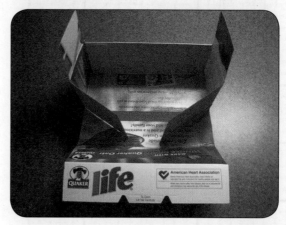

## Step 5: Glue and Fold

Use hot glue to secure the side flaps and glue the back flaps. Reverse the existing fold to form the lid.

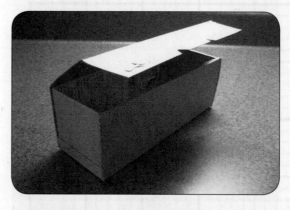

## Step 6: Finish the Box

I used a stamp to put a logo on the lid of the box, but you could paint it, use stickers, whatever. I hope J.J. is happy with the results.

# outside

This chapter will guide you in improving your survival skills, your campsite, and your own backyard! Consider the outdoors one giant rumpus room, and get started enjoying the fruits of the wilderness with these awesome projects.

# How to Build Your Own BBQ Barrel

By **johnnyblegs** John Legge
(www.instructables.com/id/How-to-Build-Your-Own-BBQ-Barrel/)

Lucky for me on my last day of work at The Bakery, the 55-gallon honey barrel I'd been waiting for was finally empty. Getting laid off wasn't going to stand in the way of my dream to make my own barbecue.

## Step 1: The Prep

First, I had to empty out all the excess honey and clean the inside. Then I borrowed a grinder from a friend and cut the opening.

## Step 2: Constructing the Stand

I had to make a base and the only things around were some old chain-link fence posts that I'd never taken to the dump and some scrap plywood I'd demoed out of a creepy room in my basement. I cut 6 posts at different lengths—2 the length of the barrel & 4 for the legs. I wanted the BBQ to be portable so the best way for that was for the barrel to sit on top of the stand. Two posts held the barrel while the 4 legs were attached by drilling holes for the carriage bolts on either end. To attach and keep the legs sturdy I secured them with pieces of plywood. Put the barrel on top and it stood tall and proud.

## Step 3: Attaching the Lid & Grill Grates

I added brackets to hold the grills and to keep the lid from falling inside, as well as a lower rack to hold the coals and allow for air circulation. Be sure to purchase stainless steel brackets and hinges.

## Step 4: Burn off the Inside

I lit a fire in it to burn off any paints or coatings or who knows what.

## Step 5: Finishing Touches

Last steps in the construction were to add a handle (plain wooden dowel from the hardware store), air vents, and a temperature gauge. I also decided to spray the barrel with a high heat resistant pant. Besides customizing the color a little, the paint helps prevent rust on the barrel. The only thing left was to test it in a real-life BBQ situation.

outside

Outdoor fires are so hot right now. Seriously. On cool summer nights, you can melt marshmallows and nibble s'mores while you lounge in an Adirondack chair, feet propped up on the rock ledge. So if you really want to light up right, do it in style. Take a few days to build your very own ring of fire.

### Shopping List

- Cast-Concrete wall stones
- Capstones
- Steel Campfire Ring (the one we used here is from Markstaar)
- 4¾-inch drainage gravel
- Patio base (stone dust)
- Masonry adhesive
- Ready-Mix Mortar (if needed) to cement a natural-stone cap onto the wall. A 40-pound bag is enough.
- Concrete bonding additive (a.k.a. "milk") to make the mortar more flexible.

### Step 1: Learn the Anatomy

A built-in fire pit is a glorified campfire, with sturdy walls of stone that help contain the flames and heat. That's especially important in the parts of the country where there's a risk of brush fires. So the first task in building any fire pit is checking local codes on open flames. The pit must be located far from overhanging trees, the house, and any other flammable structure.

To make building stone walls easier, you can use blocks made from cast concrete and molded to look like real stone (available at any home center). They're flat on the top and bottom so they stack neatly, and some interlock for added strength. Glue them together with masonry adhesive. Choose a block with angled sides, meant to form curves when butted against each other. The optimal size for a fire pit is between 36 and 44 inches inside diameter.

As an added precaution, the fire pit should be lined with a thick steel ring like the ones used for park campfires. These protect the concrete in the blocks from the heat, which can cause them to dry out and break down prematurely.

A fire pit should sit low to the ground, with walls rising no more than a foot off the ground. But for stability, the base of the wall must be buried below ground in a hole lined with gravel, providing drainage and protecting against frost heaves in winter. The gravel also creates a level base for the stones to rest on. Most concrete blocks are about 4 inches high, so if the first course and a half sit underground, and there are two and a half courses above ground with a cap on top, you'll end up with a foot-high wall—just right for resting your feet on while sitting in an outdoor chair.

### Step 2: Lay Out the Blocks

Dry-lay a ring of blocks on the fire pit site, placing them end to end until you have a perfect circle positioned where you want the finished pit to be. To adjust the size of the circle, you may need to cut a block. Hold the block over the gap it will fill, then mark it on the underside at the proper width.

Using a 3-inch cold chisel and a brick hammer, score the block on the mark, and continue the score all the way around the block. Place the block on a hard surface (flat rocks or gravel). Hold the chisel in the score line, then hit it with the brick hammer until the block splits.

outside

293

Clean up jagged edges with the tail of the brick hammer. Place the cut block into the ring.

## Step 3: Mark the Pit Location

Make sure all the joints between the blocks are tight and the front and back edges line up. Using a spade, mark a circle in the ground about an inch outside the perimeter of the ring.

Take note of how many stones make up the ring, then remove them and set them aside.

If the blocks you are using are interlocking, remove any tongues on the bottom of the first-course blocks so they will lie flat in the trench. Chip them off with the tail of a brick hammer.

## Step 4: Create a Level Trench for the Blocks

Using a spade, dig a straight-sided trench, 12 inches deep and as wide as one block, within the circle marked out on the ground. Then dig down 6 inches in the area encircled by the trench.

Lay the ring of blocks in the trench to see if all the pieces fit in a circle. If not, dig more to widen the trench. Remove blocks.

## Step 5: Fill the Trench

Fill the trench with 6 inches of ¾-inch drainage gravel. Using a hand tamper, compact the gravel. If necessary, add more gravel to keep the trench level and even.

Always make sure the blocks line up perfectly in the front and back when you lay them out; a difference of 1 inch in the circle's diameter could create a 3-inch gap between blocks.

## Step 6: Lay and Level the First Course

Place the first block in the ring. Using a 2-foot level, check that it sits level both side to side and front to back. Where the block is too high, tap it down with a rubber mallet. Where it's too low, shim it slightly with a handful of patio base. Make sure this first block is perfectly level and positioned correctly in the trench before moving on.

Lay another block next to the first one. Butt the sides together tightly and line up the front and back edges. Using the first block as a reference, level the second block side to side and front to back.

Lay the rest of the blocks in the trench in this manner until the ring is complete and all the blocks you counted earlier are used. Make sure each block is perfectly leveled and lined up tight with its neighbor before moving on to the next one. (You may have to coax the last block into place with a mallet.) Using a 4-foot level, occasionally check level across the ring.

## Step 7: Assemble the Walls

Using a caulking gun, squeeze a zigzag bead of masonry adhesive across two adjacent blocks. Lay a block on top of the

outside

glue-covered pieces, centering it over the seam between the two. Make sure any interlocking parts on the blocks fit together well. Continue until the second course is finished.

## Step 8: Fill the Pit

Fill the pit with 6 inches of gravel, which will help support the first two courses as they set up. Glue and lay the third and fourth courses, continuing to stagger the joints.

Insert the iron campfire ring into the circle. Adjust it to sit even with the top of the block wall. Fill any space between the ring and the block wall to the top with gravel.

Work quickly and only in a small area at one time; masonry adhesive sets up quickly.

## Step 9: Cap the Blocks

Loosely arrange the cap pieces on top of the pit walls. (If you are using natural stone, try to arrange the pieces together like a puzzle.) Lay one stone edge over the next and mark the upper stone where they meet. Also, roughly mark the stone for a 2-inch overhang on the outside of the circle and an inch on the inside. Using a brick hammer and a chisel, score the stone on those marks. On thick natural stone, use a grinder fitted with a diamond blade to score it more deeply.

Lay the stone on a hard surface. Split it by hitting a chisel in the score mark, or by tapping against the stone's edge with the brick hammer until it breaks. Score and split each stone this way, moving around the circle in one direction until you've made a cap that fits together tightly.

If you're using blocks, glue the pieces on top of the wall. If you're using natural stone, combine the dry mortar with enough bonding additive—not water—to make a mix with a peanut-butter consistency.

Wet the wall with some bonding agent. Lay a large mound of mortar on two blocks. With the point of the trowel, make a groove across the mortar. Lay the capstone on top, push it down, then tap it with the rubber mallet to set and level it. Continue to lay the capstones in this manner until the wall is finished. Wait two days before lighting a fire.

outside

# How to Build a Fish Pond or Garden Pond

By **metanoia**
(www.instructables.com/id/How-to-Build-a-Fish-Pond/)

I thought I would share how I built our pond in case you would like to replicate it yourself. After one false start I have have created a beautiful garden fish pond.

## Materials

Before you begin you will need the following things:

- shovel
- trowel
- garden hose
- plank of wood
- spirit level
- pond liners and liner underlay newspaper
- bricks
- landscaping rocks
- fountain pump (optional)
- black vinyl duct tape (optional)
- cement & bucket

**Note**

I live in Australia. If you live in an area where it snows you may have to take other things into account for your fish to survive. Koi fish also need specific habitats that I have not addressed in this tutorial. My total cost for this project was around $100 as I only needed to buy the liner, sand, and the pump. The pond liner cost me $40.

## Step 1: Digging the Hole

First dig yourself a good hole. I had a look at pond liners that were available first and knew that I could get one that is 2.5 × 2 m for $39, so that meant that I wanted to keep my pond less than 1.5 × 1 m and no more than 50cm deep. You can use a garden hose as a guide to work out your approximate shape.

You want to dig the sides straight down, but be careful that you don't break off parts of the wall as we want them nice and solid for later. You might want to start a little smaller than your ideal size and make it bigger as you go just incase you do accidentally collapse part of a wall. One point to realise is that once you have put on the rocks at the end it will seem smaller so don't be afraid if it looks really big right now.

Take off the crumbly top soil to a width of 4-5 inches around the hole if this is an issue for you like it is for me. The top soil for us was only about an inch thick, which gives us a solid foundation for the bricks. Use a straight plank of wood and a spirit level to make sure your sides are reasonably in line across the pond. Use a hand trowel to shave off a little more if some areas are higher than others.

Create a deep part and a shallow part in your pond. The centre of my hole is about 15cm deeper than the small area at the top. This will allow us to put in a range of plants as we desire. Some plants can only be placed in up to 20cm of water, some like it a lot deeper. Think about the fish you are going to get when you are planning your size as well as Koi need a much deeper, larger area than other fish.

Check for rocks and roots that may puncture your liner. After scraping with the shovel and removing most of the rocks I used my hands to feel around all the areas of the pond and dug out any more small rocks with the trowel.

Next, place your underlay in the hole. I used about an inch of sand in the bottom and on the ledge. You can also use damp newspaper, carpet, or special underlay that you can buy from garden centres.

## Step 2: Lay the Liner in the Hole

Lay your liner over the hole. Try not to drag the liner around too much, but with a little draping and patience, you can achieve a neat look with your liner. I took off my shoes and spent some time pushing it gently into all the corners and doing some initial pleating. You may want to use some black vinyl duct tape to tape down some of the pleats like I did to make them even less noticeable. Use bricks or stones to hold the liner down neatly all around the pond.

## Step 3: Put in Some Water

This is the step that most instructions jump straight to, though after my first attempt I took the extra time at step 2. Start to fill the pond with water until it is about half full (or 2 inches from the top of the liner). I filled it about half way up to the bottom of the bricks. As it is filling you can gently ease out the liner at any areas where you need to allow more liner to reach the bottom or fix up any pleats.

When you are happy with the liner (take your time and get it right!) place your layer of bricks around the ledge. The purpose of the bricks is so that you will be able to have the water level above the liner so you will not notice it is there. There is nothing more distracting from a pond than seeing the ugly creases in a black plastic pond liner as per our first try, dubbed "Fail Pond".

## Step 4: Secure the Liner

If you are planning on having a pump or water feature, you will want to think about its placement and where the power cables and any other hoses will go at this point. We decided to have a simple water feature, so I placed the pump in the desired position and ran the cord to the side of the pond. I did not run the cord to the back because you don't want to be looking at the cord when you are standing in front of the pond. The cord runs to the bottom and then around the bricks until it comes out the back as this is the closest point to the house. Test the water feature! It is better to ensure it works now than have to take half of the pond apart to get it back out!

An optional step at this point is to fill any gaps between the bricks with quick setting cement. I used this between each brick so that any dirt or sand packed behind would be less likely to run into the pond when it is full of water. You do not need to make it waterproof as the pond liner takes care of this. Allow your cement to cure for 3-4 hours before proceeding.

Next gently ease the liner straight up behind the bricks and pack dirt up to it like a ramp, then fold the liner down and pack dirt over top. The liner should come up to the level of the bricks and then hide and slope away from the pond. This should mean no run off (including dirt) flowing into the pond, and any overflow should flow away from it.

outside

Note also that we decided to have a "wetland" area for our pond. There is a semi-circle of sand where the liner continues flat at the level of the bottom of the bricks under the sand, and then is built up in a mound. The sand area will be constantly wet allowing us to grow plants that like wet feet, but do not like to be submerged. You could do this too, or skip this part for a simple pond.

## Step 6: Final Touches

Waiting 24 hours gives the cement a chance to cure and your bricks and rocks a chance to settle into place. Top up the wetland with more sand as the rocks will hold that in place. Now it is time to fill up the pond 1 to 2cm below the top of the bricks and add your plants. Wait at least 2 days before adding fish, or follow the recommendations from your local aquarium expert.

## Step 5: Position Rocks

Gently ease your rocks onto the sides and where possible, allow them to overlap the bricks completely. This step allows complete coverage of the pond liner and is the decorative part of the pond. It is handy to have a number of rocks to choose from so you can play with their positioning until you are happy with how it looks. Fill the pond up to the bottom of the bricks. Great job!! Time you took a break!

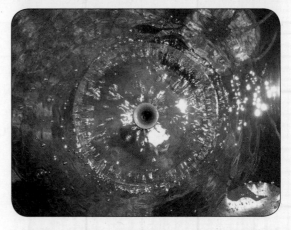

outside

# How to Build a Rain Water Collector

## By iPodGuy

(www.instructables.com/id/How-to-build-a-rain-water-collector/)

In this instructable, I will show how I made a rainwater collection system to water my garden. This helps to conserve water and make good use of a free and renewable resource.

## Step 1: The Beginning—Installing the Posts

To begin, I laid out a 55 gallon drum on the ground and dug a hole on either side in the spot that the poles (4 × 4 pressure treated lumber posts) were going to go.

With the first post in the ground, I leveled it off with a level and propped it into place with scrap wood. Then, I began to mix the concrete. This entire project took three 50lb bags of fast-drying concrete. With the concrete mixed to the right consistency, I poured it around the base of the post.

The second post went in the same way as the first. From end to end—including the posts, it wound up measuring 39 inches.

With the front two posts in place, I took a barrel and laid it back into place. This made it possible to judge where the last two posts should go.

Of course, each post got 6 screws in the base to help them stay in the concrete. All screws used in this project were 2½ inch coarse-thread exterior screws.

With the last two posts in, the concrete is allowed to dry and harden. Including the posts, the front and back both measured 39 inches and the left and right sides both measured 38 inches. However, anybody attempting this should measure and place the posts in whatever configuration that is best.

## Step 2: Building the Barrel Braces

While the concrete dried, I began to make the barrel braces. These need to be strong, since they will be supporting the entire weight of the barrels. For this, I used two pieces of 2 × 4 screwed together with 5 screws (3 on one side, 2 on the other). The pieces measured 39 inches. After that, I drilled pilot holes on both sides (centered and 1¾ inches in). Into these pilot holes, I drove galvanized lag bolts (with washers) using a ratchet with the appropriate tip. Driving the lag bolts in ahead of time will make it easier when attaching them to the posts.

outside

For a two-barrel system, I needed to make four of the barrel braces. All four of them measured 39 inches apiece.

The bottom front barrel brace went in first. I drilled pilot holes into the posts where the barrel brace was to go. The pilot holes were exactly 13 inches up from the ground. I drove the lag bolts the rest of the way with a ratchet, making sure to check with a level.

### Step 3: Installing the Pole Braces

The bottom two pole braces went in next. They went in directly under the first barrel brace and were screwed in after being checked with a level. These offer nothing by way of support for the barrels. All they do is help to maintain structural stability on the frame.

### Step 4: Installing the Barrel Braces

Next, the second barrel brace went in. These two will be what supports the bottom barrel. The pilot holes that I drilled to accept the lag bolts were 23 inches from the ground. The difference in height makes the barrel tip slightly forward. The angle helps to fit more water in the barrels as they fill and allows the barrels to drain more completely.

I tested the bottom braces with an empty barrel to be certain that the barrel would fit properly.

### Step 5: Installing the Pole Braces

After that, I cut out the top two pole braces. The top pole braces will go on the same angle as the barrels, so it is useful to measure to determine the appropriate length. Mine were 38½ inches.

### Step 6: Finishing the Frame

The last two barrel braces and the last two pole braces went in next. I drilled the pilot holes for the top two barrel braces exactly 25 inches up from the tops of the bottom barrel braces. I drove them in with a ratchet and checked with a level. The ends of the last two pole braces went up exactly 26 inches from the tops of the top two barrel braces and are held in with screws.

I then tested the frame with two barrels to be sure that they both fit comfortably. The bottom (and heaviest) barrel is slightly pinched in by the top barrel braces. This adds to the stability of the bottom barrel.

With the two barrels in their final places, I attached additional barrel supports in the fronts and backs of the barrels. All four supports measured 39 inches. I checked the supports with a level, but did not take an exact measurement of their position. They were placed where I felt that they would support the barrels best. With the four barrel supports in, the barrels are in their final positions and cannot slide backwards or forwards.

## Step 7: Installing the Barrels

I chose to use barrels with raised lips on the top. Into the lip of each barrel, I drilled two screws down into the barrel braces. This will help to prevent the barrels from rocking and shifting during bumps or windy days.

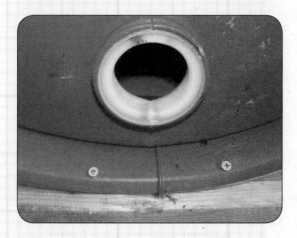

## Step 8: Installing the Plumbing

I used a barrel wrench to screw the plugs into the barrel bungs. The plugs that came with the barrels were already threaded to accept drains and other attachments. The very top bung did not get a plug as this is where the drain will go later

My barrel plugs came already threaded to accept various attachments. I chose hose bibs that were a little longer than a standard boiler drain or hose bib. However, most anything would work. To make them fit the plugs, I also needed to use a bushing to adapt them. Wrap the threads with thread tape and snug with a wrench. Other parts can be substituted at this point, such as two pipe elbows instead of hose bibs.

I made the connector hose out of clear tubing and two female hose ends. The hose ends were in the garden department as replacement parts for mending broken hoses. Make sure that the hose ends properly fit the hose bibs when shopping for parts, otherwise additional adapters may be needed.

This is the completed connection. With both hose bibs in the fully open position, water will be able to drain from the top barrel into the bottom.

outside

301

barrels should be installed high enough to get a constant flow of water.

Next, I drained the system and washed it out an additional time to be certain that I flushed out any small debris.

## Step 10: Installing the Drain

Anybody attempting this may want to consider installing gutter guards. They help to keep debris from clogging the system by just allowing the water in and dropping debris from the roof.

Detach the gutter and measure the width of the spout. You will need to know this when shopping for parts. Mine happened to be two inches.

These are the parts that I used to drain water from my gutters into the barrels. I used a 2 inch to 1½ inch rubber reducer and various pieces of 1½ inch ABS pipe. The bungs on the barrels are 2 inches wide and the extra half-inch is to allow water to drain out when the barrels reach capacity.

## Step 9: Testing the System

At this point, I decided it was a good time to check for leaks. I filled up the system through the top bung and waited to see if any water leaked out. I did notice that the top plug was dripping, so I tightened the plug a little more and all was fine.

I then tested all the hose bibs to make sure they worked properly.

I attached a garden hose to test if I was getting an acceptable amount of water pressure. There really is no pressure to speak of, since this system is gravity-fed, but the

For the new gutter drain, the reducer was clamped on to the spout and the ABS pipe clamped in. This is what all of the pieces will be built off of.

Dry-fitting all the pipes and various fittings is useful to determine exactly how a drain will be put together. A person attempting this may want to experiment with what works best as not every setup will need the same parts. Clean the pipes and fittings and apply ABS glue to cement into place (those using different types of pipe such as PVC will want to use the appropriate type of cement as well).

Make sure the pipe fits and rests comfortably on the barrel. Also, I used a piece of wire nailed to the barrel brace to hold the new drain in place. You will want to use piping that is less than the size of the bung, otherwise water will not be able to leak out and will back up your gutters, potentially causing flooding problems for a basement or crawlspace. An optional thing I did was to select a 90 degree bend with an additional outlet. Into that, I cemented a thread and cap. This will act as a temporary override during a storm if the system were to become clogged with debris and cause the gutters to become backed up with water. Simply remove the cap and the excess will spill onto the ground.

## Step 11: Finishing Touches

I used a reciprocating saw to cut the tops of the posts off, using the top pole braces as a guide. I then screwed on the roof to the frame. The roof measured 45 × 45 inches of ½ inch plywood.

## Step 12: Decoration

I chose to remove the roof and hang plastic lattice on the sides and back and used 1¼ inch finishing nails to hold it in place.

## Step 13: Finishing Touches

I began using a reciprocating saw to trim the lattice, but later switched to a hand saw because it made more even cuts. I re-attached and shingled the roof to protect the plywood and make it more attractive. I used ¾ inch roofing nails for this step.

I would like to paint the wood with a low- or no-VOC exterior paint at some point to match the house.

## Step 14: Final Thoughts

The hose that drains from the top to the bottom barrel would benefit from being wider. Water can only pass through as fast as the smallest opening can handle. If I were to re-do it, I'd try to drill or cut a wider hole to accept wider fittings and tubing. There is most likely a way to pressurize the system with an air compressor for applications that need more pressure than gravity such as sprinkler systems. The bottom barrel would most likely benefit from a small hole drilled above the water line to let out air as it gets replaced with water. This will allow the top barrel to drain into the bottom barrel faster and at a more steady rate.

outside

303

# How to Navigate with a Map and Compass

By **zwild1** Scott Wild
(www.instructables.com/id/How-to-Navigate-with-a-Map-and-Compass/)

Alright, so everyone knows a few fundamentals of navigation—north is always up, the sun rises in the east, and compasses usually point towards magnetic north. But at some point in time, outdoor enthusiast or not, you'll want to be able to find out where you are, and where you need to go.

## Step 1: Choosing a Good Map

The map is your most important tool, as you can always squeak by without a compass (not recommended!).

**USGS**

Pros: USGS maps are the standard for wilderness navigation, s scale of 1:24000 (1 inch equals 24,000 inches) and line intervals of 50 feet make them pretty detailed. They have WGS84 (lat/long) and UTM coordinate systems. Cons: The 7.5 minute maps are huge and can be unwieldy. Many maps haven't been updated since 1950.

**Custom Correct Maps**

Pros: 15 minute coverage; scale is 1:62500; derived from USGS maps, but arranged to show popular loop hikes and trails, updated more recently—1990 84; both lat/long and UTM. Cons: Less detailed; only for Washington; 100 foot contour lines.

**Green Trails Maps**

Pros: 15 minute coverage; originally based on USGS, but updated frequently; compact size; uses lat/long, UTM, UMS coordinates; scale is 1:69500. Cons: Only available for WA and OR right now, with plans for AZ, CA, NY, and NV; 100 foot contour lines.

Essentially, be sure your map covers the entire hike, has a map scale or datum that you are comfortable with, includes features like roads, boundaries, and streams.

## Step 2: Choosing a Good Compass

The compass is your second most important navigation tool, but it is also the most important to get exactly right. Unfortunately, there's not much room for DIY here. Your compass should have specific features, and they're absolutely worth a few bucks extra. It should have:

- A clear base plate—To see underneath the compass.
- A sighting mirror—To sight objects at eye-level.
- A rotating bezel, marked with 360 degrees in 2 degree increments.
- Meridian lines for map use.
- Declination Adjustment and arrow to correct for the difference between magnetic and true north.
- And there are many more features. Just be sure you at least have the basics. Compass Models: I personally recommend the Suunto MC-2 D ($40+). It works great and is fairly inexpensive. The MC-2 G (45+) is alright, and you can use it worldwide. It's more expensive and

I still prefer the MC-2 D. The Silva Ranger CL515 ($40+) is another good one.

## Step 3: Taking a Bearing on a Map

This step is pretty simple. When doing any map work, be sure you ignore your compass needle and declination arrow. Those guys are only helpful when you're using the compass in relation to the world around you. For now, consider it more of a protractor. This is the simplest of the exercises. Imagine you're on a mountain lookout. You see another mountain, what heading is it?

1. Open the compass, and lay it flat on the map.
2. Move the compass so that the base is along point A (where you are), and the mirror is along point B (the other mountain).
3. Rotate the bezel until North matches the maps north, and the meridian lines line up with a north south line (lat/long lines, UTM grids*).
4. Read the bearing at the top of the compass. **

---

*The edge of the map is the ideal line. Any lines that parallel it will work too.

**On the bottom of the compass, 180 degrees around, is the bearing from Point B to Point A.

## Step 4: Follow a Specific Bearing on a Map

Alright, you're on a mission. You know that there's a cave filled with treasure unmarked on your map, It's 308NW of your position.

1. Open the compass and turn the bezel to 308NW.
2. Orient the compass with the clear part along your current position.
3. Turn the whole compass, keeping one edge along your position, until the compass matches the maps north, and the meridian lines match North/South lines on the map.
4. The destination is somewhere along the line created by the base of your compass.

## Step 5: Taking a Bearing on a Real Object

Before we use your compass, we'll have to set the declination. First, find the declination in your area by visiting NOAA Geomagnetic Data. Then, follow the directions that came with your compass to set the declination properly. Now you can take a bearing on a real object.

1. Choose an object to take a bearing to. Ideally this is something you can do,

then reference on a map. But you can practice with objects that are a minimum of twenty feet away.

2. Stand well clear of your computer. Large, metal objects usually mess up compass readings.

3. Tilt your mirror ~45 degrees in relation to the base.

4. Hold the compass outward, level, relaxed, and at eye level.

5. Close your non-dominant eye.

6. Match the object up in the compass sights. Be sure its level!

7. Turn the bezel until the north (red) needle is in the declination arrow.

8. Read the heading from the bezel.

9. Give the bezel a spin, rinse, repeat.

## Step 6: Following a Bearing in Real-Life

Woo hoo! You know your campsite is only a mile away, at heading 40NE. But how do you translate the heading into an actual direction?

**Method One**

1. Dial the bearing in on your compass.

2. Set the sight mirror at ~45degrees, hold it level, and bring it to eye-level.

3. Close your non-dominant eye.

4. Turn your body until the north needle is within the declination arrow or box.

5. Take note of an object on that heading. Choose a peculiar tree, peak, or anything else in your direction of travel.

6. Head to that object, then re-shoot your bearing.

**Method Two**

Shoot the bearing, then have a partner travel in that direction until he's just at the edge of your sight distance. Once he's there, tell him to move left or right to get him aligned. Move to your partner, and then repeat. It's a great method if you need to be super accurate.

## Step 7: Conclusion

Hopefully you just learned four new skills. I'm not an expert, but those few things are enough to keep most people out of trouble. The easiest place to practice is around home. It may be worth finding a partner to check on your work. If you head out to the wilderness, find a spot where you can pick out a bunch of landmarks. Shoot them with the compass, then compare your bearings to the actual bearings on the map. Remember the best way to avoid getting lost is to stay found. Have fun! Acknowledgments- *Mountaineering: The Freedom of the Hills 7th Edition.* If you're serious about this outdoors, this book is a great reference.

## Sleep Warm Anywhere

By **Mother Natures Son**
(www.instructables.com/id/Sleep-
Warm-Anywhere/)

Keep in mind that most of these techniques assume dry weather. If it's raining or snowing, the steps are the same, but you'll have to do them inside your tent or vestibule. It is also assumed that you have a sleeping bag rated for around the same temperatures you're likely to be experiencing, but the techniques demonstrated here can give you some wiggle-room with that. Remember: being prepared is always step one.

Hopefully, these techniques will help you get a better night's sleep, and in doing so help you better enjoy the great outdoors.

### Step 1: Put on Your Fly

This seems like a no-brainer, especially with a mesh-canopy tent like mine, but it's very, very important in frigid conditions. Not only does your fly block wind, keep in heat, and keep off rain or snow, many tents are actually designed so that the fly helps prevent condensation, and a dry sleeper is a warm sleeper. The fly also provides a vestibule, which is an extremely useful thing to have, especially in windy or rainy situations.

### Step 2: Use a Pad

Many of the big tough hikers or ultralight junkies out there spurn the use of the pad—as

did I, until I got a bag that requires one. This is fine, normally; granite's as good as a box spring from my point of view. But when you're in extremely cold conditions, and especially when sleeping in the snow, it's a must. A Big Agnes pad is my favorite, though it takes about a half-life of plutonium to inflate, but virtually any pad will do. Closed-cell foam is obviously better for hiking in areas where punctures are a risk, and many prefer the convenience of self-inflating Thermarests. As long as you have one, it doesn't really matter.

### Step 3: Dry Off

A dry sleeper is a warm sleeper. Well, unless his boxers are full of dry ice, obviously, but it's a good rule of thumb. Before going to bed, make sure you're dry. If you just got done hiking, you could be covered in sweat, or if you washed your face before bed, you might be wet as well, though admittedly cleaner. Do what you can to get dry. If your clothes are damp, switch into a dry set.

### Step 4: Dress Warm

Since I've written this, there has been a lot of back-and-forth about whether or not this is actually a good idea. However, I must maintain my position, due in no small part to the excellent links provided by the thermally impressive gmoon, particularly this one: http://sectionhiker.com/sleeping-naked-in-a-sleeping-bag/.

I recommend a synthetic fleece vest or wool sweater and a knit cap. The vest is light, dries quickly, and is quite warm. The sweater

**307**

is even warmer and in my experience slightly more compact than fleece for the same amount of warming.

Both remain fairly insulative even when damp, unlike cotton sweatshirts, which are literally worse than nothing in wet situations. Though I prefer the wool sweater overall, synthetic fleece is nice in that it absorbs almost no moisture.

The hat is amazingly warm, and while I usually use wool knit, synthetic is also excellent.

I should also comment on the importance of the bag liner. This is a cloth (I use synthetic fleece) liner that goes inside your sleeping bag. It can improve the rating significantly.

## Step 5: Get Warm Fluids into You

This is probably the most pleasant step. Sitting out in the cold after a long day of communing with nature, there's very little that's nicer than a warm drink. I personally prefer tea, but hot coco and hot drink mixes such as apple cider or Gatorade are also favorites. The purpose of this step is twofold: it warms you up and it hydrates you. There's virtually no part of camping that is worse off for better hydration, and sleeping is no exception. Don't overdo it, though; a cup or two is good but past that you're probably in for a nighttime hike to the tree. You should also eat something, obviously, but if you haven't figured that out you probably shouldn't be camping.

## Step 6: Get Warm Fluids Out of You

You're going to be spending the next several hours getting you, your clothes, your sleeping bag and your tent comfortably warm, and all that's going to go to waste if you find yourself having to wriggle out of your bag for a tree-run. Answer the call of nature before you go to bed, and you'll be a lot happier.

## Step 7: Make a Hot Water Bottle

This is an excellent trick. Just before bed, fill a Lexan bottle with hot water and wrap it in some clothes. This is also a twofold step: It'll warm you up initially, and you can drink it if you get thirsty in the night. Just make sure that lid's on tight. Many people have suggested the use of rocks instead of a water bottle, but believe it or not, water stores more heat at a given temperature than stone. The measurement of how much heat a given volume of something stores at a given temperature is called volumetric heat capacity, and water's is about twice as high as granite's.

## Step 8: Sleep Tight

Crawl into your cozy bag and drift to sleep in the great outdoors. Keep an eye out for signs of trouble, though—when you first get in, you'll be warm, but when your body becomes sedentary it's likely to cool down a bit before your sleeping bag warms up. If you keep getting colder, you may need to add more clothes, but don't constrict yourself. Place your hands in your armpits to keep them warm. If you're shivering and stop but are still cold, congratulations! You've got hypothermia! Get moving. Make yourself more tea and a fresh hot water bottle. Use your head. Sleeping in the cold doesn't have to be dangerous, but it's always risky.

How to make your very own waterproof dryer lint fire-starter, for free.

Using only household items, you can make a 1 oz waterproof fire-starter that burns for 15 minutes. It's perfect for camping, backpacking, or even your backyard fire pit. No need to buy fancy fire starter logs, here you'll need to gather a few household items that would have otherwise been thrown in trash.

## Gather Materials

First, gather a few materials from around the house.
- Dryer lint
- An empty egg carton

- Old candle stubs (or in my case, a box of canning wax—$3, available at your local hardware store.)
- Dental floss
- Scissors
- New Belgium beer (not required, but hey, that's how it happened)

## Step 1: Cut the Wax

Whether using old candle stubs or bars of canning wax, cut them into small strips/chunks so they can be more easily melted.

## Step 2: Fill Egg Carton with Dryer Lint

Take your dryer lint and fill each compartment. Stuff a fair amount into each as it will prolong burning time.

## Step 3: Cut and Fold Compartment

Using the scissors, cut each compartment and fold the ends of each on top of each other.

outside

309

## Step 4: Tie Each Compartment with Dental Floss

Using dental floss (or any disposable string), tie each fire-starter allowing for a few inches of additional length.

## Step 5: Melt Wax

Drop your wax pieces into a disposable glass jar (or empty aluminum can) and place it into a boiling pot of water. Keep the water level low enough so the jar or can doesn't tip over. Once the water boils, you should have fully melted wax in a few minutes.

## Step 6: Lower Fire-Starters into Jar or Can

Turning off your burner, you can now lower the fire-starters into the jar or can of melted wax using the length of dental floss. Make sure the fire-starters are fully submerged until bubbles stop rising to the surface. Note: It may help to use an additional utensil to push them below the wax line.

## Step 7: Let Fire-Starters Dry

Drizzle any remaining wax onto the fire-starters. This will help ensure waterproofing. Let the fire-starters fully dry. I placed them on a paper towel to prevent a messy cleanup. After about an hour or two, they should be rock solid.

## Step 8: Light Your Fire-Starter

Now that they have dried, your fire-starters are ready to go. Just light a corner and bask in the glory. My initial test had a burn time of 15 minutes.

The goal here was to take items around the house that would have otherwise wound up in a landfill and turn them into something useful. Hope you enjoy.

outside

# Camping Shower!

By alliedmilk

(www.instructables.com/id/Camping-Shower-1/)

This is a very simple solar-heated portable shower unit to take camping. There is no privacy shade, just simply the water delivery aspect.

## You will Need

- a 9 liter rectangular water jug.
- braided poly rope. I didn't measure, but I used more than 10 feet, and less than 20.
- garden watering can with detachable spout OR a replacement spout.
- a chain shackle
- unscrewable chain link
- roll of Gorilla tape

## Tools

- (3) contractor grade glue sticks
- a glue gun
- a tiny tube of krazy glue
- thin piece of wood (I used a Redbird match stick)
- pliers
- lighter/butane torch
- scissors

## Step 1: Fitting the Rigging

First we need to tie a length of rope around the water-jug. Start by laying the jug tap side down. Run the rope through the handle and even out the lengths. Using the bottom edge of the jug as a mark, use the two sections of rope to tie a reef (square) knot, then continue running it around the length of the jug. When you get around to the other side, split the sections around the white spout of the jug and pass an end through the handle. Tie another reef knot at this position.

## Step 2: Perfecting the Spout Head

If you found the same jug as me, that's great, because this will be much easier for you. If you haven't found the same jug, all you really need to find is an attachment of any kind (even a small shower head would do) with holes in it similar to the watering can that will fit on the end of the water jug spout. I chose what I did for it's simplicity.

Remove the spout from the watering can. Insert the water jug spout end on to the water jug spout. Ensure you've got a relatively snug fit. I had about 1.3mm of a gap when I'd inserted one end into the other, which I deal with later.

Take the front end (part with the holes in it) off of the funnel part.

Place the front end face down in a vice, or a flat surface you won't mind getting hot glue on.

Once your glue gun is heated up, begin squeezing small drops very cautiously into each of the holes in the two inner rings, leaving the center hole cleared. This way

311

we'll only get water out of the center hole, and the outer ring. If the center hole gets clogged, use the match stick to clear it out.

Let it dry a while.

## Step 3: Prepare the Hanging Line

This is a simple step of a couple knots, the chain pieces, and some hot glue.

Note: You are not gluing the rope to the chain pieces.

Get your chain shackle into the vice with the ring side up, and tie a reef knot in that bad boy.

Glue the knot shut by placing drops of hot glue strategically on all sides of the knot.

Take your unscrewable chain link and do the same thing with it on the other end of the rope.

As a final step in the rope preparation, I grasped the excess ends of all the braided poly rope knots with my pliers and cut off the excess. Then I used my lighter to cure (melt) the ends of the rope to make sure they stay together.

## Step 5: Tape up Your Jug

Now we're going to put a bunch of black Gorilla tape around the jug to capture the heat of the sun. So when you go camping, fill it up in the morning and leave it in the sun all day.

Also, we'll wrap some tape around a part of the rope in order to make it sticky enough for the chain pieces to not slide around on it.

Begin taping up the jug. You can tape the rope on the front (under the spout) to

the jug, might as well keep it out of the way. DO NOT glue the rope on the back end to the jug though, or you won't be able to hang it.

On the back of the jug is the portion of rope in which you tied your first knot—tape those two sections together.

Tape as much as you like. The more the better I'd say. I'm going to leave some space to I can see the water level.

## Step 6: Test it Out!

Fill up the jug with water, walk over to an appropriate testing tree limb or other kind of cross bar.

Unscrew the shackle and place the taped up rope through it, put the screw back in, and tighten.

Lift the 9L of water into the air, with the chain link in your other hand.

Affix the rope to the tree or the jug.

Pull the air stopper out turn it on! Look at your perfect camping shower!

Note: You can alter the flow by opening and closing the water jug spout. So you can have a full on rinse or just a trickle.

Also, you can time release the flow to turn off. If you pop open the air stopper, turn the unit on then plug the air stopper again, the water will run for another 20-30 seconds, and then trickle to a stop.

You can also alter the rate of water flow by where along the taped up rope you place the shackle. I find by leaving it at the 5L mark (on the back of the jug) I get a perfect symmetrical flow right until it's about empty.

# How to Purify Water Using Iodine Tincture

By **joshf** Josh Freedman
(www.instructables.com/id/How-To-Purify-Water-Using-Iodine-Tincture/)

When you're in the wilderness, you need clean water to drink but water sources in the wilderness can carry bacteria such as giardia. You don't want giardia, trust me, and trying to carry a few jugs of Poland Spring would be extremely heavy and inefficient. Luckily, there are a number of ways to purify water, and one of the simplest, cheapest, and most effective ways is to use iodine tincture.

## Supplies

To complete this task, you'll need the following:

- Water bottle: A Nalgene (what I use here) or a metal water bottle will work best, but all you really need is any container that will hold water
- Iodine Tincture Solution: You want Iodine Tincture with 2 percent iodine and about 47 percent alcohol. Bottles of this solution should be available at your local drugstore and a 2 oz. bottle is usually $3 or less.

- An eyedropper: Counting the number of drops is the easiest way to keep track of how much you're using.
- A good water source: This can be a lake, a river, a stream, etc. If you have a choice of water sources, consider these two tips: Clear water is better than cloudy water. Flowing water is better than still water. Remember, though, that even if the water looks extremely pure and clean, it should still be purified before drinking. Looks can be deceiving!

## Step 1: Fill Your Bottle

After finding a water source, you need to fill your bottle with water. To do this, position yourself close to the water source and tilt the bottle under the water. You want to collect water from near the surface, so don't just immerse the whole bottle in the water. Let the bottle fill up and remove it. Examine your bottle of water to make sure there are not too many floating particles (called "floaties" in scientific terms). A couple of small floaties are fine, but too many large floaties can be dangerous. If this happens, you need to try filling up again. A way to solve this problem is to cover the mouth of the bottle with a bandanna or thin cloth that will allow water into the bottle but keep floaties out.

## Step 2: Add the Iodine Tincture

Dip your eyedropper into the iodine tincture and squeeze up some of the liquid. Carefully position the eyedropper over the mouth of the bottle and add 5-10 drops per 32 fluid ounces (about 1 liter) of water. The exact number of drops is a personal choice

313

(I can't make this decision for you) depending on the following factors: The water source: if your source is a lake or some other still body of water, you want to add closer to 10 drops; if the source is flowing, you can add fewer. The clarity of the water: you should add closer to 10 drops if the water is cloudy. Your own aversion to the taste of iodine: some people hate the taste of iodine (it is a little bitter, and you will notice the taste in your purified water). If this is the case, you might want to add closer to 5 drops. Personally, I'm a fan of 8 drops.

## Step 4: Wait 5 Minutes

After adding the iodine, you need to wait 5 minutes before you can continue. You can go for a quick hike, admire nature, play a game, or think up an idea for your next instructable.

## Step 5: Thread the Bottle

After five minutes, you need to purify the mouth and rim of the bottle (which touched the original water source and which will touch your mouth). To do this, you need to "thread" the bottle. Turn the bottle upside down and slowly unscrew the top until you can see a ring of water appear around the inner rim. Once you see that ring of water, you know that the water with the iodine has touched the mouth of the bottle and disinfected it. Screw the top back on and flip the bottle right-side up. A little water will probably leak out while threading, and that's not bad—it just ensures that you've fully threaded.

## Step 6: Wait 30 Minutes, Then Enjoy!

The iodine needs time to completely purify the water. You need to wait 30 minutes before you can drink the water—plenty of time to finalize that idea for an instructable. After you have waited 30 minutes, your water is purified for drinking. Revel in the cool, clean taste of your iodine-infused water while you enjoy your wilderness adventure.

There is always more work to be done in the workshop. In these pages, you'll learn how to build better shop equipment, do basic welding and woodworking, and make awesome projects you can use to fill up the other rooms of your home.

# How to Find the Center of a Circle

By **noahw** Noah Weinstein
(www.instructables.com/id/How-to-Find-the-Center-of-a-Circle-1/)

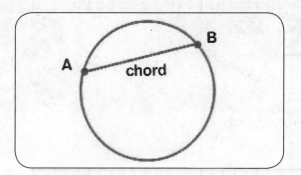

Finding the centers of things for woodworking is pretty important. Squares and rectangles are pretty easy, you simply draw two diagonal lines from the opposite corners and the point where they cross is the center of your material.

Finding the center of a circle on the other hand wasn't quite as intuitive to me, and until doing some searching of my own, I didn't know that there was a simple and easy trick. Time to share.

## Step 1: Draw Some Chords

A chord is a line that intersects any two points on the circumference of a circle.

Simply take a ruler, place it down on the edge of your circle so that it crosses the outer edge in two places, and use a pencil to mark a line.

Technically to find the center of a circle you only need one perfectly drawn chord but since people aren't machines and there's some user error in the process, draw a couple so that you can average the results.

## Step 2: Mark the Centers and Draw a Perpendicular Line

Use a ruler to find the midpoints of the chords that you just drew. If your chord measures 11" from end to end, the center of the chord is 5.5" from the ends.

Mark that point.

Then, using a square, draw a line that is exactly 90 degrees to the chord pointing towards the center of your circle. Make it a little longer then where you think the center of the circle resides.

Do this for all of your chords.

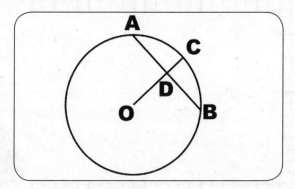

## Step 3: The Center is the Point Where They Intersect

The center of the circle is the point where all of these perpendicular lines intersect. I drew 5 different chords with 5 perpendicular lines coming from them, and they all come within about 1/16 th" from each other.

# Built-in Book Cases

By CarlS Carl Sutter

(www.instructables.com/id/Built-In-Book-Cases/)

For this project, we needed built-in book cases for a long wall. By using pre-drilled melamine laminated boards and pre-built cabinets from the local home store, we were able to build them with a minimum of tools, and get a perfect fit to the room.

## Materials

- The book cases are made from a series of frames, pre-drilled shelf hole melamine on the sides, and ¾" plywood on the tops and bottoms. All the middle ones have a pre-made cabinet under them, and the leftover space was divided in half, to have a narrower bookshelf on each end to fit the room end-to-end.
- The cabinets are pre-built and 36" wide and about 13" deep.
- Melamine laminated sides—they are sold as 12" wide, but are actually 11.75" wide. These are pre-drilled with shelf pin holes.
- Plywood top & bottom & shelf above cabinet—we used ¾" hardwood laminated—Luan or Birch is fine.
- Plinth blocks (5" high and 2.5" wide) and rosettes (2.5" square)
- Fluted molding—2.25" wide
- front edge trim molding
- bottom and top trim 1" × 3"
- shelves—¾" plywood with 1" × 2" front edges

- shelf pins and knobs for the cabinet doors
- crown molding

## Step 1: Section Frames

Each section of the book case is based on the width of the cabinets we used. The cabinets are wrapped in the frame, so the outside frame width will be the width of the cabinet plus 1.5" (¾" for each side) plus a tiny bit for the melamine veneer. So, we measured the wall, divided it up into the number of frames that will fit. There was some left over, so we made narrower bookshelves on each end (with no cabinets). In our case, we could have done one more cabinet, but the sides would have been too narrow to look good, so we used one less cabinet box and the result looks pretty good.

The cabinet frames are pretty easy to make because we didn't use any fancy joinery. The cabinets have three fixed shelves; one for the bottom of the cabinet, one for the top of the cabinet, and one at the top of the frame. The frames go from the floor to almost the ceiling, and the cabinets fit inside the frame.

The length of the fixed shelves is the same as the width of the cabinets—in our case, 36". The width of the top and bottom fixed shelves is the same as the melamine sides (11.75"). The width of the middle shelf on top of the cabinets is wider to get some overhang over the cabinets (noted below).

The top edge of the bottom shelf was set to the height of the baseboard plus ¼" for a reveal between the baseboard and the bottom shelf. Since we used 1 × 3 boards on the bottom, that's 2.5" plus ¼".

The top shelf height is set to allow room for a top face molding, and then crown molding to the ceiling above that. The height of each frame was a bit less than the ceiling height to allow for moving the frames in. For our shelves, the top edge of the top shelf was the ceiling height minus the crown molding height minus about an inch reveal to the shelf minus a ¼" reveal from the face molding to the top shelf.

The shelf above the cabinets needs to be deeper than the melamine so it overhangs the cabinets a bit. We made it 13.5" deep. It's wider than the melamine (11.75" deep) to allow for the plinth block (¾") plus a 1" overhang over the cabinet fronts.

At the top back of the sides, we cutout a notch to allow the existing crown molding to stay in place. This seemed easier than removing the molding, and since we have an older house, that crown molding is probably nicer than current materials. Maybe some future owner will tear out these bookcases and thank us for leaving the molding.

We used drywall screws to hold the sides to the shelves, and they definitely need to be pre-drilled and counter-sunk since it's going into the edge of plywood and we don't want it to split.

Each frame is not very strong, but once the cabinets are in place and they are side-by side, the whole system gets a lot stronger. Attach the top and bottom shelves, but leave the cabinet top off for now—that can be added on top of the cabinets.

## Step 2: Cabinets

Once you have the frames in the room, you can set the cabinets on the base. We set them flush with the front of the frames. Then we used a few drywall screws from the sides

to connect the cabinets to the frames. Be careful on the placement so the screws don't go into the cabinets. Once the cabinets are in, the cabinet top shelf can be added, and screwed in.

Place all the frames against the wall, and use shims to get the cabinet top shelves to line up and look straight. Once you have them lined up, use a few 1¼" drywall screws to connect the frames together on the sides so they don't shift. Pre-drill and counter-sink these holes too. We found white plugs to put in the counter-sunk holes. Wood putty and paint would probably work too—might not match the melamine finish exactly, but you really wouldn't notice once the shelves are in and filled with books.

## Step 3: Details

The shelves on top of the cabinets should all be connected together to make the impression of one continuous surface. They

could be cut with notches for the melamine sides, but we just used little blocks to fill in those gaps. Those were glued and screwed in since they were small, and we use wood putty to fill the gaps and sanded it smooth. After painting, it looks like one continuous piece. At the sides we added the plinth blocks at the bottom, the rosettes at the top, and fluted molding on the sides. Note that these do extend into the shelf space a bit, and this is by convention and design.

The baseboard is 1" × 3" pine, and the top face molding is too. Each is attached with a ¼" reveal from the bottom and top shelves. The baseboard does not need to touch the floor (but it can) since we add shoe molding on the face.

We added crown molding to match the existing room molding—some tricky cuts where they meet, but we used the coping method to match that.

On the front edge of the shelf above the cabinets, we added some trim molding—it's ¾" thick, so it matches the front of the shelf.

## Step 4: Shelves

The movable shelves are simply made from plywood with a 1" × 2" front edge glued and screwed on. The shelves need to be ¾" narrower than the sides to allow for the front piece +¼" narrower so the shelves are not pressing right against the trim molding on the sides. So, make the plywood 1" less than the width of the sides.

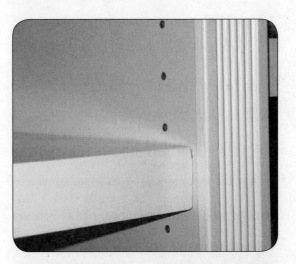

workshop

319

# Awesome Cutting Boards!

By **acantine** Andrew Cantine
(www.instructables.com/id/
Awesome-Cutting-Boards!/)

This instructable details how to make hardwood cutting boards out of maple and cherry scraps. Not only are they beautiful and high quality, they're made from materials that would have been discarded otherwise. Reduce, Reuse, Recycle!

## Get Your Materials

We used maple balusters removed during a remodel as the main elements of the cutting boards. Each piece had a few holes in the ends from where they'd been attached to the stairs/banister. We cut off just enough material to get rid of the holes, not worrying about uniform length.

## Step 1: Getting a Square Deal

After we'd removed the ends, we had to take care of the rounded edges with a quick trim on the table saw.

## Step 2: It is not OK to Eat Varnish

Varnish: good for balusters, bad for cutting boards.

We passed them through a planer to take off the outermost layers of varnish and wood

so we could get back to clean maple. We passed through each face that glue would be applied to several times to get a nice smooth surface. We left the varnish on the faces that would become the cutting surfaces to be dealt with later.

## Step 3: Check Your Work

This step is more or less concurrent with the last. Measure (for thickness) to see if the piece still has varnish on any side.

## Step 4: Make it Go Faster

I've said it before, and I'll say it again: The key to speed lies in the paint job, not what's under the hood. For a spiffy racing stripe, we used a piece of cherry leftover from a desk project. The nice thing about using cherry is that it gets darker the more you use your cutting board. We trimmed it down to size so that it matched the thickness of our maple pieces.

## Step 5: GLUE!

The important thing is to get an even coat and to make sure there won't be any air pockets lingering after they're pressed together, this is important! A nice, evenly spaced squiggle brushed out smoothly does just the trick. Also, don't worry too much about getting glue everywhere, because you will.

We used regular Titebond for this project and it's held up fine for me over the past 5 years. In the meantime I've switched to Titebond III which is their waterproof glue. It's more expensive, but I think the added protection/precaution is worth it.

## Step 6: Line 'em Up!

Once you get your glue nice and even, making sure there are no air pockets, you can start to slap the pieces together.

We left the varnish on two of the surfaces and we also didn't worry about length at this point.

Don't be misled by this last statement! For clarification, we'd decided (based on the number of pieces we had) how big and how many of each cutting board we wanted to make. I mean "not worrying about length" in terms of not being ultra-precise about the lengths of the individual pieces PER cutting board.

## Step 7: The Clamp Down

We supported the slats from the top and bottom (we did the same thing on the other end simultaneously) to keep the pieces even as we squished them together with pipe clamps. You should also keep some wood scraps between the clamp faces and where they meet the wood. If you're not careful you can end up damaging your project by leaving a depression if you clamp tightly. After you get the boards clamped from the sides be sure to remove the clamp and wood you used to keep everything in line, otherwise you'll end up with railings on your cutting board, which most users will find undesirable.

## Step 8: Sit Down and Have a Think. Or Two

So how long did we need to wait for the glue to dry?

24 hrs?

48 hrs?

workshop

321

All it takes is about 30-45 minutes! Different glues cure differently and wood glue cures in the absence of air, which is why you want to be so careful about making sure there aren't any air pockets in your glue job.

## Step 9: Operation "Reverse Clamp Down"

Once your glue is set, remove your clamps.

Grab a paint scraper and a scrap of something to wipe the glue on (it will still look wet on the surface, don't worry, it's cured between the boards themselves), and get all the excess crud that got squeezed out during the clamp-down. You only want to leave as much glue on the boards as you'd want to send through your planer.

## Step 10: The Plane Boss, the Plane!

Once we'd removed most of the glue, we sent the assembled boards through the planer to get them nice and flat. Each cutting board took several passes to remove the varnish we'd left from before.

## Step 11: Tying up Loose Ends

After a quick zip on the saw all the lengths we'd left from before were squared up.

## Step 12: Sanding

Talk about a wonderful machine! If you don't have a drum sander, have fun sanding! Alternatively, if you have a cabinet shop in your area they might be willing to run your assembled boards through for you. It's been my experience that they'll charge you around $2 a minute—this is an incredible bargain—it will only take them about 2 or 3 minutes to do, versus the 45 min to an hour (or more!) it can take using a palm sander.

## Step 13: The Finishing Touches

We added a chamfer (45 degree angle) to the boards giving them gently rounded outside edges and gave them another light sanding by hand to catch all the side-surfaces.

## Step 14: Fin

We added some tiny cork-feet to keep them from sliding around, but in hindsight this was probably unnecessary.

In terms of protecting your board, use mineral oil, or one of the commercially available products for protecting butcher-blocks. Vegetable oils will go rancid and you'll want to avoid nut oils so you don't send anyone to the hospital with an allergic reaction. Whatever you decide to use, remember that it needs to be food safe.

If your board starts to look dry, just reapply your mineral oil by rubbing it into the surfaces (every side, keep it evenly oiled) with a cloth. You really can't use too much and it probably wouldn't hurt to do it a couple times, i.e. apply oil, let it sit overnight, and hit it again the next day.

You don't want to expose these to too much water—do not put them in the dish washer, or let them soak—if you scrub it off with soap and water be sure to dry it immediately.

# Bandsaw Boxes Made Easy

By **Wood Chuck** Bruce Beatty
(www.instructables.com/id/Bandsaw-Boxes-Made-Easy/)

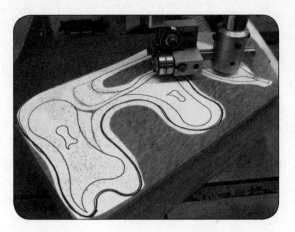

**Warning**

Bandsaw Box making can be addictive.

## Step 1: Design Your Creation

Design your creation. You are only limited by your imagination. Or search the web for ideas. The following box is a facsimile of a picture I found created by Lois Keener Ventura.

## Step 2: Prepare Your Blank

Glue up a block to fit you design—unless you keep 12/4 material around!

On this particular box I used a piece of 8/4 walnut for the core and 2 pieces of lace wood for the front and back. The total block measured 3″ × 6″ × 11″.

## Step 3

Roughly cut out your template and attach it to the blank with spray adhesive. Be sure to leave enough room to sand to your line. At this point you are only cutting the outside of your design.

Keep in mind the smallest radius you can cut is determined by the size of your bandsaw blade. I used a 3/16 or 1/4″ blade for the boxes I've made so far.

NOTE: If you fail to follow your line don't worry, just consider it a design.

## Step 4: Sand Your Creation

It is easier to sand all of the curves now before you proceed. That way the back will be identical to the main body.

NOTE: I usually make my boxes around 3″ thick so they will fit on my spindle sander!

## Step 5: Slice Off the Back

Now slice off the back of your box. Mine are around 1/4″ but that's your decision.

## Step 6: Cut Your Drawers

Decide on an entrance point and cut out each drawer (in one motion if possible.)

Or if you come to a sharp point, stop your saw and back out of the cut.

My box will be a little different: there will be two entrance points. One will be left open with the drawer exposed and the other will be closed.

## Step 7: Cutting the Drawer Openings

The middle drawer is cut out after the lower drawer is cut out, by joining the two openings with a single kerf.

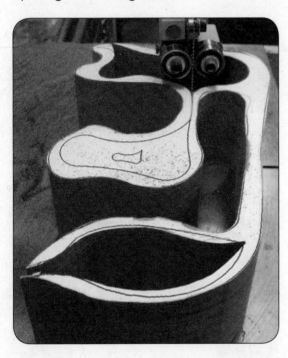

## Step 8: Closing The Gap

Then I glued my lower entrance point back together.

Depending on your design it is sometimes quite a challenge to place clamps.

## Step 9: Sand

Sand all of the inside compartments where the drawers will go. While your glue is drying you can sand the outside of your drawer body.

## Step 10: Preparing Your Drawers

Now slice a front and back off your drawer bodies. Your choice for thickness

NOTE: You might want to mark your pieces in some way so you don't get the parts reversed. This will make sure the glue up goes smoother.

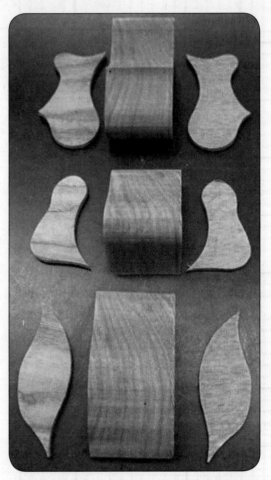

## Step 11: Design your Drawer Compartment

Mark your drawer bodies with a shape that will become the inside of your drawer.

Don't make the corners too sharp, You still want to sand the inside.

## Step 12: Cut the Drawer

Follow your pattern (roughly) and remove the drawer cavities.

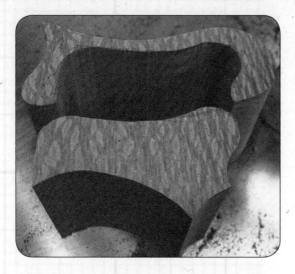

## Step 13: Sand Drawer Curves

Before drawer assembly sand the inside of your drawers.

## Step 14: Re-Assemble Your Drawers

Carefully line-up the front and back pieces of your drawers and glue them back together.

## Step 15: Attach the Rear Panel

The rear panel of the main body can be attached (actually it can be attached anytime after you glue your entrance point closed).

There will likely be a small amount of sanding along your glue line when it dries and near the entrance cut.

## Step 16: Make Your Drawer Pulls

Design and cut out your drawer pulls (if required). These are very small pieces—use extreme caution if you use a bandsaw to cut these out. I chose ebony pulls for this box just to accent the Lace Wood.

## Step 17: Attach Your Handles

Attach your handles and you're done!

## Step 18: Apply Your Finish

Finish with your favourite finish and show it off.

I hope you give these boxes a try, they are great fun to make and will make wonderful handcrafted gifts.

Depending on the complexity of your design the whole project will only take 4 to 5 hours. (not counting waiting on glue to dry).

# Turning a Baseball Bat

By **carlbass** Carl Bass
(www.instructables.com/id/Turning-a-
baseball-bat/)

Making a baseball bat is fun. It's a relatively straightforward woodturning project. As little leaguers graduate from aluminum and composite bats, it's good for them to hone their skills with a classic wood bat.

## Tools and Supplies

- 36" wood bat blank
- wood lathe
- turning tools
- square
- outside calipers
- sandpaper
- oil/varnish finish
- fine Japanese saw

## Step 1: Choosing the Wood

The first thing to do is to find a good blank of either hard maple or northern ash. The rough size should be approximately 3" across and 36" long. The straighter and tighter the grain, the less chance it will break when you use it. Material that's been graded for making bats is much better than what you find at the local hardwood store.

If you can't find a round blank, you can start with a blank that's square in cross section. Then chamfer the long edges in order to make it octagonal in cross-section.

The blank should be about 3" longer than the final length to allow for waste at both ends.

## Step 2: Marking the Center

The next step is to mark the center of the cylinder on both sides. You can use a center finder, if you have one. If not, a good trick is to use a square to inscribe a right angle inside the circle. Draw a line where the legs of the square intersect the circumference. That line goes through the center. Do the same thing again after rotating the square 90 degrees and the intersection of those two lines is the center.

At the center, use an awl to make a hole that the centers will fit into.

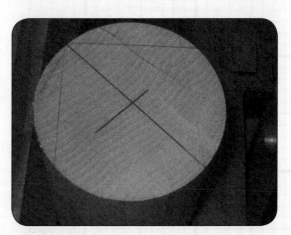

## Step 3: Roughing out the Blank

Mount the blank on the lathe. I use a live center at the tailstock and a steb center at the headstock. I mount the bat so the barrel will be closest to the headstock. I find it easier to turn this way and it seems to vibrate less but if you mount it with the barrel at the tailstock, most of the cuts are "downhill".

Turn the blank into a cylinder making sure it's at least 2.75" along its length. I use a roughing gouge to do this as I'm more interested in balancing the piece than the surface finish. If you have a lathe that can adjust speed, 800 rpm is a good speed.

## Step 4: Marking Out the Bat

I now mark out the bat by laying pencil lines every 3" on the blank, including the end of the handle and the barrel. Just hold a pencil up to the spinning blank and it will leave a clear line.

## Step 5: Gauging the Depth

Starting at the end of the barrel, I use a parting tool to make a small channel. I leave the diameter within this cut about ⅛" larger than the finished dimension. I usually cut to depth the first 3 or 4 of these marks starting from the barrel down.

If you're copying an existing bat, use the calipers to transfer the measurements. Set the calipers by measuring the existing bat. Add about 1/16" to the measurement to allow for cutting and sanding. Using a parting chisel, cut the blank until the caliper just barely slips through.

If you're working from a drawing, you can set and measure the calipers or use a dial caliper directly.

## Step 6: Shaping the Barrel

I use the roughing gouge again to remove most of the waste between the depth cuts. At this point, I usually turn the lathe up to 1200-1600 rpm. I try to keep a fair curve between the cuts by focusing on the back of the silhouette of the barrel. I then use a skew gouge to smooth the surface. While I'm mentioning the tools I like to use, other turning tools can work just as well.

I usually sand the barrel with 100 grit sandpaper (or whatever the surface finish calls for) before I move on to cutting the rest of the bat. This allows me to get a good surface before the bat gets too whippy on the lathe.

## Step 7: Shaping the Handle and Knob

Continue using the parting tool to mark the appropriate depth of the cuts. Use the spindle gouge or the skew chisel to fair the curve between the channels cut with the parting gouge.

The shapes and sizes of knobs vary greatly and are a matter of personal preference—they don't affect the performance.

## Step 8: Supporting the Center

The trickiest part of turning a bat is that down near the handle, a bat is relatively thin compared to its length. As you start cutting towards the handle, the bat will vibrate and cause the tool to bounce and make spiral chatter marks. The first thing to do is to make sure your tools are as sharp as possible. The second thing to do is to find a way to support the stock in the middle. The best and most convenient way for the experienced turner is to put your hand right behind the cut and support it.

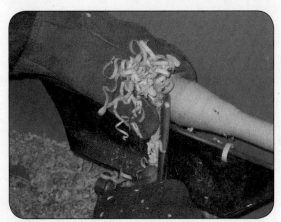

## Step 9: Sanding the Bat

Depending on the surface quality and fairness of the curve, you'll need different amounts of sanding. If the surface is rough and the profile not perfectly smooth, you should start with 80 grit sandpaper. To help smooth out the shape and not make the imperfections worse, it's helpful to back up the sandpaper with a small piece of wood so you're not merely polishing the peaks and valleys.

If the surface is better, you can start sanding with 100 or 120 grit sandpaper. I usually sand in several steps up to 220.

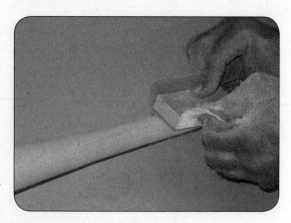

## Step 10: Applying Finish

I've found a mixture of oil and varnish to be the best finish. You can buy these types of finishes in the hardware store or make your own mixture. I usually put a few coats of finish on while the bat is still mounted on the lathe.

## Step 11: Trimming the Ends

I use the skew chisel held vertically to make super clean cuts on the end grain. I hone my skew just before making these cuts. If you're using a gouge or a scarping tool, be careful here because cleaning up the marks left in the end grain is almost impossible. Then I clear some room with a parting chisel and leave a shoulder for the saw to ride on.

I cut the protrusion at the top of the barrel to about an inch across (I'm going to make a hollow at that end of the bat) and cut the end at the handle to about ¼" (to leave as little as possible that I have to sand).

Then I remove the bat from the lathe and use a small Japanese saw to trim off the little nubs and sand the ends.

## Step 12: Hollowing the End

Most bats these days have a small hollow in the end but it's definitely optional. You can just leave the end slightly convex and sand it when you take it off the lathe.

Because I've made enough of these I've built a jig to hold the bats upright while I rout a hollow at the end. I use a ½ spiral up cut bit and guide the router with a template bushing, and then follow that cut with a 1.25 inch round nose bit following a circle template set atop the end of the bat.

Some of the commercial bats I've looked at seem to do this step with a drill.

## Step 13: Engraving the Bat

If you have access to a laser cutter, you can really make the bat look special. I mount it on a rotary device on the laser cutter and cut whatever the player wants on it. Before engraving, I cover the area to be cut with blue masking tape as it makes for a cleaner cut.

If you don't have access to a laser cutter, you can use a wood burner or you can paint logos and names on the bat.

## Step 14: Finishing the Bat

The last step is to apply more finish. I generally wet sand the finish at this point with 400 grit sandpaper and do as many coats as my patience or kids allow before one of them wants to take it out and hit with it.

# DIY Dust Collection System

By RadBear

(www.instructables.com/id/DIY-Dust-Collection-System/)

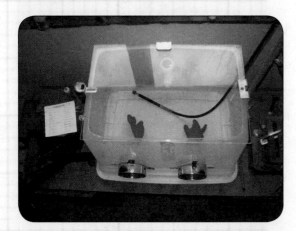

In doing a quick search of Instructables I found a passive dust collection system very similar to my idea. My system incorporates a Shop-Vac to actively draw in the dust, instead of only containing it. Aside from containing dust there is the added benefit of not having to use as much safety gear. The box will contain the dust and flying debris so I won't have to wear a dust mask or safety goggles.

If you build a passive version of this project you want it to be air-tight so that dust won't escape. If you build an active system you need the unit to allow air to flow in so your vacuum can work. Lack of incoming air could damage the motor of your vacuum.

You can allow for air flow in one of two ways:

1. You can build a specialized opening that allows air to enter while the rest of the unit is air-tight. This would allow you to also use the system in a passive mode if your vacuum was unavailable.
2. You could allow spaces around the various penetrations into the system. This would allow air to flow in along multiple paths and requires no specialized openings. The downside being that it would be messy to use it in a passive mode as dust would be more likely to escape. I went with this method as I am a sloppy cutter.

## Materials

The materials I used for this project are as follows:

- Large plastic container with a snap on lid
- Coffee can
- Vacuum cleaner nozzle attachment
- Sink drain pipe
- Pair of rubber dish washing gloves
- Hose clamps
- Piece of Plexiglass scrap metal (sheet metal and heavy duty pieces)
- Rubber gasket material
- Epoxy

The tools I used for this project are as follows:

- Drill press
- Hand drill
- ⅛" drill bit
- Round needle file
- Electric shears
- Wood burner/soldering iron
- Utility knife
- Pop riveter
- ⅛" diameter rivets
- Ballpean hammer
- Bench vise
- Dremel with grinding drum
- Jigsaw
- Hacksaw
- Can opener
- Metal punch
- Awl
- Scissors
- Marker
- Measuring tape
- Flat-head screwdriver
- Tape measure
- Ruler

## Step 1: Container Size and Placement

The first step in building the dust collection system is determining the size of container you're going to use. I wanted something that I could use on my work bench. So the limiting factor for me was the space between my bench vise and drill press.

## Step 2: Penetration Preparation and Layout

After you acquire a container that will fit your space you will need to decide where to place the penetrations (e.g. gloves, tool access, cord access, and vacuum connection). In doing this consider where the electrical outlets are in your shop and where you plan to place your Shop-Vac. Once you've chosen the locations of the various penetrations, you need to mark the locations on the container. In order to make these markings accurate you need to configure your penetrations so you can use them as accurate templates. In my case this meant cutting off a portion of the vacuum nozzle and cutting the drain pipe that will be used to provide cord access and cleaning up the edges with a Dremel. I then marked the penetrations using a marker. I also marked the outline of the material I will remove from the bottom of the container to install the Plexiglas.

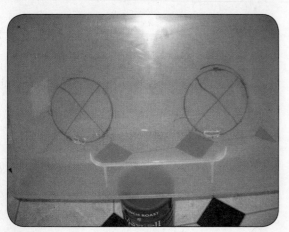

## Step 3: Cutting the Penetrations

I first used a wood burner to melt starter holes for all of my planned penetrations. Next I used my electric shears to cut out the material. With that accomplished I finished the edges with my Dremel and test fit the connections.

## Step 4: Adding the Top

Originally I had planned to get a piece of plexiglass and sand it down to fit inside the container. Then I would attach it to the container with rivets. Instead of drilling out the rivets if the plexiglass ever became too scarred by flying debris, I made a wood frame with a groove cut in it to serve as a track. That way, the plexiglass could just be slid in and out as needed.

Instead of a wood frame I decided to use some metal flaps that just bent up over the plexiglass while it rested on the top of the container.

I measured the top of the container. Then I went to the local hardware store and they cut a piece of ¼" plexiglass to the dimensions I needed. Then I placed it on top of the container to verify it was the correct size.

After I verified the size of the plexiglass I dug out three pieces of heavy duty scrap metal to make the metal flaps.

First if your pieces of metal need holes figure out where you want them. Then mark the hole locations on the metal pieces. This would also be an appropriate time to mark where you will need to bend the pieces. Once you mark them clamp the metal into a drill press and drill out the holes. After

workshop

drilling clean the sharp edges and excess material away with a Dremel and a round needle file.

When you've drilled the holes it is time to bend the flaps. Lock the metal pieces into your bench vise just below the line you drew on them. Then if it is thinner metal bend it ninety degrees with your hand. If the metal is really thick apply multiple mighty wallops with a ballpean hammer until it is bent ninety degrees.

Now that the metal pieces are bent hold them in position with your hand on the plexiglass while it rests on top of the container. Using the metal as a template mark where you will need to drill holes for the rivets. Now use an awl to make small starter dents in the plastic on these marks. This will keep the drill bit from walking. Then drill out the holes with a hand drill.

Insert rivets into the holes in the metal and plastic. Use your pop riveter to secure them. Once the flaps are in place remove the protetive covering from the plexiglass and slide it into place.

## Step 5: Flex Shaft Access

I cut a hole on the upper right side of the container to allow the Dremel's flex shaft to be used. (I chose the upper right because this is the side of my bench where my Dremel stand is located). However, I didn't want to just have an open hole in case I ever needed to use the unit passively.

To solve this dilemma I decided to use some rubber gasket type material I pulled off the outside of an old hard drive. I cut a piece of gasket material that would cover

the entry hole and marked four points. I then used an awl and drill as described in the previous step to drill holes in the plastic at these points. The excess material around the holes was cleaned away with a Dremel.

I then used these holes as a template to mark the gasket material. Using the awl I then made holes at these points.

Next I inserted rivets into the holes in the plastic. Then I slipped the rubber piece over the four rivets. With this done I popped the rivets into place.

Next pull the rubber piece off the rivets. Then mix up some epoxy and smear it around the hole and the rivets. When this is done put the rubber back in place. Use a spring clamp to hold it in place while the epoxy hardens.

Once the epoxy has set use a utility knife to cut a vertical and a horizontal slit in the rubber. This will allow the flex shaft to enter and minimize dust escaping from this point if the vacuum isn't on.

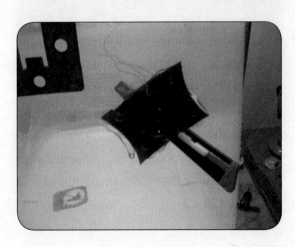

## Step 6: Glove Mounts—Prepping the Coffee Can

I chose to use a coffee can to mount the gloves to. This will work for me because I have arms like twigs.

The first step in preparing the coffee can is to get rid of the bottom of the can and the flange around the top. This is most easily accomplished by going to the kitchen and making use of an electric can opener.

Once this is done use your Dremel to grind down the sharp edges left on the can. When the edges are ground smooth use a hack saw to cut the can in half to produce two short tunnels. Use the Dremel for a second round of grinding.

## Step 7: Glove Mount Preparation—Rivet Holes & Gloves

With the glove mounts cut and ground it is time to get them ready to receive rivets. Place one of the mounts into one of the holes that we cut for it earlier. Then mark where you plan to rivet the support brackets (which we'll make in the next step) on the can and the container. I used two rivets for each end of the bracket: two on the can and two on the container.

With the rivet positions marked it is time to drill the holes. Use a metal punch to make dents at each of the rivet positions to keep the drill bit from walking. DO NOT use a hammer to do this!!! Just hold the punch and turn it in a circle while applying pressure. If you smack the punch with a hammer it will cause the can to deform.

When the dents are made secure the piece to the drill press with a clamp and drill out the various holes. I held it with my hand. DO NOT do this. I was being extremely stupid and could have lost precious bits of myself. DO NOT imitate me.

Now that the holes are done I bet you can guess what will come next . . . If you said cleaning off the excess with your Dremel and a needle file give yourself a big pat on the back.

After the excess material is gone it is time to attach the gloves to the mounts. To do this you need to stretch the glove over the end of the can. This can be a bit tricky, but it is possible. I stretched the glove opening by pulling on it. Then I held the mount between my knees and worked the glove over the end of the can.

In order to keep the glove in place we are going to secure it with a hose clamp. This will allow the gloves to change if they become damaged, while holding them securly in place.

Put the glove mount into the hole we made for it with the glove protruding into the container. Orient the mount so the glove is in the position you want. I chose to have the thumb pointed upward. Reach inside the container and place the hose clamp around the base of the glove. Use a screw driver to tighten the clamp. As the clamp tightens this will change the position of the screw which is closing the clamp. Make sure you adjust the clamp as it is tightening so that the screw mechanism is always facing up. This will ensure you will have access to loosen the clamp should you have to change out the gloves in the future.

workshop

And be sure, if your gloves are specific to the left and right hand, to put the proper one on the proper side.

## Step 8: Mounting the Glove Mounts

And now it is time to mount the glove mounts on the box. This will be accomplished with brackets made from scrap metal.

To make the brackets you'll need eight pieces of metal about ½" wide and about three inches long. Originally I was drilling the attachment holes in the container and using these as templates along with the holes in glove mounts to mark the rivet poistions. However, this was very time consuming and sometimes error would creep in and the holes wouldn't line up properly.

I found it much faster to use the following method. Use the bench vise to bend the scrap metal into an "L" shape. Hold this bracket on the outside of the glove mount and center it on a set of rivet holes. Mark the position of the rivet holes from the inside of the mount with a marker. Also draw a line across any part of the bracket that sticks out past the edge of the mount. This will show you what to trim off later.

While you're still holding the bracket in position, mark where on the upper portion of the bracket you want the rivets to pass through the bracket into the container. (Hint use a different color marker for these dots so you know which end is which).

Once the rivet holes have been marked the positions will need to be transferred to the opposite side of the lower portion of bracket. The L-shape of the bracket prevents you from drilling the holes directly on the marks with a drill press.

I transferred the marks by pressing on them with a metal punch and moving it in a circular fashion. Next I turned the bracket over and marked the positions with a marker. Then I used the metal punch to make starter dents at these locations.

With the dents made I secured the bracket to the drill press with a clamp and drilled out the holes. Then I cleaned up the holes with a Dremel and needle file. I then trimmed the excess metal away from both ends of the bracket.

With the bracket properly sized attach it to the glove mount with pop rivets. Now use the other leg of the bracket as a template to drill attachement holes in the container. Once you have done this attach the bracket to the container with pop rivets. Repeat this process until all the brackets are in place.

(I used longer rivets for mounting the top bracket to the container. The longer rivets protrude enough to keep the excess portion of the hose clamp held down out of the way.)

## Step 10: Power Cord Access

Now we come to making the access for power cords. This penetration is intended to allow you to use an orbital sander or other small power tool within the confines of the dust collection box. I chose to make this out of a curved piece of drain pipe. The curve in the pipe will lower the chances of dust particles escaping as they aren't likely to go into and up the pipe. Dust escape is decreased further by adding a rubber gasket to the top of the pipe.

Back in step four we already configured this penetration, so we'll start by adding the rubber gasket to it. The piece of drain pipe I had came with a threaded compression fitting on the end, and I chose to take advantage of this in order to add the gasket. (If your pipe doesn't have this fitting you'll have to develop another method.)

Unscrew the compression fitting. There will be a a nut and a clear plastic ring (this is the thing that gets compressed by the nut, hence the name compression fitting.) Recycle the clear plastic ring or return it to your parts stash as its services will not be required.

Place the end of the pipe on the gasket material and trace around it with a marker. Then use a pair of scissors to cut out the gasket material. Place the circle of gasket material in the nut and screw it onto the pipe. Once it is in place cut two slits in the gasket material to form an "X" shape. This will allow cords to pass.

With the gasket in place we now have to attach the penetration to the container. I did this by using the same L-bracket technique I described in the glove mount steps. I used the drill press to drill two holes in the pipe, cleaned them up with a Dremel and a needle file, and pop riveted them into place.

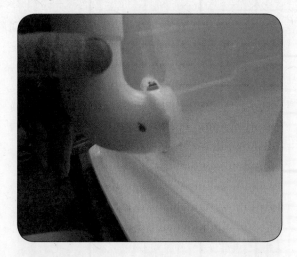

## Step 11: Insert Vacuum Nozzle

Now all you have to do is insert the vacuum nozzle. I'm going to have it held in place by the edges of the hole I made for it in the container. I may epoxy the nozzle in place in the future as sealing around it may create stronger suction. However, it is less likely to get snapped off as I take it in and out of storage. Ah decisions, decisions. In my first test I ground down a piece of scrap wood, but I wasn't able to see the particles being drawn into the vacuum. However, I didn't find them collecting in bottom of the container so I'm pretty confident it worked.

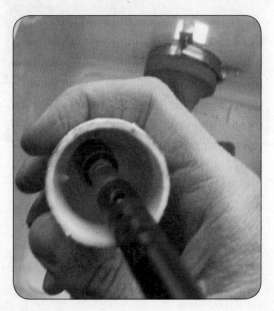

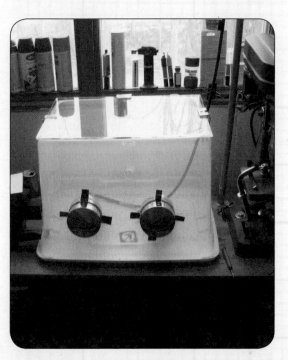

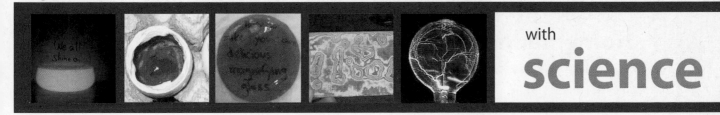

## with science

Turn your home into a laboratory with these fun experiments! Learn how to make plastic, grow bioluminescent algae, and extract your own DNA. Grow an eggshell geode, launch a hot air balloon, and even build a fusion reactor in your basement. It's time to unleash your inner mad scientist!

# Homemade Plastic

By **Coffeebot** Nathanael Phillips
(www.instructables.com/id/Homemade-Plastic/)

This is a quick and simple method for making your own general-purpose plastic. The constituent ingredients are milk and vinegar. That's it. The total cost is less than $10, possibly less than $5 if you can get a good deal.

The plastic is moldable, and has a consistency of soggy cheese (I certainly hope I never encounter cheese that's anything like this!). When all is said and done, it should take you about 10-15 minutes to make the plastic (less if you make a small amount), 10 minutes of cleanup, plus 2+ days to allow the plastic to dry. As always, your mileage may vary.

As for the final product's strength and whatnot, I would classify it as "okay." If you roll it thin (as I did in this instructable), it can easily be snapped in half, though it will probably survive a small drop on to carpet. Thicker pieces seem to be more resilient against average abuses—no problem dropping on to carpet, and if it's thick enough, you wouldn't be able to snap it in half. A blow from a hammer or other such object would quickly shatter it, though.

## Ingredients & Utensils

**Essential Items**
- Milk
- Vinegar
- Large Pot
- Larger Pot (needs to be the same size as the other, or larger).
- Spoon, preferably plastic or metal
- Strainer or Colander, the finer the better
- Stove to simmer milk.
- Paper Towels

**Handy, but not Necessarily Essential, Items**
- Wax Paper
- Aluminum foil
- Rolling pin

Before you begin making the plastic, it's important to know what you're intending to make. By knowing what you're final goal is, you can make the preparations for the mold before you have a sloppy wad of plastic on your counter.

How much milk and vinegar will you need? The basic ratio that I follow is 1 TBSP of vinegar for every cup of milk. (16:1 ratio, milk to vinegar)

1 cup of milk will produce a puck of plastic about 2" in diameter, ⅛" thick.

## Step 1: Heat It Up

If you've never heated milk before, it's important to know that if you heat it too fast, it will start to burn on the bottom of the pot. To bring it to a simmer, it's best to keep the heat down to about 50-60%.

When the milk nears boiling, you will notice a foam forming on top of the milk, as well as a little noise coming from the pot. Steam will start to appear too.

Once you reach this point, turn off the heat, pour in the vinegar, and stir. You will immediately notice chunks of casein forming. Stir it for another thirty seconds or so, for good measure.

## Step 2: Strain

Slowly pour the heated liquid through the colander and into the larger pot. Most of the chunks of casein will get caught. We pour slowly to avoid splashing the plastic-loaded liquid into the sink.

Once you've poured it out (don't worry about what's left in the bottom, we'll get to that), gently shake the strainer, and swirl it around a little. Most of the casein will lump up in the bottom, pulling itself out of the holes. Make sure a majority of the liquid is strained out, but don't press it out—the casein will just get stuck in the holes, and make it harder to get out.

Now that it's all clumped together, dump it out on some wax paper.

If you have a super-porous strainer like mine, you may want to pour the liquid through the strainer several times. Doing it a second time I pulled out a chunk about ¼ as large as the original mass; that's a nice addition.

## Step 4: Sop Up the Excess

After you've strained all of the casein out of the liquid, you'll want to soak up some of the remaining juice in the mass on the wax paper. Use a few paper towels, and press gently on the casein. The liquid will spill out like squeezing a sponge. Be careful not to make it too dry, because it will become difficult to mold if it's too dry.

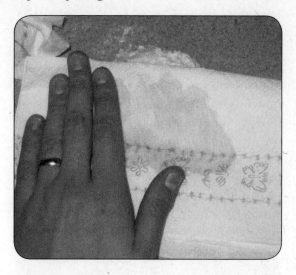

## Step 5: Mold!

At this point, you're ready to do whatever you want with the plastic.

It will take about two days to cure, but if you're using a mold where it cannot easily breathe, it will take longer.

One thing to watch out for is that the casein will warp when it's drying, especially if you have it rolled out into a sheet. It's best to put a weight on it. Watch out, though, because it will seep a milky-vinegary scented liquid into whatever is holding it in place. I used a heavy programming book . . . and it now has a funny smell to it. Awesome.

Lay another sheet of wax paper over the casein. Use a rolling pin to spread it out. If you didn't dry it too much in the previous step, it should roll nicely, without many cracks or chunks.

Give it a few days to dry, and it'll be ready to go. This is critical. Depending on how you wrap/mold your casein, you may find it takes more than a week to dry. Wrapping mine in foil took two weeks to get remotely dry. As is expected, the thicker it is, the longer it will take to dry.

I should also note that if you're making a flat piece, the plastic will curl if you remove it from its mold before its dry. I made this mistake with this project, and ended up with a piece that was unusable because it curled.

science

# Grow Your Own Bioluminescent Algae

By **ScaryBunnyMan**
Christopher Quintero
(www.instructables.com/id/Grow-Your-Own-Bioluminescent-Algae/)

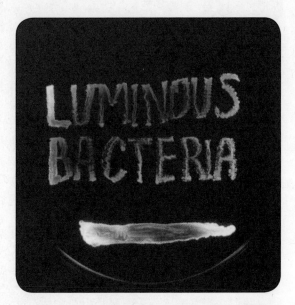

You may have memories of running after fireflies with hands outstretched on a warm summer evening. You may have even watched some Discovery Channel documentary on the mysteries of the deep sea and marveled at those "glowing" organisms featured. Chances are however, you probably haven't heard too much about the plethora of other bioluminescent creatures inhabiting this planet.

Bioluminescence (literally meaning living light) occurs within many living organisms, although, most are relegated to the deep sea. This chemical reaction involves the oxidation of Luciferin (just a name for a class of biological light emitting pigments). While related, the name doesn't come from any devilish origins, but rather the Latin "lucifer" meaning "light bringer".

Today however, we'll focus on a particular light emitting alga known as Pyrocystis fusiformis. These dinoflagellates typically do not occur in high enough concentrations among marine algae to produce a very noticeable glow. However, when the conditions are right (excess nutrients, enough sun, etc) an algal bloom can occur and populations explode.

With a little luck and a LOT of patience, you can grow your own bioluminscent algae at home.

## Gather the Materials

A number of marine enthusiasts already grow phytoplankton at home for use in feeding various species of marine life. The method we'll use is rather similar.

**To Start, You Need**

- A clear growing container (shallow containers with lots of surface area work best)
- Sea Salt: No, not from your pantry you gourmet fiend, you can get this at most pet or aquarium stores.
- A grow light and timer: You can pick up a plant fluorescent and rack for ~$10. Make sure you have a light timer.
- Micro Algae Grow: our most crucial ingredient (besides the actual algae). There are a number of nutrient formulas people have experimented with, and truthfully, I've only had mixed results with this one. Experiment with what works best.
- A Starter Culture: These can be obtained from a few places online. I recommend www.empco.org/edu.

science

## Step 1: Preparation and Mixing

Sanitation is necessary so your batch doesn't crash. After you REALLY wash out the grow container, make sure there is absolutely no residue left. Some people say swirl some diluted bleach around. Others say to stick it in the microwave after it's completely dry (won't melt or deform if it's dry . . . wet is another story). Choose your preference.

Additionally, sanitize the tubing if you're using an air pump, and anything else you're using to prepare this batch.

Mix up a batch of salt water. Use purified water as tap water can contain chlorine or other things that might kill your batch.

Mix the salt to a 1.019 specific gravity (sg) concentration. Directions on how to do this are on the back of the package. You'll need a hydrometer if you've never done it before.

Add in ~1 ml of the micro algae grow. In this case, less is more. The solution you received the culture in should already have enough nutrients to support sizable growth. If you don't want to mess with making your own solution (not necessarily a bad idea) many places that sell starter cultures will also sell culture solution.

Let both the solution and culture bag sit in the same area out of the sun for an hour or two. This is simply to let them reach room temperature. A sudden change in temp during transfer could shock the culture enough to significantly harm it. If your room temp is in the 70s (°F), you should be okay. Ideally, the water should be around 22 degrees Celsius.

Finally, transfer the algae into your bottles.

## Step 2: Growth

These dinoflagellates need a constant cycle of light and darkness for optimal growth. Put your grow light and bottles in a dark place (closet) where you can strictly control how much light they get. Set the timer so the grow light is on a cycle of 12 hours on, 12 hours off. Don't be worried if your starter culture doesn't emit light right after you receive it. They will only bioluminesce in their night cycle, so plan the light cycles accordingly for when you want to see it.

Monitor your cultures for any sudden changes in color, and give them a gentle shake every day or so or all the sediment will collect to the bottom. If you have a successful culture, you will eventually need to "split" the batch. Mix up another batch of saltwater/nutrients, and halve your culture between the new bottles.

Remember, these cool creatures will only brightly flash when disturbed and only during their night cycle. Too much disturbance can both harm them, and wear them out. They have a "recharge" time so to speak between disturbances for optimal performance.

If you're looking for something that will constantly glow, you might want to check out bioluminescent bacteria instead. You can get some from Carolina Biological supply.

Culturing this is a rather different process, but you can find some guides on the net. One bioluminescent strain is Vibrio fischeri.

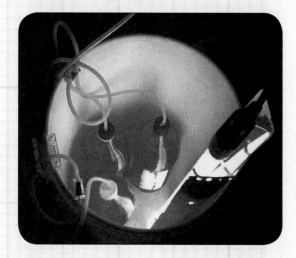

science

339

Using magnetic ink and any oil lying around your house, make a substance that's liquid when it's sitting around, but turns solid in the presence of a magnetic field

This instructable will show you how to make your own ferrofluid. A ferrofluid is a fluid with magnetic particles in it, and if the fluid is exposed to a magnetic field, all the magnetic particles will align with the field lines, and make the fluid much more dense. There's a lot of cool things you can do with this fluid.

## Get the Materials

You'll need two basic materials: magnetic (MICR) ink, and a household oil. I've tried a couple types of oils, and it seemed like a light lubricating oil works best, but any cooking oil will work fine, as well. The amount of oil you have is pretty much the amount of ferrofluid you'll get out—about 50ml is good for starters, but feel free to make as much as you want. The ink is a dry magnetic ink that's used to print checks and other documents that use magnetic character recognition. It's going out of style, so you'll have to poke around a little bit to find it. It's important to remember that you don't want a toner cartridge—just the toner.

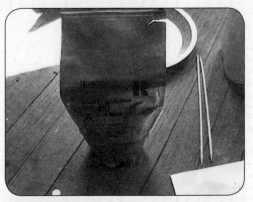

## Step 2: Mix It!

Pour some oil into a mixing cup. Add a bit of the ink, and stir it into the oil. You're making a suspension, so the ink won't dissolve in the oil. Just stir it. Keep on adding ink and stirring until you have a thick solution. There's no exact science to this. A good guideline for identifying a well-mixed fluid is that if you tip your mixing cup, the fluid should ooze rather than slosh.

science

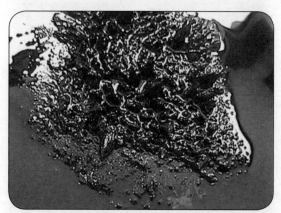

## Step 3: Play with it!

Grab your favorite permanent magnet and hold it up to the mixing cup (don't touch the fluid with the magnet, or even get close, unless you enjoy cleaning). Watch how the fluid turns from liquid to solid as you bring the magnet closer. Show your friends the horrible oily liquid you have in a cup, and then simultaneously slap a magnet onto it as you harmlessly "dump" the cup over their heads (practice this first). Buy some cheap solenoids from www.allelectronics.com and electrically change the consistency of the fluid.

## Step 4: What Other People Do with it

You can make brakes with it by putting some fluid between a wheel's axle and hub. The wheel will spin freely as the fluid acts just as a liquid lubricant, but if you apply a magnetic field, you're suddenly putting a lot of friction of the wheel's rotation. The good folks at the Univeristat Der Kunste Berlin made a ferrofluid display that can play Nibbles: www.digital.udk-berlin.de/en/projects/winter0405/main/hauptprojekt/snoil.html.

science

# 5 minute DNA Extraction in a Shot Glass

By **macowell**
(www.instructables.com/id/5-minute-DNA-Extraction-in-a-Shot-Glass/)

Despite its exotic-sounding name, DNA is ubiquitous—it can be found in every cell of every living thing and almost everywhere on the planet. In this instructable, we'll show you how to isolate your own DNA with little more than some dish soap, table salt, high-proof alcohol, a shot glass, and a bit of your own saliva.

## Materials & Set Up
- ¼ of a shot glass full of your saliva
- several drops of dish soap (look for sodium laurel sulfate in the ingredients)
- a pinch of table salt (¹/₁₆ of a teaspoon)
- some contact-lens cleaning solution
- meat tenderizer or pineapple juice (optional)
- Ice-cold 120-proof+ liquor (overproof rum works well)

## Step 1: Salivation . . . GO!
¼ of a shot glass of saliva is harder to produce than you might think! Work your tongue against your cheeks and teeth as you think of a big juicy grilled steak/tofu cube/dim sum, or muffins/baked cookies. I had to spit about 5 times to fill the glass ¼th full.

## Step 2: Add a Couple Drops of Soap
Now that we have some saliva to work with, the first step is to break open (lyse) the cells it contains. We can do this by mixing in a couple of drops of the dish soap. The detergents in the dish soap (like the sodium laurel sulfate, aka sodium dodecyl sulfate) destabilize the membranes of the cells, spilling their contents into the rest of the solution of saliva. This includes all of the cytoplasmic and nuclear proteins, sugars, and yes, nucleic acids (DNA! and RNA.) But all of this stuff is still dissolved in the saliva. The rest of the steps will cause the DNA to aggregate and precipitate out of solution.

## Step 3: Some Protease . . .
Now that we've busted open the cells, they've spilled their guts all over the place in our saliva solution. In this step we try and get rid of as much of the protein part of those guts as we can. A protease is a type of enzyme that can break down other enzymes. Meat tenderizer, pineapple juice, and soft contact lens cleaning solution all contain (different) proteases. A tiny bit of any of those should reduce the amount of protein that precipitates out with our DNA later on.

## Step 4: And a Pinch of Salt
Just add a pinch of table salt to the soapy saliva. I used less than 1/16th of a teaspoon, and that was probably too much.
So what's the deal?
Although we have freed the DNA from the cells, it's still dissolved in the solution.

To get the DNA to precipitate and solidify, we need to do something about each molecule's negatively-charged phosphate backbone.

When we dissolve the table salt in the solution, some of the positively-charged Sodium ions will interact with the negatively-charged regions of the DNA molecules and effectively shield other nearby DNA molecules from their repulsive force. This will help them all aggregate and clump together in the next step.

To visualize the idea here, imagine the resistance you feel when you begin to push the south poles of two magnets together. This is sort of like what's going on between the individual DNA molecules. Now imagine inserting the north pole of a third magnet between the south poles of the first two—the resistance is reduced. The north pole of the third magnet is sort of like the Sodium ion in our solution.

### Step 5: Pour on a Layer of the Rum

Mix the solution in the shot glass for a minute by gently shaking and rocking the glass.

Now gently add a layer of the overproof rum to fill up the shot glass. The best way to do this is by tilting the shot glass and transferring the rum over a little bit at a time using a straw. If you have a steady hand, however (or just think you do, like me), you can try and slowly pour the icy-cold rum from the bottle onto the top of the saliva in the shot glass. The key thing here is to prevent the alcohol from mixing much past the surface of the saliva.

You should see some cloudy, snot-like white stuff suddenly appear near the boundary between the saliva and alcohol as you add the alcohol. This is DNA (and probably a lot of other cellular junk) precipitating out of solution!

What's going on? DNA is not very soluble in alcohol, so some of the free DNA at the surface of the saliva solution immediately precipitates when we begin to add the alcohol. Other, deeper DNAs are pulled out of solution by the precipitating DNAs into the alcohol, and suddenly we end up with this visible floating mass of DNA.

### Step 6: Spool Your DNA

If you are in a playful mood, you can use a small rod like a toothpick to spool up your DNA. Insert the toothpick into the DNA precipitate and gently swirl it around, rotating the toothpick at the same time. You're trying to wind the filaments of precipitated DNA around the tip of the toothpick.

Once you think you've got them, you can slowly lift the toothpick out of the solution. You should see it trailing a thin strand . . . of DNA!

science

## Egg Shell Geode— Crystals

By **wombatmorrison**

Sharon Riger Morrison

(www.instructables.com/id/Egg-shell-geode-crystals/)

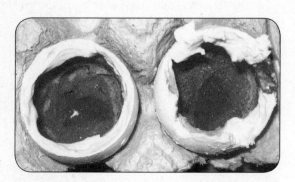

This a variation on common crystal growing techniques. Instead of growing crystals on a string, grow them inside a "geode" made from an egg shell and plaster of paris.

### Materials

- egg shells (washed)
- plaster of paris
- disposable cup
- craft sticks or stir sticks
- water
- table salt or other crystal growing material—magnesium sulfate, borax etc.
- bowl or pan
- optional: food coloring for colored crystals

### Step 1: Prepare "Geode" Shell

Carefully crack an egg in half—try to save the largest part of the shell.

Clean egg shell. Rinse with diluted bleach water, followed by plain water. You want to kill any bacteria on the eggshell.

Mix plaster of paris according to directions on package (This is usually about 2 parts plaster powder to one part water. ALWAYS add plaster powder to water, this minimizes airborne plaster dust. Stir well and thump cup a few times to force air bubbles to the surface).

When plaster starts to thicken, spread a thin layer of plaster inside the half egg shells—about ¼ inch or 6 mm. Try to get a thick edge of plaster along the edge of the shell for a more durable "geode."

Let plaster set and dry.

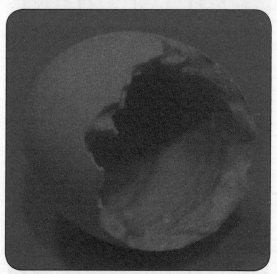

### Step 2: Prepare Crystal Growing Solution

For one egg shell geode make about ¼ cup of solution. Start with hot water and dissolve as much salt as you can. Stir well and heat water as needed to make a saturated saltwater solution. Keep adding salt until you get a few undissolved grains of salt in the bottom of the pan. Add food coloring if desired.

### Step 3: Grow Crystals

Fill plaster egg shell with crystal solution and set in a protected, out of the way place.

Wait a day or more. Crystals will form as water evaporates from the salt solution. Vary air temperature and observe variations in crystal size.

science

# Cook Up an Edible Magnifying Glass

By **Tararoys**
(www.instructables.com/id/Cook-up-
an-Edible-Magnifying-Glass/)

We shall make our very own magnifying glass. . .out of hard candy!

## How it Works

Light moves at different speeds through different materials. When it changes materials, depending on the angle it hits that material, it changes direction—something called refraction. A lens refracts light so that it makes things you're looking at seem bigger or smaller, depending on the type of lens.

The angle that light hits glass is also important. It's just like you if you dive off a diving board. If you dive straight in, you go straight down. However, if you dive at an angle, the surface of the water deflects you in a different direction. Don't believe me? Try belly-flopping.

So we're going to make a lens. All you need is some transparent substance, like glass or plastic, and a mold for the lens.

We shall make a plano-convex lens, which is a fancy Latin name for a lens with a flat bottom and a curved top. And as for the transparent material, well, my transparent material of choice is inexpensive, easily accessible, easily polished, lightweight, low-melting-point, non-toxic, biodegradable, edible, and delicious.

In other words: hard candy.

## Supplies
### Food Supplies
- 1¾ cups sugar
- 1 cup water
- ½ cup corn syrup (optional)
- ¼ teaspoon cream of tartar (optional)
- flavoring (optional)
- 2 16oz boxes of cornstarch
- no-stick cooking spray

### Cooking Supplies
- smallish saucepan
- candy thermometer (somewhat
- optional)
- 1-inch deep cake pan (or bowl, or something suitably deep)
- candy-pouring crucible: either make one or use a glass measuring cup

### Other Supplies
- spherical object ( I used a ladle)
- a couple children (optional, for the polishing step)
- an air-conditioned home without much moisture in the air or a nice, clear, NOT humid day. (Ever wonder why hard candies get chewy over time?

## Step 1: Making the Mold

I like to set up the mold before making the candy, because making hard candy and pouring requires quick work and you don't want to be distracted trying to make your mold while you've got molten candy on your hands.

science

345

Take your one-inch deep pan and fill it full of corn starch. My particular pan is an eight-inch diameter pan, and it took two 16-oz boxes to fill it.

Level it off a bit so that it's full, but not overflowing.

Take your round object—in my case, my two-inch-in-diameter ladle and press it deep into the corn starch. Like a meteor hitting the earth, you're going to displace a lot of starch, so it will sort of mound up over before leaving a big crater. The bottom of the crater will probably be somewhat cracked or have imperfections. No problem, simply spin your spherical object in the hole to smooth it out. That's the advantage of making a round object mold, you don't run into big displacement problems.

And honestly, having a perfect mold does not matter in the slightest—from what I can tell, corn starch is not supposed to be used as a mold for things this big because huge imperfections show up when you cast your candy if it's too large. On the other hand, it works just fine in this specific case, because we get rid of those huge imperfections in the polishing stage later.

## Step 2: Making the Candy

Let's get cooking.

Get your ingredients around. You need:

- 1¾ cups sugar
- 1 cup water
- ½ cup corn syrup (optional)
- ¼ teaspoon cream of tartar (optional)
- flavoring (optional)

This is the most dangerous part of the process. Liquid candy is charmingly called culinary napalm because it's hot and sticks to everything. Be careful. Wear an apron. Safety goggles would not go amiss. Remember, being a mad scientist means you destroy them all, not yourself.

I don't like to pour molten candy from a heavy pan directly into my mold, so I made myself a candy-pouring crucible. I made my candy crucible out of an aluminum can, an awl, a three-foot piece of thin wire, and a wooden skewer. I like my design because when you pour candy into it, the molten candy will bubble up as the last bits of water vapor try to escape it. Since my hole is in the bottom of the crucible, there are not as many air bubbles in the stream of molten candy flowing out the bottom.

Mix the sugar, water, corn syrup, and cream of tartar in your saucepan. Stick it on your stove, and turn your stove up to high. I got out my wooden spoon and stirred my mixture to make this particular batch, but a professional cook recommends never stirring your mixture for better candy.

When the candy starts to boil, put in your thermometer. If you don't have a thermometer, you can use the cold water method to check how done your candy is. Make sure the bulb of the thermometer is in the candy. If it doesn't reach, you will have to tilt the pan and cover the bulb occasionally to check what the temperature of your candy is.

You will notice that at the very beginning, your candy solution looks like boiling water. Near the end, however, it looks like boiling oil: the candy is very thick and viscous, and it has turned slightly golden. It will take ten to fifteen minutes to get up to temperature.

While you're waiting, be sure that you have your mold nearby, as well as a cookie sheet or plate sprayed with no-stick for anything left over.

When your candy reaches about 290 degrees, turn off the stove. Hard candy is made at 300 degrees, and the pan will heat

science

your candy up the additional few degrees. You do NOT want to go over 310 degrees because that's when the candy starts to burn. I don't even like to go over 300 degrees. This is the point where you want to stir in a few drops of any flavoring you want.

Take your candy off the stove and pour it into your crucible. Let the bubbles settle for about half a minute, and then, gently, very gently, start pouring the candy into the mold.

If your candy starts to set up while your pouring, and you're using a microwave-safe crucible to pour, go ahead and stick it in the microwave for fifteen to thirty seconds to loosen it up again, then continue pouring.

Now . . . we wait. Depending on how thick the candy is, it can take anywhere from ten minutes to an hour to fully harden. Because they're pretty thick, I give my lenses an hour to set on the counter.

## Step 3: Polishing the Lenses

Your cool lenses have cooled—now it's time for the fun part!

Lift your lens from its bed of corn starch. You'll notice that there's a bunch of corn starch stuck to the bottom of it, and that the hard candy cracked your mold and formed a bunch of ridges on the bottom of your lens—it's impossible to see through it!

Never fear. It's time to polish it!

Make sure to hold your lens by the edges—otherwise you'll get fingerprints all over the lens, which will make it hard to see through, and you'd have to polish them off. Given HOW you're going to be polishing them, it's best to not get your dirty fingers all over the lens in the first place.

So, to polish, get out your high-precision mark 1 portable sugar polishing tool, also known as your tongue. Start licking.

The corn starch doesn't taste that great, but soon enough you'll get to the good stuff. This is where it pays off to flavor your candy. Plain hard candy is kind of dull.

This is also the part kids love, and, if you've kidnapped the neighborhood kids, you can always tell their parents that you weren't feeding them candy, they were helping you manufacture precision optics.

Tip for parents: if you've ever wondered how to get your kid to stop chewing on lollypops and to start licking them, make them into lenses!

How many licks does it take to polish a lens? Honestly, I don't know. I lost count after about 500.

Once you have your lens polished, with no bumps, scrapes, fingerprints, or other surface-marring features, your lens is now ready to use as a magnifying glass.

DON'T put your lens directly on what you are trying to magnify. The lens will be sticky, especially after you got done polishing it. Instead, place a clear plastic sheet, like a sandwich baggie, on top of what you are trying to read, and put the lens on top of that.

Et Voila! Instant magnification!

science

## Step 4: Unanswered Questions

Your lens will be a clear yellow color, not completely white. I don't know if there is a hard candy recipe out there that lets you make transparent lenses without the yellow color, although I searched for days on Google. I did make a transparent lens by stopping at the soft-crack stage, but the clear candy was taffy-like, and in a few minutes my lens slumped and did not hold its shape.

I don't know how long they will last. Conventional candy wisdom says that candy can last indefinitely in cool, clear conditions, but if you expose them to head and/or water, they will warp and dissolve away. Sugar is hygroscopic, which means that it likes to attract and absorb water. This is why, if you leave sugar out for too long, it will form a sticky film. In our case, that may actually be a good thing: the water softens the top layer of the lens, and it starts flowing a little bit. According to my experiment, this little bit is just enough to smooth out any remaining surface irregularities and bring your lens to a nice, high shine.

Now, fellow mad scientists! Go forth, armed with your magnifiers, and remember, they can take away your chemistry lab, but they can NEVER take away your kitchen!

# Mokume Kireji-DIY Woodgrain Composites

By **festeezio**
(www.instructables.com/id/Mokume-Kireji-DIY-Woodgrain-Composites/)

Here's an easy alternative to Mokume Gane that the average maker can put together in their garage without the need for fancy tools.

Mokume gane, Japanese for "woodgrain metal" or "burl metal" is a technique of metal-working developed by Denbei Shoami in 17th century Japan for the adornment of the guards (tsuba) of Samurai swords. The wood-grained effect is achieved by working diffusion bonded stacks of dissimilar metal plates. The contrast between the metals can then be accentuated with chemical treatments called patinas. It has more recently found use in the west to create beautiful jewelry. Although mokume gane can be made at home by the DIY'er, it takes some pretty heavy equipment to make it happen. Wouldn't it be nice to be able to achieve a similar wood-grained effect with simpler techniques? Enter our old friend the composite.

Back in 1910, Westinghouse developed a composite of resin-impregnated fabric trademarked as MIcarta® (now a registered trademark of the Norplex-Micarta company). The name micarta (with a small "m") is sometimes used as a generic term for any resin impregnated laminate of linen, canvas, paper, carbon fiber, or glass fiber. These composites are generally strong, waterproof, resistant to many solvents, and are great electrical insulators. They have been used as knife handles, grips for firearms, printed circuit boards, electrical insulators, pool cues, and guitar fretboards.

In this instructable, we'll use simple techniques to produce micarta-like laminates with Mokume Gane style patterns out of cheap bed sheets and epoxy resin. You can use these laminates for computer case modding, steampunk projects, costume jewelry, knife handles, and a host of other things. I call these laminates Mokume Kireji (wood grained fabric).

## Gather Your Materials

Here is a list of materials needed to make your own wood-grained composites:

**Safety**

- Respirator or Mask: Sanding, filing, or grinding on composites generates nasty fumes, smells, and dusts. You must wear respiratory protection when working with composites.
- Gloves: I used cheapo disposable nitrile gloves to keep the epoxy off of my skin
- Eye protection: You know better than to use chemicals and tools without eye protection. Foresight is better than no sight.
- Clothes you don't mind ruining: No matter how OCD you are, you will almost certainly get epoxy on your clothes. Wear something you don't mind messing-up.

**Components**

- Resin: I used West Systems 2-part epoxy. This stuff cures slowly (hours) which gives me more time to work. Do not use quick curing resins like "30 minute epoxy" because they will harden before you have a chance to finish your work.
- Plastic Wrap: I used Saran Wrap. Epoxy does not like to stick to Saran Wrap and this will be used to your advantage.

- Fabric: I used cheap cotton bed sheets. Select at least 2 contrasting colors (more is OK).
- Scissors and/or a paper cutter: Something to cut the fabric with
- Clamps and/or a press: You need to compress the layers of fabric together. If you don't have a shop press, don't sweat it; you can use some inexpensive C-Clamps and wood to make a functional press for small projects. Some of my examples are made using a 20-ton shop press; the others are made using four 5 inch c-clamps (about 5 bucks each) and 2 planks of 1 inch thick wood. No need to buy fancy/expensive equipment if you don't really need it.
- Sander/files/sandpaper: You will need to sand, file, or grind away parts of your composite. You can do it by hand, but it will take some time. A small power sander will make the work go faster. Use coarse grit paper to "hog out" larger amounts of material and fine grit paper to smooth out the surface and make it all pretty.
- Advanced technology resin application devices: to mix/apply the resin. Wooden popsicle sticks or tongue depressors work just fine
- Mixing containers for epoxy: I used disposable soup and salad containers; epoxy doesn't like to stick to these either; when the residual epoxy cures, pop it out of the container and you can reuse it (for more epoxy, not for food please).
- Patterning material: This can be anything from dried beans to toothpicks. You'll see what I mean in just a few steps.

## Step 1: Get To The Chopper!

Using a paper chopper or scissors, cut your fabric into appropriately sized pieces. Keep in mind that the edges of your composite will be wonked up by excess resin, so you should plan on making your fabric slices at least 10 to 15 percent larger in area than what you need for your final size. It will also need to be thicker. How much thicker? That depends on what you use to create your pattern. The thicker the patterning material, the more material you will have to remove to get both surfaces flat and parallel. This will make much more sense in the following steps. In any event, it is a good idea to make a small test piece in order to get your measurements the way you want them.

This is also when you need to decide what your color scheme will be. Will it be alternating layers of black and white? Three layers of red to every one layer of brown? How about red, white, and blue? How many layers thick do you want your composite to be? Figure this out now and cut enough fabric for your project. Also keep in mind, that the tint of your resin will slightly alter the color of your fabric. My resin had a bit of a yellow cast to it, and this tended to give my white fabric a bit of an olive tint. When in doubt, make a small test piece to ensure you're going to get the results you really want.

## Step 2: Lay Up Your Composite: Birdseye and Ladder Patterns

Now let's put the components to work. Let's make a single piece of composite with two different patterns: The birds eye pattern, and the ladder pattern. This one will be made out of 15 pieces of black fabric alternating with 15 pieces of white fabric.

If you're using a press, wrap your press-plates in Saran wrap. If you're using c-clamps, wrap your pieces of 1 inch thick wood in Saran wrap. This will keep your press plates from sticking to your work.

science

Place a single sheet of your fabric down on the press plate. This will serve as a template to help you place your patterning materials accurately.

Arrange your patterning materials on the template sheet. For the ladder pattern mokume, I used several pieces of plastic filament about 3mm in diameter, lined up in a row (toothpicks would have worked too). For the birds eye pattern, I used steel BB's (4.5mm diameter) arranged randomly.

Cover your patterning materials with a sheet of Saran wrap so that they don't become glued to your composite.

Mix a batch of epoxy resin according to the manufacturer's instructions

Place your first sheet of black fabric on top of your patterning material and coat it with a thin layer of freshly-mixed epoxy resin. The entire sheet should be lightly coated.

Now add a sheet of white fabric and gently apply another thin layer of epoxy.

Continue this process: black sheet, epoxy, white sheet, epoxy, etc until you have used up your fabric (30 pieces in this example).

Take your other press plate (make sure it's covered with Saran wrap) and lay it on top of your stack of epoxy-coated fabric.

Clamp tightly and evenly using your c-clamps (or press in your shop press)

Wait for the epoxy to fully cure

**Words of Wisdom**

- Make sure you let the epoxy fully cure, or the next step will be a disaster.
- When you clamp your press plates down, excess epoxy will come smooshing out the sides of the press. Make sure you lay down some plastic to catch the excess resin, or you will have one heck of a mess.
- Don't rely on paper towels or newspaper to catch the excess resin. Just enough will bleed through to permanently fuse the paper to your floor and/or work surface. You must never ask me how I know this.

## Step 3: Reveal the Pattern: Ladder and Birdseye

Once the epoxy has cured, remove your masterpiece from the press/clamps to reveal: a turd. Your composite will look ugly, with chunks of resin hanging off the edges and no signs of the beautiful woodgrain pattern that you were expecting. Don't sweat it, you're not done yet. Using files, a power sander, a saw, etc, remove the ugly tattered edges, leaving behind the nice uniform center. Now using a sander or files, begin to slowly remove material from the surface of your slab of composite. For my project, the ladder-pattern part of the composite was cut away from the birds eye-pattern part for greater clarity. Also note that the BB's stuck in the composite were wedged into the composite but were not epoxied to the slab thanks to that piece of Saran wrap. The stuck BB's were easily pried out prior to sanding.

As you sand down the surface, you will begin to see the pattern appear. The patterned surface will appear dull and matte, but we'll fix that shortly.

Now is probably a good time to fashion your piece of composite into your project of choice. Cut out a piece in the center and make an uber cool picture frame. Maybe an escutcheon plate for computer case modding? Perhaps a component of your next steampunk creation? This stuff cuts like wood, with simple hand tools. Don't worry about making sharp 90 degree cuts, if you radius the edges with files or sanding (instead of leaving them sharp) the mokume pattern will become even more dramatic.

## Step 5: Finish the Surface: Ladder and Birdseye Patterns

Now to bring out the shine.

Prepare a small batch of epoxy and apply a coat to the sanded surface and allow it to cure.

Any irregularities in this clear coat can be sanded out, and the surface re-coated with fresh epoxy.

Polish as desired. Admire your work, as you are indeed "all that".

## Step 6: Bonus Pattern: Grid Pattern

But wait, there's more!

Sure, you can come up with all kinds of patterns on your own, but isn't nice to start with a palette of basics?

This grid pattern was created with a piece of the brittle plastic sheet that is used to cover fluorescent light fixtures. A 2 × 4 foot sheet of the stuff set me back about 6 bucks at a home improvement store.

This is a really fun one as it serves a double purpose. I created a demo piece using alternating sheets of black and white fabric (again, cheep cotton sheets) with a piece of the textured light-fixture plastic as a patterning layer.

The left side of the piece has not been sanded and has a beautiful "quilted" appearance. It could be used as-is. The right side of the slab has been sanded and then re-coated with epoxy to reveal the white layers underneath.

Sweet.

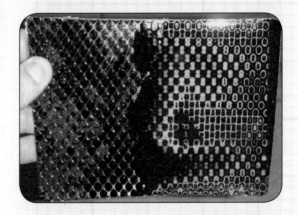

# Candle Powered Hot Air Balloon

By **ewilhelm** Eric Wilhelm
(www.instructables.com/id/Candle-Powered-Hot-Air-Balloon/)

Build a candle powered hot air balloon using painter's plastic, balsa wood, and birthday candles.

## Step 1
### Cut the Plastic and Heat-seal the Edges

Layout your materials on a large sheet cardboard. Pull out approximately 6 feet of the painter's plastic and cut it forming a sheet 9 x 6 ft. It's important to have plastic that is ½ mil (12 microns) or thinner. Thicker plastic is too heavy to fly. Fold the sheet in half along the 9 ft side forming a two-ply sheet 4.5 x 6 ft. Use a hot knife to seal the two 4.5 ft edges. An electric hot knife makes this really easy, but it can also be done with an old metal knife heated over a flame. Check your edges and correct any large holes. A few small holes won't cause problems.

## Step 2
### Melt Candles Together and Attach them to Balsa

Again, an electric hot knife makes this step a breeze. A heated fork can achieve the same results. Make sure to do both sides. Once the candles are attached together, melt them to the middle of a piece of balsa wood ³/₁₆ x ⅛ x 36 inches.

## Step 3
### Assemble the Balsa Frame

Make an "H" with the 36 in balsa and candle piece and two ³/₁₆ x ⅛ x 30 in balsa sticks. Make the joints with a small piece of clear tape.

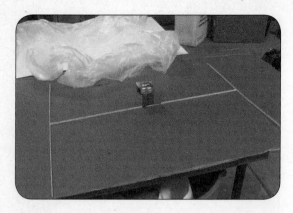

## Step 4

Tape the balloon to the balsa frame.

## Step 5

Use a stick inside the balloon to hold the plastic away from the candles and light them. Keep holding the plastic up until enough hot air has filled the balloon to inflate it.

## Step 6

It's an amazing feeling when your creation first gets lift and starts to take off. At this stage, there's about ten thousand things that could go wrong. Carefully think everything through before you actually do it. I tied some thread to mine so I could fly it inside our warehouse without it getting away and setting the place on fire. It will drip a lot of hot wax, so keep it over the cardboard if possible. Also, if you let the candles burn all the way down, the balsa will catch on fire.

science

354

This instructable will show you how to make one of those cool lightning globes with about $5.00 worth of parts. WARNING: This makes use of some very high voltage. It could be potentially lethal, especially if you are standing in a puddle of water.

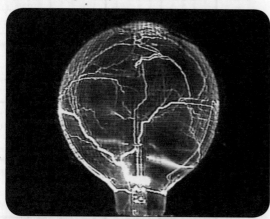

## Supplies

- Large, clear light bulb: Not just any light bulb will work. It must be one that has been gas filled. Typically, anything 60 watts or higher should work. Lower wattage bulbs typically have a vacuum. 60 watt and higher usually have an argon nitrogen mix, which lights up nicely! I found a 5 inch 60 watt bulb for about $2.49 at the hardware store.
- Aluminum screen, painted black. The aluminum screen will be our ground to attract the high voltage. Instead of shelling out a bunch of money for an entire roll of aluminum screening, just look for an HVAC vent with some right on the back. I found mine at the hardware store for about $1.50, and the screen was already painted black!
- A cheap black plastic pot. This is going to be the holder for the globe. Since it

will be used at night, it doesn't need to look pretty. I found a black plastic pot for about $0.79, you guessed it, at the hardware store.
- A high voltage power source. This is what makes the magic happen. I used the same monitor as the one in my Electric Fence Monitor Hack Video. With people upgrading to LCDs like crazy these days, you can easily get a 15" monitor from someone for free. WARNING: Color monitors put out close to 30,000 volts. This voltage can harm you and quite possibly kill you, depending on the depth of the water you are standing in or how old your pacemaker batteries are. Seriously, though, be careful.

## Step 1: Prep the Screen

The screen is our grounding plane for the high voltage. It will be wrapped around as much of the light bulb as possible, without causing unintended arcs. Trim the screen as needed. You should be able to fold the screen in half and still be able to fit the bulb inside tightly. The screen I used was painted black, so I scraped off some paint with an x-acto knife. Since we need to attach a wire to it, pick a good spot on the edge of the screen—right in the center. You'll need to scrape paint off of both sides of the screen and on both edges. Then fold the screen in half, poke the stripped ground wire through both pieces, wrap it around the edge as tightly as you can get it, and then solder the ground wire to itself. Since the screen is aluminum, you won't be able to solder the wire directly to it. That's why it's very important to tighten the ground wire around the screen. Use pliers if you have to.

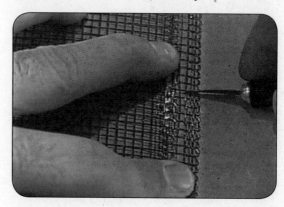

to the bulb. Now slide the bulb into the pot and it's done. It's not pretty to look at, and it's not supposed to be. It's for use at night.

## Step 2: Fit the Screen Over the Bulb

Next, I trimmed the screen on the top and bottom to be sure the high voltage wouldn't arc unintentionally. Then I made several cuts evenly spaced around the screen so I could fold it to the shape of the globe. To make it easier, you can make one cut the proper length, remove the bulb, then make the rest of the cuts. At that point, simply bend the screen flaps down and then slide the bulb inside. That will make it nice and tight. Do the same for the top, and then use your hands to gently squeeze the screen around the globe so it's form-fitted.

## Step 4: Test it Out!

Now it's time to hook it up and test it out! Refer to the Monitor Hack instructable for instructions on how to connect the aluminum wire to the anode. Be sure to pay attention to the part where you carefully discharge the high voltage! The ground wire needs to go to ground, of course. The easiest place to attach the ground wire to is the inside of the monitor at the same place the high voltage was discharged to. Turn it on and test it out!

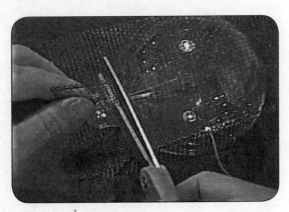

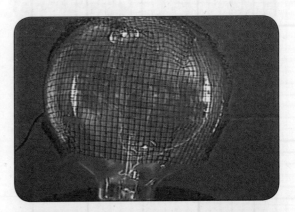

## Step 3: Prep the Stand

To prep the stand (cheap plastic pot), cut out a hole in the top the size of the light bulb stem. You'll also need to cut a slot on one side to allow the high voltage wire to pass through. Cut a small hole in the side of the pot about four inches off the ground. The high voltage wire will pass through here, so it must be high enough that it won't try to arc to ground. Feed the wire through the side hole, then through the top and attach it

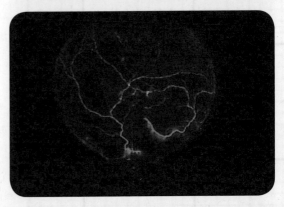

science

# how to do absolutely everything

## with
## electronics

Electronics can be intimidating until you try it. Learn the basics, then get started making cool and useful projects that will surprise and delight your friends. You too can harness the power of the great and wonderful ohm.

# Make a Vibrobot

## By **randofo** Randy Sarafan
### (www.instructables.com/id/Make-a-Vibrobot/)

A vibrobot is perhaps one of the quickest and easiest bots that you can build. In almost no time you can make a fun little bot that makes its ways to and fro across the floor. It is so easy, in fact, that it wouldn't be hard to make a few at once.

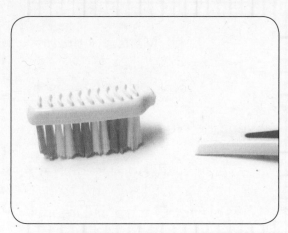

## Go Get Stuff; You will Need
- 3VDC Micro-Vibration Motor
- CR1220 Coin Cell Dip Type Battery Holder
- Enercell™ 3V/225mAh CR2032 Lithium Coin Cell Battery
- Toothbrush

## Step 1: Strip Wires
Trim the wire leads of the vibrating motor shorter. Strip away a bit of the protective jacket to expose the copper wires.

## Step 2: Solder
Solder the red wire of the 2032 battery holder to the positive pin of the battery holder.

Solder the black wire to the ground (minus) pin of the battery holder.

## Step 3: Cut
Use your diagonal cutters to cut the toothbrush head from the toothbrush handle.

## Step 4: Hot Glue
Hot glue the motor and battery holder to the flat plastic part of the toothbrush head.

## Step 5: Power!
Insert the 2032 battery and watch it go.

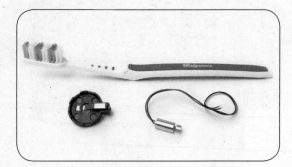

# How to Solder

By **noahw** Noah Weinstein
(www.instructables.com/id/How-to-
solder/)

This guide focuses on soldering for the beginner and explains how you can solder a variety of components using a few different techniques—from the classy to the downright caveman.

## Tools and Materials

Soldering is the process of using a filler material (solder) to join pieces of metal together. Soldering occurs at relatively low temperatures (around 400 degrees Fahrenheit) as compared to brazing and welding, which actually melt and fuse the materials themselves at higher temperatures. In soldering the filler material becomes liquid, coats the pieces it is brought into contact with, and is then allowed to cool. As the solder cools it hardens, and the two materials are joined. Soldering is a quick way to join many types of materials, from copper pipe to stained glass. It creates an electrically conductive strong bond between components that can be re-heated (desoldered) if you should ever want to disconnect two items joined together.

As with many skills, having the right tools for the job affects the quality of the work being done. When it comes to soldering you can end up using a lot of fancy tools, or just a few simple items you can pick up at the hardware store for a couple of bucks.

At the very minimum you will need the solder and a heat source to melt it—preferably something small which can get to 600-800 degrees Fahrenheit. If you've got that, you're ready to make a connection. I got together a solid supply of soldering tools by raiding the Squid Labs soldering station. Here is the complete list of what I used:

### 1. Soldering Iron

Most people opt for using a soldering iron to solder. It's a great heat source that heats up and cools down quickly and can maintain a pretty constant temperature. Soldering irons can be purchased from a variety of places. I have picked up some at RadioShack some from the hardware store, some from garage sales and a bunch more from retailers online. Low wattage (15-40 watt) soldering irons work best for soldering components on circuit boards while more powerful (60-140 watt) soldering irons work well joining thicker materials like braided speaker wire. If you use too powerful of a soldering iron on a circuit board you might damage the components you are trying to join. I like to keep a low-wattage iron around for detail work, and a high-wattage iron that I can use when I am not too concerned about exposing the material I am working with to high temperatures. It's a real pain to solder thick wires without a powerful soldering iron.

The soldering iron in most of the pictures is made by Weller, and has a variable temperature control. This is the best of both worlds since you can set the heat exactly where you want it, but it's significantly more expensive than fixed-temperature irons. If you're just going to do some occasional soldering it isn't a must have by any means. Anyone interested in modding a soldering iron should check out DIY Hot Air Soldering Iron by charper.

### 2. Solder

There are lots of kinds of solder available. They come in different thicknesses from around .02" to some really thick stuff you would only use on copper pipe with a butane torch. You use thin solder for detailed work like putting resistors onto circuit boards and thicker solder for joining larger materials like speaker wire. I use solder around .025" for most jobs. Most solder is made from a combination of tin and lead—it's about a 60 percent tin, 40 percent lead mix depending on what solder your using.

Some solder will contain a small amount of silver. This pushes the melting temperature up a bit, but the silver helps the solder to flow and makes a stronger joint. If you are worried about burning whatever your working with, try to stay away from solder with silver in it, but it works very well if you're just joining wires or something that won't be easily damaged. The last thing to know about solder is that you want to use a solder that has a rosin core. The rosin acts as a flux when soldering and helps the connection—it's also the kind that's most readily available at the hardware store and from electronics suppliers.

### 3. Soldering Iron Tips

Soldering irons come with a tip, so you don't have to go out and get a special one, but it's important to know the differences between them and make sure you're using the right tip for the kind of soldering you're doing. Some small-wattage irons come with conical pointed tips for detail work, while most high-wattage irons come with a flatter screwdriver-style tip that works well on wires. You want your tip to be a little smaller than whatever you are soldering so you have good control of what you heat up and what you leave alone.

### 4. Soldering Iron Holder and Cleaning Sponge

It's nice to have a safe place to put the soldering iron down in between soldering. A soldering stand safely holds the iron and gives you a place to clean the tip. Some soldering irons come with their own holders. The stand isn't a necessity for learning how to solder, but it does help.

### 5. Tools to Work with Wires

I have a go-to stock of tools that I round up when working with wires or electrical components. They consist of wire cutters, a wire stripper, needle nose pliers, and an automatic wire stripper. The automatic wire stripper is really convenient if you're going to be stripping lots and lots of wire, but by no means necessary. I have stripped lots and lots of speaker wire using my teeth (not the best idea, I know I know.)

### 6. Clips to Hold Your Work

Often called "third hands" or "helping hands," these little guys help a whole lot when soldering. You have to hold the soldering iron with one hand and the solder wire in the other, so it really helps to have something else to hold the components you're actually trying to join. You can use alligator clips, clamps, or even some tape to hold things in place if you need to.

### 7. Exhaust Fan

I do most of my soldering at a soldering station that is equipped with an exhaust fan. It's really not such a good idea to breathe in solder fumes, and soldering does produce fumes. Any kind of ventilation/fan you can rig up will help.

### 8. Safety Goggles

I hadn't ever used goggles before while soldering, but while doing research for this post I saw it mentioned elsewhere and agree that it's a good idea. Little molten bits of solder tend to fly out of the soldering joint when you're feeding in the solder, and if it landed in your eye it wouldn't feel too good.

### 9. The Materials that You Want to Join Together

I was just messing around, and mostly soldering for the purpose of this instructable so my materials didn't necessarily make anything. You can solder wire, electrical components like resistors and capacitors, circuits, breadboards, electrodes, small pieces of metal and whatever else you can think of.

## Step 1: Getting Ready

Once I get my tools rounded up I like to plug in my soldering iron and let it heat up while prepping my materials.

First things first, the tip of the soldering gets hot—up to 800 degrees Fahrenheit, so don't touch it. I know this seems obvious, but many people seem to burn themselves at some point while soldering.

If you're using a new soldering iron you will want to put a small amount of solder on the tip of the hot iron before you start working. This is called tinning the iron and you only have to do it with a new iron. Once you start using it will usually have some solder on it already and be ready to go.

Once the iron reaches temperature (some irons take minutes to do this and some irons take seconds), I like to clean the tip of my iron on a wet sponge. You can wet the sponge on your soldering base if you have one, or you can just use a damp sponge or steel wool. Gently touch the tip of the soldering iron to the sponge and clean off any old bits of solder that might be stuck to it. It will sizzle a bit; this is normal.

I asked Mitch, a soldering expert for some tips. Mitch showed me a good idea for how to hold solder wire: he cuts a piece of it off the roll, and then makes a coil at one end with a short lead at the other. This helps him hold it steady and apply just the right amount of solder. This is a way better idea than trying to hold the whole spool of solder or grab onto just one thin strand.

Next it's time to pay some attention to the material you're soldering. If you're soldering wire, you'll need to strip back about ½" of insulation to expose the bare wire. If your joints are going to be wire-to-wire or wire-to-lead, you can twist them together tightly before soldering. Electrical components placed on a circuit board don't need much prep work; just seat them where you want them and find a way to hold them in place with clips or by bending the leads outward slightly so they stay put when you turn the circuit board over.

Finally, place what you want to solder into the clips on the helping hand, or on a surface you don't mind getting a little burn mark on—scrap wood works well. Basically you just don't want the components moving around on you when you go to solder them.

Hopefully your soldering iron has reached temperature by now, because you're ready to solder!

## Step 2: Soldering Wire

I started soldering just two pieces of wire together because it's the most forgiving way to learn. You can't really get the wires too hot—the insulation might start to melt a bit, but you're not going to hurt the wire.

With the wires you want to join twisted together and held in place, pick up your soldering iron in one hand and your solder in the other.

Touch the tip of the soldering iron to the wires and keep it there.

The wires will begin to heat up. At some point over the next 2-10 seconds (depending on how hot your iron is) the wires will be hot enough to melt the solder. You can touch the solder to the wires (not to the tip of the iron!) periodically to see if it's hot enough. It's tempting to just touch the solder to the

electronics

361

tip of the iron and melt it right away, but don't! You will end up making what's called a cold solder joint. This occurs when you melt the solder around the joint, but you aren't melting the solder into your joint or onto your components to make a good connection. It's much better to wait the few seconds and melt the solder onto the hot wire itself.

If you touch the solder to the wire and it begins to smoke and melt, the wires are hot enough. Add the tip of your solder to the joint as necessary. You want to introduce enough solder to cover the wires, but not so much that you create a big glob of solder at the bottom of the joint.

Once you've got what you think is enough solder on the joint, pull the solder away and then remove the soldering iron. If you're using a gun style soldering iron like I was, release the trigger to turn it off. If you're using the kind that doesn't have a trigger the iron will stay hot, so just place it back into the holder.

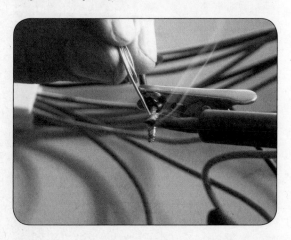

## Step 3: Soldering Components Onto a Circuit Board

Up until pretty recently I spent most of my life soldering speaker wire and crossover components for speakers. This meant mostly wires twisted around wires or big resistor leads twisted around inductors and capacitors. At that level soldering doesn't really get any more complicated than what I did in the previous step. Lots of the projects on Instructables, however, use smaller electrical components and circuit boards, so I figured I would give that a try too.

Soldering on a circuit board takes a little more care and attention, but it's still very

doable. I pushed a few of the leads from some spare LEDs and resistors through some open holes in a circuit board that was lying around. I soldered the leads onto the bottom of the circuit board where the electrodes push through. This is called through hole component soldering.

To solder the LEDs and the small resistors to the circuit board I switched to the adjustable temperature soldering iron. The tip was smaller so it would be easier to get the solder right where I wanted it, and using the soldering gun on a circuit board is probably way more heat than necessary and it could end up damaging the components. I set the temperature of the iron to 675 degrees Fahrenheit and waited for the tip to heat up. I then loaded the circuit board into the alligator clips and got myself ready to solder—iron in one hand, coil of solder in the other.

When soldering leads into circuit boards you want to heat the metal contact on the board and the lead itself. Applying too much heat can damage the circuit board or even your components. The surfaces being joined in this application were much smaller than the twisted wire, so things heated up a lot faster.

I touched the tip of the iron to the crack between the lead and the metal pad on the circuit board. After waiting a couple of seconds, I dipped the tip of the solder into the joint and placed a very small amount of solder at the connection—no more than the head of a pin or so.

Once the solder pooled a bit and soaked into the joint I removed the solder wire and then the iron. I remove the solder a second or two before I remove the iron so that the tip of the solder doesn't get stuck to the joint. The solder begins to harden as soon as you remove the iron.

Using the proper amount of solder is more important while soldering small components on a circuit board than when soldering wires. If you apply too much solder and it pools up outside of the metal pad, it can cause a short. Too little solder and your component won't make a good connection with the circuit board and might not work the way you want it to. When you've got the right amount of solder it looks like a small

electronics

ant hill that forms right at the base of the lead and the circuit board.

## Step 4: Cutting the Leads

Once you've got your components soldered into the circuit board, you can go back and cut off the excess leads. Just a few quick tips before you snip: It's best to use a sharp wire cutter that has just one side of its cutting edge beveled. This way you can get a smooth flat cut when you cut off the lead. It's also a good idea to cut the leads pretty close to the circuit board to minimize the risk of creating a short.

Holding onto the excess lead when you cut it off is a good way to keep the little ends from getting all over the place. Once you've got your leads cut you're pretty much done with soldering and ready to move on.

## Step 5: Surface Mounting Components Onto a Circuit Board

Many circuit components need to be surface mounted on circuit boards, which forces you to be a little more precise then when you can work on the bottom side of the board.

To solder something onto the surface of a circuit requires a process called tinning. Tinning is when you apply a small amount of solder onto the materials you are joining before you connect them. In this case, it involves putting some solder on a contact on the surface of the circuit board then attaching the component to the solder pool. Mitch showed me how this process is done.

First he touched the tip of the iron onto the small pad on the top of the circuit board.

He then introduced a small amount of solder onto the pad and took the iron away.

Then, a few seconds later he picked up the component he wanted to solder with a set of tweezers, heated up the small glob of solder that he had just placed down, and gently lowered the contact on the component into the pool of hot solder.

He took the iron away, held the component in place a few seconds longer, and released the component from the tweezers.

He then went to the other side of the component and finished making the connection by soldering the remaining two contacts together.

Surface soldering is done like this because you need to lower the component into place by hand, so it's hard to hold the iron, the tweezer and the solder all at the same time. Additionally, tinning is just a good thing to do while soldering small components. I didn't tin the wires before I soldered them because they were so big I was sure I was going to apply enough solder to make a good connection. However, when soldering small components or doing surface mount soldering like this, tinning can be really helpful because you basically already have your solder applied to your pieces before you go to connect them.

## Step 6: Soldering with a Lighter

Everything that I have explained how to do up until now has hopefully been pretty close to how things should be done "the right way" when soldering. Soldering, however, is just a process of joining things together to make a connection. If you don't have all the

363

tools to solder, but still want to learn how to solder something, never fear, with just solder and some wire you can practice bare bones soldering.

Bare bones soldering comes in handy when you're stuck on a desert island and you need to make a repair to your headphones so you can watch the sun go down while being serenaded by your most recent whale songs cd. It's also a cool trick to pull off next time your decide to be MacGuyver for Halloween.

I took some pieces of wire and stripped them with my teeth—the best method for doing this I have found is to use my molars. I just grab the insulation with my teeth, try to sever the insulation a bit, and then pull on the wire. It's easiest to do with braided wires, and it certainly takes a little practice to apply the right tension so you don't just rip the wire apart entirely. But once you get the hang of it it's actually a pretty functional method. (WARNING: I do not encourage stripping wire your teeth at all, and it will probably lead to expensive dentistry work if you do it enough.)

Once I had the wires stripped and twisted together I got a lighter and a bit of solder and went to work heating up the wires I wanted to join. It took the lighter about as long to heat up the wires as it did when I used the iron. I then fed a little solder into the joint, continued heating the wire to smooth things out, and then turned off the flame.

It worked just as well as it would have had I used an iron. Of course it's harder, if not impossible ,to use this method on circuit boards, but it sure does the job on wire. I have heard that using matches also works well when soldering wires.

## Step 8: Desoldering: Fixing Mistakes and Extrapolation
### Desoldering

Desoldering is the process of removing solder at a joint to disconnect two components, wires or materials. You might have to do this if you want to replace a component that's gone bad, or if you want to change something about your design once it's already soldered into place. To desolder wires you can usually just heat up the connection and wiggle them around until they come free.

With leads that are mounted through holes on a circuit board it takes a little more finesse. To desolder something delicate its best to use a desoldering pump, or bulb which will actually suck up the molten solder and remove it from the joint.

### Fixing Mistakes

Soldering is pretty forgiving, and its usually pretty easy to fix a mistake. If you put down a little too much solder or position something incorrectly you can usually reheat your joint, melt the solder, and then reposition your component as necessary. Solder can be heated and cooled as many times as you need to get your joint the way you want it.

### Extrapolation

Soldering is a pretty straight forward process but there is no limit to what you could create with it. It works well for making jewelery, doing basic arts and crafts with small metal objects, or re-wiring your toaster into a heating element for an infra-red sauna.

## Everyone Needs a Multi-Meter

By **Phil B** Phil Bohiken
(www.instructables.com/id/
EVERYONE-Needs-a-Multi-Meter/)

A multi-meter can save the average person a lot of money over a few years. You will often be able to solve many problems yourself in less time than it would take to get a technician to come to your home. This instructable will show how to do that simply and easily.

A multi-meter is the tool every home ought have. They eliminate the guess work from so many things and can save a lot of money.

### Step 1: Will I Electrocute Myself?

No, that will not happen if you follow a few simple precautions. Most home uses of a multi-meter will be done with the power disconnected, or with very harmless low voltages. Regardless, you will always handle the probes by their well-insulated, completely safe plastic "handles." Usually, you will hold one in each hand.

The black probe is normally associated with the ground or negative terminal. The red probe is normally associated with the "hot" or positive terminal.

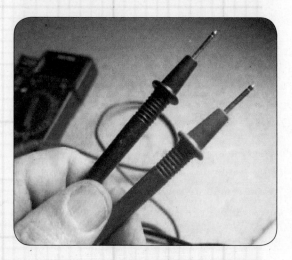

### Step 2: So, What Can a Multi-Meter Do?

You can test common batteries, but that is only the beginning of what you can do with a multi-meter. Notice the symbols for AC (alternating current) voltage and for DC (direct current voltage). Batteries use only DC voltage. Household batteries like AA and AAA are rated at 1.5 volts. On this meter, select the 4 volt range on the DC scale for common batteries. If I were testing a 9 volt battery with this meter, I would need to move the selector to the 40 volt range.

Touch each end of the battery with a probe. Ideally, the red probe touches the "+" end of the battery and the black probe touches the "−" end of the battery, but in practice it does not matter for this purpose. A minus (−) sign will appear in front of the numbers if the red and black wires are reversed when testing the battery. You are interested in only the numbers. A 1.5 volt battery is "dead" when it registers 1 volt or less. If a device does not work, but the 1.5 volt battery registers (for example) 1.38 volts, a new battery will not make it work. There is another problem to be solved. A 9 volt battery is "dead" when it falls to read about 7.5 to 8 volts. But, when a battery is "dead" also depends on the application. I use a 9 volt alkaline battery in a wireless microphone. I have learned by experience that a battery with a voltage below 8.5 volts will not last through a one hour church service.

### Step 3: Your Car Battery

One morning you turn the key in your car, but the motor turns over too slowly to start. You suspect the battery may be dead. Set the meter selector to 15 volts DC or more. Touch the meter probes to the terminal posts on your car battery. The meter will read 12 to 13 volts, but you want to know what the voltage reading is when the battery is under a load. Have someone turn the key while you watch the meter. If the meter reading drops to around 9 volts or less, you need to charge the

electronics

365

battery and see if that solves the problem. If you still get a reading of about 9 volts under load after a sufficient period for charging, you probably need a new battery for your car.

## Step 4: Corrosion?

Your car battery may be in good condition, but the starter still barely cranks the engine. The problem could be corrosion at one or both of the battery terminals. Sometimes you will see white or blue powder around the terminals, but often the corrosion is not visible. Set the voltmeter to a DC setting slightly in excess of 12 volts. Have a helper turn the key to crank the engine. If the battery connections are good, the voltmeter reading should remain at zero (0). If the battery connections are corroded, they will provide a high resistance, perhaps even an open circuit, and current will try to go through the voltmeter as an alternate route. The voltmeter reads the difference in voltage between one probe and the other.

That means the voltmeter will show a reading equal to the voltage of the battery. Clean or replace the battery terminal by taking it apart, dissolving the corrosion with baking soda in water, and scraping the parts of the connection.

## Step 5: Light Bulbs

Is your light bulb burned out, or is there a problem with your lamp? The first test is to check for a circuit through the light bulb. Use a low resistance or a CONT setting. This test will not work with the compact fluorescent bulbs, nor with fluorescent tubes. Those do not have a continuous conductor running through them, like an incandescent light bulb.

If the bulb tests good, some further checks on the lamp socket are necessary. Set the meter to the 400 volt AC selection. Touch one probe to the side of the bulb socket. Touch the other to the tip at the bottom of the socket. The meter should read about 120 volts.

You may find the expected voltage in the bulb socket and also the bulb are good, but the lamp still does not light. If the socket is older, the contact tip at the bottom of the socket may have lost its springiness and it may not make dependable contact with the center tip of the bulb. Use a popsicle stick to lift the tip. If you can be sure there is no electrical power to the socket, you may use a screwdriver. Then screw the bulb into the lamp socket and it should work.

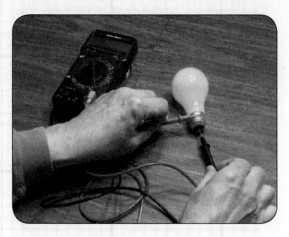

## Step 6: Fuses

Many devices use fuses, from your automobile to your household air conditioning system. A fuse is an electrical conductor designed to fail when a pre-determined threshold of current is present in the circuit. Their purpose is protect the rest of the circuit from a current load that would destroy it.

Sometimes fuses are out in the open where they are visible. Sometimes they are under a cover marked "Fuses." Sometimes they are inside an appliance with no notice of their presence. This is true of some microwave ovens and some television sets. Open the case and look for a small cartridge fuse. The fuse will usually be near where the electrical cord comes into the appliance. You may have thought you need a new microwave, but the real problem may be only a small fuse costing less than a dollar.

The fine wire in cartridge fuses is often so fine that it is difficult to see with the unaided eye. Some fuses have a solid body that blocks vision. When testing fuses set the multi-meter to CONT. for continuity. Touch the probes to the ends of a good fuse when on this setting and you will hear a shrill tone indicating there is a continuous circuit through the fuse. No sound means a bad fuse.

WARNING: If you open the case on a television or a microwave, be careful not to touch components other than the fuseholder. There are parts that retain a high voltage electrical charge. It is not likely you would touch these, anyway; but, if you did, they can kill.

## Step 7: Your Air Conditioner Unit

Air conditioning systems always seem to fail during the hottest, most miserable weather. No one wants to spend a muggy night trying to sleep with no air conditioning. If the problem is only a fuse, your meter can save you the cost of a service call by a technician, and you can have your system up and running again before the house has even warmed up inside.

Your air conditioning system may have more than one set of fuses protecting it. There may be a set of circuit breakers in your main electrical panel. Check to see that the circuit breaker toggles have not moved to the "off" position due to a sudden overload. Go to the air conditioner unit outside your house. Look for any cable conduits (metal pipes, some flexible). Follow them with your eye and look for any metal boxes that might contain fuses. The fuses will likely be mounted in a fuse block that can be pulled from the box. Use the continuity setting to check the fuses.

electronics

Set the meter to the 400 volt AC setting. If you place one probe on A and the other on B, the meter should read about 230 volts. That is true whether the switch in the box is "on" or "off." Place one probe on A and the other on C. The meter should read about 115 volts. Place one probe on B and the other on C. The meter should again read about 115 volts. Readings between F and C or G and C should also each give a reading of about 115 volts when the switch is "on." These readings indicate the fuses are good. With the switch in the "off" position, readings between F and C or G and C should be zero volts.

If you wish to check the fuses without them being electrically charged, move the switch lever to the "off" position. Set the meter to CONT. Touch one probe to D and the other to F. You should hear the meter's shrill chime tone. Now place one probe on E and the other on G. You should hear the tone again. This also indicates the fuses are good. If one of the fuses does not test good, be certain the switch is in the "off" position. With your fingers or a pair of pliers or a wooden stick to pry, remove the bad fuse. Take it with you to a hardware or building supply store and get a replacement.

## Step 8: The Electric Clothes Dryer Does Not Dry

The wet clothes in your dryer are still wet after running for the full cycle. The drum turned. The dryer went full cycle. What could be wrong? First check for a clogged filter or vent pipe. If those things are good, the problem may be electrical, and a multi-meter can help you find and fix it.

Dryers operate on two different circuits at two different voltages. The motor that turns the drum works on 115 volts. The heating element works on 230 volts. The electrical outlet behind your dryer that powers the dryer looks like this.

Set your meter selector to 400 volts AC. Put one probe into the "A" slot. Do not touch the other probe, but insert it into the "B" slot. The fit may not be tight. You may need to wiggle the probes to touch the metal inside and get a reading on the meter. The meter should show 230 volts. "C" is the neutral wire. "D" is the ground wire. Place a probe into "A" and the other probe into "C" or "D" and the reading on the meter should be 115 volts. The same should be true of a reading between "B" and "C" or "D." If you do not get these readings, check to be sure one circuit breaker or one fuse is not blown. There is the possibility that the dryer's heating element could be burned out, but that is not as likely. You can access it from the back of the dryer. Remove a cover over its terminals. Be sure the power to the dryer is disconnected. Use an Ohms setting on your meter and check for an open circuit. Testing an oven element in your stove is very similar. Remove the screws that hold the element in place and pull it from the oven. Do a resistance check on the two terminals.

## Step 9: Electrical Outlets

Sometimes you need to check an electrical outlet, or replace it. Set the meter to 400 volts AC. Place a probe in the "hot" slot and another in the neutral slot. The meter should read about 120 volts. Place a probe in the "hot" slot and in the ground slot. The meter should read 120 volts. Place a probe in the neutral slot and in the ground slot. The meter should read zero volts. Check outlets with your voltmeter before removing the cover and beginning to work on them. You want to be certain the power is "off."

## Step 10: Cords and Other Things

I have added alligator clip attachments to the probe ends on my meter. They are a very handy accessory I got at Radio Shack. They are like an extra hand.

Whether it is a toaster, or a phone charger, or a power cord for a computer; cords often fray internally within an inch or two of the plug. This is very understandable. That is the area of the cord that is frequently flexed back and forth. If something, like a phone charger, works some of the time, but not at other times; attach the meter with a resistance scale setting. Gently flex the cord back and forth near the plug end. Make fairly sharp bends. Watch the meter reading to see if it fluctuates between a normal reading and no connection. If it does, ask someone with a soldering iron to cut the cord back and reattach the plug end for you.

## Step 11: Lightning and Your Telephone

During the 1980s I was the pastor of a church in a rural setting. Lightning sometimes struck the utility company's power distribution lines and jumped to telephone lines running into our building. Once our telephone would not work. Twice the phone answering machine would not work. I was able to use my meter to rescue the telephone. I was also able to rescue the answering machine once, but not the second time. After the second strike we added a surge protector and had no problems after that.

The selector is set to the diode checker. Diodes are one way electrical valves and are very sensitive to surges of electrical current, especially with things like lightning. The arrow with a line across the arrow point is the standard symbol for a diode. Not every meter has a diode checker setting. Because diodes are very sensitive to current overloads, the diode checker limits the current in amperes that flow through a diode while testing it.

When testing a diode, you are looking for a relatively high current reading when the red and black leads are attached one way, but a relatively lower reading when the connections are reversed. The black probe is now above the red probe and the reading is one-third the previous reading, which is considerably lower. These readings are the sign of a good diode.

Often a diode can be checked without removing it from the circuit. Sometimes the readings are confusing. Chances are current is feeding through some other electronic component to cause an undependable reading. Then it becomes necessary to desolder one of the diode leads to isolate it from the circuit for accurate readings.

In the lightning incident I mentioned, there were only a couple of diodes. One of them failed its test. For less than a dollar I was able to replace the defective diode and the phone was good ever after. At the time a new phone was about $20.

electronics

## Step 12: Reading Amps. (current draw)

Although often used interchangeably in this Instructable, and wrongly so, "current" and "voltage" are actually different from one another. Voltage concerns the pressure at which electrons flow, like water pressure in a pipe. Current (amps. or amperes) deals with the volume of electrons flowing at the operating voltage. A device may appear to work, but makes an unusual noise or quickly overheats. A check of the amps. drawn by the circuit can tell you if there is a problem, even though it will not identify the exact problem.

First, check the device specifications. Look for a plate or label on the back or bottom of the device. It may tell you the device is designed to draw (for example) 2.3 amps. at 120 volts. Or, it may tell you the device uses 276 Watts at 120 volts. (Watts equals volts multiplied by amps., so divide Watts by volts to determine the proper amps.) If this device were found to draw (for example) 4.5 amps., you would know immediately something is wrong.

Reading amps. is different from reading voltages. Voltage readings are the drop in electrical "pressure" across two points in a circuit, or a whole circuit. The meter is not part of the circuit, but reads what happens across or between two points in the circuit. When reading amps, the meter must become a link in the circuit, just like a link in a chain. See the graphic showing how you can make a sandwich with two conductors and a piece of plastic between them. This sandwich can be placed between two batteries in your

device to see what the current draw is. The alternative is to break the circuit by cutting a conductor and connecting the meter to the ends of the cut conductor. You would need to reconnect the cut connector when you are finished. Set the selector for DC amps in the desired range.

You may need to change the holes into which the probes connect on the meter.

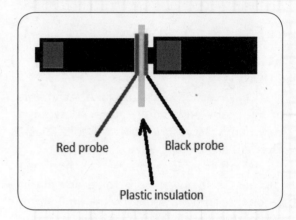

Red probe  Black probe

Plastic insulation

## Step 13: Shocking, Simply Shocking!

My father had a small electrical business when I was in high school. I was often his helper. Many of his customers lived on farms. A frequent complaint was a tingle (mild electrical shock) when taking a shower bath. Invariably, there had been a lightning strike nearby recently, and the lightning surge had shorted an electric water heater element to ground through the water inside the water heater tank. Turn off the power to the water heater at the circuit breaker. Remove the cover plates over the heater elements and pull the fiberglass insulation back. Disconnect the wire from one of the terminal screws on the heater element to isolate it from any possible feedback through another part of the circuit. This is to avoid false readings. Set the Ohms scale to a high range. Look for this symbol: Ω to identify the Ohms or resistance scale. Touch one probe to one of the heater element terminal screws. Touch the other probe to bare metal on the side of the water heater tank. If the element is not shorted to the water inside the tank, the meter reading should indicate an infinite resistance (no current flow, an open circuit).

A few years ago we had a neighbor who avoided having grandchildren visit because anyone who touched the built-in kitchen stove received a mild electrical shock. I set my meter to an AC voltage setting in the 150 volt range and placed one probe on the chrome oven handle and one probe on a sink faucet. My meter told me the electrical current registered about 40 volts AC. It took me some time, guess work, and checking; but I found someone had disconnected the thin green wire that connects the metal frame of the stove to that home's grounding circuit. When I reconnected the wire, the stray voltage disappeared. The green ground wire was located on the back of the oven.

## Step 14: Auto Ranging Meters and Reading the Meter

It is easy to forget to set the meter to the right range for the type of reading you will be making. With an analog (needle indicator) meter, that could be fatal to the meter. Some digital meters are "auto-ranging." That means the meter automatically makes the right setting. My meter has circuit protections built into the meter. Part of this is two fuses designed to "blow" before the circuitry can be harmed. I try to keep extra of these fuses on hand, just in case.

On my meter the digit "3" indicates an open circuit (= no path for electrical current). If I am using the Ohms (resistance) scale, the digit "3" appears until I attach the probes to the device I am testing. Sometimes the digit "3" remains when attached to a device known to be good. There should be an actual reading, but the reason there is not is that I have the meter set to an incorrect range.

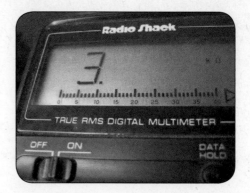

## Step 15: Accessories and Features

I have already mentioned two accessories available for my meter: insulated alligator clips and spring clips for grasping electronics component wires. I used my alligator clips to connect to the red and green wires on the pigtail. If all is well, the voltmeter should read about 50 volts DC. This can be a big help when you are reporting a service outage. The pigtail has two other conductors. I taped them so they would not touch anything and create a short.

Sometimes you need an extra hand. Multi-meters come with a fold out stand on the back of the meter. These usually can also be flipped up to function as a hanger for the meter. This frees both hands for manipulating the probes, especially if the voltages could harm someone.

Sometimes you may be able to reach terminals with the probes, but may not be able to read the meter. If you can manage to press the Hold button and release it, the meter will freeze the reading so you can move and see what the meter recorded.

electronics

This instructable shows how to wire up one or more LEDs in a in a basic and clear way. Never done any work before with LEDs and don't know how to use them? It's OK, neither have I.

## Step 1: Get some LEDs

So I wasn't completely honest—I have used LEDs once or twice before for simple applications, but I never really knew what I was doing, and since so many projects on instructables use LEDs, I thought I might as well teach myself and post about it too.

I know that there are many projects already posted that contain information about how to wire LEDs for simple projects—LED Throwies, LED Beginner Project: Part 2 and 9v LED flashlight—the best evarrr!, but I think that there could still be some use for a detailed step by step explanation about the basics of LEDs for anyone who could use it.

The first step was to buy some supplies and figure out what I would need to experiment with. For this project I ended up going to Radioshack because its close and a lot of people have access to it—but be warned their prices are really high for this kind of stuff and there are all kinds of low cost places to buy LEDs online.

To light up an LED you need at the very minimum the LED itself and a power supply. From what I have read from other LED instructables wiring in a resistor is almost always a good idea.

## Materials

- LEDs—I basically just reached into the drawer at RadioShack and pulled out anything that wasn't more than $1 or $2 per LED. I got:2760307 5mm Red LED 1.7 V2760351 5MM Yellow LED 2.1 V2760036 Flasher Red LED 5 V2760041 2 Pack Red LED 2.6 V2760086 Jumbo Red LED
- 4VPower Supply—I really didn't know what I would need to power them so I bought some 9V batteries and some 1.5V AA's. I figured that would allow me to mix and match and make enough different voltage combinations to make something light up—or at least burn those little suckers out in a puff of smelly plastic smoke.
- Resistors—Again, I wasn't too sure what I would need in terms of resistors here either. Since I got a whole bunch of different LEDs with various voltages I knew that I would need a couple different types of resistors, so I just bought a variety pack of ½ Watt Carbon Film Resistors (2710306).
- I gathered up a soldering gun, solder, needle nose pliers, electrical pliers, some primary wire and electrical tape too since I thought they might be useful.

## Step 1: The LED

LEDs come in different sizes, brightnesses, voltages, colors and beam patterns, but the selection at Radioshack is pretty small and so I just picked up a couple different

LEDs from what they had in a few different brightnesses and voltages. I kept close track of what LED was what voltage because I didn't want to accidentally send too much current through one of the low voltage LEDs.

The first thing I did with the LEDs was figure out which wire (its called an electrode) was positive and which was negative. Generally speaking the longer wire is the positive electrode and the shorter wire is the negative electrode.

You can also take a look inside the LED itself and see whats going on. The smaller of the metal pieces inside the LED connects to the positive electrode and the bigger one is the negative electrode. But be warned—in the LEDs I picked up I didn't always find this to be true and some of the LEDs had the longer electrode on the negative when it should be on the positive. Go figure—its OK though, if it didn't light up I just flipped it around.

Once I knew what was positive and what was negative I just had to remember what the voltage of each LED was.

All my LEDs recommended 20mA of current. 20mA is standard for most LEDs.

## Step 2: Power Supply

To make the power supplies I just soldered some wire onto the ends of the batteries I had bought so that I could easily attach the LEDs to them. The 9V battery served as my 9V power supply, one AA battery made a 1.5V power supply and three AA batteries bundled together made a 4.5V (1.5V + 1.5V + 1.5V = 4.5V) power supply. I didn't use alligator clips on the ends of the wire, but they would have been helpful here.

## Step 3: Resistors

I opened up the assortment pack to find that resistors aren't labeled with what value they are. The pack said it contained a whole bunch of different resistors from 100 ohms to 1 Meg ohm so I set out to see what was what. When I poked around online I found that all resistors have a coding system on them that tells you what value they are. Here are two pages which explain in depth about how to calculate resistor values. Do it yourself http://wiki.xtronics.com/index.php/Resistor_Codes, or Have it done for you. I'll go through the examples of how I calculated the values myself in the next few steps when I start wiring up my LEDs. For the time being I just admired their little colored stripes and moved on to trying to get just one LED to light up.

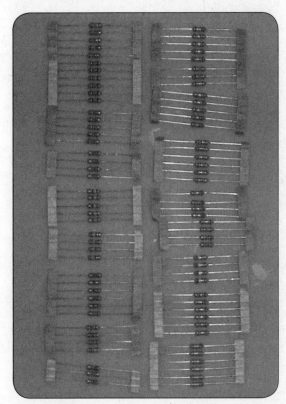

## Step 5: One LED, No Resistor

LEDs require sufficient voltage to light them. Sometimes if you give them too little voltage they wont light at all, other times they will just shine dimly with low voltage. Too much voltage is bad and can burn out the LED instantaneously.

So ideally you would like the voltage of the LED to match the voltage of your power

electronics

373

supply, or even be slightly less. To do this you can do a couple of things: change your power supply voltage, change the LED your using, or you can use a resistor that allows you use a higher voltage power supply with a lower voltage LED.

For now I just wanted to get one lit up so I chose my the power supply that had the lowest voltage—the single AA battery which outputs 1.5V.

I chose to light the red 1.7V LED since the battery outputs 1.5V and I knew I wouldn't kill the LED with too much power.

I wrapped my positive wire from the battery to the positive electrode of the LED and wrapped the negative wire from the battery to my negative electrode and presto—let there be LED light!

This first experiment was pretty easy to do—just some wire twisting and enough knowledge to know that the 1.5V power supply would light the 1.7V LED without need a resistor.

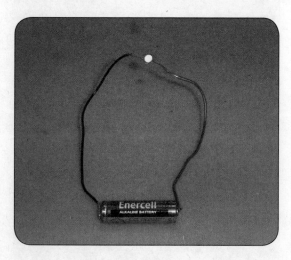

## Step 6: One LED With a Resistor

It was just a coincidence that I bought an LED that was 1.7V and that it ended up working being able to be powered by my 1.5V power supply without the use of a resistor. For this second setup I decided to use the same LED, but up my power supply to the three AA batteries wired together which output 4.5V—enough power to burn out my 1.7V LED, so I would have to use a resistor.

To figure out which resistor to use I used the formula:

$$R = (V1 - V2)/I$$

where:

V1 = power supply voltage

V2 = LED voltage

I = LED current (usually 20mA which is .02A)

Now there are lots of calculators online that will do this for you—and many other instructables reference this as a good one, however, the math really isn't too hard and so I wanted to go through the calculation myself and understand whats going on.

Again, my LED is 1.7V, it takes 20mA (which is .02 A) of current and my supply is 4.5V. So the math is . . .

$$R = (4.5V - 1.7V)/.02 A$$

$$R = 140 \text{ ohms}$$

Once I knew that I needed a resistor of 140 ohms to get the correct amount of voltage to the LED I looked into my assortment package of resistors to see if I could find the right one.

Knowing the value of a resistor requires reading the code from the color bands on the resistor itself. The package didn't come with a 140 ohm resistor but it did come with a 150 ohm one. Its always better to use the next closest value resistor greater than what you calculated. Using a lower value could burn out your LED.

To figure out the color code you basically break down the first two digits of the resistor value, use the third digit to multiply the first two by and then assign the fourth digit as an indicator of tolerance. That sounds a lot more difficult than it really is.

Using the color to number secret decoder website found here, a 150ohm resistor should have the following color code . . .

Brown because the first digit in the value resistor I needed is 1

Green because the fifth digit is 5

Brown because in order to get to 150 you have to add one 0 to 15 to get to 150.

Gold—the resistors I got all have 5% tolerance and 5% is represented by gold

Check out the decoder page link above if this isn't making sense.

I looked through all the resistors, found the one that was brown, green, brown, gold, and wired it in line on the positive electrode of the LED. (Whenever using a resistor on an LED it should get placed before the LED on the positive electrode.)

Low and behold, the LED lit up once again. The 150 ohm resistor stopped enough of the 4.5V power supply from reaching the 1.7V LED that it lit up safely and kept it from burning out.

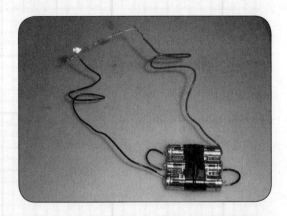

## Step 7: Wiring up Multiple LEDs in Series

Now that I knew how to wire one LED with various combinations of LED voltages and power supplies, it was time to explore how to light up multiple LEDs. When it comes to wiring more than one LED to a power supply there are two options. The first option is to wire them in series and the second is to wire them in parallel.

LEDs wired in series are connected end to end (the negative electrode of the first LED connects to the positive electrode of the second LED and the negative electrode of the second LED connects to the positive electrode of the third LED and so on and so on . . . ). The main advantage of wiring things in series is that it distributes the total voltage of the power source between all of the LEDs. What that means is that if I had a 12V car battery, I could power 4, 3V LEDs (attaching a resistor to each of them). Hypothetically this could also work to power 12, 1V LEDs; 6, 2V LEDs; or even 1 12V LED if such a thing existed.

Ok, let's try wiring 2, 2.6V LEDs in series to the 9V power supply and run through the math.

R = (9V – 5.2V)/.02A
R = 190 Ohms
Next higher resistance value—200 Ohms

Now the variety package of resistors didn't come with a 190 or 200 Ohm resistor, but it did come with other resistors which I could use to make a 200 Ohm resistor. Just like LEDs, resistors can be wired together in either series or parallel (see next step for an explanation on wiring things together in parallel).

When same value resistors are wired together in series you add their resistance. When same value resistors are wired together in parallel you divide the value of the resistor by the number of resistors wired together.

So, in the most simplified sense, two 100 Ohm resistors wired together in series will equal 1 200 Ohm resistor (100 + 100 = 200). Two 100 Ohm resistors wired together in parallel will equal one 50 Ohm resistor (100/2 = 50).

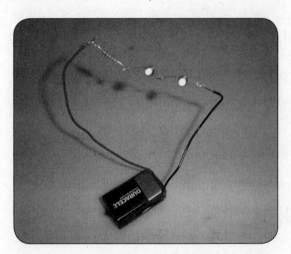

## Step 8: Wiring up Multiple LEDs in Parallel

Unlike LEDs that are wired in series, LEDs wired in parallel use one wire to connect all the positive electrodes of the LEDs your using to the positive wire of the power supply and use another wire to connect all the negative electrodes of the LEDs your using to the negative wire of the power supply. Wiring things in parallel has some distinct advantages over wiring things in series.

electronics

If you wire a whole bunch of LEDs in parallel rather than dividing the power supplied to them between them, they all share it. So, a 12V battery wired to four 3V LEDs in series would distribute 3V to each of the LEDs. But that same 12V battery wired to four 3V LEDs in parallel would deliver the full 12V to each LED—enough to burn out the LEDs for sure!

Wiring LEDs in parallel allows many LEDs to share just one low voltage power supply. We could take those same four 3V LEDs and wire them in parallel to a smaller power supply, say two AA batteries putting out a total of 3V and each of the LEDs would get the 3V they need.

In short, wiring in series divides the total power supply between the LEDs. Wiring them in parallel means that each LED will receive the total voltage that the power supply is outputting.

And finally, just some warnings . . . wiring in parallel drains your power supply faster than wiring things in series because they end up drawing more current from the power supply. It also only works if all the LEDs you are using have exactly the same power specifications. Do NOT mix and match different types/colors of LEDs when wiring in parallel.

I decided to do two different parallel setups.

The first one I tried was as simple as it could be—just two 1.7V LEDs wired in parallel to a single 1.5V AA battery. I connected the two positive electrodes on the LEDs to the positive wire coming from the battery and connected the two negative electrodes on the LEDs to the negative wire coming from the battery. The 1.7V LEDs didn't require a resistor because the 1.5V coming from the battery was enough to light the LED, but not more than the LEDs voltage—so there was no risk of burning it out.

Both of the 1.7V LEDs were lit by the 1.5V power supply, but remember, they were drawing more current from the battery and would thus make the battery drain faster. If there were more LEDs connected to the

battery, they would draw even more current from the battery and drain it even faster.

For the second setup, I decided to put everything I had learned together and wire the two LEDs in parallel to my 9V power supply—certainly too much juice for the LEDs alone so I would have to use a resistor for sure.

To figure out what value I should use I went back to the trusty formula—but since they were wired in parallel there is a slight change to the formula when it comes to the current—I.

$R = (V1 - V2)/I$

where:

V1 = supply voltage

V2 = LED voltage

I = LED current (we had been using 20 mA in our other calculations but since wiring LEDs in parallel draws more current I had to multiply the current that one LED draws by the total number of LEDs I was using. 20 mA × 2 = 40 mA, or .04A.

And my values for the formula this time were:

$R = (9V - 1.7V)/.04A$

R = 182.5 Ohms

One last note about wiring LEDs in parallel—while I put my resistor in front of both LEDs it is recommended that you put a resistor in front of each LED. This is the safer better way to wire LEDs in parallel with resistors.

The 1.7V LEDs connected to the 9V battery lit up—and my small adventure into LED land was completed.

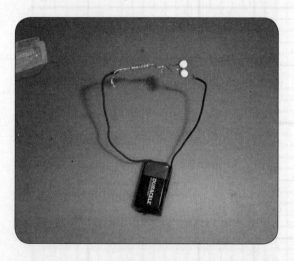

# Table for Electronic Dreams

### By **andydoro** Andy Doro
(www.instructables.com/id/Table-for-Electronic-Dreams/)

Table for Electronic Dreams is a table which reveals the hidden electrical activity of nearby electronic objects.

## Gather Parts!

You will need:

- 15 circuit boards
- 15 LM324 quad op amp
- 15 14-pin sockets
- 60 white LEDs
- 60 induction coils* Currently I am using coils from Digikey part number M10013-ND. The inductance is 4.7mH. They do not look like the ones pictured in this instructable.
- 60 10 ohm resistors
- 60 10M ohm resistors
- 60 1K ohm resistors
- 30 100K ohm resistors
- 15 10μF capacitors
- 60 0.1μF capacitors

You could change these numbers if you want to make a smaller table. There will be 1 quad op amp, 4 LEDs and 4 induction coils for each board.

For the Table:

- ¼ inch translucent white acrylic 33" × 21"
- ¼ inch clear acrylic 33" × 21"
- aluminum u-channel

For op amps I am using a quad op amp LM324, but you can use any op amp chip.

## Step 1: Plan Circuit

Follow the schematic and connect the components properly.

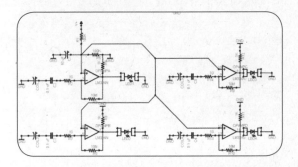

You can do this on a perfboard or a printed circuit board if you want to be fancier. I am selling printed circuit boards , please see my website for details on ordering boards.

Essentially the coil picks up a voltage, which is amplified by the op amp, which drives an LED.

I have placed the coil next to the LED so there is more of a one-to-one correspondence between detected field strength and LED brightness.

## Step 2: Assemble Circuit

Assemble components onto a printed circuit board. You can also use perf board. The board should run on between 3 to 5 V DC current. Use a voltage regulator (7805 or 3940) in order to get a steady voltage.

## Step 3: Test the Board
Oh look, it's working!

## Step 4: Repeat!
You can keep making circuit boards!

## Step 5: Mount Circuit Boards
I mounted the circuit boards to some transparent acrylic. I placed the boards so that the LEDs are in a 3 inch pitch grid. You can then connect the powers and grounds of each of the boards together with some wire.

## Step 6: Test the Circuits
You can test the circuits' responsiveness to electronic devices. I used a cell phone, but it works best if the cell phone is in use. You can try calling a friend or checking your voicemail.

## Step 7: Build Table
You can install these circuits into an existing table, or build your own. Actually, it doesn't have to be a table at all . . .

## Step 8: Finishing Touch
Now you can place a sheet of translucent white acrylic above the layer of circuits to diffuse the light from the LEDs. I used small white vinyl bumpers for the acrylic to sits on top of.

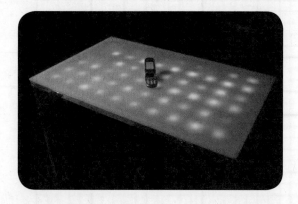

## Step 9: Done!
For more information and a video, please see www.andydoro.com/table/ Thanks!

electronics

# Electromagnetic Floater

## By J_Hodgie
(www.instructables.com/id/
Electromagnetic-Floater/)

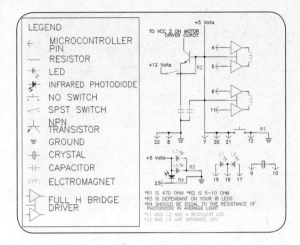

This Instructable will show you how to make a device that can float almost any object with a magnet in it.

It is much like the floating globes you can buy, except it works by balancing the forces of permanent magnets with electromagnets, rather then simply using combinations of permanent magnets.

This is done by using a microcontroller and an IR sensor to detect where an object is floating below. Then based on a set value, the microcontroller uses the electromagnets to to hold the floating object at a given height.

The place the object floats at depends on the weight of the object and the power of the magnets in the object. The height is set by holding the object under the magnets and sensor and pushing the button.

The object floats at the point where the force of gravity down equals the force of the magnets pulling up, which allows it to use non-industrial electromagnets and less power to float. The program also dynamically adjusts so the object is always at the perfect height.

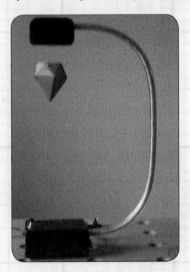

## Materials
- ATMega168 Microcontroller
- 1 16-20 MHz Crystal
- 28 Pin Socket
- Dual Full H Bridge IC
- 1 Power NPN
- 2 Electromagnets
- 1 Bicolor LED
- 2 IR LED
- 1 IR Photodiode
- 1 5V Regulator
- 2 Leveling Capacitors
- 1 SPST Switch
- 1 NO Button
- 1, 470 Ohm Resistor
- 1, 5 Ohm Resistor
- 1 Universal Breadboard
- 2 Cases
- Plexiglas
- Solder
- Hot Glue
- Steel Wire
- Vinyl Tubing
- 3 or more ¼" diameter × ¼" thick rare earth magnets (for the base)
- 2 or more ½" diameter × ⅛" thick rare earth magnets (for the objects)

## Tools
- Soldering Iron
- Hot Glue Gun
- Desoldering Pump
- 3rd Hand
- Plexiglas cutter

## Step 1: Prepare the Base

Once the materials are gathered, the cases needs to be prepared. For my base I used a project box to house the electronics, and a ring box to house the magnets and sensor assembly.

First you need to drill a hole in the back of each box for the support wire to go through. Also cut holes for the power switch, power input, set height button and LED indicator. You also need to cut most of the bottom of the ring box out, just leaving a lip on the bottom.

Support the ring box above the base box by using some heavy gauge steel wire, bent to the shape and height you want. Next, wrap the electrical wire around the steel wire, then cover all of it with the vinyl tubing (optional) as seen below.

Next, bend the bottom end of the support in a zig zag pattern and use hot glue to secure it to the inside of the bottom case. I secured the ring box to the top of the support wire by using a magnet, but it could also be stuck on by hot glue.

## Step 3: Install the Magnets and Sensor

This step is pretty straight forward, first solder the electromagnets to 4 of the wires. As you attach the parts be sure to use a continuity tester to find and label the corresponding wires on the other end. At this point it is not too important which way the electromagnet coils around the magnet, it can be adjusted later. But be sure to connect both electromagnets the same way.

When you put the electromagnets in the box when finished, put the permanent magnets inside the coil.

Next cut a piece of Plexiglas to fit inside the bottom of the ring box but so the bottom lip holds it up. The next step is to attach the IR emitters and sensor to the Plexiglas as seen in the pictures below using hot glue then finish attaching and labeling the wires.

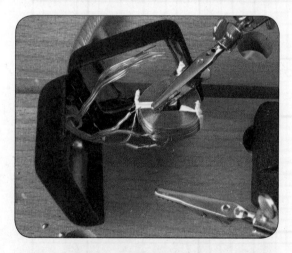

electronics

## Step 4: Build the Electronics

For this step you probably should assemble the electronics on a solderless breadboard before soldering them together. The schematic to build the circuit is attached along with the hex file to load on the microcontroller. The Arduino—007 code file can be found at instructables.com/id/Electromagnetic-Floater/, and you can tweak or make changes as you need.

It is very important to plan where all of the parts go, so all of the electronics will fit in the box the first time, If not it could be very frustrating and cause much grief.

It is also important to note that the NPN power transistor(s) will heat up. To overcome this I mounted them to contact the aluminum base of my project box. This way it acts as a heat sink, preventing a spectacular fire. You will also need to come up with something similar to remove most of the heat from the box.

Once the electronics are built, there is a section of code in the program to uncomment and then load onto the chip to test the orientation of the coils. It pulses the coils off, pulling up, and pushing down, also indicated by the LED. If you hold a magnet under the electromagnets and it doesn't follow the pattern, reverse the wires.

## Step 5: Make Some Objects to Float

This part is only limited by your imagination. I have found that if the objects to float are too small, or two short relative to the width, are harder to get to float.

## Step 6: Start Floating

All that is left to do is start floating the objects.

This is done by holding the object under the magnets and slowly bringing it up. When It nears the point where it wants to float up, push the button. This will set the level to float at to the current height.

Next, hold it just below where you set the hold height, so the LED lights up. Hold it there until it simply floats out of your hand. This happens because the microcontroller slowly adjusts the hold height up, to where the electromagnets have enough power to control the object.

You may also notice some buzzing coming from the electromagnets. This can be easily fixed by inserting some padding around the electromagnets.

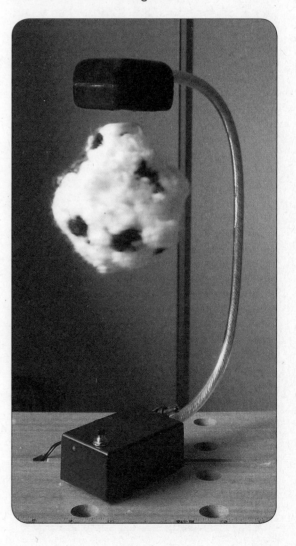

electronics

# MintyBoost! Small Battery-Powered USB Charger

By **ladyada**
(www.instructables.com/id/
MintyBoost!---Small-battery-
powered-USB-charger/)

This project details a small & simple, but very powerful USB charger for your mp3 player, camera, cell phone, and any other gadget you can plug into a USB port to charge!

The charger circuitry and 2 AA batteries fit into an Altoids gum tin, and will run your iPod for hours: 2.5 × more than you'd get from a 9V USB charger! You can use rechargeable batteries too.

Some numbers . . .

iPod video (tested, using alkaline batteries): 3 hours more video (1 full recharge)

iPod mini (tested w/rechargeables): 25 hours more (1.5 full recharges)

iPod shuffle (unverified): 60 hours more (5 full recharges)

Weight (with 2 × AA): 3.5oz

This project is suitable for beginners, some soldering tools are necessary but even if you've never soldered before it should be pretty easy. You can etch a circuit board and/or breadboard this up, or simply buy the kit from the adafruit webshop.

## Step 1: The Process (Meta documentation)

This next 10 steps detail how I went through the process of coming up with the idea, hardware, design, etc. for this project. It's not 100% correct but it's pretty close. I also include the schematic/layout files in Eagle format. The prototype one is best for etching at home (its single sided)

## Step 2: The Process: Come up with an Idea

OK so where does an idea come from anyways? It's the only important question & the most difficult. I guess I'd have to say it was prompted by looking at these half-dozen projects:

- *Aaron Dunlaps 9V USB charger
- *Another 9V + 7805 USB charger (Instructables)
- *Jason Streigel's 9V+7805 USB 'battery' (hackaday)
- *Ians Firewire switching charger (Instructables )
- *Chris DiClerico's 9V+AA's firewire charger

OK, there's probably even some I'm missing. So what's the overarching theme here? Almost all use 9V batteries and a 7805 (an extremely common linear 5V regulator: makes a solid 5V from 7-18V input). This design works great because, well, 7805's are awesome and 9V's provide 7-9V depending upon how 'dead' they are.

However, there's one thing about 9V's that I've learned (from lots of bad experiences). One is that they don't have a lot of amp-hours: that is, how much current (amps) they can provide and for how long (hours). A Duracell 9V provides -about-500mAh over its lifetime. That's 500 mA (or .5A) for one hour or 100mA for 5 hours. That number is somewhat idealized but it's a good starting point.

Another problem is that they don't like to supply a lot of current, because they have high internal resistance (~2ohms), but basically that just means that if you want a lot of current (say to resuscitate a drained device) the 9V won't provide all 500mAh, but maybe more like 400. (Say you're drawing 250mA, then .25A*2ohm = 0.5V lost to internal resistance. For more info on 9V, read the Duracell datasheet )

Another problem with the 9V+7805 scheme is that a 7805 is a linear regulator. That means if you want 100mA at 5V (basically, USB power) then you're taking 100mA at 9V and then losing the 4V*100mA = 400mW (.4W) difference as heat.

As the battery wears down to 7V the heat loss goes down to (7-5V)*100mA=.2W but you're still getting bad efficiency. At best the efficiency is 72% (5V/7V) and at worst its 55% (5V/9V) That means you're losing about a third of the battery power to heat!

I'll also throw out that the 7805 itself has a quiescent current of about 5mA so you're always losing 5% (5mA/100mA) efficiency just for regulation! (& that's at least since if you're trickle charging the battery at 50mA then the 5mA quiescent is 10%)

OK so basically the 7805+9V solution works but the efficiency is startlingly low, say 60% or so, and provides only 300mAh at 5V.

We can engineer better!

## Step 3: The Process: Engineering a Better Solution

From experience, I know that AA's are great. They are cheap, have lots of power, very low internal resistance and are easily available everywhere. Whereas a 9V has 500mAh (for a total of 9*500 = 4.5Wh power) two AA's have 3000mAh each for a total of 2 * 1.5V * 3000mAh = 9Wh, about twice as much power. The only problem is that 2×AA's provide 3V and what we need is 5V. With a 9V battery we can use a linear regulator because 5V is greater than 9V but, sadly, we can't use a linear regulator to

turn 3V into 5V. Instead we will need to use a boost regulator (also known as a DC/DC switching/step-up regulator)

The process of how a boost regulator works is somewhat beyond the scope of this document, suffice to say they work great but are a little more annoying than linear regulators because you have to pick out an inductor and wire up some extra parts. You can get a lot more info about Boost Converters at Wikipedia which is also where I stole the boost topology image from.

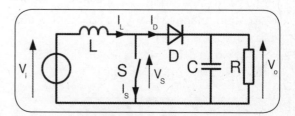

## Step 4: The Process: Enclosure Selection

So at this point I start thinking about enclosure and size. Most people think of this last, and that's a bad idea. If there's one thing I've learned from hacking on electronics, its that you should try and select the case first because it dictates a lot of the electronics and interface.

I know that the parts for the kit must be all through-hole (no surface mount) and easy to work with. I also want AA batteries, 2 is good although I know from experience that most boost converters will work with any number from 1 and 3 just fine. I have a predilection for Altoids tins and I also know that I can fit ~2 AA's into a gum tin so I pull out a tin and take some measurements.

OK 2 AA's fit well, so now I rummage through my collection of battery holders and find one (PCB-mount) which seems to be pretty good. It doesn't have a switch but I don't need one anyway (see quiescient calculations, later on).

So I take some measurements . . . Looks like I have about 1.25" × 0.7" semicircular PCB space at the top for the circuit board.

I also try out another battery holder I have, this gives me more space, 1.25"×0.85" . . . but the batteries go in sideways so one would have to remove the holder to change the batteries. I'd prefer that you can just take them out directly, so I don't go with this one (it also turns out I don't need that extra space).

(I now do a little hack to turn the PCB mount 2xAA battery holder into a wire-lead one. Basically I just solder on red and black 6" wires and clip off the PCB through-hole leads. This is actually a little difficult because the plastic melts and you have to sort of keep it in place while you solder. Its not suggested.)

Now that's done I'm ready to think about what I can cram into that space.

## Step 5: The Process: Boost Chip Selection

So now it's time to design the boost supply. Since I don't have much space, I'm going to try to make my circuit as tiny

as possible but still be easy to solder. That means I want a boost chip that is 8-DIP (smallest though-hole), with an internal MOSFET switch (1 less part) and is high frequency (to keep the inductor small). I also need to be able to supply 100mA at 5V and it should run on as low as 2V input. Also I want to be able to buy it online from a common supplier.

- 8-DIP package
- Internal FET switch
- 100mA output @ 5V
- 2V minimum input voltage

OK, lets search Digikey. I start with "DC/DC converter 8-DIP" and check "items in stock"

I then select 1 output, 8-DIP (to differentiate between 18-DIP) and select all the current-outputs >=100mA and apply the filter. There's still about 40 options. So then I select the all voltage input ranges that start with 2V or less. Also I select all the Adjustable, and 5V-inclusive output voltage options.

Looking over this list, it looks like I have a lot of options so I'm going to go back and select only the chips that can be preset to 5V (as opposed to adjustable ones that use 2 resistors to set the voltage). 5V is very common so every reasonable DC/DC chip will be available with such an option.

Now there are about a dozen options. The LT1073, LT1111, LT1173 and LT130x as well as the MAX751 & MAX756. They're all pretty much the same, so I basically make my choice based on price at 100 pieces (since I'm planning to kit it up). I also know that Maxim is great about sending samples so I decide to go with the MAX756 (datasheet) which is $2.32/100. Note that I could have gone with any of them, so this a somewhat arbitrary choice.

According to the datasheet, I can supply up to 200mA @ 5V, run off input voltages as low as 0.7V and the efficiency is about 85% with 2 AA batteries. The chip also runs at 500KHz which is pretty fast and means that the inductor can be pretty small (~22uH) Anyway, I've used this chip before and its worked out well for me.

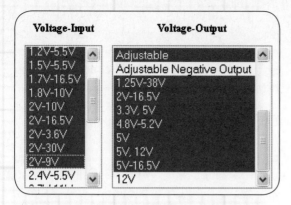

## Step 6: The Process: Inductor Selection

The next step is to choose an inductor. This can be a bit of a pain, and there is a lot of math you can throw at the problem. However, the datasheet suggests (under "inductor selection") to get a 22uH inductor, with a ~1.2A saturation limit, and DC resistance of 0.02 ohms.

What we want is through-hole, which actually means its going to be hard to find an inductor; almost all inductors are surface mount. But I'll take a look at what digikey has to offer. I search for "fixed uH inductor ~smd ~smt" which means I don't want SMT/SMD (surface mount) and I want a non-adjustable inductor that is in the uH range (not mH or nH). I then filter out inductors with 1-3A current and 18-27uH inductance.

That filters it down to about a dozen choices. The SLF inductor is actually surface mount, and we're going to outright ignore the ones that cost more than $2.50. Inductors for small electronics like this should cost around $1-$2, as a guideline. That leaves us with the DN7418-ND "INDUCTOR 27UH POWER AXIAL" and the 6000-220K-RC "INDUCTOR HI CURRENT RADIAL 22UH." Both of these look good, with about ~1.5A saturation current and 0.07 ohm DC resistance.

I also check out Mouser. The online search for mouser isn't as nice as Digikey's so I end up looking at the paper catalog instead. I only found one inductor, really, the 18R223C (22uH radial power inductor) and/or the 18223C (axial version) that also has plenty of power capacity and a 0.03ohm DC resistance.

So, I order 2 of each of these.

## Step 7: The Process: Rapid Prototyping

In reality, what I did was look through the Digikey catalog, where I only found the DN7418 inductor (the other one was somewhat hidden in the RF inductor section). And it showed up before the Mouser box, so I spent an hour or two making up a prototype.

The circuit itself is simple, I want one large electrolytic cap for low frequency smoothing on the battery, and an output cap pair (electrolytic and one ceramic cap for high freq. smoothing). I also need the chip, a reference voltage capacitor, the inductor and a schottky diode to finish off the boost regulator. I happen to have some 1N5818's, which are often used as schottky diodes in boost regulators. I also need a USB type A female jack, of course, and two holes to solder the battery pack into. You can compare the schematic to the topology diagram in step #3 keeping in mind that this chip has an internal transistor switch.

All these parts must fit into the space left over from the battery pack. I make EagleCAD library parts for the inductor and chip (the rest are already there) and lay out the board. I'm not going to detail making library parts in eagle or pcb layout, others have done so already. Use whichever software you want, I like Eagle because there's a free version available for download if you're just making small PCBs.

Since I know this just a prototype version, I make the PCB single sided -- for easy etching. I also make the traces really large. I print out a paper version of the PCB and punch the parts through to verify that they're the right shape/package.

I get my etching setup together, turn on the heater for the etching tank, and print out a bunch of tiled PCB layouts on toner transfer. I transfer the toner onto a single sided PCB and etch it in the tank

Then I clean off the toner transfer, drill the holes with a dremel drill-press with carbide drill bits, and cut out the shape.

**electronics**

Then I solder the parts in, and fit it into the case with the battery pack, using double-sided foam sticky tape to hold down both the battery holder and the PCB without shorting the PCB to the metal tin.

OK, done!

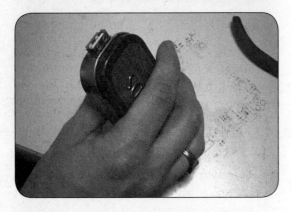

## Step 8: The Process: Prototype Testing

Now we test to see if it works! With the two batteries inside, I measure the voltage on the USB connector: about 5V, which is good. I send off this version to a friend with once of each kind of iPod, including the newest 4G video iPod, for real-world testing: both to verify the iPod will charge and also how long it will run with the additional pack.

Its also time to verify the math for efficiency: how good is it, after all?

So, in theory, we should be able to calculate the efficiency of the boost converter from datasheet info. We're basically boosting 2.5-3VDC -> 5VDC at around 50mA-100mA. Looking at the MAX756 datasheet, note the efficiency graph.

So we should be getting around 85% efficiency, perhaps a little more. I think the only thing that can really change this number a bit is the inductor. (Below, I verify I'm getting 82% efficiency)

If we're getting 82% efficiency conversion from $2 \times 3000$mAh Duracells, that means we get (2 * 1.5V) * 3000mAh * .83 = 7.38 Watt hours. Compare that to a single 9V as we calculated before: $(1 \times 9V)$ * 500mAh * .65 = 2.93 Wh. So we're going to get about 2.5x more power out of these two AAs than a single 9V.

With rechargeable batteries, we get (2 * 1.25) * 2200mAh * 81% = 4.45 Wh (about 50% more than an alkaline 9V and 3x more than a rechargeable 9V)

Next, lets verify the efficiency using test equipment, and try out the different inductors to see if they make a difference. Instead of using batteries, I'll provide 3V from a bench supply that will also tell me how much current is being drawn. And instead of an iPod I'll fake the load with a resistor. Since the standard USB current draw is 100mA from 5V, that means I need a 5V/.1A = 50 ohm load. I can't just use a tiny resistor because 5V * .1A = ½W and most resistors are ¼W. So instead I take two large 100ohm 'power' resistors, and twist them together. I also check the resistance to verify that together they are 50ohms. I also find a 20ohm power resistor. This will allow me to not only test a 100mA load but also a 250mA load.

I perform 4 tests with 2 inductors: 100mA load for both 2.5V in and 3V in (rechargeable and disposable batteries) and 250 load for both.

It looks like inductor #2 is little more efficient, probably due to the fact it has a lower DC resistance (30 milliohms instead of 70mohm of the other inductor). It's also a bit cheaper so I'll go with that inductor.

Regardless, it looks like the efficiency is around 82% which is about what I expected.

Another thing to note is that I don't put an on/off switch in like you'd need with a 9V+7805 regulator. That's because the quiescent current of the MAX756 is very low, on the order of 100uA (0.1mA). I measured this myself and got about 75uA.

That means that the self-discharge rate is ~2000mAh/0.1mA = 20,000 hours, more than 2 years. Most batteries don't last that long! Therefore, we don't need a switch; when nothing is plugged in, almost no power is being used.

(In the end, I found another radial inductor that was cheaper and as efficient, which is what I use in the kit).

## Step 9: The Process: Kit Budgeting

So now that I've verified that the project works, I have to figure out whether I want to sell it, how many I expect to sell, and how much I want to charge. Lots of people have different techniques for this. I tend to go with my 'gut' which usually means there's a lot of information I use but its difficult to express it.

I tend to decide whether I want to sell something based on how popular/useful/easy it is. I think that this kit will be pretty popular and useful because lots of people have stuff that charges/powers over USB. Also, it seems like other people are selling similar things (like the 9V + 7805 type charger, or Griffin's 9V charger, or Belkin's 4xAA charger) It's easy to make because all the parts are through-hole and there's not a lot of them.

I'm going to basically assume I'll sell 200 or so within a few months, and I'll order parts in batches of 100, so I should budget that way. (I often buy more than 100 PCBs at a time because of the scale economies involved in PCB manufacture.) It turns out so far that I can sell a couple hundred units of a kit in a few months, particularly if it gets picked up by a blog or web site. This may or may not be true for you, however if you cant afford to make 25 kits at once you're going to find that its hard to make any money in the process.

To figure out how much to charge, I make up a table with different quantity prices

To calculate the PCB costs, I used Advanced Circuit's insta-quote service.

These prices are for 2 PCBs, which I'll cut in two, because its cheaper (probably because they don't like dealing with very small circuit boards). I usually go with 2 week turn prices. Note that the PCB quote doesn't include the $150 one-time tooling NRE fee, which adds $3 to the /50 price and $1.50 to the /100 price. Advanced Circuits is a little expensive, but they're very good on quality and they're good at catching mistakes. Anyways, you can try going with a cheaper shop but I can only vouch for these guys.

There's also shipping prices included, maybe $1/per. In general, I double the parts cost to come up with the 'retail' cost. In this case, I'll charge $19.50. Anything less than $10 or $20 is great because $20 are considered to be stuff/food coupons, really.

## Step 10: The Process: Finishing up!

There's a bit more work to do. First, I redesign the board since I'm going with a radial inductor instead of an axial one. I actually do another etch test, to verify everything one last time. Then I tile two boards together (cheaper) and generate gerbers. I use gerbv (free software) for viewing and verifying the gerbers. On windows, I use GC-prevue I always check the boards with www.freedfm.com before I ship them off to be made. I used 4pcb.com so it's the same company but even if you don't go with 4pcb.com as your PCB manufacturer, it's a neat service. A week later (depending on your turn time) a box shows up with the circuit boards! Then I sit in front of a computer and do a lot of website stuff. I also take a lot of photos a good photo setup will make documentation easy. I have a simple 150W ECT bulb + diffuser setup at EYEBEAM. A tripod is key! See how to put it all together at: www.instructables.com/id/MintyBoost!—Small-battery-powered-USB-charger/

electronics

# How to Make a Solar iPod/iPhone Charger—a.k.a. MightyMintyBoost

By **Honus**
(www.instructables.com/id/How-to-make-a-solar-iPodiPhone-charger-aka-Might/)

I wanted a charger for my iPodTouch and the MintyBoost was definitely my first choice. I wanted to take it a bit further and make it not only rechargeable but also solar powered.

Apple has sold over 30 million iPodTouch/iPhone units—imagine charging all of them via solar power. . . . If every iPhone/iPodTouch sold was fully charged every day (averaging the battery capacity) via solar power instead of fossil fuel power we would save approximately 50.644gWh of energy, roughly equivalent to 75,965,625 lbs. of CO2 in the atmosphere per year. Granted that's a best case scenario (assuming you can get enough sunlight per day and approximately 1.5 lbs. CO2 produced per kWh used.) Of course, that doesn't even figure in all the other iPods, cell phones, PDAs, microcontrollers (I use it to power my Arduino projects) and other USB devices that can be powered by this charger—one little solar cell charger may not seem like it can make a difference but add all those millions of devices together and that's a lot of energy!

There are some really nice features about this charger:

It's solar powered!

It's small.

Large battery capacity—3.7v @2000mAh

On board charger charges via solar, USB or wall wart. Accepts input power from 3.7v to 7v.

Remove the solar cell after charging and you have a nice compact USB power supply.

Unplug the solar cell and use the Velcro to secure the MightyMintyBoost inside a backpack or messenger bag—now plug in a larger solar cell attached to your bag for even faster charging. Using a slightly larger solar cell (6v/250mAh) you can generate enough power to fully charge an iPhone in about 5.5 hours and an iPodTouch in 4 hours.

Safety note and general disclaimer: Be careful cutting the Altoids tin as it can have some really sharp edges—file them smooth if necessary. Assemble this at your own risk—while it is really easy to build, if you mess something up there is the potential to damage the electronic device you are trying to charge. Be careful in your assembly and soldering work and follow good safety practices. Only use a type of battery charger specifically designed for the type of battery you are using.

## Step 1: Tools and Materials

Here's what you'll need to build your own MightyMintyBoost:

**Tools**
- Soldering iron
- Scissors
- Wire cutters
- Pliers (or multi-tool)
- Multimeter
- Metal shears
- Clear packing tape

**Materials**
- MintyBoost kit from adafruit.com
- Lithium polymer battery charger
- 3.7v 2000mAh Lithium Polymer battery

- JST connector/wire
- Small solar cell
- 2" × 3" adhesive backed Velcro
- Small double sided adhesive squares
- Altoids tin

Adafruit now also sells all the parts you need to make this a bit more mighty. Have a look at: www.adafruit.com/blog/2010/07/09/how-to-make-a-solar-mintyboost-a-solar-power-charger-for-your-gadgets/

Adafruit recently introduced a new LiPo charger that is specifically designed for solar charging that has much better performance. It's not as small but the performance gains would make it worth it. Have a look and read about the design at www.adafruit.com/products/390.

### Some Notes

The single cell Lithium Polymer charger can accept input power that ranges from 3.7 to 7v maximum. When the cell reaches full charge the charger will automatically switch to trickle charging. When charging using the mini USB port, the charging current is limited to 100mA. When charging using the barrel plug jack, the charging current is limited to 280mA.

The solar cell maxes out at approximately 5v @ 100mA in bright sunlight. If you need faster charging simply use a larger solar cell—a 6v cell @ 250mA would work very well and they are easily obtainable and inexpensive. I used the size of solar cell that I did because I wanted it to be super compact.

assemble—even a complete novice can do it. Instead of connecting the battery holder in the kit, we're going to solder a JST connector to the MintyBoost PCB. This tiny connector will then allow the MintyBoost circuit to connect to the Lithium Polymer battery charger circuit. Make sure you get the polarity correct! Test the MintyBoost by connecting the battery pack (make sure the battery pack has a charge) and charger circuit. The MintyBoost connects to the connector marked SYS on the charger board and the lithium polymer battery connects to the connector marked GND. Now cut a notch in the Altoids tin for the USB port and use some double sided adhesive to mount the PCB to the Altoids tin.

### Step 2: Add the Battery and Charger

Now cut a notch out of the other side of the Altoids tin to fit the charger and secure the charging circuit to the bottom of the Altoids tin with double sided adhesive. Reconnect the battery and the MintyBoost PCB to the charging circuit. Make sure nothing on the bottom of either one of the circuit boards is touching the bottom of the Altoids tin.

### Step 1: Build the Minty Boost Kit

First build the MIntyBoost kit according to its instructions. It's really easy to

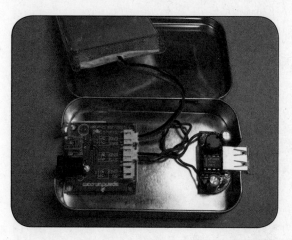

electronics

## Step 3: Add the Solar Cell

There are a couple of different ways to connect the solar cell. The first is by simply shortening the connector leads and plugging the barrel plug into the barrel jack on the charging circuit.

The second method is to replace the connector with another JST connector and plug it into the third connector marked 5v on the charging circuit. I didn't have another JST connector handy so I just soldered a salvaged two pronged connector to the charging circuit where there are two open pins on the 5v line.

Using the second method certainly is a bit cleaner since you don't have the big barrel plug sticking out of the side of the tin.

UPDATE—Since the original charging circuit has been discontinued, the best way to connect the new version Sparkfun LiPo charger is to splice a mini USB cable to the solar cell wires so it can plug directly into the charger. There is a simple guide on how to do this at http://ladyada.net/make/solarlipo/

Now attach the solar cell to the top of the Altoids tin using some 2" wide Velcro. I wrapped the battery pack with a layer of clear packing tape to help protect it. Then the battery pack is simple set down on top of the two circuit boards—it's a near perfect fit.

Now set your MightyMintyBoost out in the bright sun and charge it up! You should see a little red LED on the charger board light up. Once it's fully charged connect your iPod/iPhone/USB powered device and enjoy!

## Step 4: FAQ and Additional Info

Here's a list of frequently asked questions:

Q: Is it possible to overcharge the Lithium Polymer battery?

A: No—the charger will automatically switch to trickle charging and then shut off.

Q: Is it possible to drain the Lithium Polymer battery completely and damage it?

A: No—the battery has its own low voltage cut off circuitry that will prevent it from completely discharging—the low voltage cut off is around 2.8v

Q: How long will it take to fully charge the Lithium Polymer battery and how long will it take to charge my iPod/iPhone?

A: How long it will take to fully charge depends on the amount of sunlight available but as a rough guesstimate it would take around 20 hours using the small solar cell in direct sunlight. Using a larger solar cell could easily take half if not one third the amount of time. Those same figures would apply if you were charging it over USB or using a wall wart power supply. Charging your iPod is much faster. How fast it does it depends on your device's battery capacity. An iPod Touch has a 1000mAh battery so it should fully charge it in around 2 hours. A 3G iPhone has a 1150mAh battery so it will take slightly longer, and a 2G iPhone has a 1400mAh battery, so it will take around 3 hours.

Q: The Lithium Polymer charger has an input voltage range of 3.7v minimum to 7v maximum—what if I want to use a higher output solar cell for faster charging?

A: To use a solar cell with a voltage output greater than 7v, you need a voltage regulator to drop the voltage to a level that the charger can handle. You could use a 7805 voltage regulator to limit the output to +5v—they only cost about $1.50 and are very simple to wire up. The 7805 will give you a fixed +5v and is usually good up to 1A current. You could also use a LM317T which is an adjustable regulator, but it would involve a bit more circuitry to use. Some people also use diodes to drop voltage, since many diodes have a voltage drop of .7v. There's a lot more info here: http://en.wikipedia.org/wiki/Linear_regulator. The other option would be to use a 6v/250mA solar panel. This will stay within the current input range and voltage input range of the Lithium Polymer charger. Remember that you can also connect smaller solar cells in parallel to increase the available current—two 5v/100mA solar cells connected together in parallel will give an output of 5v @200mA.

Q: How would I connect the more powerful charger—there doesn't appear to be a clear way to do this?

A: To use the more powerful 1A charger you would need to wire a two way switch to the battery so that in one position the battery would be connected to the charger and in the other position the battery would be connected to the MintyBoost circuit.

Q: Will this work with USB devices other than iPods and iPhones?

A: You bet! There's a list here: www.ladyada.net/make/mintyboost/

Q: Won't the inside of the Altoids tin short out the circuit?

A: No—using double sided foam tape to mount the circuit boards keeps the bottom of the board from coming into contact with the inside bottom of the tin. If you're really worried you can cover the inside bottom of the tin with clear packing tape.

Q: How much does this cost? Can I build it for less? Is it cost effective?

A: If you buy everything as listed it would cost $70.75 (not including the Altoids tin or shipping.) If you wanted to scratch build it using the MintyBoost PCB from Adafruit, building your own charging circuit, and supplying your own parts from various sources you can save quite a bit. Both the charging circuit and the MintyBoost circuit are available online—just go to the web pages listed in the tools and materials section—they're also listed at the bottom of this page. Both Maxim and Linear Technology supply free samples (according to their websites) of their ICs so you just need to provide all the other bits (available from places like Mouser and Digikey.) Using a slightly smaller solar cell and a 2200mAh battery it is possible to build it for a lot less. After adding up the small parts for the MintyBoost circuit, a small blank PCB for the charging circuit (you would have to etch the board yourself) and a mini USB connector, you could conceivably build this for around $21.00 (not including shipping or an Altoids tin). It wouldn't be exactly the same of course, but it would be functionally the same. I don't know if the 2200mAh battery would fit into an Altoids tin either. It would be a LOT more work of course, and there could be a fair bit of troubleshooting if you're not experienced in building these types of circuits or soldering surface mount components. So is it cost effective? Absolutely—it just depends on the amount of work you want to do. Either way, you get a very useful and versatile solar powered charger.

electronics

# LED Chess Set

## By Tetranitrate
(www.instructables.com/id/LED-Chess-Set/)

It all started with an idea I had many years ago.

I had just picked up a cheap-o glass chess set at my local arcade for the low low price of only 15,000 tickets. The novelty of playing with glass pieces quickly wore off, and I wondered how I could make it better. The thought of illuminating the set seemed very appealing, but there were so many different ways that could be done.

I could put alternating colored lights under the board following the checkerboard pattern. The light would shine up through the glass board and make the pieces glow. The problem with this design is that the pieces would change color with each move, and (since the difference between the two sides is not black / white but frosted / clear) this would make game play somewhat confusing.

I could put a small battery and light inside of each piece, so the two sides would each be different colors. This would probably be the simplest way to get glowing pieces; however, this design is not without its problems. The batteries would need to be replaced. Their lifespan could be extended if a small sensitive on/off switch, activated by the chess piece being in an upright position, were added. This would complicate the design though, and still only be a temporary solution, as the batteries would need to be replaced eventually. This design (with the switch) does have one more advantage. It gives the chess pieces two states, on and off. I liked the idea of the chess pieces being illuminated while they were in play (upright and on the board), and dark while they were out (dead and off the board).

The final design I chose was to have each piece contain an LED that would be powered by a conductive board. The board is plugged into an outlet, so there is no need

to worry about the power running out. While the pieces are on the board they are "live" and illuminated, and while off the board they are "dead" and dark.

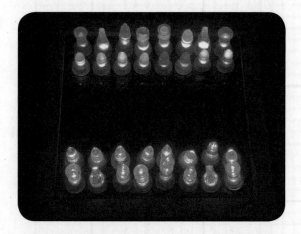

## Step 1: How it Works

Sixteen blue LEDs and sixteen green LEDs are glued inside the hollow recesses in the base of each chess piece. The positive contacts for the LEDs are wired to copper washers attached to the base of each chess piece. The negative contacts for the LEDs are clipped to be made flush with the rest of the base. A conductive chessboard is made from a sheet of copper. The sheet is wired to the positive lead from a power transformer. Insulated holes through the center of each square on the board allow magnets to pass through. The magnets connect and hold a negatively wired steel plate underneath to the negative leads from the LEDs.

## Step 2: Materials

This project uses a wide range of materials and tools, so I separated the two lists into individual steps. The materials include:

- Glass chess set—I bought a couple so if I broke some of the pieces I would have extra. The chess pieces should have a small cavity in the bottom covered by some circular felt stickers, to prevent them from scratching the glass chess board.
- LEDs—Twenty 5mm blue and twenty 5mm green LEDs. I ordered mine from superbrightleds.com.
- Magnets—I used ⅛" tall ¹⁄₁₆" diameter cylindrical neodymium magnets. Since

three were used in each square on the board, 192 were needed all together. Of course the magnets could be ³⁄₈" tall and only 64 would be needed.

- Wood—A thin sheet (~¼" thick) with the same area as the copper plate, used both as an insulator and as a structural backing for the copper. Thicker pieces of wood are also needed to make the final box/enclosure for the chess board, but the dimensions do not matter too much, as almost any scrap wood will do.
- Copper plate—A square copper sheet around ¹⁄₁₆" or ¹⁄₃₂" thick, and with an area at least that the size of the original chess board. I found mine on eBay.
- Copper washers—The outer circumference should be the same size as the outer circumference of the base of the chess pieces. The inner diameter is not as important, but should be large enough to easily wire an LED through.
- Steel plate—Should be exactly the same dimensions (length and width, thickness doesn't matter too much, but around ¹⁄₁₆" or ¹⁄₃₂" would be ideal) as the original chess board (only the 8 × 8 grid of squares, not counting any extra border). If each square on the chess board is 1" by 1" then the steel plate should be 8" by 8".
- Copper foil tape—Again the exact specs change depending on the size of your chess board, but a few feet (~6') of tape should be good. The width of the tape should be half the width of one square on the chess board (1" chess board squares=½" copper foil tape)
- Acrylic sheets—It doesn't really need to be acrylic, but that was the building material available to me at the time. One square will be to sandwich the steel and copper plates together, and to hold the wires in place. The other square I used as a bottom to the chess board box.
- Power supply—I used a wall wart with a 120V AC input and 3V 300mA DC output to power the chess board.
- Gaffers tape—To tape stuff in place
- Glue/epoxy—To hold the copper plate to the wood sheet. Wood glue is also used to make the box.

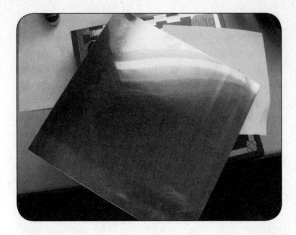

## Step 3: Tools

There are many different tools needed to make this project exactly the way I describe it. That being said, this project can most likely be completed without most of the tools I list. Improvisation is the name of the game.

- Sandblaster—You can either use a professional "real" sandblaster, or you can make your own using a paint sprayer, rubber hose, and bucket of garnet following Star's instructable. I highly recommend making your own. It is dirty, it is simple, and it is fun.
- Soldering iron—Used for doing the obvious.
- Deburring tool—Used for burring De's. Deez what? Deez nuts.
- Drill and bit set—Some carbide tips are useful if drilling out the glass chess pieces is necessary.
- Multimeter (optional)—Used to measure the voltage given off by the board, once constructed.
- Dremel and bits—Various dremmeling needs
- Steel wool—To polish the copper plate
- Metal file—For breaking out of prison, and to help with deburring.

## Step 4: Starting the Copper Plate

The copper plate is the positive (+) contact for the chess pieces. I had a difficult time thinking of the best way to get the checkerboard pattern on a single conductive surface. The plate could easily be divided into 64 uniform squares, but that would look terrible. I briefly considered using two separate conductive metals (copper & steel,

electronics

or similar), and making a checkerboard pattern by alternating squares of them, but that would take too much time and effort. I finally decided that sandblasting, the same technique used to make the original glass chessboard (I think, although it may have been chemical etching), would be the best way to get the pattern down on a conductive metal surface. Sandblasting a checkerboard pattern into the copper sheet will result in 32 squares with the original shiny copper gleam, and 32 frosty squares that were exposed to the abrasive. The hardest and most time consuming part about this step was not sandblasting, but setting up a stop.

A stop is what prevents the abrasive material from etching/frostifying unintended areas of the plate. There are many ways of setting up a stop. The technique I describe involves using a large format printer with a vinyl sticker medium. While this method is probably inaccessible/unfeasible for most of the people reading this, the entire process should not be too hard to replicate with common household tools and materials (printer, x-acto knife, tape, and, at most, a trip to Kinkos). Like always, the pictures say a thousand words, and are much more descriptive then I could ever hope to be with written instructions).

Polish the copper sheet—Polish the nicer of the two faces of the copper sheet with some steel wool, so that it is shiny. Shiny things are fun. Create a checkerboard pattern file—Using Illustrator, I made a checkerboard pattern file with the same dimensions as the original glass chessboard. The printer I used was able to cut the lines on the adhesive sticker medium, so, once printed, all I needed to do was peel off every other square from the pattern. If you do not have access to a printer with automatic cutting then you can use a regular printer to print out the pattern onto an adhesive medium, and trace the lines with an x-acto knife. The vinyl sticker paper I used was a perfect material for this job because it can be peeled off without leaving behind any residue, but it is strong enough to stay attached to the copper while being

sandblasted. Make sure to test your material before using it, otherwise you will either end up with adhesive residue left behind on the copper plate, or a fuzzy edged out of focus looking checkerboard pattern (The out of focus appearance will happen if the edges of the square stickers begin to peel up while being sandblasted).

Transfer the adhesive checkerboard stickers to the copper plate—I used a large sheet of transfer paper to get the vinyl sticker pattern squared perfectly with the copper plate. Transfer paper is just like very large masking tape. If transfer paper is unavailable, overlapped masking tape can be used instead. Overlap the tape so that it so it forms a large square which is a bit bigger than the checkerboard sticker. Place the non-adhesive side of the checkerboard sticker against the adhesive side of the transfer paper, so that both sheets are sticky side up. Remove the backing on the checkerboard sticker, and peel away every other square. Lay the checkerboard sticker/transfer paper combo on a hard flat surface, sticky side up (duh). Carefully lay the copper sheet directly over the checkerboard sticker, so that the sheet aligns with it perfectly, and press down firmly. When you are confident that sticker has completely adhered to the copper sheet, flip it over and peel away the transfer paper at a sharp angle. Make sure all the checkerboard pattern stickers remain completely stuck to the copper sheet.

Sandblasting—By far the most fun part of this step. If all the preparation was done correctly, the process of sandblasting is hard to screw up, and provides very impressive visible results. One of the good things about sandblasting (copper at least) is that it is hard to overdo it. Unless the stickers start to fall off, it is almost impossible to "overfrost" the copper. You will reach a certain level of "frostiness" and will not be able to go beyond it. It is possible to "underfrost" though, and once you take the stickers off it is hard to go back, so just be sure that every exposed part of the board is evenly blasted. From this point on you should probably handle the copper plate by the sides, as fingerprints have a tendency of turning into nasty black smudges.

## Step 5: Drilling the Copper Plate

The purpose of this step is to get holes into the copper board that will allow the negative (-) contact points for the chess pieces to pass through the copper plate. If you know a more effective or better way of getting holes through the copper than what I describe here, feel free to use your own technique. Mark off the center point of each square—The holes will go through the center of each individual square on the board. There are many ways of marking off the center points.

I decided to draw an X on one of the remaining unused square stickers, line that square up with the squares on the board, and poke it with something that would leave a mark. A crossbow bolt is what I had, so a crossbow bolt is what I used. Do this for all 64 squares on the board. Drill through the board—The goal is to get ¼"; holes through the center of each square. I used a hand-held drill with regular bits to do this.

Before drilling, clamp the copper plate down to a flat piece of scrap wood, so the bit will have something to drill into once it passes through the copper. The scrap wood will help prevent the copper sheet from bending out of place while it is being drilled. It is best to use clamps with rubber feet, so they do not scratch the copper. If a metal clamp must be used, put a piece of cardboard between the foot and the copper.

Keeping the drill perfectly perpendicular to the plate, drill out all 64 holes. Clean up the plate—After drilling, many of the holes will have burrs on them. Remove these either with a metal file, or a deburring tool. I found the deburring tool to be much more effective . . . I wonder why.

## Step 6: Making the Board

This step describes adding a wooden backing to the copper plate. The backing will provide both structural support and act as an insulator between the (+) copper plate and the (-) magnets/steel plate.

The wood—Like everything else in this project the specifications depend on exactly what parts you used and how you used them. If you happened to use thicker copper, then it may not need structural support, and a small veneer insulator backing would probably work. The copper I used was thin and pretty flexible, so I needed to back it with a sturdy piece of wood. I had this pretty nice ¼" thick polished wood laying around, so that is what I used.

Prepare it—I lay the copper sheet on top of the wood, and traced the area out with a fine tip sharpie. I then cut off the excess wood with a chop saw, and smoothed the sides with a belt sander. Scuff up the back of the copper plate and one side of the wood.

Glue them together—I wish I had put more thought into this step before I went ahead and got epoxy everywhere. Almost any method of gluing the copper and wood

electronics

395

together would have been better than what I did. I just spread/mixed the epoxy out on some aluminum foil, and smeared the back of the copper sheet and the wood in it. Doing this allowed epoxy to go through the holes in the copper plate and mess up the front. If I were to redo it, I would cover the front with masking tape or transfer paper to completely prevent any glue from going through the holes (On second thought, the front of the copper plate should probably be shielded with some sort of adhesive cover right after drilling. Doing this will help prevent scratches and smudges, and will also keep the glue from going through the holes). I would have also painted on the glue on the back of the copper plate to prevent it from ever even getting near the holes. When both the copper sheet and piece of wood have glue on them, press the two faces together and hold/clamp firmly until they set.

Drilling the wood—After the glue has dried completely it is time to drill through the wood. The diameter of the drill bit should be the same as the diameter of the magnet. The magnets I was using were 1/16", so the bit I used was also 1/16". Drill holes through the wood in the center of the hole in the copper. Place the magnets in the holes to make sure they fit.

## Step 7: Wiring the Board

I thought of three different ways of wiring the board before I finally settled on the one I will describe in this step. My first idea was to individually wire each of the 64 squares on the board to a power supply, but I figured there had to be an easier way. My second idea was to wire up eight strips of metal in series, have the magnets hold them in place, and connect the very ends of the metal strips to the power supply. My third idea is what I actually used.

Preparing the steel plate—Thoroughly clean one side of the steel plate. Place magnets in each hole on the board. I needed columns of magnets three tall, to get through the combined thickness of the copper plate and wood backing. Place the steel plate squarely underneath the wood (The clean side of the steel plate should face the wood and copper). The magnets should jump from the holes in the wood to the steel plate. Their location on the steel plate will indicate where to lay rows of copper tape.

Laying the tape—Cut eight strips of copper tape to the length of the steel plate. Lay them down on the clean side of the plate directly under the location of the magnets. Cut two longer strips, and lay them down so they overlap with the tops and bottoms of the eight rows. These two strips should be long enough to wrap around to the back of the plate.

Wiring the (-) plate—Cut two 2' segments of wire. Solder them to the copper foil that overlaps on the back of the steel plate. They should be soldered on opposite corners of the plate. Optional: To help keep the wire from pulling the copper tape off the board, duct tape the wire to the plate a few inches away from the solder points.

Wiring the copper board—Clamp the copper sheet/wood to a sturdy work surface, and drill two holes into opposite corners. Make sure to drill into the copper and then through the wood. If you do it the other way, you risk pushing or bending the copper sheet away from the wood. The diameter of the holes should be just large enough to allow the wires to pass through. The holes should also be in the two corners that are not occupied by the wires connected to the steel plate. Put the ends of the wires through the holes and solder them to the copper plate.

Putting the pieces together—Put magnets into each square on the copper plate. Place the steel plate on the bottom of the wood, so that all the magnets line up with the rows of copper tape. The magnets will snap to the steel plate, and (as long as you lined everything up correctly) the magnets should sandwich the copper foil tape. The magnets will also hold the steel plate to the bottom of the wood/copper sheet.

Optional—Although unnecessary, I found this final step part very helpful. Cut a sheet of acrylic to the same size as the chessboard (thickness of the acrylic does not matter). Line up the sheet of acrylic with the bottom of the chessboard, and mark off where the four wires come from the board. Drill out these spots with bit the same diameter as the wires, and "thread" the wires through the holes in the acrylic. This will help keep the wires and the steel plate in place, as well as organizing all the "functional" parts of the chess set into a single package.

## Step 8: Starting the Box

The main purpose of the box is to shelve and protect the chessboard, but it also helps cover all the wires and even out the base. The box I made for this project was produced entirely out of scrap wood.

Prepping the wood—Four even pieces of wood, each slightly longer in length than a side of the copper plate, are needed to form the sides of the box. Measure the combined thickness of the copper/wood plate, and cut a shelf of that thickness into the wood. The shelf should be as high up the wood as possible, but have a thick enough overhang that it will not snap or break when

the chess board is being pushed into it. The reason for the overhang is to hide the two wires soldered to the board. Cut the ends of the four pieces of wood at 45 degree angles. On two of the pieces of wood, shave a bit of the underside of the overhang and cut a small groove into the shelf, so the soldered wires have room to fit in when the box is closed.

Putting the pieces together—Lay out a strip of painters tape sticky side up. The length of the tape should be a few inches longer than the combined length of the wood sides. Lay the four wood sides down on the tape, making sure to line up the orientation of the two notched sides with the two wired corners of the board. Put the board into one of the sides, and put wood glue on each of the 45 degree angle cuts. Fold the side pieces around the board, and use the excess tape to hold them in place. Square all the corners (using a rubber mallet if need be), and place clamps across all four sides. After the glue has set remove the clamps and tape.

## Step 9: Wiring the Box

This step describes the process of connecting the (+) copper plate and the (−) steel plate to the power supply.

Drill—Drill a hole (of the same diameter as the wire from the power supply) into the side of the box. Put the wire through the hole, strip an inch and a half off the end, and separate the two different polarity wires. Using a multimeter, determine and mark which wire is the positive and which is the negative.

electronics

397

Solder—Solder the two wires from the steel plate to the negative wire from the power supply, and solder the two wires from the copper sheet to the positive wire from the power supply. Cover the soldered bits with electrical tape to prevent shorting.

Tape—Tape everything to the underside of the steel plate, or (if you made the optional square to organize the wires) tape everything to the bottom of the acrylic. Gaffers tape is always a good choice.

Test—Using an LED, test the board to make sure that it is wired correctly and working.

## Step 10: Finalize the Box

The box is pretty much done at this point, so this step is somewhat optional. In this step I will describe the process of adding an acrylic bottom to the box that will be held in place with magnets.

Creating a ledge—I used a milling machine to create a ledge on the underside of the box. If you have access to a milling machine and choose to use this method, make sure to clamp both sides of the box, so it stays nice and solid during the milling. If you do not have access to a milling machine, then you can use a dremel, or some similar tool to work away a ledge deep enough to fit a sheet of acrylic in.

Make the bottom—I cut and fit a sheet of acrylic to the same area as the inside of the ledge. I had a handful of magnets left over after wiring the board, so I decided that is what I would use to hold the bottom in place. I turned the box chess face down,

and placed the acrylic bottom into the ledge. Using a drill bit with the same diameter as the magnets, I drilled two holes in each corner, straight through the acrylic into the wood.

Magnetize the bottom—Eight holes in the acrylic and eight holes in the wood makes for a total of sixteen magnets. I glued the magnets in with some gel super glue, alternating the polarity, so the bottom could only fit in one way. I cut up an old hard drive ribbon cable and glued it to the acrylic to make a pull tab for the bottom.

## Step 11: Preparing the Pieces

There is really not much to this step.

Remove felt—The chess pieces probably have a black felt circle on the bottom to prevent glass on glass action. Remove this piece of felt. Remove any remaining adhesive using some acetone.

Test depth—The chess pieces should have a small cavity underneath the felt. I am pretty sure this is an artifact from the molding process. None of the cavities are the same depth, so you should take an LED and test each piece to make sure the cavity is deep enough to completely hold it. If it is not, you have two options. You can either spend your time carefully drilling out the piece with a quarter inch carbide tipped drill bit, or you can buy another set. After drilling a few pieces, I figured it would just be easier to get another set since they are so cheap.

electronics

## Step 12: Making the Pieces

When I purchased the original copper sheet for the board I decided to buy a spare, in case one was jenky. It turns out that it was a good idea since one of them was kind of crummy. I made the board from the nicer of the two, but then I had an extra sheet lying around. I figure instead of buying very specifically sized conductive washers for this last step, I would waterjet the extra copper sheet I had into washers. No access to a waterjet? No worries, just buy some copper washers online. They have very specific sizes.

Gluing the LEDs—Using the gel superglue I glued sixteen blue LEDs into the clear pieces (I chose blue for the clear pieces because it would resemble ice), and sixteen green LEDs into the frosted pieces. While gluing, try to make sure the negative lead (the longer one) is directly in the center of the piece because it will be making contact with the magnet that is in the center of the square.

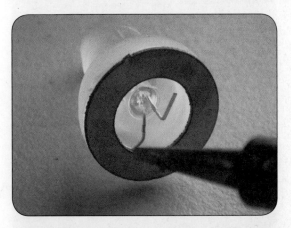

Trim the leads—Bend the positive lead to the rim of the base and clip the excess. Clip the negative lead so that it is just slightly extending past the bottom of the piece, and bend the excess at a 90 degree angle, so it will have some area that comes in contact with the magnet.

Glue the washers on—I covered ¾ of the bottom of the chess piece with glue. The remaining quarter was the area near the positive lead. I left it unglued because I did not want to risk ruining the connection to the washer. Firmly press the washers onto the glue (but do not rotate!) and let sit undisturbed until the glue is dry.

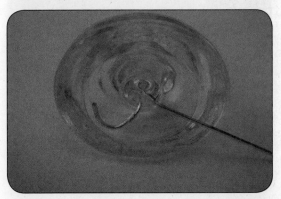

Solder the lead—Solder the positive lead from the LED to the inner rim of the copper washer. This will be a delicate, slow going operation, but be patient and do each one carefully.

YOU ARE FINISHED!!!—Plug the board in, and put the pieces on it to make sure they all work. Sit back and bask in your awesomeness which is a direct result of my awesomeness.

**electronics**

## Hand Lights
By **Grathio** Steve Hoefer of
Grathio Labs
(www.instructables.com/id/Hand-
Lights/)

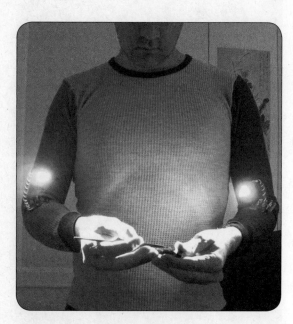

If you work with your hands and want to have more light where you're working, these hand lights (okay, forearm lights) work great and are pretty simple to make.

I like to work on stuff in my living room, because that's where all the comfortable furniture and the good music system is. Unfortunately there's not a ton of light.

So I made these. They'll give you light right where you hands are, wherever you move them. Wearing one on both arms makes sure there's always enough light on everything, and they're pretty light and comfy.

These instructions are for making one, but you'll probably want two.

### Total Cost
About $8 to $12, including the batteries.
### Parts
- 1 Battery holder for 3 AAA batteries.
- 3 AAA batteries.
- 1 mini toggle switch.

- 18 inches of 2 conductor stranded wire. 20 gauge or so.
- 18 inches of Velcro. Hook or loop.
- 1 inch of Velcro (the mate of the Velcro above)
- 3 White LEDs: (I used 3, 7000mcd 3.5v, 25mA LEDs, though fewer, brighter LEDs would work too.)
- 3 resistors, 47 ohm. (Or whatever your LEDs need.)
- 18 inches of 9 or 11 ½ gauge aluminum wire. AKA armature wire.
- Solder Hot glue
- Electrical tape/heat shrink tubing.

### Tools
- Soldering iron.
- Hot glue gun.
- Wire cutter/strippers.
- Pliers.
- Scissors.

## Step 1: Collect All Your Parts and Tools

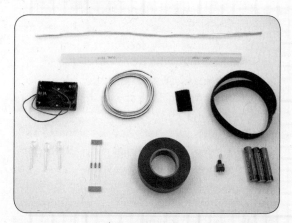

## Step 2: Create the Support Arm
First I put little pieces of electrical tape over the visible metal bits of the battery holder to prevent shorts from our armature wire. Don't use too much tape because it'll conflict with the hot glue we use later. (You want to apply hot glue to the plastic, not to the tape.) Skip this step if you're using a less cheap battery case. Take the armature wire and bend it around 3 ⅓ sides of the battery case. It should generally be snug, but leave a small (⅛") gap along the "inside back". That's the side that will be

closest to your chest and closest to your shoulder. That gap is where you'll secure the adjustable strap, so make sure your Velcro strap will fit through it. Note that this one is a right-handed light. For a left-handed one wrap the wire the other way. When you're happy with it, hot glue it in place. Make sure you don't put any glue on the part where the strap will go. And don't get any glue inside or you'll have a hard time getting batteries in.

end of the LED goes to the +, short to −.If they all check out then solder the three LEDs together. (Or if you got one big, bright LED you skip this step.) Solder all the free ends of the LEDs together along with one side of your two conductor wire. Similarly connect the free ends of the resistors together with the other strand of your wire. Apply some electrical tape or shrink tubing to prevent short circuits. Now would be a good time to test it again and make sure they all light up and you don't have any short circuits.

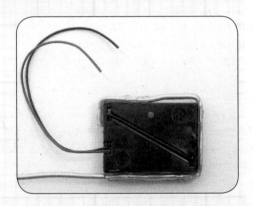

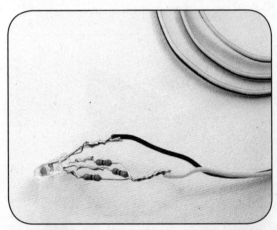

## Step 3: Wire up Your LEDS

Solder the resistors to your LEDs. Since 4.5 volts is too much for most LEDs you need to put a resistor in there to keep them from burning out. In most cases a 47 ohm resister on each will work. Use an online LED resistor calculator to be sure. (The values for my LEDS: 4.5 volts, 3.5 forward volts, 25mA forward current, and 3 LEDs.) It doesn't matter if you put them on the long or short end of the LED, just put them all on the same end so you don't get mixed up and have to spend 20 minutes desoldering them. (Like I did.) Now would be a good time to check them with your battery pack to make sure you've got it right. The long

## Step 4: Create the Velcro Strap

Make sure you have enough Velcro to fit around your forearm with a several inches to spare. For me 15 inches was enough, but I don't spend lots of time at the gym. Hook or loop doesn't matter, as long as you have a long piece of one and a short piece (an inch or so) of the other. Hot glue one end of the long strip to the bottom of the battery enclosure.

Make sure its hook or loop side facing the battery holder. Put it on the "up the arm" end, farthest away from where the armature wire sticks out, and pointing away from our little gap we left for our strap. When the glue cools, put the strap through the strap hole we left in step one. Then hot glue the short bit near the end of the strap. Leave about ½ inch to make it easier to pull off. Glue it on the hook or loop side, not the smooth side. (You could also stitch it, but the glue gun is already hot . . .) You should now have an adjustable strap that will secure it to your arm.

## Step 5: Finish Connecting the LEDs

While you're trying the strap out, bend the remaining bit of the armature wire to a good Brontosaurus neck shape, and cut it to length. When you find a length you like, hot glue the lights in place and wrap the trailing wire around the armature a few times to keep it out of the way.

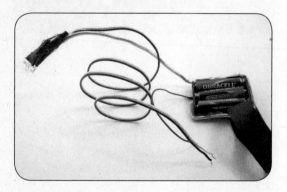

## Step 6: Connect the Switch

Note for the lazy: You can get a battery enclosure with a built in switch, or simply skip the switch and just take the batteries out to turn it off. But why wouldn't you want to add a toggle switch? Toggle switches are awesome. Connect your switch between one of the leads from the battery holder and your LEDs. Connect the other battery lead directly to the LED wire. Again check to make sure that everything is wired the right way before soldering into place. Try to keep the leads as short as possible so you don't have to worry about them catching on stuff. Hot glue the switch into place. I also covered the wire with glue to prevent shorts, keep it from catching on stuff, and because hot glue is one of the most fun ways to get first degree burns.

## Step 7: Use!

Put it on your arm and fire it up! Tweak the position of the armature wire and make the individual LEDs to make sure they direct light where you want. I wear them just below the elbow, half way between the inside and side of the arm. And lastly: Make another one, they work better in pairs. And your second one will go much faster.

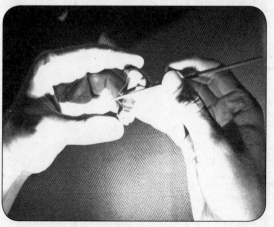

# Make a Fire Breathing Animatronic Pony

By lvl_joe

(www.instructables.com/id/Make-a-Fire-Breathing-Animetronic-Pony-from-FurRea/)

For Maker Faire Detroit 2011, I displayed a hack I made to a FurReal Friends Butterscotch Pony. My fellow LVL1 Hackers and I had taken control of the motor control system of the toy and added a flame thrower to it. It seemed to go over really well with the crowd, so I am putting up the information for anyone to make their own. Just remember that this project uses **Fire** and should only be built and operated by no less than 2 adults with appropriate experience in fire safety and proper fire safety equipment on hand.

## Get It Before You Hack It

At one time, Butterscotch and S'more ponies both sold for around $300, but they seem to be discontinued. Thankfully, there is a fairly steady stream of them showing up on Craigslist and second hand stores. I purchased my first Butterscotch off Craigslist for $20.

## What You will Need

Hardware
- FurReal Butterscotch or S'More Pony
- Arduino Mega
- Wire 18g
- Solder
- Electrical tape
- Wii nun-chuck
- Wii Nunchuck breakout adapter
- 0.1" 16-pin strip male header
- ⅛th OD ptfe tube (trade name Teflon)
- Bowden cable (brake cable for the back wheel of a bike)
- Scrap PVC tube around 3" at about 1' long
- Scrap Plexi glass

Tools
- Wire Strippers
- Razor blade
- Phillips head screwdriver
- Flat head screwdriver
- Multimeter
- Soldering Iron
- Computer to program the Micro Processor (Any OS)

## Step 1: Removing the Skin: Head First

Before you get into the really fun parts, you will need to skin your pony. I started at the head as it already has a zipper. Move the mane out of the way, and locate the zipper at the base of the neck. You will find that the zipper pull has a cap over it to prevent it from unzipping. Simply break off this cap and unzip the skin from around the head.

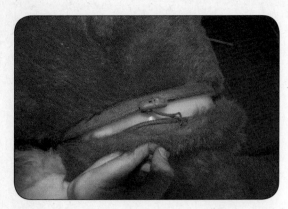

## Step 2: Removing Skin: ENT

Now we are going to remove the skin from around the face. The face is attached in 4 areas: the ears, eyes, nose, and mouth. Pull the skin up the back of the neck so you can get inside the back of the ponies head.

The ears break off easy (one was already missing when I got to this point). The other broke off when I was trying to get the skin off. This is not a problem as you can glue them back on easily. If you wish to keep the ears attached, you can cut the cloth around the ear holes with a razor. If you are OK with taking them off, a hard tug should pop them right off. Once the ears are removed, pull on the fabric where it tucks into the head. This will rip the seams, freeing it up.

Roll the skin further down, and you will get to the eyes. The fabric is sewn into the top and bottom of the eyes. Simply cut the stitches here to detach the fabric. Try to not look your pony in the eyes when you do this, as you may start feeling bad about what you are doing.

Moving down to the pony's nose, there are 2 pegs holding the rubbery snout on. One in each nostril. These slide out without much trouble, away from the body in a parallel fashion.

## Step 3: Remove Skin: Straight From the Horse's Mouth

The last step of peeling your pony's face off is to removed the skin from the mouth. The skin on the upper and lower jaw are both connected in their own way.

To remove skin from the upper jaw you just need to fold the face down until you see a horse shoe shaped piece of plastic around the mouth. It will have 4 pegs pushed up into holes with 3 legs that close around them. You will just need to bend 2 of the legs on each peg back and they will pop right out.

The bottom jaw will most likely have popped off by this point. We need to remove the jaw plastic from the rubber. It for the most part will pull off but it will take some time. I also had to cut some spots with a razor that where to fused.

After you get the lower jaw removed slide it back into the slot under the chin and glue it into place.

## Step 4: Remove Skin: The Body

Removing the skin from the body is a lot of the same. There are a few more places where they sew the fabric to the plastic. I followed the seam in most parts. just cutting a little bit of the thread and then pulling it apart.

On the underside, pull the Velcro open. In the back side where the Velcro ends you will find a zipper leading up to the tail. There will be stitches at each end holding it together but no slider. Cut the stitches and it will come unzipped. There will only be a small area holding the zipper area to the Velcro area. Cut this small bit of fabric and we will move to the front.

electronics

The front end of the Velcro has a small stitch leading to a T intersection. Unstitch this area then unstitch along both sides of the untill you get to the legs.

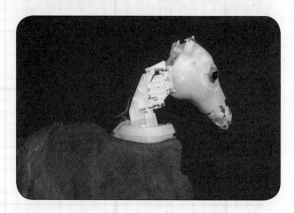

## Step 5: Removing the Skin: The Legs

There is an inner seem along each leg. Snip the stitch and tear down each of them untill you get to the feet. The feet are held on with a different fabric that is then looped around a rope inside of the hooves. Just cut around the bottom of the leg removing this other fabric and freeing the rest of the leg.

At the top of each leg you will need to remove some stitching leading around the intersection of the inner leg and the lower side of the body. When you get close to the stitches running along the bottom of the pony that you have already cut, snip away the fabric in between. You should not be able to lift the skin up all the way around the head.

## Step 6: Removing the Skin: The Neck

The very last step is to remove the part that is holding the fabric to the neck. I did

this by cutting through the lighter, fur-less fabric at the neck. After I removed it, I found that it was held on by a zip tie inside of that loop of fabric. You can do it my way, or you can insert the wire cutters into the fabric at the nap of the neck and simply cut the large zip tie. This should allow you to remove the skin completely.

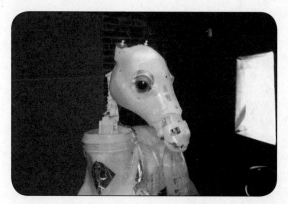

## Step 7: Removing the Face

To get to the main circuit board in the head, you need to removed the left side of the face (the pony's left, not yours) There are quite a few screws that you will need to remove to do this. There is also a clip that holds the snout onto the rest of the face. This clip was difficult to remove and I ended up marring the face a bit with a screwdriver and wire snips.

Under the face you will find that the circuit board is held in place by 4 screws. Remove these screws, as we will do most of our work from the lower side.

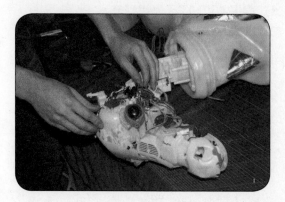

## Step 8: Getting Access to the Circuit Board in the Lower Body

I removed every screw I could find from the pony and still could not get the body open. I could not see any clips I could open, or anything else I could remove to release it, so I did the next best thing and dremeled a hole in the stomach. This ended up working out in the end as it provided a good place to put the fuel for the flame thrower. You will want the hole large enough to allow your PVC tube to just slide in.

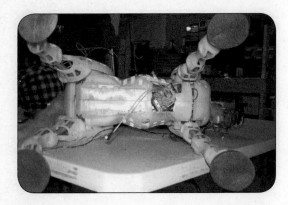

## Step 9: Cutting the Power to the Microcontroller

To take control of the pony we will cut the power and the ground to the Microcontroller that is currently controlling the pony. There are two controllers in the pony, one in the head, and one in the body. The one in the head sends commands to the one in the body so we will only be cutting power to the head, and this will take care of both.

To do this, cut the trace going to the 4th and 5th pin on the larger of the two boards sticking out at a right angle. The traces will be on the back side of the board. The 4th pin should have a white wire soldered to it. Using a razor you should be able to cut the trace without a problem.

## Step 10: Tapping Power for the Arduino

Now we need to power our Arduino, but there is no need to add another battery when we already have the 6 C cells powering the pony itself. Tapping into the power being pulled into the circuit in the pony's head will give us around 9v. I had a few 9v wall warts laying around so I cut the cable off of one with 5.5mm/2.1mm barrel jack on it. I tied this into the connectors going to the

head. You can also purchase an adapter from adafruit as that will be much easier.

## Step 11: Tapping the Lines into the Motor Control Circuit

You will need to tap into the lines coming out of the motor control circuit coming out of the micro-controllers. We will do this at 4 spots on each of the Circuit boards.

On the board in the pony's head you will need to solder your wires into R14, R15, R27, and R28.

R14 and R15 move the head up and down plus open and close the mouth.

R27 and R28 move the head move left or right as well as move the eyes and ears.

On the board in the body, you will want to solder you wires onto R10,R42 and R11,R41.

R10/42 move the head left and right

R11 Moves the tail (only one way)

R41 bobs the head up and down at the neck (moves one way around in a circle like the tail).

## Step 12: Taping into the Encoders

There are 4 encoders that will tell you the position of the head. Two of them are located in the head and 2 of them are located in the body. The two in the head are easy since you can see them when you take the pony's face off.

Solder ~2' long wire to each of these encoders. I used 18g wire.

For the encoders in the body, I was unable to find an easy way to get to them, so I cut the end off the wire. We will solder the wires from this cable right into the bread board so strip them and you are finished with them for now. Try to leave these wires as long as you can.

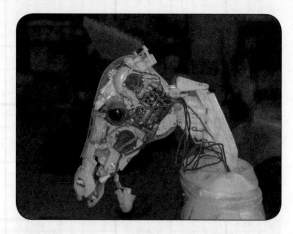

## Step 13: Getting the Motors and Sensors Connected to the Arduino

For the current code you will want to have the pins as such:

Resistor label—Pin on the Arduino
R14  Pin 23
R15  Pin 25
R27  Pin 27
R28  Pin 29
R10  Pin 37
R11  Pin 35
R41  Pin 31
R42  Pin 33

To get the pins connected I soldered them to the end of .1 male header.

## Step 13: Connecting a Wii Nunchuck into the System

Now you will need to connect the Wii nunchuck breakout board from adafruit. If you want to run the wii nunchuck at 5v you can just use the .1 pitched pins that are on the breakout board. You can set the input pin 19 as 5v output and pin 18 as input. I connected mine with wires and chose to play it safe by running it at 3.3v.

On your mega, connect it as such:
Gnd: Ground
3.3v: 3.3v
Data: 20
Clk: 21

## Step 14: The Arduino Code

The code (found at instructables.com/id/Make-a-Fire-reathing-Animetronic-Pony-from-FurRea/) should be loaded on the arduino mega using the arduino IDE. Before doing so, you will need to put the modified wii nunchuck file into your arduino libraries folder. It should be in the root of your arduino IDE install. It should look something like "C:\User\joe\arduino-0022\libraries\WiiChuck\WiiChuck.h." Make sure that you put it inside of a folder named WiiChuck so that it can be found by the Arduino. After you load this on your Arduino, you should be ready to start moving the pony around.

The sketch has to bit bang the PWM sent to the motor controls as there are too many pins to do it on PWM pins. I think it runs too slow for the Arduino to do it with hardware anyways.

**Current Controls Work Like This**

• Push the joystick one way and the head will start moving that way from a dead stop.
• Move it the opposite direction from the way it is currently moving and it will stop moving.
• Move it up or down and it will move that way from a dead stop.
• Move the opposite direction then the head is moving and it will stop moving.
• C moves the tail.
• Z shakes the head.
• The mouth moves when the head is moving up and down.
• The ears and eyes move when the head is shaking.

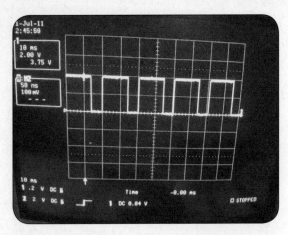

## Step 15: Getting the Fuel to the Head

The fuel we are using for the fire is automobile starter fuel.

To attach the fuel source, we will connect one spray cap from the starter fluid to a Teflon tube that runs from the hole in the belly up along the neck and then out just over the nose where we will place our igniter. The tube will not be the right size to fit into the cap so use a drill bit that is the same diameter as the tube to bore it out until it fits.

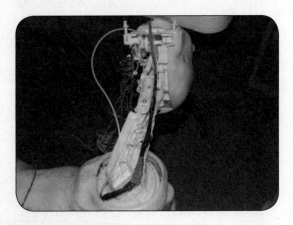

## Step 16: Building an Ignition System

The ignition system is an electric grill igniter that has had the leads on it extended. Just over the mouth (or wherever you want the fire to come out) we have attached a metal plate that is connected to one lead of the igniter. The Teflon fuel tube is epoxied right over this lead. Finally, the other lead off of the igniter is connected to a wire on the other side of the fuel tube, so that the spark will arc across the tube.

When modifying the igniter you will want to connect one 6 foot wire to each lead. Ours had 4 leads. If you have the same type you can put electrical tape over the other two so that they do not spark inside of the body. You will also need to insulate the leads that you extended with tape, shrink tube, or hot glue to keep it from sparking at the igniter rather than at your extension leads.

## Step 17: Remote Fuel Trigger

The remote fuel trigger uses a bowden cable to pull down on a sheet of hinged plexiglass, which pushes the spray nozzle on the fuel can. A bowden cable is the type of cable that is used in bike brakes. This allows it to be flexible in the middle, but still allows it to transfer force in relation to its end points.

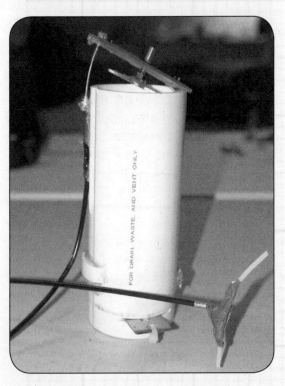

# The Plasma Speaker

By **Plasmana**

(www.instructables.com/id/Build-A-Plasma-Speaker/)

A plasma speaker is a device that generates a high voltage electrical arc that makes purple light and music! Without any speakers or any moving parts! Sounds too good to be true? Well, you're wrong, the high voltage arc really does 'sing' by vibrating in the air. (Of course, you will need to give the device musical audio for it to work.)

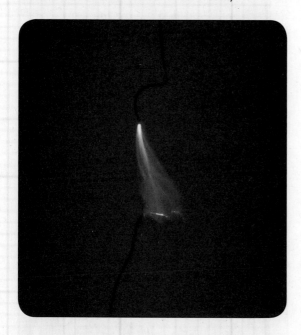

## Step 1: The Dangers You Must Know

A plasma speaker is no toy . . .

### Health Hazard

Unlike the ordinary speakers, the plasma speaker are dangerous high voltage device. Do NOT attempt to build this device unless you know what you are doing. And do NOT even attempt to build one if you have heart problems, a weak heart, or are wearing a pacemaker, because one little shock from this thing can put you out.

I am not responsible for any injuries or deaths caused by this device.

Why should you know all of this? It is because you ONLY live once.

If you think that you shouldn't build one, just watch movies of it working instead, much better than risking your life to build and operate one.

If you think you are okay to build one without killing yourself, then move on to the next step.

### Hazard to Electronics

Since the plasma speaker generates high voltages, there is a chance there will be high voltage spikes on the low voltage side of the device, which can get onto the audio line and damage (or destroy) the player.

## Step 2: Schematics

The schematic was quite complex and buying four MOSFET's is a little too expensive for me.

So I simplified the design to using one MOSFET.

I just recently found out that the manufacturer who makes the components sells the best quality MOSFET to other manufactures and sells the poorer quality ones to the whole sellers and retailers. For this project, the best grade MOSFET is critical, and it can only be gotten by salvaging old electronic devices, unless you are willing to pay for thousands to the manufacturers for the components.

## Step 3: So, How does it Actually Work?

Okay, you must be very curious how the plasma speaker works. Note: This information is technical, skip this step if you don't understand. The TL494 acts like an oscillator and a modulator, it generates a high frequency (5KHz to 45KHz) to drive the flyback transformer to make high voltage arcs. Then when you give it audio, the TL494 modulates the audio frequency into the main high frequency. Now the flyback transformer is being driven by the high frequency and the audio frequency, and when the arc is produced, the arc vibrates the air with both the audio and high frequency creating sounds. If you tune up the 22K potentiometer, the high frequency increases, when it goes higher than 20KHz, we cannot hear it, but only the audio frequency.

## Step 4: What You will Need . . .

You will need quite a lot of stuff to make the plasma speaker . . .

Parts

- TL494 chip (Datasheet for TL494)
- 200 uF (or 220uF)—50v electrolytic capacitor
- 47 nF—250v (or similar voltage ratings) capacitor
- 100 nF—50v capacitor
- 10 nF—50v capacitor
- 2.2 K—¼ W resistor
- 10 ohm—¼ W resistor
- UF4007 diode (or other fast diode that is rated 1 A (or more) and 500v (or more)
- 10 K—¼ W potentiometer (same thing as a variable resistor)
- 22 K—¼ W potentiometer (same thing as a variable resistor)
- Audio jack
- Wires
- IRF540 MOSFET (other MOSFET's with similar ratings should work)
- Large heatsink
- Flyback transformer (can be found from old CRT.)
- 12v power source (for TL494 oscillator, I used a 9v battery)
- 12v to 40v power source (for the flyback transformer)

- Breadboard (for testing)
- Veroboard

Tools

- Soldering iron
- Wire strippers
- Wire cutters
- Pliers
- Helping hands
- Hot glue gun

Abilities

- Good with a soldering iron.
- Can read schematics.
- Know what you are doing when you are dealing with high voltage.

## Step 5: Build the Prototype on the Bread Board

Do what the title says . . . Build the circuit on the bread board! Why on a bread board and not build it directly onto the veroboard? Well, it is a very good idea to build the prototype on the bread board before you solder the components onto the veroboard because you will get a better idea on how to build a 'real' one on the veroboard. You can make sure all the components are working fine, if not, you can replace it easily. You can modify or tweak the circuit a bit to give the plasma speaker a better performance.

## Step 6: Test the Prototype

After you have built it, go ahead and test it! If it does not work, don't get all frustrated or anything like that, go back and check your circuit closely, make sure there are no missing connections, and check the components are properly connected to the circuit.

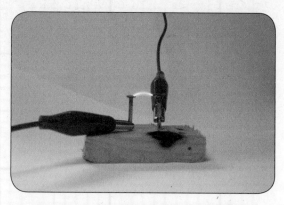

## Step 7: Build the Circuit

After you have tested to make sure everything is working, start building the prototype onto the veroboard. I use a 16 pin socket for the TL494. It is a really good idea to use sockets for the ICs because you won't risk heat damage from soldering, and if the IC fails, you can easily replace it instead of desoldering it and soldering another one in. I also added an LED indicator, which is a good idea so that you know whether the circuit is on or off. The LED indicator is connected to the TL494's power supply line. After you are done soldering, make sure you made nice shiny solder joints and they are no solder bridges. If you think it is all good enough, add some dab of hot glue onto the loose components and wires for strain relief.

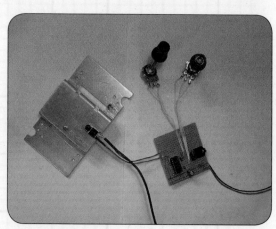

## Step 8: Final Test

Okay, you are very close. Test your plasma speaker to make sure if it is working or not. If it's working, let out a sigh of relief that you did it! If it's not working, don't overreact (I know it is very frustrating when something does not work). A few things can go wrong with this circuit:

Solder bridge—That is the most common problem in soldering. Some connections missed out.

Another common problem: Damaged components. Try to find and fix the problem, there is no point giving up unless you are really lazy.

## Step 9: Enjoy and Impress Your Friends!

Go ahead and pump in your favorite music then listen and watch the arc dance with the music and admire what you built. Then show it to your friends and family, I can guarantee you they will be greatly impressed.

## Step 10: How to Use the Plasma Speaker

Here is how you can control the plasma speaker with the two potentiometers. The 10K potentiometer is used to change the TL494's internal oscillator frequency—from 5KHz to 50KHz. If you want to play music on the arc, tune the frequency up until you don't hear it and play the music. Note: The 10K potentiometer does NOT affect the input audio (music). I am not too sure what the 22K potentiometer's job is, but it seems to change the volume of the audio. Fiddle with the 22K potentiometer until you can hear the music loudly. Note: Making the music louder will shorten the length of the arc.

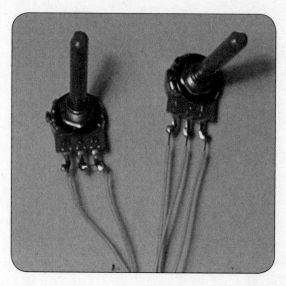

411

# also available

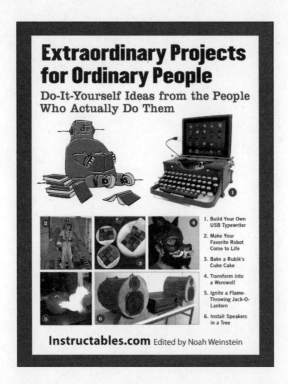

Collected in this volume is a best-of selection from Instructables, reproduced for the first time outside of the web format, retaining all of the charm and ingenuity that make Instructables such a popular destination for internet users looking for new and fun projects designed by real people in an easy-to-digest way.

Hundreds of Instructables are included, ranging from practical projects like making a butcher block counter top or building solar panels to fun and unique ideas for realistic werewolf costumes or transportable camping hot tubs. The difficulty of the projects ranges from beginner on up, but all are guaranteed to raise a smile or a "Why didn't I think of that?"

Numerous full-color pictures accompany each project, detailing each step of the process along the way. It's an invitation to try a few yourself, and once you're done, see if you don't have a couple of ideas to share at Instructables.com.

US $16.95 paperback 978-1-62087-057-0